W9-CMG-404

THE ENGLISH LANGUAGE IN AMERICA

The English Language in America

By

George Philip Krapp

Professor of English in Columbia University

Volume I

The Century Co.

FOR THE MODERN LANGUAGE ASSOCIATION OF AMERICA

New York MCMXXV

PRINTED IN U. S. A.

PREFACE

Though American histories of other kinds abound, of politics, of diplomacy, of painting, music, even of furniture, the American language has strangely escaped historical treatment. Perhaps it has generally been assumed that the language of America enjoys the felicity which is said to be the lot of persons and states without a history. But the life of the English language in America has covered three hundred years, and so long a stretch of static happiness certainly could not be expected in any thing human. In truth American English extends over just those periods in which the English language, reflecting new and complicated developments in social and economic conditions, has undergone some of its most interesting changes. In these changes the English language in America has shared to as great an extent as the American people have shared in the development of the civilization of the modern world.

In their immediate day and hour the facts of current American English have not infrequently challenged attention. But such studies of American English as have been made reflect for the most part an impressionistic or polemic interest in the speech of the day, and though often animated and amusing, and sometimes the vehicles for a certain amount of valuable information, they have offered very little in the way of systematic elucidation of the English language in America. Perhaps most attention has been paid in these treatises, both by Britons and by Americans, to the ever-burning question whether American English is as good as British English. Among recent discussions of the relations between British and American English the most elaborate as well as the most independent is contained in Mencken's *American Language*. Studies of this kind, however, have usually been more significant as inquiries into social prejudices than into linguistic history.

One may question whether even now the time is ripe for writing a history of the English language in America. If by ripeness one means that the details for the definitive history of the American language have all been collected, certainly the time is not ripe, but as certainly it never will be so. Historians have frequently lamented that history lags so far behind happenings. The history of an event cannot be written until too late to know about it, until immediate knowledge has been simplified and "interpreted" by viewing the event in the accumulated opinion of tradition. But if this is a necessary condition under which the historian must work, the time for writing a history of the English language in America will never arrive until our speech is a dead language and its history is written by a representative of some new and alien civilization. A less dismal way of approaching the question, however, may be that of asking whether an author who attempts the subject is as ripe for the undertaking as he may well hope to be. In answer all the present author can say is that he has devoted years of interested study to the subject, that he presents such materials as he has collected and such conclusions as he has reached not as final, but as salvage from the wastes of time which it seems advisable to tow into a harbor while opportunity permits.

The historical study of English in America has the double effect of bringing the past closer and at the same time enriching it with a distant and strange content. History both deepens and shortens perspective. It relieves a flat chronology by filling it with detail, but by filling it, at the same time it makes the past seem less extensive. Nothing is so long as a vacant half hour, and imagination alone can make a distant perspective. It can make even a remote golden age. As one studies detail, however, one realizes that no moment of the past was golden, but every moment was real and human. As historical knowledge grows the remote comes nearer, and humanity is seen not to have been as different one hundred, two hundred or three hundred years ago as it was supposed to be. It is so at least in the historical study of the American language. Perhaps one cannot quite say that there is nothing new under the sun in speech, but one can say that what seems new in American speech will most often be shown on further examination merely to be something old in a new surrounding.

It would be quite practicable to take American English as the point of departure for ventures into the general history of the whole past of the English language or even into general psychological linguistics. Neither of these purposes has been present in the composition of this book. It would seem that a more limited and immediate field of interest and duty lay before the student of American English. By limiting the treatment one is enabled to present a greater abundance of local detail than otherwise might be appropriate. But even with this excuse the author has been compelled to ask himself not infrequently if he has not burdened his story with too ample collections of fact. The historical student in one corner of his heart is not altogether unlike the stamp or curio collector. He finds it hard to resist the charm of a specimen. A specimen attracts for various reasons, the situation in which it was found, the shading of value which it acquires from context, or merely because it has never before been put on record. And after all the historian has the best right to be something of an antiquary. No one surely has a better opportunity than he to collect for the museums. In the matter of exhaustive citations it has seemed better, therefore, to err on the side of inclusiveness than on that of exclusiveness. In a work of historical reference, it is annoying not to find what one is looking for. The author of this treatise does not hope that he has saved his readers infallibly from this annoyance, but at least he has not neglected his opportunities to be as inclusive as possible. The same may be said with respect to the citation of authorities. It has seemed better to be specific than vaguely general, even at the expense sometimes of being needlessly specific. Examples and illustrations have not been cited therefore without indication of their origin, whether from some other study, from some document, or if no literary source is given, from personal observation.

This history has therefore been made documentary so far as possible by direct quotation of passages. The study of words in the chapter on the American vocabulary treats in detail only words for which documentary citations or direct evidence can be given. The only way to save the treatment of vocabulary from degenerating into a medley of chatty and amusing and doubtfully accurate remarks about words is by constant reference to actual usage. The great advance of Thornton's *American Glossary* over older books on Americanisms lies in the fact that Thornton gives title, page and date for every word he discusses. The method is sound and every one who will study American vocabulary intelligently must start from Thornton and make such additions as his opportunities enable him to make.

A preface is not the place to dwell on these topics at length, but attention may be called to the many glimpses of the changing state of American culture which one gets through the study of the language. One realizes intimately in this way the early dangers which confronted the Union, the dangers of disintegration which, as many hoped, language and the study of language were to remove. The hope was not vain, for undoubtedly language has been one of the strongest binding forces in American experience.

One sees also the struggles and conflicts in social ideas as they made for uniformity and as they determined values. The notion that usage could be regulated by an authority appealed strongly to the sympathy of Americans in the late eighteenth and early nineteenth centuries—unfortunately has not altogether ceased to appeal. But there seems to be a peculiar and pathetic significance in the general acceptance of Walker in the early nineteenth century and in the attempts to live up to Walker. This feeling for Walker was different from the earlier respect for Dr. Johnson, and on the whole less intelligent. Dr. Johnson was accepted as a source of positive information, as one who could tell you how to spell words and how to define them. But Walker was accepted as a source of social distinction, to be acquired by appropriation if one had it not by nature.

So far as general standards of culture are concerned, it is quite obvious from the study of the language that, since the days of colonization, a great change has come over American ways of regarding this particular social activity of speech. This change can be seen to a certain extent still in progress. Among an unschooled older generation of speakers, certain liberties and variabilities of vocabulary, syntax and pronunciation are present which the newer generation, socialized and normalized by experience in the public schools, condemns or charitably overlooks. Standards of speech have become more regular and severer than they formerly were. An educated man who should now assume the pose of rusticity would arouse the suspicion of cheap trickery, for rusticity of speech no longer characterizes the average citizen, but only those noticeably below the average. In the seventeenth and eighteenth centuries, however, even through the first half of the nineteenth century, the conditions must have been different. In a seventeenth or eighteenth century village, or even town, the number of conventionally educated persons would be small, perhaps only the minister and the schoolmaster. This means that the standards of the conventional education could not apply to the general life of the community. Pronunciation, grammar and spelling were not then tests of respectability, of democratic equality, in the degree to which they have since become. What seems now like illiterate speech, the speech of persons who do not reflect how they speak, was then merely the normal speech of the community.

The town records of the seventeenth and eighteenth centuries are doubtless fairly representative of the average cultural level of American life of the times. These records were not usually kept by a learned person but by some respectable citizen of the community. They are rich mines of information to be derived both from direct statement and by inference. The conscious struggles of the recorders as well as their inadvertences are instructive, though this evidence must always be treated cautiously, since even the so-called illiterate person may have his highly literary moments. Thus in the *Hempstead Records, farm* acquires a kind of Hellenic look when it is spelled *pharme* (1664). For *home* the spelling *whome* is very frequent in several records, and one at first wonders whether this spelling represents a real pronunciation or is merely a semi-learned extension of the spelling of *whole.* In this instance other evidence supports the conclusion that *whome* was really pronounced with the initial consonant of *whim,* the final bit of evidence being the inadvertent spelling *wome.* But these unconventional spellings are not always so deeply significant. In the *Hempstead Records* for 1659 one finds *kow ceeper* and *cow ceeper*, and in 1664, *cep* and *sep* for *keep*. The spellings here mean nothing for pronunciation, though their logic is perfect. If *c* can have the value of *k* in *cow*, and if *c* can have the value of *s* in a word like *receive*, then *s* can have the value of *k* in keep. This shows clearness of mind, but sometimes the spellings indicate merely uncertainty, as when in these same records, 1660, 1661, *particular* is spelled *piticler*, *piticlur*, *pitucler*, *pitculler*, *partickler*, the first probably standing nearest to the recorder's actual pronunciation.

Much of this irregular spelling, syntax and pronunciation of a century or two ago still persists, the important change which has taken place being one of attitude toward it. To regard these and similar unconventionalities as being the genuinely native elements in American speech, the real American language, would be absurd both from the historical as well as the psychological point of view. Good grammar ordinarily has as ancient a history as bad grammar, and popular or illiterate English can be carried back to British sources no more and no less definitely than standard English. The stabilizing of standards which has taken place in American English is by no means peculiar to this country, but the same development has been characteristic of the whole modern period of the English language.

This history was not written to cover a special plea for a distinctive American language, illiterate or otherwise. On the contrary the author feels, as every disinterested student of American English must feel, that historical study brings American English into a closer relation to the central tradition of the English language than is commonly supposed to exist by those who have not looked at English in America from the historical and comparative angle. At various times of heated sentiment, attempts have been made to manufacture tradition, to construct a peculiar American language when none existed. Thus immediately after the Revolution, many advocates arose of what they were pleased to call a Federal English —an engaging name, though the thing itself was difficult to put down in black and white. Later Walt Whitman grew eloquent over the notion of a reconstructed language for These States, though he failed to give the prescription for it. Most frequently the genuine American language has been supposed to be a speech markedly different from the standard English of cultivated conversation or the body of English literature—in short a popular and more or less illiterate dialect. But why popular speech should be considered more genuine, more essentially American, than standard speech it is difficult to see. Indeed striving towards standardized forms of speech would seem to have been one of the most constant and characteristic of American impulses. The parallel between America in the last one hundred and fifty years and Italy in the time of Dante is more than superficial and accidental. In America as then in Italy, we have been striving to attain an "illustrious vernacular," an English speech lifted above the level of any local or class dialect. This illustrious vernacular has been a standardized and more or less manipulated speech, to a certain degree an artificial and literary speech. But it has been nevertheless for the last century and more the norm by which other forms of American English have been estimated. Popular life is interesting and popular speech is interesting, and both by contrast are also often amusing, but in its usual manifestations, the so-called "real American language" is nothing more than a kind of literary class dialect, made by peppering normal English with a certain number of popular violations of conventional grammar and pronunciation. It is vivacious enough and may be true enough as an element in dramatic characterization, but to say that this is the real American language is equivalent to saying that all persons who are not garage keepers or shopladies or factory hands, all persons who do not disrupt every convention of propriety that occasion offers, are frauds and impostors. But American English is certainly larger than the speech of one class, even than that of the superbly self-satisfied class of the illiterates. Popular American speech is no more the real American language than the speech of the London coster is the genuine speech of England or than Apache Parisian is the only genuine French. Any dialect may of course be genuine when it is genuinely used, but of the many forms of a highly developed language like English, who shall say which is the quintessentially genuine? or who shall insist that the crude only may be genuine?

In the matter of bibliography the author's main endeavor has been to prevent the bibliographical machinery from becoming too burdensome. Books referred to only once or twice are ordinarily treated as casuals, their titles are given in the body of the text where the reference occurs, but are not included in the general bibliography. The names of such authors are of course in the index. The general bibliography consists of titles of books which have been mainly and more or less constantly useful in the composition of the history. Titles frequently referred to in the text are given at such places only in abbreviated form, but fuller details, like dates and places of publication, can easily be found in the alphabetical list of the bibliography. An exhaustive bibliography of the whole subject of American English would have been extremely bulky and would itself fill a large volume. The bibliography here given can be supplemented by the several bibliographies contained in the volumes of *Dialect Notes.* Tucker, *American English,* pp. 332–345, also has a bibliography, and the very useful bibliography of Mencken's first edition, pp. 323–339, appears conveniently classified and enlarged in the later editions. Attention may be called likewise to the forthcoming *Bibliography of the English Language,* by Professor Arthur G. Kennedy, of Stanford University. And finally, almost any library or cataloging index will furnish abundant titles on American English, though many of these titles, especially in journalistic and magazine literature, will be found to be of little value. It seems true that many persons are inclined to rush into print on questions of language without an adequate foundation of knowledge. Their comments are often more interesting to the student of human passions and perversities than they are to the historical student of language. In some instances titles of books not specially important in themselves have been included in the bibliography. These have been mentioned for their representative value as titles of types of books which the student of historical American English is compelled to examine. The author will remark, however, that he has in his own card indexes scores more of such titles of antiquated grammars and spelling books which he has refrained from thrusting upon the attention of his readers. Some time a complete bibliography of American English must be made, but that is a subject for a book in itself.

A word of explanation may be given of the author's occasional use of the word British in a phrase like British English to contrast with American English. Englishmen themselves do not now commonly use the adjective British in this way, though they do speak of the British Empire, and certain schools advertise themselves as being conducted exclusively for British boys. Englishmen would not however speak of a certain usage of speech in England as British to distinguish it from Canadian or Australian or American. To them it would be merely English, the thing itself. But if students of English in England do not feel the need for distinguishing terms for the several aspects of the language, including their own, students of English in America do feel this need and can scarcely avoid using terms which make these distinctions clear. The word British is an obvious one to use, and it has been employed in this history because it is practically convenient. Others have done the same, and the word has acquired a certain standing as an Americanism. A similar excuse may be made for the word American as an adjective limited in application to the United States. In strict logic such a use is not justifiable, but common practice and understanding have long since put the word beyond the jurisdiction of logic.

Economy and the demands of a moderate degree of exactness have necessitated the use of a phonetic alphabet in the discussion of sounds and pronunciations. The reasons for this necessity have been set forth more at large at the beginning of the second volume, in the chapter which discusses pronunciations, and there also readers unfamiliar with the notation of the International Phonetic Association will find the symbols briefly described. The system of notation employed is simple and the few minutes devoted to understanding it will be amply repaid by increased ease and swiftness in reading.

CONTENTS

THE ENGLISH LANGUAGE IN AMERICA

THE ENGLISH LANGUAGE IN AMERICA

THE MOTHER TONGUE

Long experience in one's native speech causes it to seem so obvious and natural, like elemental things, wind and rain and sun, like breathing and walking, that it makes no urgent demands for explanation. "It needes not," said Sir Philip Sidney, "that a man should be put to schoole to learne his mother tongue." Perhaps not—at least in Sidney's day. In later times, and especially in America, speech has not been taken for granted quite so easily. On closer examination this familiar activity of speech is seen to be extraordinarily complicated and subtle, in the end often inexplicable. A complete account of the American idiom, if one could give it, would go far towards explaining the whole spiritual history of the American people. But this chapter does not pretend to give any such complete account. It attempts the more possible task of setting down some of the most significant features of that background of experience, hidden or open, against which thoughtful Americans project their speech when it becomes for them a matter of conscious reflection. It is true that speech in the main rests upon a foundation of feeling, not of reflection, and these less conscious attitudes cannot be disregarded. That their feeling for a mother tongue and their opinions concerning it have been the same among all Americans at any given moment, it would be folly to suppose. They have been sufficiently present, however, and sufficiently unified for at least two hundred years to permit one to speak of an American mother tongue, of a general and standard American speech. The American people realize themselves as a nation in part through the possession of a distinctive speech. This distinctive speech, this mother tongue, the general background of which it is proposed here to examine, is obviously English, but it is, first of all, the English of America.

Immediately the questions arise, however, whether Americans have generally viewed their mother tongue in some relation to older British English, and if they have not, what they have substituted for this pious tradition. But the mere asking of these questions shows that language is not a thing apart. It is an inseparable element in the whole of a people's life and has intimate connections with politics and other activities. Before the United States came into being, it would scarcely have occurred to anyone, either on this side the water or on the other, to think of the English language in America as anything but an extension of British English, different in its local habitation from the speech of the home country, but not different either in present character or future prospects. Does not a son remain a son, wherever he may dwell?

A son, however, may become a man, hungry for personal rights and privileges, and when the colonies began to claim the dignity of manhood, even the gentlest prick served to burst the bubble of this assumption of homogeneity which hitherto had been so comfortably accepted on both sides of the water. Instead of fixing attention upon similarities, both British and Americans now began to notice the differences that separated them from each other. Both were surprised to find these differences so great, and naturally this same discovery of fact, or supposed fact, led to opposite interpretations in theory. The Americans were inclined to see in these differences a mark of their peculiar virtue and claims to consideration, while the Britisher was often moved to look upon them as indications of an unsuspected deterioration and degradation which circumstances had suddenly brought into clear light. So far as the language itself is concerned, both of these extreme views were wrong. Colonial English had developed no remarkable gifts or powers, nor had it degenerated from a purer and more perfect type of speech which was only carefully preserved in England. After the Declaration of Independence, American English remained as it always has been, a closely related but differentiated branch of the English language, connected by the most intimate bonds of tradition with the parent speech. The narrow partisanships which were drawn into the consideration of speech arose not from that activity itself, but from entirely different occasions for an indulgence in emotions of loyal pride or prejudice.

Though the English language in America did not experience a new birth with the separation of the colonies from Great Britain, that event nevertheless provides a reasonable starting place for the consideration of what we must from that time call American English. Deep rooted though it was in the past, this English of eighteenth century America came then to be regarded from a new angle, and though the language in itself may not greatly have changed from what it was before, as in all other human social institutions the changing opinions which man held with respect to it must be counted as a part of its essential character. The special history of American English as something consciously separate and distinguishable began, therefore, with the realization of the existence of an American nation. In the third quarter of the eighteenth century Americans began to feel that their mother tongue was something near and intimate, the speech which gave to them a unity upon their own American soil.

National or standard languages have seldom developed under the control of conscious intention, and to this rule the English language in America is no exception. In its present state, apart from what it has inherited from older traditions, which is obviously a great deal, American English is the result of a variety of impulses and tendencies, often crossing each other in a bewildering fashion and never for long uniting into a large and clearly defined purpose which the American people have held before them as an ideal towards which in their language they should aspire. It would have been surprising had it been otherwise. Languages grow and change only as they accompany the daily activities of men and women in the communication of their thoughts to each other. They are, moreover, the least conscious of the social possessions of peoples. Political and ethical ideals may be formulated, even in the earlier stages of their development, with a certain degree of definiteness and clearness. But a nation as a whole rarely gives thought to the trend of development of its speech, is rarely conscious that there is a trend of development. Its language may be deeply affected by the general tone of its life and thought, but the language itself is a resultant by-product of these general influences, and only in slight measure does it determine their character or weight. Language in the main is an echo of life, not a motive power in it.

At times, however, theorists and reformers arise who attempt and in some degree are able to give language a more active significance. When the American colonies at the end of the eighteenth century finally detached themselves from their older political associations, the occasion seemed unusually propitious for the formation of a native American speech which should not only be distinctive for American life but should also help the new nation to a realization of those inner purposes and aspirations which were still engaged in the struggle for existence. The beginnings are seen in an article by an unknown author (see Albert Matthews, *Transactions of the Colonial Society of Massachusetts*, XIV, 263–264), addressed to the Literati of America and published in the *Royal American Magazine* for January, 1774. In this article the writer proposes a society to be called Fellows of the American Society of Language, "for perfecting the English language in America." The author expresses the conviction that America will soon be "the seat of science." Perhaps the writer of this address to the literati of America was John Adams, for a few years later, after several very significant events had happened, in a letter to the "President of Congress," dated September 5, 1780, John Adams proposed an academy for "fixing and improving" American English, *Works*, Boston, 1851, Vol. VII, p. 249. He remarks that the British have occasionally tried a similar project, but have failed: "so that to this day there is no grammar nor dictionary extant of the English language which has the least public authority." "The honor of forming the first public institution for refining, correcting, improving, and ascertaining the English language," he continues, "I hope is reserved for congress; they have every motive that can possibly influence a public assembly to undertake it. It will have a happy effect upon the union of the States to have a public standard for all persons in every part of the continent to appeal to both for the signification and pronunciation of the language. The constitutions of all the States in the Union are so democratized that eloquence will become the instrument for recommending men to their fellow-citizens, and the principal means of advancement through the various ranks and offices of society." The project is described a few weeks later in a letter to Edmund Jenings, September 30, 1780. "After Congress shall have done it," that is, shall have established the academy, says Adams, "perhaps the British king and parliament may have the honor of copying the example. This I should admire. England will never more have any honor, excepting now and then that of imitating the Americans. I assure you, Sir, I am not altogether in jest. I see a general inclination after English in France, Spain and Holland, and it may extend throughout Europe. The population and commerce of America will force their language into general use."[1]

Adams returns to the subject later, *Works*, Vol. IX, p. 509, and again expresses the opinion that "English will be the most respectable language in the world," largely because of the number of people who will be speaking it. A contemporary Frenchman, Roland de la Platière, addressing the Academy at Lyons in 1789, went as far as Adams and spoke enthusiastically not merely of English, but specifically of the language of the United States, as the possible universal language of the future.[2]

[1] See Matthews, *ibid.*, p. 262. Language like this explains why similar statements still being made have such a hauntingly familiar sound, as when Walter Hines Page, *Letters*, I, 144, writes as follows, October, 1913, from the American Embassy in London to President Wilson: "The future of the world belongs to us. A man needs to live here, with two economic eyes in his head, a very little time to become very sure of this. Everybody will see it presently. These English are spending their capital, and it is their capital that continues to give them their vast power. Now what are we going to do with the leadership of the world presently when it clearly falls into our hands? And how can we use the English for the highest uses of democracy?"

[2] See Baldensperger, "Une Prédiction Inédite sur l'Avenir de la Langue des États-Unis," in Modern Philology, XV, 475–476.

A similar high patriotic purpose underlay the ideals with respect to an American language which Noah Webster preached with energy, with as much scholarship as his day afforded, and with not a little common sense. In his earliest utterances, in the *Grammatical Institute*, Part I, 1783, which later became the *American Spelling Book*, one observes still a good deal of the heightened feeling of the war just ended. "The author wishes to promote the honour and prosperity of the confederated republics of America," wrote Webster, p. 14, "and chearfully throws his mite into the common treasure of patriotic exertions. This country must in some future time, be as distinguished by the superiority of her literary improvements, as she is already by the liberality of her civil and ecclesiastical constitutions. Europe is grown old in folly, corruption and tyranny—in that country laws are perverted, manners are licentious, literature is declining and human nature debased. For America in her infancy to adopt the present maxims of the old world, would be to stamp the wrinkles of decrepid age upon the bloom of youth and to plant the seeds of decay in a vigorous constitution."

Only rarely, and only after the fervor of the Revolution had somewhat cooled, was a milder voice raised in support of the continuity of the ancient traditions of the English language in America. Thus a writer in the *Monthly Magazine and American Review*, Vol. III, 1–4, July, 1800, in an Essay "On the Scheme of an American Language," protests against the notion that "grammars and dictionaries should be compiled by natives of the country, not of the British or English, but of the *American* tongue." And instead of endeavoring to insulate themselves from their ancestors, he advises Americans to direct all their labors to the opposite purpose. On the whole he sees little difference between American and British English, and prophesies confidently that "the future bards of Potowmac and Messouri shall be said to write English." It is his conviction that the literary tradition will be a sufficiently strong binding force to hold the language of the English and American people together. "Books," he declares, "are the only adequate authority for the use of words," and good American English must be the speech of those "whose dialect is purified by intimate intercourse with English books."[1]

On the whole, however, most persons agreed with Webster that the isolation of America from England and from the rest of Europe was bound to result in the development of an entirely new speech in the New World. Webster was convinced that this isolation would produce, "in a course of time, a language in North America, as different from the future language of England, as the modern Dutch, Danish and Swedish are from the German, or from one another," *Dissertations* (1789), p. 22. Thomas Jefferson thought it not improbable, *Writings*, ed. Washington, VI, 188, that the changes in American English would in time "separate it in name as well as in power, from the mother-tongue." These prophecies were not unreasonable. When one considered the great differentiation which had taken place among the Teutonic dialects of Europe, closely related geographically, it must have seemed, from the point of view of the eighteenth century, all the more certain that two countries so widely separated as England and America must diverge widely in their common speech. The forecast has turned out to be false because a student of Webster's or Jefferson's day could not foresee the international and highly literary character of American civilization as it has developed in the century and a quarter since they wrote.

This certainty of the formation of a new language in America, Webster welcomed whole-heartedly. He believed that the language of England had passed the point of its highest development and was already in a state of decline. The life of language seemed to him to be like that of the forms of organic life in the world of nature. A seed after it was planted grew, under favoring conditions, until it reached the limits of its possible growth, the plant then remained stationary for a moment, but immediately it must fall into decay. The stage of improvement or growth in the English language corresponding to the natural growth of a plant, Webster considers to have commenced with the age of Queen Elizabeth and ended with

[1] See also *ibid.*, III, 173, and III, 184–185.

the reign of George II. "It would have been fortunate for the language," he adds, "had the stile of writing and the pronunciation of words been fixed, as they stood in the reign of Queen Anne and her successor. Few improvements have been made since that time, but innumerable corruptions in pronunciation have been introduced by Garrick, and in stile, by Johnson, Gibbon and their imitators," *Dissertations*, p. 30. The taste of her writers "already corrupted, and her language on the decline," Webster regards England as no longer providing a worthy model to follow. He would have Americans take a fresh start in this cyclical process of the life of language. Here was a fresh people, in a new country, with untried ideals, an entirely new life was here to be worked out. It was not only the opportunity, it was the duty of the American people to develop a peculiar language of their own; "as a nation," he declares, "we have a very great interest in opposing the introduction of any plan of uniformity with the British language, even were the plan proposed perfectly unexceptionable," *Dissertations*, p. 171. As America was now a self-constituted nation, he considered that American honor required that America should have a system of her own, in language as well as government. Will not the Atlantic Ocean, the pride of an independent nation, he asks, restrain our rage for imitating the errors of foreigners? To Webster, Englishmen were foreigners, and what have we to do, he asks, with the customs of a foreign nation?

The elements from which Webster would construct the new American speech he found ready to his hand. The American people, as he viewed them, were a race of simple folk, neither rustics nor peasants on the one hand, nor aristocrats on the other, corrupted by the false refinements of stage and court, in Webster's phrasing, as these refinements flourished in the effete monarchies of Europe. It was the speech of this folk that Webster would make the basis for his new American English, especially the speech of the New England colonies as the region in which education and literary culture were most highly developed. He presents an engaging picture of the state of culture in New England in his day, which other authorities confirm as true, showing the wide extent of reading even among village folk, and the vivid interest in all matters of education which has been the great gift of New England to the American nation. It should be remembered that the New England settlers, even those who tilled the soil, tended to congregate in towns where social intercourse was possible, not to be sparsely scattered over vast territories, as were the settlers in other sections of the country.

But Webster was not intent upon advocating a local New England standard as the general model for American English. He insists that the standard shall not be local but national, and that it shall be the standard set by the most enlightened, that is, the educated members of the several communities, not the most ignorant. Here at least, among much spread-eagle patriotism, we find a clear enunciation of principles which have ever been active in determining the character of the mother tongue of the American people. The advocacy of a national and literary standard for American speech was a logical response to the novel conditions in the new country. The standard of British English having been rejected, both for patriotic reasons and also because it was too remote to be applied, as Webster himself was aware, there remained only the choice between the speech of one geographical or social community, to be elevated above all the rest, and the speech of no community at all, that is, a manipulated generalization of speech habits which should cover the nation as a whole. It should be pointed out in passing that Webster understood quite well that this national speech must be to some extent theoretical and unreal, and that his advocacy of it was contrary to his general principle, that it is the duty of the student of the English language "to find what the language *is*, and not how it *might have been made*," *Dissertations*, p. ix. He compromised with his general principle, however, because a certain amount of artificial manipulation seemed necessary before the language could arrive at that ultimate uniformity short of which a democratic society cannot rest. In a passage in his *Grammatical Institute*, Part I, 1783, p. 6, Webster discusses the local variations in American speech which he thinks should be harmonized, and as this is the earliest reference in which the differing details of American speech are described, the passage deserves to be quoted in full:

"Not to mention small differences, I would observe that the inhabitants of New-England and Virginia have a peculiar pronunciation which affords much diversion to their neighbours. On the other hand, the language in the middle States is tinctured with a variety of Irish, Scotch and German dialects which are justly censured as deviations from propriety and the standard of elegant pronunciation. The truth is, *usus est Norma Loquendi*, general custom is the rule of speaking, and every deviation from this must be wrong. The dialect of one State is as ridiculous as that of another; each is authorized by local custom; and neither is supported by any superior excellence. If in New-England we hear a flat, drawling pronunciation, in the more Southern States we hear the words *veal*, *very*, *vulgar* pronounced *weal*, *wery*, *wulgar; wine*, *winter*, etc., changed into *vine*, *vinter; soft* becomes *saft;* and *raisins* and *wound*, contrary to all rules and propriety, are pronounced *reesins*, *woond.* It is the present mode at the Southward, to pronounce *u* like *yu*, as virtyue, fortyune, etc., and in a rapid pronunciation these become *virchue*, *forchune*, as also *duty*, *duel*, are changed into *juty*, *juel.*"

In the *Dissertations* Webster later desires the New England "yeoman" to alter his "drawling nasal manner of speaking," and likewise when he says *marcy* for *mercy*, or *kiow* for *cow*, he would have him change these pronunciations to accord with the more general custom. "Vast numbers of people" who in Boston and Philadelphia say *weal* and *wessel* for *veal* and *vessel* are asked to resign their peculiarities for the sake of uniformity. The Virginian is asked to pronounce his final *r's* more fully, and all persons who cherish fashionable distinctions of pronunciation are told to put away such undemocratic affectations.

Though this kind of compromise which Webster found it necessary to advocate in order to establish his standard of national use remains as much a necessity to-day as it ever was, national use based upon the speech of educated speakers abides as the only general standard which has recognized value in American English. The bearing of this upon American speech was realized early by those who gave careful thought to American conditions. Cooper, in his *Notions of the Americans* (1828), analyzed the situation thoroughly and soundly. He declared that in America, "while there are provincial, or state peculiarities, in tone, and even in pronunciation and use of certain words, there is no patois," *Notions*, I, 62. An American, he avers, might distinguish between a Georgian and a man from New England, but a foreigner could not, and he adds that though Americans pass for natives every day in England, "it is next to impossible for an Englishman to escape detection in America." The reasons why it is impossible, in Cooper's opinion, for an Englishman to escape detection are that in England not only are local distinctions more highly developed and fully preserved, but also a "slang of society" exists there with a "fashion of intonation . . . which it is often thought vulgar to omit," with the result that speakers who escape the local dialects are likely to fall into this fashionable dialect. Cooper clearly recognized the futility of attempting to estimate American speech by a British standard. "If it be assumed," he remarks, *Notions*, II, 123, "that the higher classes in London are always to set the fashion in pronunciation, and the best living writers in England are to fix the meaning of words, the point is clearly decided in their favour, since one cannot see on what principle they are to be put in the wrong." Cooper acknowledged that for England the standard of speech is to be found in London, since there congregate those "whose manners, birth, fortune, and political distinction make them the objects of admiration." So powerful was the authority of the cultivated society of the metropolis of British life, that it seemed to Cooper absurd to suppose that in comparison with this authority, either the church or the stage or education exerted any but a slight influence upon British speech. In other words, Cooper believed that England had a so clearly recognized and admired social aristocracy, an aristocracy of birth, wealth, and wit, centered in London, that it easily provided the standards for all things of the spirit. In America, however, he thought a different state of affairs existed. "If we had a great capital, like London," he observed,

Notions, II, 124, "where men of leisure, and fortune, and education, periodically assembled to amuse themselves, I think we should establish a fashionable aristocracy, too, which should give the mode to the forms of speech. . . . But we have no such capital, nor are we likely, for a long time to come, to have one of sufficient magnitude to produce any great effect on the language. . . . The habits of polite life, and even the pronunciation of Boston, of New York, of Baltimore, and of Philadelphia, vary in many things, and a practised ear may tell a native of either of these places, by some little peculiarity of speech. There is yet no predominating influence to induce the fashionables of these towns to wish to imitate the fashionables of any other. If any place is to possess this influence, it will certainly be New York;" but even this Cooper thinks will not come to pass, and that "an entirely different standard for the language must be established in the United States, from that which governs so absolutely in England." Where is that standard to be found? Cooper's answer is that it must be found in the speech of the nation as a whole, that in fact it already is found there. For if the people of America were like the people of any other country on earth, "we should be speaking at this moment a great variety of nearly unintelligible patois," whereas in reality the American people speak the English language "as a nation better than any other people speak their language." "This resemblance in speech can only be ascribed to the great diffusion of intelligence, and to the inexhaustible activity of the population, which, in a manner, destroys space." "The distinctions in speech between New England and New York, or Pennsylvania, or any other State," he continues, "were far greater twenty years ago than they are now," a change which cannot simply be explained as due to migration, since migration "would often introduce provincialisms without correcting them, did it not also, by bringing acute men together, sharpen wits, provoke comparisons, challenge investigations, and, finally, fix a standard."

For the last twenty years, concludes Cooper, it has been a matter of hot dispute in which of the large towns in America the best English is spoken. "The result of this discussion has been to convince most people who know anything of the matter, that a perfectly pure English is spoken nowhere, and to establish the superiority, on one point in favor of Boston, on another in favor of New York, and so on to the end of the chapter." Social standards being thus disposed of, as well as fashionable society, the church, the stage, Congress, the court, "for there is none but the President," and the fashions of speech in England, the only guide to a standard speech which Cooper finds to be left is reason, and he is convinced that "in another generation or two, far more *reasonable* English will be used in this country than exists here now."

These opinions were expressed, it will be remembered, before Cooper's return to America from his seven year's residence in Europe. His notions of America expressed after his return are much less optimistic. "Without a social capital," so he wrote in the Preface of *Home as Found* (1838), "with twenty or more communities divided by distance and political barriers, her people, who are really more homogeneous than any other of the same numbers in the world perhaps, possess no standard for opinion, manners, social maxims, or even language." The truth lay between these two extremes of statement. A national standard is, to be sure, not a perfectly realizable standard, and in that sense the people of America possessed no standard of speech. What they possessed, however, in this conception of a national speech, was a guide to conduct as effectual as any recognized or formal rule could be. Perhaps also Cooper's opinion of American speech as governed by reason calls for some interpretation. What he evidently meant to do was to distinguish between an instinctive social and traditional attitude towards speech, and one in which habits are determined to a greater extent by choice and intention. The latter he regarded as the attitude of Americans towards their speech, and in this sense their language might justly be called a "reasonable English."

In the earlier years of the American republic, this insistence upon the importance of a uniform and independent national speech was a logical result of the fear of disintegration which must always beset those interested in maintaining a federation of independent states. "But this I will presume to affirm," wrote Alexander Hamilton, *Works*, ed. Lodge, II, 38, "that from New Hampshire to Georgia the people of America are as uniform in their interests and manners as those of any established in Europe." The frequency with which one comes upon assertions like this is evidence that the fear of the contrary could not have been remote.

One of the few utterances of the Philological Society, which flourished during the first years of the republic, is contained in a letter, dated New York, July 4, 1788, and signed by Josiah Hoffman, president, approving Webster's *American Spelling Book* and "recommending it to the use of schools in the United States, as an accurate, well digested system of principles and rules, calculated to destroy the various false dialects in pronunciation in the several States, an object very desirable in a federal republic." This letter was frequently reprinted by Webster in editions of his spelling book. It may seem a little strange that mature and important citizens should concern themselves about anything so insignificant as an elementary spelling book. But to their minds, the elementary spelling book carried a burden of deep meaning. Anything that might decrease the danger of disruption was eagerly seized upon in those troubled years. Not only the writers, grammarians and dictionary makers of the early years of the republic, but the statesmen as well expressed themselves emphatically on the importance of maintaining a uniform national speech in America. With the large increase of migration and the expansion of the country westward in the early nineteenth century, the necessity for the cultivation of a national standard seemed to many observers more pressing than ever. Commenting on one of the minor recommendations of his pronouncing speller, the first edition of which appeared in 1819, Cummings remarks, p. x, that "if we consider the great importance of preserving uniformity in our country, and of avoiding what already begins to be called northern and southern pronunciation, no attempt to preserve harmony in the republic of letters will be regarded as too minute." "As we become more extended," he observes, "the greater is the probability that our language may one day be broken into a variety of provincialisms, as is common with the language of other countries." To secure uniformity, one must have a "system" of pronunciation, and Cummings accepts Walker, because "at present there can scarcely exist a doubt" that Walker's system is the best. Rather than be divided among themselves, Americans like Cummings were willing to impose upon themselves inflexible British authority.

"It is an important object, in this country," said Webster, *Elementary Spelling Book*, New York, 1843, on one of the fly leaves, "to have a uniform national language, to which all foreigners settling in this country, should conform." "In the early years of our independence," continues Webster with his usual modesty, "much was done to promote this object by Webster's Spelling Book . . . and the effects of the general use of Webster's book, for more than thirty years, are visible at this day, in the remarkable uniformity of pronunciation among the citizens of the United States." One may doubt that this uniformity, if it existed, was so exclusively to be attributed to Webster's Spelling Book, and Webster himself in this same passage, notes with approval a discovery he made on the occasion of his visit to England, "that pronunciation in England is not regulated by books, or by any book, but by the usage of the higher classes of society."

As time has passed, the claim of any higher class, or any local standard, for example that of New England, has had increasingly less chance of receiving general acceptance in America. Perhaps there is, or at least has been, a tendency for the West to look up to the East in matters of speech, as newer communities are always inclined to look with respect upon the traditions of older settled regions. But the terms West and East are confessedly vague—no one knows where the West begins—and the respect of the West for the East is a sentiment which is likely to pass unchallenged only when it is not brought into too close relation to concrete action. The threefold requirement that good American English must be present English, national English, and reputable English, good repute being defined in terms of educational standards, has not only passed into a truism of the rhetorics and guide-books which abound for the direction of American students, but it has become, one may say, an element in the sub-conscious life of the language. The prescription was old, as old at least as Campbell's Rhetoric, and even the phrasing of it which has passed current in America was borrowed from England. "That usage," says Creighton, *Dictionary of Scripture Proper Names*, p. 21, quoting from Crombie's *Etymology and Syntax* (1802), "which gives law to language and which is generally denominated good, must be *reputable, national,* and *present.*" This was the conventional way of stating the point as it was established by Campbell. But the difference between this statement as applied to England and as applied to America is that it has meant a great deal more for America than it has for England.

The result in America has not been to destroy existing distinctions in local speeches or to prevent new ones from developing as new conditions have arisen, but rather to put all local distinctions on the same level as compared with the general standard speech. In the latter, because of the definiteness of the standard, an astonishing degree of uniformity has developed, and cultivated speakers who have given any thought to the matter of standards and who have not wilfully retained their local customs of speech, even in their own localities speak and write a language which is but slightly differentiated from that of other regions, whether the locality be on the Atlantic or Pacific coast, whether it border on the Great Lakes or the Gulf of Mexico. As compared with the language of most countries, national uniformity and the striving towards national uniformity may certainly be regarded as one of the notable characteristics of the American mother tongue.

The modifications of the ideal of a general national standard which have just been made are, however, far from being unimportant. Though no local dialect presumes to take upon itself the authority of general standard, many local dialects are regarded not without honor in their own communities and are used by many speakers of cultivation without apology and even with pride. This must necessarily be so, since a citizen of a federated nation must first be a member of some local community, and only on special occasions will he be called upon to put aside his local customs and duties in favor of more general and abstract national demands. It results, therefore, that many features of local dialects have what may be called a very high local standard value as the speech of cultivated persons, and that the contentment and satisfaction of the several communities in their local speech has, in each case, a claim to toleration which can be set aside neither by the claims of the national standard nor those of any differing local standard. In a democratic society there is always a tendency towards disintegration, and this tendency has been, and still is plainly exhibited in American speech.

National standards, conscious or sub-conscious, manifestly cannot be manufactured out of whole cloth. They must have a considerable foundation in common experience before they can be made to seem effective as general guides to conduct. In spite of the theoretical rejection of a local culture or a local speech as affording an adequate national standard, it remains true that the culture of New England, and to a less degree, the speech of New England, have most fully represented to Americans, viewing themselves historically, the aspirations of the country at large. It will be interesting to examine the reasons why New England speech should have been exalted to this position of theoretical prominence.

In the first place, the speech of New England started with a strong initial advantage in that the colloquial idiom of the New England colonists was in large measure that of southeastern England and of London. "To prove that the Americans have a corrupt pronunciation," wrote Webster, *Dissertations*, p. 127, note, "we are often told that our ancestors came from the western counties of England." "This is but partly true," he continues, and he maintained that "many of the principal settlers came from London and its vicinity, some from the middle counties . . . and a few from the northern counties." Other evidence of various kinds confirms Webster's statement. The New England colonists gladly and rightly thought of themselves as a stream issuing from the central fountains of English life.

Narrow patriots might maintain with all the passion they could muster that the new country must detach itself completely from the culture of the mother country, but their contention proved vain. There was something stronger than theories of government, and that was the bond which intimate social tradition establishes, the kinship of blood, of speech and of sentiment which cannot be set aside by decree or by intention. In moments of exalted feeling Americans sometimes declared their complete emancipation from British standards, but in reality they had no desire to forego their ancient inheritance. Webster himself was proud of the fact that his fellow-New Englanders spoke, as he thought, the language which Britain had established as its approved refined and literary speech. Had the New England colonists come mainly from Yorkshire or from Scotland, or from the western counties, and had their familiar speech thus been one of the northern dialects of English or of Somerset, it is doubtful if New England speech would ever have been taken into critical favor. But fortunately, it agreed in the main with the generally accepted cultivated standard in Great Britain, and was thus spared the struggle which any contemned local dialect must have undergone in the endeavor to establish itself in opposition to the powerful influence of the speech of London and southern England. Moreover, the speech of the New England colonists thus stood in fairly close relations to that of the southern, especially the tidewater Virginian colonists. To a certain degree the Virginian colonists represented a different social class from that of New England. The organizers of this Virginian colony stood in more intimate relations to the higher official life of England than did the founders of the New England colonies. They were perhaps to a greater extent men of the world, gentlemen and younger sons of gentlemen, and as such could not have viewed with favor any speech which deviated widely from the customs of the court speech with which they had been familiar in their own group. For reasons peculiar to its own life, Virginia exerted a less general and less energetic influence than

New England upon American social customs in their earlier formative and expanding period. But again the character of New England speech saved it from a stronger opposition than that which it would have been compelled to meet had it been a less respectable dialect than the one current among the settlers of Virginia.

New England standing thus close to Old England has always held an honored place in American opinion as the transmitter of a highly prized race tradition. As time has passed, British and American English, at those points where they came in contact, which would obviously be mainly in the printed and literary language, have drawn close to each other and have not fulfilled the early prophecies that the two languages would drift far apart. Among those who have given any thought to the matter, there has rarely been one who had any desire, whether in New England or elsewhere in America, to make of American English a separate speech. Occasional theorists, like Walt Whitman, in his *American Primer*, written about 1850, have proposed that "the etiquette of saloons" should be "discharged from that great thing, the renovated English speech in America." Whitman, however, did scarcely more than express this desire, and few other theorists who have agreed with him have done much more. When it came to the actual use of the language for literary purposes, Whitman could not forget "the etiquette of saloons," the cultivated tradition of the past. There have been undoubtedly extremists in both directions, those who would altogether reject British English, and those who would prescribe it as a refined and inescapable necessity. But the American attitude in the main has stood halfway between these extremes. Though there has been little direct knowledge of British English among Americans, there has been no eager desire to escape from it, no scorn or contempt for it. On the contrary, perhaps there has been too much acquiescence on the part of the average American in the opinion that British speech, in some undefined way, is better than American speech, that the Britisher has a native right in the language which the American enjoys only by favor of the original proprietors. This provincial feeling towards England has been stronger in New England than in the rest of the country, because in the rest of the country, New England in large degree has taken the place of Old England. The "muscular classes," "the young men of These States," when they turn their attention from sport and business to culture are much inclined to look elsewhere than at home for what they are seeking. They look to New England for the remote and perfect English, if not to practice it, at least to admire it; or if New England is home, even if Boston is home, a still more perfect perfection may be sought beneath the shadow of St. James. In the quest for culture, it has sometimes been found difficult, even by sensible persons, to draw the line at the right point between sound respect for tradition and abject provincialism. There is consolation, however, in reflecting that only a violent radicalism in American speech could have saved it from any appearance of provincialism.

In general, the relatively compact and highly organized social life which developed early in the northern colonies gave to the ideas prevalent in New England an exceptional carrying power. Several of these ideas, whether we look upon them as spreading from New England or only as typically represented there, have been of very great significance in determining the feeling of Americans for their mother tongue, and these call for further examination.

One of these characteristically American ideas was that of the equality of social rank. Great differences of rank did not exist in New England. Ministers, lawyers, teachers, and doctors stood slightly above the average level, but the learned professions were recruited directly from the populace, who felt themselves inferior to none. Webster bids Englishmen take notice that the "American yeomanry" are not to be compared to the "illiterate peasantry" of their own country. "The yeomanry of this country consist of substantial independent free-holders, masters of their own persons and lords of their own soil," *Dissertations*, p. 288. Among this yeomanry, certain of the finer interests were cultivated with enthusiasm. It is true that the imagination had little play, whether in poetry, or painting, or music, or prose narrative, or drama. The arts cultivated were those of a relatively intellectual or practical character, but owing just to this limitation, they were arts within the reach of all members of the community. Whatever culture existed was accessible to all. Timothy Dwight, *Travels*, I, 302, gives an engaging picture of New England, the whole country covered with villages, and every village with its church and "suit of schools." "Nearly every child," he continues, "even those of beggars and blacks in considerable numbers, can read, write, and keep accounts. All the people are neighbors; social beings, converse; feel; sympathize; mingle minds; cherish sentiments; and are subjects of at least some degree of refinement." In his generous description of the people of New England, Cooper declares, *Notions*, I, 94, that "beyond a doubt nowhere is to be found a population as well instructed, in elementary knowledge, as the people of these six States." "It is equally true," he added, "that I have nowhere witnessed such an universality of that self-respect which preserves men from moral degradation." These statements are all the more significant as coming from one who was not a native of the region described, indeed was not an ardent lover of it.

In hill town and valley town, upon the coast and in the interior, a remarkably homogeneous civilization developed. Now that so much of this has passed away, the modern student is constantly surprised to find in what out-of-the-way places printing-presses flourished in New England, how abundant books once were where now no books are found at all. "I am acquainted," wrote Webster, *Essays*, Boston, 1790, p. 339, in the reformed spelling which he at this time affected, "with parishes, where almost every householder haz red the works of Addison, Sherlock, Atterbury, Watts, Young, and other similar writings; and will converse handsomely on the subjects of which they treet." If this sounds a little like Yankee self-esteem, it can be confirmed by Cooper, *Notions*, I, 97, who remembered that copies of standard English authors were repeatedly to be found "in retired dwellings where one would not expect to meet any production of a cast higher than an almanac, or a horn-book." Webster calls attention also to the common custom of establishing parish libraries, the progenitors of the later public libraries, which were supported by subscription. He notes as of similar significance the relatively greater extent to which newspapers were circulated in New England as compared with other sections of the country. In the year 1785 he found the number in Connecticut alone "to be neerly eight thousand; which waz equal to that published in the whole territory, south of Philadelphia." [1]

The two binding institutions which most effectively held together the elements of the democratic social life of early New England were the church and the district school. Every village of any size had its own church and its own resident minister or clergyman. Living in direct contact with the people and delivering sermons as they did with unflagging assiduity, the clergy exerted a powerful influence in maintaining the intellectual tone of the life of their respective communities. It was, moreover, not a popular but a learned clergy whose voices were heard in the New England meeting houses. In the earlier years of the colonies, there was some danger that the church might successfully assume a kind of autocratic and Calvinistic authority which would have made of it merely a stern judge and lawgiver, exalted above the familiar life of the people. By the end of the seventeenth century, however, the character of the New England ministry had undergone a change. The extremes of early Puritan doctrine and discipline had been modified, the church had been compelled to give up its hold upon civil affairs, and the church as a whole had become a more democratic social institution than the early church promised to be. It would be stretching the point perhaps too far to say that the growth of church life in America has been determined by the church in New England as its origin and point of departure. Too many other elements have entered since the colonial period which found no part in the New England church to permit of so simple a disposition of the matter. But it is true that the general character of the congregations and churches

[1] *Essays*, p. 338. He refers to weekly papers, and evidently to the number of copies issued, not to different newspapers.

as they have developed their organizations throughout the country has remained essentially the same. No branch of the church has assumed or even vigorously attempted to assume the position of an authorized or established church. As divisions and sects multiplied, it became manifestly absurd for any one branch of the church to claim authority as the sole accredited conserver of religious truth. The very independence which led to the organization of the early Puritan church led also to separation from it, and in the end to toleration of Quaker, Baptist, Methodist, or any other kind of doctrine or organization which it might suit the fancy of any group of citizens to support. Here again one may note the powerful disintegrating tendencies of democracy, if not upon the essential purposes for which the church exists, at least upon the manner of its organization. Differentiation results, however, only from difference of opinion and the discussion which difference of opinion generates. It would be difficult to show in detail that American speech has been directly affected by the popular nature of the American church. One may point out, however, that the various churches in America have never been degraded to a place of social inferiority by contrast to any official church, that they have always been a very direct expression of a general will in the communities which support them and have thus responded to the community's sense of propriety and dignity. The American public has ever been church-going and has participated actively in the conduct of its churches. The indirect influence which the church has exerted upon speech and the feeling for speech, as upon other social customs, one may suppose to have thus been considerable, and many a community which has had no other means of formulating its ideals of proper convention and refinement has been enabled to do this with more or less effect through its churches. The church has been the guardian of respectability in America, and in matters of speech, if its influence has not been exalted, it has at least tended to counteract the tendency toward the crudely familiar and local which is always likely to become unduly prominent in a mixed and democratic society.

Still more significant than the church, both for its own local community and as a tradition passed on to other large sections of the country, was the New England interest in education. Though other regions of colonial America did not altogether neglect the subject, nowhere was it a matter of such concern and respectful attention as in the two northern mother colonies, Massachusetts and Connecticut. In this region a complete system of education was provided from the primary school to the university, one which was thus adequate for all the needs of the community. Cooper remarks, *Notions*, II, 96, that "the gentlemen of the middle and southern States, before the revolution, were very generally educated in England," and that after the Revolution, lacking higher schools of their own, the middle and southern States for a time fared badly in the matter of higher instruction. But in New England the two universities were early established and uninterruptedly met the demand for advanced scholarly and professional training. Elementary instruction also was an essential part of the New England scheme of things, sometimes grudgingly provided for, but never completely neglected, even in the rough period of the earliest colonization.

At first the school was an appendage of the Puritan church, not of equal rank with it, but a handmaiden to assist the church in preserving its stores of knowledge from the attacks of "that old deluder Satan" and from the corruptions which the "false glosses of saint-seeming deceivers" might bring about, Updegraff, *The Origin of the Moving School in Massachusetts*, p. 52. The Puritan church exerted a minute and strong control over its schools, and wherever the church went, the school went with it. By a law of 1647 it was ordered in the colony of Massachusetts that every township, "after the Lord hath increased them to the number of fifty house-holders, shall then forthwith appoint one within their town to teach all such children as shall resort to him to write and read." The records of early New England towns are full of accounts of "visitations" by the selectmen of the town on those heads of families in the town who were reputed to be slack in the matter of putting their children to school. And it was further ordered that "where any town shall increase to the number of one hundred families or householders, they shall set up a grammar school, the master thereof being able to instruct youth, so far as they may be fitted, for the university," Updegraff, p. 52; Mathews, *The Expansion of New England*, p. 39. Failure to meet these requirements was punishable by fine. Every child was required by the church to receive at least elementary instruction, either at home or in the elementary schools. Supplementing the lower schools came in time numberless local academies and grammar schools, and at the top the colleges and the two universities. The New England town revolved about its church, its school, and its academy or college.

In the latter half of the seventeenth century, however, the hold of the church upon its schools was relaxed, and with the separation of the church from civil affairs, the school ceased to be a function of the church and passed under the control of civil authority. The church school thus became the district school, conducted not in the interests of any ecclesiastical or other group except the community at large. In the period of transition, when the school was passing out of the hands of the church into the hands of the democratic people, there seems to have been a decline of interest in the schools. "The old sanction was gone and a new one had not as yet taken hold of the people with sufficient force to cause them to provide schools of their own initiative," Updegraff, p. 114. But this state of affairs was of brief duration, and by the end of the seventeenth century interest in the schools revived, and with the expansion of the population, the number of schools largely increased throughout New England. As colonists from Massachusetts established new communities elsewhere in New England, they carried with them their plans for the organization of schools, and always the "civil school of the church-state had become the civil school of the civil state," p. 117. Yankee education soon became a standard commodity of the country. The Yankee schoolmaster, like the Yankee pedlar, traveled everywhere, and wherever the Yankee pedlar went, the spelling-book went with him. It became as essential a part of the sustenance of all youth as their daily bread. In Woodworth's

Forest Rose (1825), Jonathan, a Yankee storekeeper, tells what he has for sale: "Everything: whiskey, molasses, calicoes, spelling-books, and patent gridirons." Halleck, *Poetical Writings*, p. 171, describes a typical Connecticut Yankee as "wandering through the Southern countries teaching the A B C from Webster's spelling book."

In Connecticut, Webster records that "every town, or parish containing seventy householders, shall keep an English school at leest eleven months in a yeer; and towns containing a less number, at leest six months in a yeer," *Essays*, p. 337. The district schools were held during the winter, and in the summer, "a woman iz hired to teech small children, who are not fit for any kind of labor." In the large towns, schools, either public or private, were kept the whole year, and in every county town, a grammar school was established by law. The striking thing about these schools is that they were common schools, open to all children of the community on equal terms and supported by public funds. Instruction in them was given in the simpler subjects, reading, writing, arithmetic, history and geography, and the schools were not regarded merely as propædeutics to colleges or the learned professions. They were devised to give all members of the community a foundation knowledge in their own language and history which might serve as the point of departure for higher studies, but which need not necessarily do so. They were devised to make citizens, not scholars.

Webster notes with disapproval "a too general attention to the dead languages, with a neglect of our own," *Essays*, p. 3ff. He advocates little attention even for living languages other than English, for "men whose business is wholly domestic, have little or no use for any language but their own, much less for languages known only in books." The masters in these schools, even of the humbler kind, were often graduates of the colleges who frequently used their teaching positions as stepping-stones towards one of the learned professions. Very many New Englanders of note in American history have been at one stage of their career teachers in the common schools, and the statement remains true even for the country at large.

The schoolmaster occupied a respected social position in the community, and Webster again comments on an interesting contrast between the state of affairs in New England and in the southern states. He points out that in the South "gentlemen of property, residing on their plantations at a distance from a village," will sometimes procure private tutors for the younger members of their families. But these instructors, for the most part, must be "vagabonds," as "the gentleman will not admit that a *skoolmaster* can be a *gentleman*, in consequence of which opinion, most or all teechers are excluded from genteel company." An exception is noted, however, in the case of grammar masters, "for a man who can teech Latin, they suppose, may be a *decent* man, and fit for gentlemen's company," *Essays*, p. 362.

To attempt to trace in detail the influence of the New England school upon the system of public school instruction as it has developed throughout the country would be a large and complicated task. As the system has grown, many compromises with the New England system, and additions to it, have been made. But the essentials have not changed. The common school, with English as the basis of its training, is a necessary part of the life of every American community, not only in those regions which were settled by New Englanders, but even in regions remote from such direct influence. It would be almost impossible to exaggerate the effect which these schools have had in the gradual process of realizing that ideal of a national speech which the country holds as its standard. English has been for a century and more the backbone of popular instruction in the common schools. At times it may have lost itself in futile exercises in grammar and parsing, but defects of pedagogic method have never obscured the aim of instruction in the native speech, which has been to correct illiteracy and to replace provincialism by something approximating general custom in speech. The process still continues, complicated by the presence in the schools, not only of Americans of different social and local origins, but in many schools also by the presence of large numbers of children of foreign birth. Though the results accomplished fall short of the ideal, when one measures these results not by the test of the ideal but by the test of what has been practically achieved with the heterogeneous material that has poured into the schools, the results certainly justify the efforts that have been put forth to attain them. Few children leave the public schools without at least a vision of the meaning of standard and literary English. The vision may later become obscured and some students may fall back to the level of provincial and illiterate English, but it does not seem that this is generally or frequently the case. Later habits, in business, in social intercourse, in further academic training for the fortunate few, tend to confirm the habits already formed. It is still possible to compare an older generation in some communities which had but little "schooling," with a new generation that has passed through the elementary schools, or through both elementary and high school, and the two generations, so far at least as speech is concerned, quite obviously belong to different levels of culture. Whether or not the new generation stands on a higher level of culture altogether than the old may be a matter of opinion affected by a variety of considerations. But the culture of the new generation is at least normalized and socialized to a degree which would have been impossible if it had not experienced the discipline which the common schools provide. This process has been going on for eight or nine generations. It was the possibility of this kind of discipline which has been the significant contribution of the New England school to the development of American speech. Among all the centrifugal tendencies of democratic American society, none has exerted a more powerful centralizing effect than the public schools.

A third characteristic New England institution, the town meeting, has maintained itself with remarkable vitality upon the soil of New England, but so far as it was transmitted to other regions, it has been so completely merged into different customs as largely to have lost its identity. When the early emigrants passed from their old homes in Massachusetts and Connecticut into New York, Pennsylvania, Ohio and other parts of the Northwest Territory, they carried with them their town meeting and for a time this institution flourished in regions where it is now unknown. It was not, however, practically adapted to conditions in the new settlements, where the local political units were larger than they had been in the New England towns and where the settlers were scattered over a wide extent of territory. Moreover, as population increased, the town meeting became unwieldy. A group of fifty or a hundred householders might profitably come together to arrange the local affairs of the towns, but as the number grew from hundreds to thousands, representative government of the local communities became a necessity. Wherever it has flourished, however, the town meeting has been a notably democratic institution. The meeting was a place where every householder might freely express his opinion, and it may be noted that even in early New England, the liberties of the town meeting were wider than those of the general government of the colony. Only members of the church were admitted citizens or "freemen" of the colony, but every householder had a vote and a voice in his local meeting.

As these town meetings were gatherings of equals, of neighbors and friends, to discuss and pass upon matters of very immediate and practical concern to all, they were not favorable training grounds for orators, and it does not seem that the town meetings were ever much inclined to encourage flights of eloquence. The orator can expand only when he has a large and helpless audience at his mercy. But the New England town community did not provide such an audience, nor was its business profitably to be transacted by means of speechifying. Dwight, *Travels*, I, 215, notes, in describing the Connecticut town meeting, that "the sober, busy citizens of Connecticut are . . . very little inclined to commend, or even to listen to, the eloquence which is intended only for show. He who would be heard with approbation, or mentioned with praise, must speak only because there is occasion to speak, must speak with modesty, with brevity, to forward or improve the measures proposed, or those which he substitutes; and not to show that he can speak, however ingeniously." The significance of the town meeting for the student of language lies in the fact that it provided a common meeting place for members of the community of varying social or local origin, where they might speak their minds as equals, and in the process, inevitably shape their speech, if peculiar, to bring it into conformity with the more or less recognized customs of the group.

It would be an interesting subject of speculation whether or not the ideals represented in the life and social customs of New England would have been so widely influential in America if the population of New England had remained within its narrow geographical confines. The interest of the subject must be entirely speculative, however, since migration from New England began as soon as there was any wider America to affect and was itself the most significant single factor in the westward expansion of the country. In his famous account of the Yankees, Irving, *Knickerbocker History*, Book II, Chapter VIII, points out that to this "Arab of America" the notion of settling himself in the world meant "nothing more nor less than to begin his rambles." In fact many of the very earliest settlers seem to have been restless persons, moving from one town to another often four or five times. At first migration within New England, that is from the mother country in Massachusetts to neighboring regions, could take place only with the consent of the church and under its constant inspection. These restrictions were soon thrown off, however, and the colonists moved freely, to Rhode Island, Connecticut, New Hampshire, and Vermont, and then outside New England to New York and Pennsylvania. Commenting on the possibility of the disruption of the American confederation, Timothy Dwight, *Travels*, IV, 513, remarks that if this should take place, "New-England and New-York will almost of course, be united in the same political body. The inhabitants are now substantially one people." From three-fifths to two-thirds of the inhabitants of New York State, he says, *Travels*, III, 252, originated from New England, and "the proportion is continually increasing. New York is, therefore, to be ultimately regarded as a colony from New England." In New York and New England, Dwight found "the same interests of every kind inseparably united," *Travels,* IV, 527. These statements will be somewhat qualified when we remember that Dwight's impressions were derived mainly from travels in Central New York. In the Hudson Valley and in the neighborhood of New York City, New England influence was not so prominent.

At the close of the Revolution and with the opening of the Northwest Territory, the great tide of westward migration began. In the Western Reserve of Ohio a "second Connecticut" came into being. At Marietta and at Granville the towns were born as full-fledged New England villages. What happened at these places, happened in scores and hundreds of other places throughout the Middle West. The migrations were not always direct from New England, for a dweller in Ohio may first have sojourned for a few years in New York or Pennsylvania before passing on to a new promised land. Where opportunities were many, it was easy for a settler to pick up his few portable belongings and set out for the better land that seemed always beckoning just a little beyond. On the whole, the New Englander seems to have had little of that feeling for "ancestral home" which was so marked a characteristic among Southerners. But many of the more steady and prosperous members of the new settlements remained after the restless ones had departed and soon established centers of widely radiating influence. Another significant feature of New England migrations, which likewise distinguishes them from the Southerner's method of seeking new homes, was that of moving in groups. When Granville was settled in Ohio, the church was first organized in its old home in Granville, Massachusetts, and was transplanted with pastor, deacons, and members, to its new surroundings. The same thing happened in numberless instances, and to this day one finds communities, not only in the Northwest Territory, but across the Mississippi in Iowa and beyond, which often seem as much like New England as New England itself. The compact organization of these communities, and their skill in institutional administration acquired through long experience, made them exceptionally effective in drawing together and giving direction to the heterogeneous elements of which frontier society was composed.

When one considers all these various streams of influence which have issued from New England and have irrigated the whole continent of American spiritual life, one may be not unprepared to believe that American speech also is but a child of New England speech. But the respect which America has always had for New England has not carried with it unquestioning acceptance or imitation of all New England customs. One may admire without exactly copying, and it must be said with respect to New England that its influence in America has been in determining the tone and aspirations of American life, not in establishing the detailed practices of American social habits and customs. Thus in the matter of speech, ever since students began to take a critical interest in the subject, New England speech in the rest of the country has been felt to be distinctly local, often rustic and provincial.

One of the first local types of character to appear in American literature was the comic New England native, with his numerous and strange but mild expletives, his vocabulary rude and doric, his drawl and twang. With all his respect for New England, Cooper thought, *Notions*, II, 130, that the best English in America was spoken "by the natives of the middle States, who are purely the descendants of English parents, without being the descendants of emigrants from New England." The provincialisms of New England, as Cooper heard them, consisted of intonations, pronunciations, and meanings of words, and he mentioned some eight or ten details of this sort. Yet he concluded that with these few exceptions, "the people of New England speak the language more like the people of Old England than any other parts of our country"—a statement of the case which most persons would agree to even to-day. But this very similarity of the speech of New England to the speech of Old England has been one of the things which has marked New England speech as provincial, or at least as different, when it has been compared with the speech of the rest of the country.

Because of its geographical position, New England from the start tended to become detached from the rest of the country. The center neither of American political nor of American commercial activity was ever in New England, and intellectual leadership, always open to doubts and dissensions, was but a poor substitute for these as a practical carrying power. Furthermore it must be remembered that the speech of New England was not itself uniform. When one thinks of the leadership of New England, one usually thinks of Eastern Massachusetts, and it is the speech of this region which corresponds to the type commonly known as New England speech. Yet none of the distinctive marks of the pronunciation of Eastern Massachusetts has been transferred from that region to the whole country. The pronunciation of *a* in *path, calf, dance,* etc. as [ɑː], of *o* in *hot, pod,* etc., as [ɔ], of *part, heart,* etc. as [pɑːt], [hɑːt], etc., of *o* in *stone, home,* etc. as an unrounded shortened vowel, popularly written *stun, hum,* these have become universal neither in the whole of New England nor in the rest of the country. They are familiar to all persons who take any interest in matters of speech, but this familiarity has not led to an acceptance of them in practice. Even communities which through immigration are mainly of New England origin soon ceased to be distinctively like New England in speech. If one were seeking for what is commonly apprehended as the general type of American speech one would not seek for it in New England, but somewhere between the Alleghanies and the Rockies. Or perhaps one may phrase the point better by saying that if two cultivated speakers, one from Nebraska and one from Eastern Massachusetts were both asked to discard those features in their speech which seemed to them to bear distinctive local color, the speaker from Eastern Massachusetts would in most cases have to yield more than the speaker from Nebraska.

One may say that in America three main types of speech have come to be recognized, a New England local type, a Southern local type, and a general or Western speech covering the rest of the country, and also all speakers in New England and the South at the moments when their speech is not local in character. This general speech has been the result of a great variety of influences, the most important probably being the mixed racial and local origin of the people among whom it has arisen. In this mixture of races the foreign element seems not to have affected American speech in any great degree, but the mingling of Scotch and Irish and of Englishmen from the north as well as the south of England has been of the greatest importance. The resultant speech is one which stands in many significant respects closer to the speech of central and northern England than it does to that of southern England, and by consequence, to that of Eastern Massachusetts. This threefold division in American speech is a matter of common though not always of clearly analyzable feeling on the part of Americans. Merely as a fact of pragmatic experience, the average American realizes three large and representative types of speech which he ordinarily designates as Eastern, Western, and Southern. He may realize also a number of other less extensive local types, but there is no other type which he would be inclined to place upon the same level as these three in comprehensiveness and in significance. The geographical terms, Eastern, Western and Southern, are commonly used, to be sure, without any implications of clearly defined geographical boundaries between the several types of speech. Neither is it ordinarily implied by this use of terms that all speakers in any community speak uniformly. It is recognized that there may be as much difference between a speaker from Eastern Massachusetts and one from Western Connecticut as between one from Eastern Massachusetts and one from Ohio. The terms Eastern, Southern, and Western are merely used to designate several types of speech which, though not finally and scientifically differentiated either socially or geographically in the popular mind, are nevertheless in practice distinguishable in the experience of every observant American.

The details of speech which occasion this feeling of difference are usually details of pronunciation and intonation, less often details of vocabulary. So far as vocabulary is concerned, the speech of all educated persons in America is remarkably uniform. One may occasionally observe a word which by its meaning reveals a local custom, as when one gives the words *evening* or *gallery* the Southern senses of *afternoon* or *porch*, or when one calls the enclosure around a house, as they do in New England, a *door-yard,* or calls a *farm* a *ranch,* as they do in the Far West. But the occasions for expressing the ideas which may call for the use of peculiarly local words are obviously less frequent and therefore less revealing than pronunciations, or cadences, which affect all words, whether they are local or not. Moreover, the conventional spelling of modern English, though it is adequate to universalize vocabulary through the printed pages of books, magazines and newspapers, by the very fact that it is conventional is made powerless to normalize pronunciation or to prevent increasing differentiation in it.

Some of the more distinctive marks of difference in the pronunciation of American English may be briefly summarized as providing the clues by which one recognizes the several large types of American speech. These types may be most conveniently designated in the terminology commonly current as the Eastern, the Southern, and the Western, or General types. Further historical and descriptive details concerning the sounds here tabulated will be found under the discussion of the several sounds in a later chapter. They are presented now merely as elements in the general background of feeling for the mother tongue. It is perhaps not necessary to point out that a sound posited as characteristic of a certain type of speech is not necessarily peculiar to that type. The quality of a style of speech is determined by the combination of characteristics which it exhibits as well as by the characteristics in themselves.

The most distinctive and generally recognized marks of the Eastern type of American speech are:

(1) loss of *r* [r] before consonants and finally

(2) tendency to pronounce *a* before [f] [s] [θ] [ns], etc., as [ɑː]. Though by no means universal throughout New England and the East, this pronunciation has established itself as one of the commonly accepted features of the Eastern type of American speech.

(3) tendency to pronounce *o* as [ɔ] in closed syllables in which the vowel is followed by a stop consonant, as in *hot, rock, drop,* etc.

(4) tendency to pronounce *o, ou,* as [ɔː] in *court, port, more,* etc., with the *r* of course lost in pronunciation.

(5) tendency to pronounce *u* as [uː] in words like *duty, tune, mature,* etc. This pronunciation is not uniform in Eastern pronunciation, but is more frequent there than in Southern or General American English. In earlier periods and in present rustic New England speech, it resulted in the pronunciation of *t* as [t] instead of [tʃ] in words like *nature, creature,* etc., popularly spelled *nater, natur, critter, creatur,* etc. This latter pronunciation has completely disappeared from cultivated New England speech, but it lingers in popular tradition.

(6) the pronunciation of the vowel of *stone, home, whole,* etc., shorter and less round than it is elsewhere pronounced, a sound popularly represented by the dialect spellings, *stun, hum, hull,* etc. This pronunciation is disappearing from cultivated speech and in many words has completely disappeared, though it is still not infrequent in others. In 1889, Professor Grandgent bore evidence that in his pronunciation *whole* and *hull* were very slightly different, much to the surprise of James Russell Lowell, to whom it seemed that "the short *o* which you get in *whole* is the rustic pronunciation and that whōle is the urban pronunciation," see *Publications of the Modern Language Association,* V, XXXVI. Cultivated usage was probably more divided in the pronunciation of this particular word thirty years ago than it is now, but in other words, as in *Holmes, colt, coat,* etc., a pronunciation with a short and very slightly rounded *o* remains in cultivated eastern New England speech. In Phyfe, *18,000 Words Often Mispronounced,* the *o* of *only, whole, wholly,* is marked as being properly halfway between the *o* of *odd* and the *o* of *old,* and as being frequently, and incorrectly, confounded with this latter sound.

(7) tendency to pronounce final unstressed *a* in such a way as to produce the acoustic impression of [r] as in *idea, Hannah,* etc., represented in popular dialect spelling by *idear, Hanner,* etc.

Some distinctive and generally recognized marks of the Southern type of American English are:

(1) loss of [r] before consonants and finally.

(2) *a* pronounced as [æ] before [f], [s], [θ], [ns], etc. In Eastern

Virginia, words of this type have "two equally authorized standard pronunciations," one with [æ], the other with [ɑː]; both of these are traditional "in certain of the best families," and they are sharply divided "on the same lines among the lower classes," Primer, *Pronunciation of Fredericksburg, Va.*, p. 196. But aside from these survivals of [ɑː] in Eastern Virginia, the normal pronunciation is [æ] in the South. Eastern Virginia and Eastern New England both had the pronunciation [ɑː] by inheritance from the same source, and of course also the pronunciation [æ]. Self-conscious New England speech, however, which we have called the Eastern type of American English, established the pronunciation [ɑː] as desirable and to be imitated in a way which was not possible in the less highly organized and critical South. The South thus tends toward the pronunciation of the General type in these words, and New England towards the Eastern type. In Thomas Nelson Page's *In Ole Virginia* the old-fashioned negro body servant in *Marse Chan* regularly has [ɑː] as in New England speech, but the author remarks in a prefatory note to the volume that "the dialect of the negroes of Eastern Virginia differs totally from that of the Southern negroes."

(3) tendency to pronounce *o* as [ɑ] in *hot, got, lot,* etc.

(4) tendency to pronounce *u* as [juː] in *duty, tune, mature,* etc.

(5) tendency to preserve in approved local standard use pronunciations different from those of general standard American use, for example, the Virginia ['gjɑːdn] for *garden;* the Georgian, Alabamian, and Mississippian ['tɪnɪs], [mɪn], for *tennis, men;* the very general Southern diphthong [æu] for [au] as in *down, town,* etc.; the pronunciation of words like *ear, hear, here, deer, dear,* etc., with the same vowel as that which appears in General American *hare, dare, tear* (verb), etc.; the pronunciation of *au* in words like *haunt, jaunt, gaunt,* as [æ], [æː], see Primer, *Pronunciation of Fredericksburg, Va.*, p. 196. These pronunciations are all survivals from older more general pronunciations, and though perhaps none of them can be taken as universally characteristic of Southern American, taken together they establish the position that Southern American speech is

likely to be more archaic, and to the uncritical observer to seem more peculiar, than any other type of American speech.

(6) tendency toward a lax articulation, especially of final consonants after continuants, as in *land, first, pest, soft,* etc. With this may perhaps be connected in general a soft and low timbre of voice and a relatively slow tempo in speech.

(7) certain characteristic cadences, for example stressing the final instead of the second word in the phrase *I think so.*

The distinctive and commonly accepted marks of the Western or General type of pronunciation are:

(1) retention of *r* before consonants and finally, either as an audible [r], as in *far, part, lord,* etc., pronounced [far], [part], [Lɔrd]; or as the reverted vowel [ə] with the consonantal quality of the *r* sometimes remaining, sometimes disappearing, as in *first, herd, hurt,* etc., pronounced [fərst], [hərd], [hərt], or [fəːst], [həːd], [həːt].

(2) *a* pronounced as [æ] before [f], [s], [θ], [ns], etc.; and as [ɑː] only under Eastern influence.

(3) *o* pronounced as [a] in *hot, got, lot,* etc.

(4) *a* pronounced as [ɑ] after [w], as in *water, watch,* etc., pronounced ['watər], [watʃ], etc.

(5) *u* pronounced either as [uː] or [juː], perhaps equally divided, in words like *duty, tube, new,* etc.

(6) a greater amount of nasalization of vowels in the Western General type as contrasted with typically Eastern or Southern American speech.

(7) a "hard" and "unmusical" quality of voice.

It is obviously much easier for an American to call up in his mind a kind of image of the Eastern and Southern types of American speech than of the Western or General type. The reason for this is that the Western or General type is a composite type, more or less an abstraction of generalized national habits, whereas the Eastern and Southern types, in their most tangible and recognizable forms, developed at the first as the speech of definitely localized and highly characteristic social communities, and have remained so. The New England type of speech had for its center that life of Eastern Massachusetts and Connecticut which by the end of the seventeenth century had passed out of experimental uncertainties into an organic social unity such as could have been found at no other place in the North at that time. The striking characteristic of the New England of the early colonists was its unity, but as soon as one stepped beyond the bounds of the original settlements, the striking characteristic of all communities was their heterogeneity.

The same thing was true in the South. The earliest seventeenth-century settlers of tidewater Virginia were in general of the same kind. They all came at about the same time and with the same purposes. They developed their own civilization within their own limits and they gave to this civilization, by reason of its appreciable local color and social unity, a typical quality which to this day is the best expression of a kind of life in America which both the historical and the practical imagination love to dwell upon. The eastern Massachusetts towns and villages and the plantations of the James and Rappahannock established themselves as fixed but radiating centers for cultural influence before the great movements westward began and before the great tides of European immigration set in. The population of these two communities was relatively small, but their social significance has been great. This it is which has given to the speech of eastern Massachusetts its representative quality for the Eastern type of American speech, and to the speech of tidewater Virginia its representative quality for the Southern type of American speech. No other locality can be fixed upon as standing as indisputably for the Western or General type of speech, as these two regions do for their own types. The reason is that the Western or General type did not assume its form in one locality. It does not belong to one locality, but to the nation as a whole. Manifestly what belongs to so heterogeneous a thing as the American nation as a whole must itself be heterogeneous. Such unity as it has is not slight, but it is not a unity which resulted from generations of life upon a circumscribed native soil, such as was the life of colonial Massachusetts and Virginia. The General type of American speech is therefore not racy of the soil of a particular locality, but if one may be permitted the tautology, it is racy of the life of the race. It has grown, and is growing, in a thousand different places, by mixture, by compromise, by imitation, by adaptation, by all the devices by which a changing people in changing circumstances adapt themselves to each other and to their new conditions.

The provincialism or localism of New England, which was mentioned above, affected the speech of New England itself in several ways. As a clearly defined local dialect developed in New England, the natives of this region, if their self-confidence had been sufficient, might have exalted their local dialect to a position of standard or literary authority. They might have rested content in it, or even have become proud of it, and as Dante established the dialect of Florence as a literary speech by writing in it, so some early New Englander of genius might have established the familiar speech of that community as the literary language of America by composing in it a great work expressive of the feeling for nationality in the new country. Some such aspiration was present in Webster's mind in his endeavors to put on record what he called the American language. But like all educated persons, Webster did not really conceive the possibility of resting contentedly on the practices of popular speech as it existed among his own townsmen and neighbors. Before his eyes there always shone the ideal of a remote literary language, which was to be modified and perhaps enriched by incorporation within it of certain local practices in speech, but which was not to be replaced by a new idiom. In consequence, the local speech tended to take on more and more the position of a homely dialect, and wherever sophistication flourished, an artificial speech tended to assume greater importance.

Now it is characteristic of New England that it is to-day, and formerly was much more, a region of one city. Boston has always been so much more important than any other city of New England that it has been the preëminent leader in the expression of all urban refinements. Boston has been, so far as New England is concerned, the center of culture, and to the extent that New England may be taken for America as a whole, the center of American culture. This central position, however, has obviously been more important for New England than it has for the country as a whole. As cultural aspirations tended to become localized in Boston, the rest of the New England region tended to become more and more provincial. On the other hand, to save itself from being swallowed up by the surrounding ocean of provinciality, Boston was driven to cultivate the more strenuously those marks of distinction which glorified it as being different from the native simplicity by which it was surrounded. This was the light in which Boston and New England in their inter-actions appeared to Henry James, viewing them from the angle of New York and Europe in the sixth decade of the nineteenth century. Here and there, says James, *Notes of a Son and Brother*, p. 350, were found personalities which exhibited "a state of provincialism rounded and compact, quite self-supporting, which gave it serenity and quality, something comparatively rich and urban." But such personalities were comparatively rare. One gazed usually "straight into those depths of rusticity which more and more unmistakably underlay the social order at large and out of which one felt it to have emerged in any degree but at scattered points." "Where it did emerge, I seemed to see," the analysis continues, "it held itself as high as possible, conscious, panting, a little elate with the fact of having cleared its skirts, saved its life, consolidated its Boston, yet as with wastes unredeemed, roundabout it, propping up and pushing in—all so insistently that the light in which one for the most part considered the scene was strongly coloured by their action."

To save itself from the invading barbarism of provincial New England, Boston made a cult of culture itself, and in nothing more strenuously than in speech. The American schools of elocution, oratory and vocal expression, now abundant and ubiquitous in the land, are a gift from Boston to the rest of the country. But as soon as one stepped out of this magic circle of cultivated Boston speech nto what one may perhaps call natural and familiar New England speech, one immediately descended to the regions of the rustic and provincial. How tantalizingly near this rustic native speech lay to the cultivated speech is evidenced by the use of the native speech which was made by writers like Holmes, Lowell, and others, who endeavored to express homespun character in homespun speech. Though this native speech was felt to be vigorously expressive, may even have been felt to be the real speech of New England, yet it was always used with a reluctant admission that the reality was not good enough for the highest purposes. It is doubtful, however, if Lowell ever expressed himself more sincerely than he did in the *Biglow Papers,* and time and again in Holmes, when he good-humoredly permits himself to forget the literary pose, glimpses of the essentially local, provincial New Englander, wise, kindly, and simple, show in the language he uses. This sense for double personality has existed nowhere else in the country so completely as in New England. Local dialects of course exist everywhere, but supplementing the General or Western type of speech there is no dialect speech which expresses familiar reality as the rustic dialect of New England supplements the refined dialect of Boston. In fact when writers elsewhere have written in dialect, they have always written in what is but a very slightly modified form of rustic New England dialect.

To detach itself more effectively from the hinterland of rustic New England, it was natural for Boston to strengthen the bonds which united Boston and England. The relatively close connection between the speech of Boston and the speech of England was noted as early as the latter eighteenth century, when Dwight, *Travels,* I, 465, remarked that the people of Boston "with a very small number of exceptions . . . speak the English language in the English manner." Since then many others have made similar observations. Boston is the only city in America in which *boots* is a common equivalent for *shoes, calico* for *unbleached muslin,* and *shop* a common name for *store.* In the mid-nineteenth century, according to many competent observers, the respect for things British in Boston might fairly be called a craze. It was Boston which in the sixties of the nineteenth century introduced to Americans "a new and romantic possibility" in afternoon tea. "The tone of Boston society," says Henry Adams, *Education of Henry Adams,* p. 19, speaking of this same period, "was colonial. The true Bostonian always knelt in self-abasement before the majesty of English standards; far from conceding it as a weakness, he was proud of it as his strength." Adams declares that almost alone among his Boston contemporaries, he was not English in feeling or in sympathies.

It will be readily understood that when Adams speaks of his Boston contemporaries, he by no means signifies all Boston. "True Bostonians" constituted an inner and upper circle, entry into which was jealously guarded and rarely effected. Surrounding the "true Bostonians" there dwelt the world of "blackguard Boston," presumably made up of all those ordinary citizens who might not aspire to be called true. By the middle of the nineteenth century, great numbers of Irish dwelt within the geographical limits of Boston, who assuredly did not kneel in self-abasement before the majesty of English standards. Boston, in the narrow sense, has come to be to the American a name for a state of mind, not for a civil organization or a local region. As a city, Boston was never entirely homogeneous. But as an ideal, it realized itself in parts with remarkable clearness in the early and mid-nineteenth century.

The effect of all this tradition and endeavor has been to place Boston in a peculiar position as compared with other seats of culture in the country. A community which claims for itself special distinctions is likely in many instances to have these claims recognized, but is just as likely to arouse hostility and to have such claims denied. Perhaps most Americans interested in the criticism of American speech would agree, however, in regarding what is commonly known as Bostonian English as exemplifying a special technique in language, as skilled virtuosity rather than natural habit. The influence of this ideal has been for good in showing that speech may be cultivated as a fine art, but on the other hand not for good in deflecting attention and respect from native idiom to the acquirement of remote and artificial practices in speech.

As a result of the circumstances under which it arose, the American mother tongue, especially in its General type, has attained an unusual degree of currency. No American popular dialect, except perhaps that of some backward negro community or the speech of some geographically isolated groups of people, differs widely from cultivated speech. An unsophisticated native of no community in America would have much difficulty in understanding a native of any other, such, for example, as an unsophisticated native of Yorkshire might have in understanding one from Somerset. After noting that "educated American English is now almost entirely independent of British influence, and differs from it considerably, though as yet not enough to make the two dialects—American English and British English—mutually unintelligible," Sweet, *New English Grammar*, I, 224 (1892), adds that "American English itself is beginning to split up into dialects." But this latter statement shows a misunderstanding of the situation. The splitting up of American dialects is an ancient inheritance from British dialects, and the rifts have not increased, but have grown fewer and smaller on American soil.

This tendency towards uniformity in American speech has long been noticed. President Witherspoon of Princeton, writing in 1784, *Works*, IV, 459, says that "the vulgar in America speak much better than the vulgar in Great Britain, for a very obvious reason, viz. that being much more unsettled, and moving frequently from place to place, they are not so liable to local peculiarities, either in accent or phraseology. There is a greater difference in dialect between one county and another in Britain, than there is between one state and another in America." Describing the state of New Jersey, *Works*, IV, 407, he remarks that "people from all the other states are continually moving into and out of this state, so that there is little peculiarity of manner"; and commenting on local phrases and terms in general, *Works*, IV, 469, he observes that "there is a much greater variety of these in Britain than in America," and adds the more penetrating observation that "if there is a much greater number of local vulgarisms in Britain than America, there is also for this very reason, much less danger of their being used by gentlemen or scholars. It is implied in the very nature of the thing, that a local phrase will not be used by any but the inhabitants or natives of that part of the country where it prevails. However, I am of the opinion that even local vulgarisms find admission into the discourse of people of better rank more easily here than in England." In other words, though Witherspoon would agree that speech was more uniform in America than in England, he believed also that the general level was lower. The question whether or not American speech would continue to be estimated by the British standard was one that Witherspoon left open, though he was inclined to think, *Works*, IV, 459, that "being entirely separated from Britain, we shall find some center or standard of our own, and not be subject to the inhabitants of that island, either in receiving new ways of speaking, or rejecting the old." It is interesting to find opinions somewhat similar to these of Witherspoon repeated by Marsh, *Lectures* (1860), p. 666, who remarks that "it is a trite observation that, though very few Americans speak as well as the educated classes of Englishmen, yet not only is the *average* of English used here, both in speaking and writing, better than that of the great mass of the English people; but there are fewer local peculiarities of form and articulation in our vast extent of territory than on the comparatively narrow soil of Britain. In spite of disturbing and distracting causes, English is more emphatically *one* in America than in its native land, and if we have engrafted on our mother-speech some widespread corruptions, we have very nearly freed the language, in our use of it, from some vulgar and disagreeable peculiarities exceedingly common in England."

Webster also bears witness to this uniformity in American speech, though this happy state he fears has been endangered by the publication of conflicting but supposedly authoritative statements in dictionaries. "Before the publication of Sheridan's Dictionary," he remarks, *Compendious Dictionary* (1806), p. xvi, "the pronunciation of words in the northern states of the United States was so uniform, that it is doubtful whether the gentlemen of education differed in fifty words; and this uniformity still exists, among those who have made no use of any standard author [by standard authors Webster means the standard dictionaries]. Yet the standard authors themselves and those who follow them, differ in some thousands of words.

It is further to be remarked that the common unadulterated pronunciation of the New England gentlemen is almost uniformly the pronunciation which prevailed in England anterior to Sheridan's time, and which, I am assured by English gentlemen, is still the pronunciation of the body of the English nation: the pronunciation recommended by Sheridan and Walker being there called the London dialect, and considered as a corruption." Here as ever, Webster takes an exaggerated view of the effect of dictionaries upon the practice of speech. The truth is that in this matter of uniformity in speech, very much depends upon the direction in which one turns the head. If one is looking for uniformity, one finds it easily, but if one looks for diversity, diversity will never be lacking.

The question of the relative excellence of American English as compared with British English is also much dependent upon point of view, certainly is not susceptible of a positive and absolute answer. Expressions of opinion on this question have always been much colored by patriotic fervor or by prejudice. Early boasts on the part of Americans that the English language was spoken in a purer form in America than in England were numerous, though not more numerous than the scornful denials of this statement by Englishmen. When Sam Slick, *Sayings and Doings* (1836), Chapter XI, says that "it's generally allowed we [the Americans] speak English better than the British," this is to be put down merely as humorous spread-eagleism. But when one meets in serious writing with a bald statement like this by Clapin, *A New Dictionary of Americanisms*, p. vi, that "as a matter of fact and as regards the great bulk of the people of the United States, there can be no question but that they speak purer and more idiomatic English than do the masses in the Old Country," one can only faintly hope that there may have been some truth in it. Tucker's *American English* (1921) defends the same thesis. On the other hand, Mrs. Trollope, the first edition of whose *Domestic Manners of the Americans* appeared in 1832, is illustrative of those who went much too far in the other direction. She declared, *Domestic Manners* (New York, 1901), I, 65, that very seldom during her whole stay in America had she heard "a sentence elegantly turned and correctly pronounced from the lips of an American. There is always something either in the expression or the accent that jars the feelings and shocks the taste." On another occasion, Vol. II, p. 31, she remarks, with presumably the same degree of penetration, a peculiarity "in the male physiognomy of Americans"—that their lips are almost uniformly thin and compressed, an acquired trait which she thinks came from the necessity of keeping the quid of tobacco in the mouth. And again, Vol. II, p. 170, she informs her readers that Americans are convinced that "one of their exclusive privileges is that of speaking English *elegantly*." She gives two reasons to explain this conviction: "the one is, that the great majority have never heard any English but their own, except from the very lowest of the Irish; and the other, that those who have chanced to find themselves in the society of the few educated English who have visited America, have discovered that there is a marked difference between their phrases and accents and those to which they have been accustomed, wherefore they have, of course, decided that no Englishman can speak English."

It is obvious that any one attempting to estimate the relative values of British and American English must go at the matter in a different spirit from that exhibited by the writers from whom quotation has been made. It is obvious also that any such estimate will have to do with questions of profit and loss in details and will not lead either to general condemnation or to general approval of either type of English speech.

Another popular and erroneous notion not infrequently expressed with reference to English in America is that American English being by origin provincial is unusually archaic. Stated more compactly, this notion often takes the form that American English is the English of Shakspere. The supposed explanation of this supposed fact is best given in the language of quotation:

"The colloquial speech of the educated class in America is to some extent archaic, compared with that of the similar class in England. This is due to the operation of certain causes, which are well known to students of language. A tongue carried from one land to another, and keeping up no communication with the tongue of the mother country, undergoes what is technically called an arrest of development. The words and phrases and meanings in use at the time of separation remain fixed in the language which has been transported. On the other hand, changes are constantly taking place in the language which has been left behind. It abandons words and phrases once widely employed; it introduces words and phrases hitherto unknown. In this development the transported speech does not share. It clings to the vocabulary with which it started; and as regards the terms constituting it, and the meanings given them, it is apt to remain stationary."[1]

The main statement of this paragraph, that transplanted languages undergo an arrest of development, that is, tend to remain as they were at the time of transplanting, if true at all, could be true only metaphorically. For languages are not like trees or plants, objects of the external world. A language does not exist apart from the mental activities of individuals. One cannot transplant languages, therefore, but only individuals who use languages. The question then widens, and one must ask, do transplanted groups of individuals undergo an arrest of intellectual development? In the main, obviously they do not. The history of language, as of other social institutions, shows conclusively that periods of migration, during which traditions are naturally unsettled and new combinations of individuals with new influences upon each other are constantly being formed, are just the periods in which extensive changes are likely to take place. It is true, of course, that a transplanted group may in its new home become completely separated from its old home, or may become isolated from all contact with what to it is the outside world, and thus like any other isolated community, may tend to transmit without modification its speech and other social traditions

[1] J. F. Lonnsbury, in *The International Magazine*, May, 1880, quoted by C. F. Smith, *The Southern Bivouac*, I, 344. The source of most expressions of this opinion is Ellis, *Early English Pronunciation*, Part I, p. 19 (1869); see Bryant, *On the Conservation of Language in a New Country*, p. 277 ff.

from generation to generation. Such communities in America are found in the Kentucky and Tennessee mountains, and in other outlying regions. The speech of these communities is archaic, however, not because it is transplanted speech but because the communities in their general social life have had few social contacts. Thus the speech of Iceland is archaic as compared with that of Norway. But the same cannot be said of America as a whole, or of the English language in America. In very many respects the language has changed, in pronunciation and in vocabulary, since the arrival of the early settlers. Perhaps it has not changed more than British English, for both have been the expression of a vigorous and developing civilization. Neither can be said to have undergone an arrest of development. If certain archaisms appear only in American speech, this merely means that these features of speech, through the accidents of circumstances, have chanced to survive in America and not in England. On the other hand, the speech of England also has its peculiar archaic survivals, preserved through the force of their own circumstances, which do not appear in America. And if one might hazard a guess on a point not established by statistical evidence, one would say that there are vastly more archaic survivals, for example in heraldry, in official and institutional life, in England than there are in America. American survivals, being peculiar to America, are merely by this fact brought into exceptional prominence by the critic who is looking for things peculiar to America.[1]

But though neither the spirit nor the form of American English may be said to be a continuation of English in Elizabethan England, there exists nevertheless an extraordinary resemblance in some respects between the two. The explanation is to be found in the fact that the conditions of life in America during the past hundred years have been not unlike those in England in the latter sixteenth and early seventeenth centuries. Life in America has been a great adventure. A spirit of freedom, of independence, of experimentation has been

[1] Bryant, pp. 286–287, discusses a few British archaic survivals, *fruiterer, draper, mercer, costermonger, poulterer, beetle* (in a generalized sense like American *bug*), *biscuit, coverlet, autumn, casket, squash, creek* (an inlet in the seacoast), *hustings, luggage, copse, cony, close* (as in a cathedral close), *goloshes*.

in the air ever since the astonishing expansion of the country in population, in territory, in practical and intellectual interests began early in the nineteenth century. In this exuberant development the English language in America has shared. The language has been treated playfully, sportingly, violently, in all the strange medley of manners which Americans have exhibited in their attitudes towards the changing circumstances of life by which they were surrounded. American vivacity and picturesqueness of expression have resulted in a rich vocabulary of slang to match which in the English language one must go back to the days of Shakspere and Ben Jonson. Ingenuity and inventiveness in speech have not been held in check in America by the restraining sense of conventional propriety to the extent that they may have been in eighteenth and nineteenth century England, where the conventions of speech were established by a respected and obeyed upper class. In America speech has taken form more directly in response to immediate impulse. Every American citizen has felt that the language is as much his property as it is that of anybody else. He has considered himself free to treat the language as he felt inclined, even to the extent of taking liberties with it. Dithyrambic orators, inspired "inkslingers" with nothing to say but with iridescent language to say it in, writers of journalistic extravaganzas, sporting editors, punsters, rimesters, slangsters of every description, all these have flourished in the wild jungle of free American expression. Side by side with this license there has to be sure always existed in America a strong sense of authority, a strong feeling of respect for classical and traditional standards which has kept the language in its more serious uses from deviating too far from the ancient and honorable models of English expression. When English has been extravagantly used in America, it has been so with full realization of the difference between free and traditional, between normal and eccentric expression. The Elizabethan quality in American English is not an inheritance but a development on American soil.

Not as much light is thrown upon the causes of dialectal divergences in America by the comparative study of American pronunciations as might be desired. It is abundantly clear that many local dialectal differences are traceable directly to local dialectal differences in England which were transferred from England to America. Much more detailed study of dialects from this comparative point of view is necessary, however, before one can make many generalizations with assurance. It will probably be found in almost every instance that American dialects are very mixed, especially those dialects which have enjoyed any wide extent of use. It may be possible to discover here and there in American speech islands of limited extent which because of their isolation have maintained a homogeneous existence. Charleston, South Carolina, and certain groups dwelling in the Tennessee, Virginia, and Kentucky mountains are supposed to be communities of this kind. Special historical studies of these several communities are much to be desired, and it is only after such studies have been made that one could assert that their speech is or is not homogeneous, or could hope to discover the precise origins of the several types of speech represented by them. When one passes from the consideration of such restricted local communities to larger groups, it immediately becomes evident that all American dialects are so mixed that a parallelism between any single British dialect and any single American dialect becomes impossible.

The statements of the earlier students of American speech on this question of the local origins of American speech in England are contradictory and often the merest guesses. Webster was inclined to connect the speech of New England more closely with the speech of the south than with that of the north of England. In this he was probably right in the main, though he made no collection of details to support his conclusion. Bartlett, p. xxxviii, however, seems convinced that New England English was derived from northern British. "The numerous words employed in New England," he declares, "which are not heard in other parts of the country are mostly genuine old words still provincial in the north of England: very few are of indigenous growth." Now and then in the body of his dictionary, Bartlett speaks of New England idioms as being derived from "Northern British," but he gives no further reasons why he thought they were thus derived.

A similar vagueness of statement appears in De Vere's *Americanisms*. "All the provincialisms," he declares, p. 427, "of the Northern and Western counties of England have been naturalized in the New England States, thanks to the Pilgrim Fathers, who had left the banks of the Trent and Humber, and subsequently by the new colonists, who followed from Norfolk and Suffolk." "They brought not only their words," continues De Vere, "which the Yankee still uses, but also a sound of the voice and a mode of utterance which have been faithfully preserved, and are now spoken of as the 'New England drawl,' and the high metallic ring of the New England voice (Charles Wentworth Dilke). The former is nothing but the well-known Norfolk 'whine,' the proverbial annoyance of visitors from the 'shires.'" Elsewhere, p. 627, speaking of the southern loss of *r* in America, De Vere declares that this sin ought to be laid "upon the shoulders of the guilty forefathers, the first English settlers, many of whom came from Suffolk, and the districts belonging to the East Anglians, and, no doubt, brought over with them this disregard of the letter *r*."

Senator Hoar, "The Obligations of New England to the County of Kent," in the *Proceedings of the American Archaeological Society*, New Series, III, 344–371 (1885), discusses mainly the political and legislational debt of New England to Kent, a debt which he finds to be definitely provable in several instances. With respect to language, he merely takes Holloway's *Provincial Dictionary* (1838), and notes a number of instances in which Kentish speech agrees with New England speech; but the inference of New England indebtedness to Kent is somewhat invalidated by the looseness of the method employed to establish it. The same criticism must be made of Thomas Wentworth Higginson's study, "English Sources of American Dialect," in *Proceedings of the American Antiquarian Society*, New Series, IV, 159–166 (1886). Higginson examined Grose's *Provincial Glossary* (1st ed., 1787, 2nd ed. 1790) and Pegge's supplement to Grose in his *Anecdotes of the English Language* (1814), noting the characteristic words of New England as they were localized in these lists. "On the whole," he concluded, "the vast balance of numbers seems to me an indication, so far as it goes, that the strain of our New England ancestry came more largely from the North of England than from Kent."

The chief conclusion to be drawn from such studies as these is the need of a stricter scientific method of investigating the question than has hitherto been employed. The *English Dialect Dictionary* has now made available a great body of material concerning contemporary British dialects, and it may be that an exact comparative study of American vocabulary in relation to British vocabulary as here recorded would yield results of value. A comparative study of contemporary dialects, however, would not provide a safe basis for conclusions concerning the relations of British and American dialects three hundred years ago. It would seem that the best beginning in such a comparative historical study could be made by approaching the question from the side of ethnology, of the local origins of the families which settled in various parts of America. "No list has yet been made," says Senator Hoar, p. 368, "which shows, by shires, the origin of the emigrants who came to New England in the first thirty years of the settlement, even so far as the knowledge we have might enable it to be done." Until such lists are made, covering all the available sources of information, it would be futile to attempt to determine racial origins by the study of dialectal differences. Dialect may confirm conclusions drawn from documentary genealogical studies, but it cannot take the place of them. English and American dialects have always been so mixed that they can be used as circumstantial evidence, often in a strikingly confirmatory way, but with little or no independent value.

An excellent beginning in this method of genealogical investigation is made in the admirable study by Orbeck, *Early New England Pronunciation*, Chapter V, "The Sources of New England Speech." In a total of 1652 pioneers in the towns of Plymouth, Watertown and Dedham, pioneers being settlers who came from England in the first wave of migration, Orbeck has been able to trace 685, or 41.47

per cent to their English homes. There is no reason to think that the persons thus traced are in any way peculiar, or that inferences based upon them would not apply to greater numbers, if information concerning the origins of greater numbers were available. The place of origin of these pioneers is given in the following table:

TABLE A

Yorkshire	42	Surrey	5
Nottinghamshire	7	Berkshire	4
Lincolnshire	8	Hampshire	29
Leicestershire	4	Wiltshire	8
Rutland	7	Dorsetshire	7
Northamptonshire	4	Devonshire	2
Cambridgeshire	9	Somersetshire	12
Norfolk	98	Worcestershire	5
Suffolk	206	Warwickshire	3
Essex	77	Shropshire	7
Hertfordshire	4	Lancashire	4
Bedfordshire	4	Isle of Man	1
Buckinghamshire	3	Scotland	1
Middlesex	5	Wales	1
London	83	Ireland	3
Kent	28	Holland	9

The first observation one would make in reviewing this table is that the origin of the early New England settlers is extraordinarily diverse, but the second is just the opposite, that the larger part of the settlers came from a small number of closely related localities. "The center of the exodus," says Orbeck, "was certainly Suffolk, and omitting London, the two adjoining counties, Norfolk to the north, and Essex to the south, come next. Indeed 67.73 per cent came from the coast counties from (and including) London to the Wash (i.e., Norfolk, Suffolk, Essex, and London)." "There were twice as many," continues Orbeck, "from the counties south of the Suffolk line as from the territory north of the line. It is interesting to note also that 599 came from the coast counties as against 72 from the inland counties. There were very few from the middle western counties, only four from Lancashire, and none whatever from the four northernmost counties. From the Scrooby region—

southern Yorkshire, northern Nottingham and Lincolnshire—there were not a great many besides those who came to Plymouth by way of Holland." The obvious inference to be made from this tabulation, as Orbeck points out, is that "we are to look for the roots of Eastern Massachusetts speech in the eastern dialects of England."

The distribution of place names may also provide some evidence concerning the local origins in England of groups of early colonists in America. The value of this evidence may be estimated from the summary of Dexter's essay on "The History of Connecticut as Illustrated by the Names of Her Towns," in the *Proceedings of the American Antiquarian Society*, New Series, III, 437. To the question whether the study of place names helps one to know from what parts of England Connecticut was peopled, his answer is that this evidence corroborates other sources of information concerning Connecticut stock. "What this stock was, the experiences of the New Haven Colony well illustrates; the first settlers in the town of New Haven represented at least three distinct neighborhoods—one part from London, one from Kent, and one from Yorkshire—the last colonizing in the quarter which our modern 'York Street' marks. Guilford was mainly settled from Surrey and Kent, and Milford from Herefordshire in the west. Here we have then a mingling of streams, from the metropolis, the southeastern counties, the distant northeast, and the western midland; and this partial view is typical of the whole. In populating Connecticut, not only London and the eastern counties, but in less degree the southwest, the midland, the northeast, all bore their part, and all contributed their fair share to our treasury of town names." A more discriminating and extensive study of town names might be useful, however, in indicating the relative proportions of American colonists from the several regions of England.

American English shares with British English a noticeable tendency to make the spoken or auditory forms of words conform to the written or visual forms. This is characteristic of all highly developed literary languages, and the tendency in general grows as the printed and written aspects of language become more prominent in the language consciousness of a people. Thus we find that many words which now have but a single standard form in both American and British English became established in this form under the influence of spelling and within the modern English period. Examples of this are *wreck,* formerly pronounced [rɛk] or [ræk], but since the end of the eighteenth century, only [rɛk].[1] So also *mesh* formerly varied between [mɛʃ] and [mæʃ], but now has settled on only the former. In *get, yet, yes,* the eighteenth-century pronunciations [gɪt], [jɪt], jɪs] have completely given place to one with [ɛ] in accord with the spelling. In *sward,* recorded by earlier phoneticians as [sɔrd] and [swɔrd], the spelling with *w* has made the latter pronunciation universal, though the *w* in *sword* has not made its way into pronunciation. Many similar examples of adaptation of the spoken form to the written form of words will be found in the chapter on the American pronunciation of English. But though this tendency is a necessary tendency in all modern languages which take their speech into the mind to a considerable extent through the eye as well as the ear, it seems in American English to have found a field specially favorable for its development. Since the standard in America has not been the spoken language of any particular locality or class of society, but one based on a theoretical national custom, necessarily it made its appeal largely through literature, wherein national custom is most comprehensively expressed. In other words, American English replaced social tests by literary educational tests in speech, the latter being almost altogether tests applied through the printed page. In this way American English has become in many instances more rational, that is, more subject to analogical rules, than British English. In the latter, pronunciations often persist through the sanction of social custom which grotesquely contradict the ordinary and expected conventions of spelling. Thus in England for *chemist* one may still hear [ˈkɪmɪst], for *clerk* one may hear [klaɪk],

[1] For further historical details concerning the pronunciation of these sounds, see the discussions in the second volume.

for *falcon* one is more likely to hear a pronunciation with the *l* silent in England, but pronounced in America; in *asthma, isthmus,* the more general pronunciation in England gives *th* the value of *t,* but in America almost universally the letters *th* have their ordinary value as a voiced or voiceless continuant.

The contrast between the British and the American attitude towards this question of harmony between pronunciation and spelling is still more marked in proper names. In America the rule is that pronunciations have been modified to accord with the common analogies of spelling, or spellings have been modified to accord with pronunciations. Thus *Berkeley, Berkshire, Hertford,* and many similar family and place names, are pronounced in America with the value which *e* before *r* and a consonant ordinarily has, but in England these words have [ɑː]. If the pronunciation with [ɑː] is retained in America, then the spelling would normally be made to conform, as *Barclay, Hartford.* In England the word *Greenwich* is commonly pronounced [ˈgrɪnɪdʒ], but the almost universal pronunciation in the town in Connecticut of that name is [ˈgriːnˌwɪtʃ]. The name of the town *Worcester* in Massachusetts is of course pronounced [ˈwuːstə] as in England, but *Wooster* in Ohio, though it retains the old pronunciation, changes the spelling to agree with the pronunciation. Thus also original *Beaufort,* a not uncommon Southern name in America, is sometimes written as pronounced, *Buford,* and older *Beauchamp* is written *Beecham.* The proper name *Ralph,* when so spelled, is pronounced [rælf] in America, but often [reːf], [reɪf] in England. For *Jenny* only [ˈdʒɛnɪ] would be heard in cultivated speech in America, but in England, [ˈdʒɪnɪ] perhaps more frequently than [ˈdʒɛnɪ].

In many other proper names respect for the spelling seems often to encourage a fuller pronunciation of the relatively unstressed parts of the words in America than in England. The word *Hobart,* said to be pronounced [ˈhʌbət] in England, Michaelis-Jones, *Phonetic Dictionary,* p. 180, would be pronounced [ˈhoːˌbɑrt], [ˈhoːˌbɑːt] in America, or in rapid speech [ˈhoːbət]. Words like *Ayscough, Avebury, Eddystone,* would seem to American ears more naturally pronounced as [ˈeːsˌkɔf], [ˈeːvˌbɛrɪ], [ˈɛdɪˌstoːn] than in the British fashion as [ˈeɪskəf], [ˈeɪbərɪ], [ˈɛdɪstən].

Examples similar to these might be added in large numbers, enough certainly to justify the conclusion that though both British and American English strive in many instances to bring the visual and the spoken forms of the words of the language into harmony, the effort seems to have worked more fully and effectively in America than in England. If Americans appear more reasonable and less conventional than the British in this respect, the explanation is to be found not in the peculiarly practical nature of the American people, but in the special conditions of English speech in America, especially in the influence of elementary popular education upon speech, and in the exaltation of literary and theoretical standards of speech above the social traditions of spoken language.

Mixture of races in America has had much less direct effect upon the feeling for the American mother tongue than might be expected. The American nation is a composite of many peoples, but its language has shown no tendency to become polyglot. So far as pronunciation is concerned, it is doubtful if in a single instance the pronunciation of normal American English has been modified by the influence of a foreign language. There are to be sure many foreigners in America who speak "broken English," who speak with an "accent," but the character of this kind of English is always unmistakable. Henry James, in *The American Scene* (1907), p. 223, describes an occasion on a certain afternoon in Boston, when he listened to the conversation of "a continuous passage of men and women," none of whom spoke English. Some spoke "a rude form of Italian," others "some outland dialect" unknown to the observer. "No note of any shade of American speech struck my ear," the passage continues, "save in so far as the sounds in question [i.e., of the foreign speakers] represent to-day so much of the substance of that idiom [i.e., of American speech]." But what elements of the "substance" of American speech to-day come from Italian, or from Polish or Russian or Lithuanian, or any other "outland dialect"?

Called to a strict account for his remark, Henry James could not have pointed, one may be quite sure, to a single specific instance in which any sound of a foreign speech has been taken over into American English, or has modified in any degree the sounds of American speech. No doubt some sounds of American English may be found in foreign languages—in any foreign language. But there is no sound of American speech which cannot be traced back to periods much earlier than those in which foreign contaminations have been possible.

In vocabulary a few words from foreign languages have been taken over into American English, more from the Indians, with whom, strangely enough, the white people have never had very intimate or extensive social communication, but who have always appealed to their imagination, than from any other source; but the number of distinctly American foreign borrowings is less than the language as spoken in Great Britain reveals, where colonial relationships and international commerce have been particularly favorable to the borrowing of foreign terms. So far as syntax and idiom are concerned, it is again doubtful if a single instance of a foreign construction which has made its way into general or standard use at any time can be pointed out in American English. The explanation of this fact is that American English, in spite of the presence in the body politic of large numbers of people speaking foreign languages, has never been really exposed to contamination with foreign idioms. Immigration of other than English-speaking peoples began early, but from the start the foreign elements have been quickly assimilated to the native. In the seventeenth century, after the revocation of the Edict of Nantes, a number of French Huguenots sought a refuge in America, but they soon dispersed and disappeared in the body of the population. Before the end of the century, large numbers of Germans had settled in Pennsylvania and the Valley of Virginia, and there they have maintained a kind of separate existence to this day, retaining a modified German dialect still widely in use for colloquial purposes and also illustrated to some extent in a literature of their own.

The Pennsylvania German dialect, however, exhibits the development which always takes place when the language of a people of relatively lower cultural and social standing comes into contact with that of a higher, that is, it has been deeply affected by English but has not exerted a corresponding, or even an appreciable, influence in the opposite direction. This statement applies not only to the German of the early emigrants, but likewise to that of the vast numbers who came later. The Germans in America have been more tenacious of their continental traditions than any other class of emigrants, and German has occupied a more important position in the instruction of the public schools than any other living language of continental Europe. But the effect of German upon American English has been negligible. The statement of Richard Grant White, *Atlantic Monthly*, November, 1879, that "with all our German immigration, there is not a single German phrase current among us" is still true. By the same token the following statement of Bartlett, *Dictionary of Americanisms* (1848), p. xxxvii, was never true: "The great extent to which the scholars of New England have carried the study of the German language and literature for some years back, added to a very general neglect of the old masterpieces of English composition, have had the effect of giving to the writings of many of them an artificial, unidiomatic character, which has an inexpressibly unpleasant effect to those who are not habituated to it." German was studied with some enthusiasm by a few persons in New England in the second quarter of the nineteenth century, and Germany then seemed to many New Englanders not only a fresh fount of philosophic wisdom but also a land of poetry and romance. It is not apparent, however, that any New England writers consciously or unconsciously went so far as to fashion their style after German writers.[1]

To the generation of Americans of German parentage born upon American soil, German has seemed almost as much a foreign

[1] For a discussion of the knowledge of German in New England, see Goddard, "German Literature in New England in the Early Part of the Nineteenth Century," in *Studies in New England Transcendentalism*, pp. 202–206. The *Monthly Magazine and American Review*, II (1800), 284–287, has an essay "On the Study of German," giving reasons for the study of that language.

language as French or Italian, to be learned with the same assiduity and labor. This statement applies even more strongly to other groups of Americans of foreign parentage. Northern Teutons from Denmark, Sweden and Norway, southern Europeans from Italy and Greece, eastern Europeans from Poland, Russia, Hungary and the smaller states, even Asiatics from Armenia and Turkey have come in steady streams, and for a time in limited communities have maintained a civilization of their own. In every instance, however, these bodies of foreign emigrants have come from relatively low social levels. Even in their own countries they had not, as a rule, assimilated the highest culture which their native surroundings afforded, nor had they exerted such a controlling part in it that they could feel it as a precious possession to be cherished at any cost. They came to America with an initial readiness to accept the institutions of their new homes. Undisciplined in the control of public affairs, they were not prepared to take a constructive part in the organization even of their own life in America, and have thus been, to the present time, the led rather than the leaders. The main result of foreign emigration to America has consequently been to add to the number of native born illiterates a very large number of illiterates of foreign parentage. So far as the American standard of national use is concerned, it matters little whether illiteracy is native and provincial or colored by recollection of foreign idioms. The great problem of instruction which by general agreement has confronted and still confronts the educational forces of the country is to correct the one as much as the other, and to the solution of this problem, the public schools have turned their attention with such intelligence and energy as to make speakers of standard American out of foreigners as readily as out of provincial Americans. In many instances, indeed, their success has been greater with children of foreign parentage than with native Americans, for the former, aware of a heavy social handicap to overcome, put forth special exertions, whereas the latter, inclined to think themselves as good as any one else, refuse to have their eyes opened to conditions which might destroy their personal satisfaction.

The question of climate inevitably arises when one attempts to consider the formative influences which have determined the character of a national language. The weather is always an engrossing subject of interest, and every community is likely to be so impressed by the peculiarities of its own particular style of weather as to ascribe to it powers and effects which extend wide and deep. Such ascriptions, however, are very rarely susceptible of positive proof, nor do they, on examination, often seem plausible. In the case of American English, for example, if one were to seek for an effect of climate on speech, with what climate would one begin? From Maine to Florida, from the Great Lakes to the Gulf of Mexico, from Oregon to New Mexico, the greatest diversities of climate are to be found. One may pass from the tropical climate of the south to the sub-Arctic climate of the far north, from mountain to prairie, from sage-brush desert to forest, and in no one of these regions would one find what might be called the typical "American climate." The distinctive feature of American climate, as of the social life of the country, is diversity, rather than uniformity. Diversity of social life may well be a significant element in determining the character of American speech, but it is difficult to see how diversity of climate can produce any effects except such as are purely local. But even in localities, it is doubtful if climate can be regarded as an effective cause of local characteristics of speech. The most plausible case could perhaps be made for Southern American English as contrasted with Northern. The languorous climate of the South has been thought to account for the slow soft voices of the Southerners, their general loss of the sound of *r* final and before consonants, and perhaps for a tendency to obscure unstressed syllables to a greater extent than is customary in the North. As to slowness of speech, something will be said later in the discussion of the American "drawl," but for the moment it will be sufficient to point out that observers have generally found this to be a characteristic not only of Southern but all American speech. The Yankee drawl has been the subject of comment for generations. Furthermore, if a warm climate be regarded as having produced a languorous manner of speech in the American South, the principle involved must be one applicable to human society in general. The evidence of Italy and Southern France alone, however, is sufficient to disprove that a Southern climate produces a slow and lazy speech. The loss of the sound of *r*, again, cannot be regarded as due to Southern climate, for exactly the same phenomenon appears in some Northern American communities, notably in New England and southern New York, and it is of course one of the well-known characteristics of standard British English. The same applies to the slurring of unstressed syllables. In many instances, and probably this statement could be made universal, what might be regarded as peculiar to Southern America finds parallels in usages of other regions with very different climates, and in every case a better explanation could be made for the several features on the basis of the effect of social relations than on that of the effect of climate.

One general description of American English has often been given which is at the same time an accusation against it, the blame for which has frequently been laid upon the climate. The statement usually runs that the American voice is hard, inflexible, lacking in resonance and over-tones, that it is monotonous and dry. To a certain extent Americans themselves acknowledge this, though fain to deny it when their attention is called to it by the alien critic. The statement is also often made that the cultivated Southern American voice stands in strong contrast to the voice of the cultivated Northern or Western speaker, that it has a different and more musical quality. It would be a rash person, however, who should say that a hard and inflexible voice is universally or even generally characteristic of the North or West. It cannot be regarded as one of the natural products of these regions. The division in this matter of the speaking voice is not to be made on the basis of locality, but more reasonably on the differences of temperament and habit. Men of affairs who have given themselves up to the bitter competition of business, who have fought first to gain a position and then to maintain it in the face of remorseless opposition, may not infrequently reveal in the harshness of their voices the severity and social inhumanity of the struggles through which they have gone. Such men often fill in a democratic community positions of greater importance than their social virtues qualify them to occupy. They are often rich men, and consequently part of that traveling American public prominently seen and loudly heard in conspicuous places. They are indeed a characteristic product of American conditions, and if their voices seem not to possess the quality and modulations of a gentle speech, the explanation is to be found in the fact that their activities have not been in the regions where the milder and easier social adaptations have had weight. A hard, domineering habit of mind will show itself in the same way in the voice of the speaker, whether he be a Northerner or a Southerner, an American, an Englishman, or of any other race. The barometer by which the fluctuations of speech are measured is an extremely sensitive one, but its records are to be interpreted in terms of social atmosphere, not often in those of wind and rain and weather.

Though a summary such as has been attempted in this chapter cannot pluck the heart out of the mystery of American English, it provides pegs nevertheless to which we may attach impressions. The feeling for a mother tongue must always rest upon distinctive national traditions. Few of the principles brought forward in this chapter to account for the existence of an American idiom would be equally applicable to the speech of England, France, Italy, Russia, or Germany. Nations make their own histories, and American speech, for better or for worse, is the child of the American people. But in this matter of the formation of a standard or generalized national speech, among western nations perhaps the closest similarity is to be found between the United States and Germany. A standard national speech may be based, first, upon the particular dialect of a locality, generalized and extended to the whole people; or second, upon the speech of a special social class, accepted and imitated by all other classes as providing the approved model of speech; or third, upon neither a local nor a class dialect, but upon the formally recorded, that is, the relatively fixed and visual aspects of the language. Manifestly American standard English is not primarily an extended local dialect. Neither is it the speech of any social class, a gentry, a nobility, or even a peasantry. The main supporting foundation for the feeling for a standard speech in America is to be found in the written language, not of course in the ingenious literary devices of the professional literary style, but in what may be designated as the normal daily uses of the written language. Each new group of American citizens has entered into possession of the language not as a natural inheritance, not as a privilege, but as an acquisition, as something to be gained through intelligent application and study. In America, as in Germany, the chief task of language in the last four or five generations has been to provide some kind of amalgamating medium to hold together a great variety of elements geographically, socially and culturally disparate, assembled suddenly and without preparation. The problem of language in America has therefore been a problem of organization. Out of heterogeneity, unity had to be produced, not by century long processes of slow development, but quickly and efficiently. To attain this end, the surest and speediest way was to base the feeling for the national idiom upon what are in some respects the more mechanical sides of speech, that is, upon reading and writing as the most readily comprehensible among the necessary accomplishments of all good citizens. It is on the foundation of education in these elemental, but profoundly significant aspects of the use of speech, that the main structure of American linguistic unity has been reared.

VOCABULARY

The vocabulary of the English language in America has always been in the main the same as the vocabulary of the English language in England. In other words, both American English and British English are constituent elements in a unity which must be designated the English language. This is the unity of the English-speaking communities. But such a bald statement immediately raises the questions in what this unity consists, what it is that gives the English language of the English-speaking peoples its distinctive and essential character, and what it is that enables one to relate the several aspects of the language, for example, British and American English, to the central and unifying idea of its nature. In effect this is merely the question of dialects, of their definition and relationships.

Two ways of establishing a central character or idea of the English language are possible. One may say that an actually existent form of the language has been by common experience, and therefore by right, established as the preëminent authority for the language. If any such claim were to be made for the English language, obviously it would be the language of England, or some particular form of the language of England, which would be elevated to this supreme position. Without entering into debate of the reasons which might be adduced as justly supporting or denying any such possible claim, one may more profitably consider the question of fact here involved. The question of fact is whether all those or any great majority of those who must be said to use the English language do thus in practice look upon the English of England as having provided the final court of authority, the home to which all errant forms of English speech must return finally for paternal blessing and approval. The answer to this question is obviously that a feeling for a fixed center of the English language in the real speech of any English community does not exist strongly enough to be a determinant in the many and varied uses of the speech. The mother tongue of all those who use English is not the English of any particular region or of any defined section of society. It is something vastly more comprehensive and subtle than this. The many different varieties of English speech are evidences of the practice of those who are equals in the enjoyment of their linguistic inheritance. One form of English speech does not exist by sufferance of another form, but each form, by the fact of its existence, is an element helping to determine the nature of the whole.

The central nature of the English language not being determined by the real practice of any locality or group, it remains that it must be determined by an idea. It is in fact a concept, a state of mind, and not an objective reality. When one thinks of the English language as a unity in this way, one is prepared to take a reasonable view of those details of language commonly designated Americanisms and Briticisms. Is the notion of the English language in America so different from the central idea of the English language that one must give a special name to it and call it the American language? Or in other words, must one establish a new central idea and feeling for the language which shall give to that speech a unity and character of its own? Where do the bounds of sympathetic inclusion within the nature of the English language end?

Now students of psychology have always maintained that no two individuals can ever be exactly alike, and one may extend this statement to speech and say that the language of no two individuals can ever be exactly alike. Whatever generalization one makes, therefore, on the basis of the speech of a group of individuals, even if the group contains only two, must allow for a greater or less area of negligible variation in the speech of these several individuals. A generalization of the speech habits which the group has in common, that is the determination of the unity of the group, can be made only by eliminating from the generalization those habits which the group does not have in common. This necessity confronts the systematizer, no matter how small or how large the group.

The extent of the area of negligible variation which one permits in language depends very much upon feeling. A single word or intonation in a particular set of circumstances may cause one to expel violently the user of the word or intonation from the circle of one's sympathy. Under other circumstances, however, one may find this word or intonation both acceptable and grateful. One forgives much where one's sympathy is engaged, but where it is not, a little spark of occasion may kindle a mighty conflagration of scornful denial.

It is for this reason that one meets with extraordinarily diverse statements of the difference between American and British English. One observer finds them, to repeat the words of the opening of this chapter, essentially the same. Another finds them altogether different, the user of the one language unintelligible to the user of the other. Thus on the one side, we find Richard Grant White, *Words and Their Uses* (1870), p. 56, declaring himself as follows:

"If in an assemblage of a hundred educated well-bred people, one half of them from London, Oxford, and Liverpool, and the other from Boston, New York, and Philadelphia . . . a ready and accurate phonographer were to take down every word spoken during an evening's entertainment, I feel quite sure that it would be impossible to distinguish in his printed report the speech of the Britons from that of the Americans, except by the possible occurrence of acknowledged local slang, or by the greater prevalence among the former or the latter of peculiar words, or words used in peculiar senses, which would be acknowledged to be incorrect as well by the authorities of the party using them as by those of the other party. In brief, their spoken language, reproduced instantly in writing, could be distinguished only by some confessed license or defect, peculiar to one country, or more prevalent there than in the other. . . . The standard in both countries is the same. . . . But although the written speech of these people would be to this degree indistinguishable, an ear at all nice in its hearing would be able to separate the sheep from the goats by their bleat. . . . Among those of both countries who had been from their birth accustomed to the society of cultivated people, even this distinction would be made with difficulty, and would, in many cases, be impossible."

On the other side, we hear Fitzedward Hall, an American, declaring that "though I have lived away from America upwards of forty-six years, I feel, to this hour, in writing English [that is British as contrasted with American], that I am writing a foreign language, and that, if not incessantly on my guard, I am in peril of stumbling. . . . Not for five minutes can he [the American] listen to the conversation of his fellow countrymen, or for that length of time read one of their newspapers, or one of such books as they usually write, without exposure to the influence of some expression which is not standard English"—that is, which does not belong to the central idea of the English language, or feeling for the language, as these figured in Fitzedward Hall's experience.[1] It is difficult to disburden the author of so extreme a statement of the charge of wilful determination to discover differences at all hazards. And in fact when Hall had the temerity to collect many illustrations of "solecisms, crudenesses, and piebald jargon" in the writings of respectable American authors like Mrs. Stowe, Howells and others, it was not difficult for his critic to point out, in most cases, precisely the details of practice which Hall brought forward to prove the un-English character of American usage in the writings of standard British authors, and to maintain convincingly that only patient search would be required to find abundant parallels to the remainder of Hall's examples. In the same spirit as Hall another critic declared that he was almost completely bilingual. "I can write English," he says, "as in this clause, quite as readily as American, as in this here one," Mencken, *The American Language* (1919), p. vii. But such criticism is made ineffective by its manifest perversity. The truth must lie somewhere in the middle.

When one says, however, that American and British English to the impartial observation are essentially the same, that they are

[1] Fitzedward Hall, "The American Dialect," in *The Academy*, London, March 25, 1893, pp. 265–7, discussed and reprinted in R. O. Williams, *Some Questions of Good English*, pp. 107 ff.

elements in the unity of the English language, this is not equivalent to saying that they are identical. Just as an exaggerated view of the difference between the two may lead to the discovery of differences where in normal experience no sense of difference exists, so an exaggerated view of the similarity of the two may lead to a lax regard for such distinctions as common experience really recognizes. These latter distinctions are of course the ones which should be made the basis of discussion when one sets out to consider the significant relations of American English to the speech of any other specialized groups in the general unity of the English language.[1]

It is significant that the word Americanism did not come into existence until after the Revolution. It was coined, according to his own assertion, by President Witherspoon of Princeton. Writing in 1784, *Works*, IV, 460, he says that "the word Americanism, which I have coined for the purpose, is exactly similar in its formation and signification to the word Scotticism." The term was devised to designate the discussion of "an use of phrases or terms, or a construction of sentences, even among persons of rank and education, different from the use of the same terms or phrases, or the construction of similar sentences, in Great Britain." Witherspoon did not assume an altogether condemnatory attitude towards his Americanisms. "It does not follow, from a man's using these," he declares, "that he is ignorant, or his discourse upon the whole inelegant; nay, it does not follow in every case, that the terms or phrases used are worse in themselves, but merely that they are of American and not of English growth." In detail, however, Witherspoon's own observations are not numerous or important. The instances of Americanisms which he cites are few in number and not of great significance. As Witherspoon was a Scotchman by birth, he probably came to America with an ear already cocked for the detection of provincialisms of speech, and it is therefore remarkable that he did not discover more than the few examples which he mentions.

[1] For a collection of opinions on the relative degree of differentiation or identity in British and American English, see Mencken (1921), pp. 1–38.

In general the attitude of Americans in the period immediately following the Revolution was one of cordial welcome to all that might be regarded as distinctive for American speech. The new nation was felt to be in need of a new idiom. Noah Webster's persistent advocacy of an American language has already been noted. Even more emphatically did Thomas Jefferson express his faith in neologism. Always hostile to "the Gothic idea that we are to look backwards instead of forwards for the improvement of the human mind," Jefferson gladly welcomed what seemed new in language. "I have been not a little disappointed," he says, *Writings*, ed. Washington, VI, 184, "and made suspicious of my own judgment, on seeing the Edinburgh Reviewers, the ablest critics of the age, set their forces against the introduction of new words into the English language; they are particularly apprehensive that the writers of the United States will adulterate it. Certainly so great growing a population, spread over such an extent of country, with such a variety of climates, of productions, of arts, must enlarge their language, to make it answer the purpose of expressing all ideas, the new as well as the old. The new circumstances under which we are placed, call for new words, new phrases, and for the transfer of old words to new objects. . . . But whether will these adulterate, or enrich the English language? Has the beautiful poetry of Burns, or his Scottish dialect, disfigured it?" The enlargement of the English language, Jefferson contends, "must be the consequence, to a certain degree, of its transplantation from the latitude of London into every climate on the globe; and the greater the degree the more precious will it become as the organ of the development of the human mind." This enlargement will come "not indeed by holding fast to Johnson's Dictionary; not by raising a hue and cry against every word he has not licensed, but by encouraging and welcoming new compositions of its elements." But in England Jefferson fears that "the dread of any innovation . . . and especially of any example set by France has palsied the spirit of improvement." "Here [in America] where all is new, no innovation is feared which offers good. . . . And should the language of England continue stationary, we shall probably enlarge our employment of it, until its new character may separate it in name, as well as in power, from the mother tongue."

These quotations from Jefferson indicate fairly well the attitude of the more liberally minded Americans towards the question of vocabulary in speech. There were some conservatives, for example, Dwight, who declared himself, *Works*, IV, 278, unwilling "to see the language of this country vary from that of Great Britain"; and there were of course hostile critics in England, like those of the *Edinburgh Review*, who treated American English with scorn and reviling. But when one examines the charges of the earlier British critics, and the confessions or apologies of the American critics, one finds them both strangely deficient in definite detail. There is usually no question of the feeling involved, but the grounds of this feeling are not made evident. A few stock examples of Americanisms occur again and again, such as *belittle, clever, lengthy,*[1] *locate, improve* (in the sense merely *to make use of, employ*), *guess, fix, progress,* as a verb. Some of these may be regarded as characteristic of the vocabulary of English in America, but the examples usually brought forth illustrate the state of mind of the critic much better than the state of the English language in America. Thus a British critic in the *Monthly Mirror,* for March, 1808, remarks that American authors make use of new and obsolete words, "which no good writer in this country would employ." "And were it not," he continues, italicizing the reprehended words, "for my *destitution* of leisure, which obliges me to hasten the *occlusion* of these pages, as I *progress* I should *bottom* my assertion on instances from authors of the first *grade;* but were I to render my sketch *lengthy,* I should *illy* answer the purpose, which I have in view," see Cairns, *British Criticisms*, p. 37. Doubtless an American who had formed his style by the study of Holofernes might have written thus, but doubtless there was never such an American. For a summary of British criticisms of American speech, see Mesick, *The English Traveller in America* (1785–1835), Chap. VIII.

[1] Discussed in detail in "The Trial and Condemnation of Lengthy," *Monthly Magazine and American Review*, III (1800), 172–174.

A reasonable conception of the term Americanism must obviously be arrived at before it is possible to examine the distinctive elements in the vocabulary of the English language in America. In any such conception a very large group of differences will immediately occur to the observer which must be characterized as in themselves having very little distinguishing value, whether for British or for American English. These are differences between American and British practice which rest merely upon what may be called the accidents of convention and which are therefore significant only when one of these forms of the English language is compared with the other. These conventional differences are of the kind which ordinarily in polite society fall by consent within the area of negligible variation. It is true that such differences have often been the centers about which the most violent storms of social prejudice have raged. To take an extreme example, not of vocabulary, but of spelling, the difference between American *honor* and British *honour* is one that rests entirely upon a difference of convention. All spellings are established only by convention, and the form of a word which is agreed upon must needs be the form of the word. On logical and historical grounds perhaps as good a case could be made for one of these forms as for the other, and if some elements of feeling not dependent primarily upon linguistic considerations were not imported into the discussion of the spellings, one's attitude towards them would be colorless and unprejudiced.

Many words and locutions of this sort immediately strike the attention when one compares American with British usage, especially when one compares the concrete English of every-day intimate life in America with the English of the same life in England. Thus in America the common usage is *coal,* when one speaks of the fuel to be put *on a grate,* but in England it is *coals* which are put *in a grate.* The difference is merely that in America coal is used as a mass-word, like iron, stone, wood, etc., whereas in the British coals, emphasis is laid upon the fragmentary character of coal utilized as fuel. Perhaps, however, American usage has gained slightly in distinctiveness, since coal means the fuel before it is burned, leaving coals to designate the separate pieces of coal when incandescent. But in words of this type it nearly always takes an ingenious analysis to make out anything characteristic for either British or American English. It merely happens that convention, through the accident of circumstances, has generalized upon one form in England and upon another form in America. A similar development continually takes place in all aspects of language that are divisible into terms of social grouping. The speaker from a southern region in America is likely to have, in a great number of instances, a set of conventional habits different from those of a speaker in New England. Perhaps the one may say *I reckon* and the other may say *I guess*, or the one may speak of a veranda when the other speaks of a porch. These habits extend to the most subtle and minute details of speech, and a really exhaustive analysis would make them extremely numerous. Such an analysis would not, however, make them individually any more important, and in the end they would merely illustrate more fully the fact that in a very great number of words the conventional habits which a group establishes are significant only because they have been established by convention. In a list of two hundred words chosen by Mencken (1921), pp. 113–116, to illustrate the difference between British and American English, in most instances the words could be transferred from one list to the other without violence to what one might feel to be the proper character of either type of English. Thus does it make any essential difference whether one speaks of a *brakeman* (American) or a *brakesman* (British) on a train? of a *coal-scuttle* (said to be American), or a *coal-hod* (said to be British)? or a *poorhouse* (American) or a *workhouse* (British)? The list of such doublets in which usage is divided but indifferent might easily be swelled to numbers far in excess of two hundred. In the end their significance might be great, because an accumulation of details of this kind might become heavy enough to destroy that sense of security and harmony in the use of the idiom which one has in relation to all those whom one takes to be fellow citizens in the republic of English speech. Whether or not this point has been reached in the differentiation of British and American English, whether or not the area of variation has become so great as no longer to be possibly negligible, depends very much upon individual choice and view. Certainly differentiation has not proceeded so far as to result in unintelligibility. Whether it has gone so far as to destroy the sense of sympathy and intimacy between one who uses American English and one who uses British English depends largely upon the degree of sanctity one attaches to *coal-scuttle* as contrasted with *coal-hod*, or *brakeman* as contrasted with *brakesman.*[1]

In some words the wavering of convention before it became settled is definitely traceable. The history of such words as *gotten* and *got*, of *guess* in the general sense of *think*, *suppose*, would carry one back to Anglo-Saxon times. For both of these words examples could be found in British use, at various times, so close in kind to the American use that it would take a hair-splitting analyst to distinguish between them. What alone could make the American usage distinctive would be the more frequent, that is more conventionalized use of *gotten* as participle and *guess* in the sense of suppose, and also the fact that the critic has directed attention to *gotten* and *guess*, among other words, and thus has made them more or less conscious uses. In England *bug* and *bloody* have also taken on certain conventionalized meanings which define their use in polite society more strictly than the words are defined in American usage. The phrasal preposition *back of*, for which Thornton gives citations beginning with 1774, has apparently more general usage in America, in the sense of *behind*, than it has in England. It also has a variant form *in back of*, which completes the analogy to *in front of*, this latter being unquestioned usage both in England and America.

Other expressions which one interested in the gradual fixing of convention and habit in British and American speech may study in the examples cited by Thornton, supplementing these by the *New English Dictionary*, are *allow*, *reckon* and *calculate*, in local and familiar use as practical synonyms of *guess*, *suppose;* the phrase *at that*, as

[1] With respect to *coal-scuttle* and *coal-hod*, it may be noted that the Fowlers' *Pocket Oxford Dictionary of Current English* (Oxford, 1924), gives *coal-scuttle* as present British use, but does not record *coal-hod.*

in "our food was of the most unwholesome kind, and scant at that;" *bureau*, meaning a chest of drawers; *chores*, meaning odd jobs about the house; *clever*, in a variety of senses which shade into each other so gradually that often it is difficult to tell where one type of usage begins and another ends; *cracker* for *biscuit; homely*, not infrequent in British use, but so much less general in England than in America that it may ultimately disappear from British standard speech and remain only as an Americanism; *raise*, as in the phrase, "I was raised, as they say in Virginia, among the mountains of the North," Paulding, *Letters*, I, 102, though the usage is not limited to Virginia and is applied to animals and plants as well as human beings; *rooster*, for *cock*, with which should be compared *roost-cock*. Examples of *roost-cock* occur early, though there is no record of a word *roost-hen*, and the American *rooster* seems to be merely a variant development from *roost-cock*. The word *calico* may mean in England a white cotton cloth, but in America it means only cotton cloth stamped with a pattern.

Though all such variations of use as those just cited are of great importance to the dictionary maker, the listing of forms of American speech which derive their interest by reason of contrast with British speech is nevertheless but a small part of the task of the student of the American vocabulary. His more important concern is to describe the vocabulary directly in relation to American life, to attempt to give in some degree a record of the American mind as reflected in words. This is manifestly a large undertaking, and the categories presented in the following pages are to be regarded as suggestive, rather than exhaustive. They are set forth here as indications of some of the directions which special studies of American vocabulary may take in anticipation of that day when we shall have a really satisfactory knowledge of this important subject.

The history of any language which covers as long a period of time as the three hundred years of the English language in America must be to some extent a history of words and expressions which have become obsolete. Some examples will be cited to show that there is material for the lexicographer and historian in older American texts. In many instances words have fallen completely out of use; in others the word survives with a loss of some of its earlier meaning, or survives now only in local or rustic use. Often the word has passed out of British as well as American use, which means probably that it was never well established in any form of English speech. Thus one finds the word *bolts*, as in the phrase "boards and bolts," *Braintree Records*, p. 4 (1646), frequently used in the early town records in the sense of timber sawed into lengths ready to be split into clapboards, a meaning no longer current in English. The *New English Dictionary* cites only two occurrences of this word in England, one for 1688, the other for 1753. In *Dedham Records*, III, 47 (1638), appears the word *stover*, "those which haue not stover enough for the cattle they nowe possesse," a word which occurs in Shakspere, and which may still be heard rustically in America. A word *haver*, meaning hay, also occurs occasionally in the early records, but is known now only in names, as in Haverstraw, on the Hudson, Haverhill, in Massachusetts. The *Easthampton Records*, I, 112 (1657), speak of "pease wheat and selfe at the whom [home] lott," but a word *self* or *silf*, in a sense appropriate to this passage, is not found in the dictionaries and probably is not now anywhere used. These records frequently use *while* in the sense of *until*, as in I, 10 (1650), "noe man shall set any gun but he shal loke to it while the starrs appeare." This use occurs also in the *Braintree Records*, p. 5 (1652), of a road "to rune through his ground while it come to Martine Sanders ground." Sherwood, *A Gazeteer*, p. 82, cites this as a Georgia provincialism in 1837.

The word *spong*, a topographical term, has now completely passed out of American use, though it was current in the seventeenth century in the forms *spong*, *spang*, *spung*. It meant a strip or section of meadow, as in the *Groton Records*, p. 136, "two parcells or spongs," "the northernmost spang of Buck medow," "severall spongs or angles." It occurs also in the *Southold Records*, I, 56 (1658), "a spang of meadowe," and a late use of the word in the phrase "spang of Creekthach," II, 484 (1719). In these records, II, 185 (1682) we also have "spong or slip of meadow."

The word *hole*, which still survives in various place names in New England, was formerly used in much the same sense as *spong*. Thus we read in the *Plymouth Records*, that "Mr. Howland desired a smale hole or pcell of meddow neare his land graunted him formerly by the toune," I, 46 (1662), and later that "hee hath pitched upon foure acrees of meddow in a hole mowed by Captaine Bradford," I, 59 (1663). The records also describe a grant of "3 holes of meddow" to Francis Cook, I, 208 (1655). They mention place names like *swan hold*, I, 81 (1655), *hobshole*, I, 110 (1668), *Billingtons holes*, I, 155 (1677), *giles holes*, I, 219 (1673). The *Groton Records*, p. 136, mention *skull holl*, and also use the word in the sense of a section of meadow. The word is no longer in general use and no doubt the more common sense of *hole*, meaning a depression or hollow, as in a hole in the ground, a bog hole, etc., has tended to crowd out the use of the word merely in the sense of meadow or section of meadow. Perhaps transitional forms are to be seen in the *Southold Records*, where we read of *a flagge hole*, II, 58 (1685), a phrase which appears a little more clearly in *flaggy hole*, I, 455 (1686). In these records, I, 453 (1684), Joshua Horton sells "all the holes of water and meadows" belonging to him. A further application of the word *hole* is occasionally met with in earlier American usage, one which survives in some place names, like Wood's Hole in Massachusetts. In this sense the word means a narrow inlet or cove of the sea. In the Rocky Mountains, as in *Jackson's Hole*, the word *hole* means an open park-like region.

The word *pan* as a geographical term is now in common use in the phrase *hard pan*, a hard sub-stratum of soil which holds water. In the sense of a shallow pool, the word is also on record in *salt pan*, *oyster pan*, and the *New English Dictionary* records other uses in South Africa. In the United States the word has never become widely current, though we read in the *Southold Records*, II, 276 (1645), of a *fresh pann* on Long Island. In this connection it may be noted that the word *hummock* is often used in these records to designate a much larger body of solid ground than would now be called by that name. Thus in the *Southold Records*, II, 246 (1694), we read of "a small humuck of kreekthatch," being one acre or thereabouts. The word appears also as *hommock* and *hammock*, II, 143 (1690).

Concerning the word *meadow* itself, the editor of the *Groton Records*, p. 135, remarks that "the first settlers of the town did not attach the same signification to the word meadow which now belongs to it in New England, where it means low, swampy land, without regard to the mowing. They called by the name meadow all grass-land that was annually mown for hay, and especially that by the side of a river or brook, and this meaning of the word was the common one in England, whence they brought their language." Yet in the *Plymouth Records* one often finds reference to *meadows* or "*meadowish land*," apparently with reference to swampiness. We still have surviving the term meadow in the sense of swamp in local names; as in the *Great Meadow* in Maine, the *Hackensack Meadows* in New Jersey, the *Tuolumne Meadows* in California, etc. The truth seems to be that the early settlers in New England had no specific word for what now would ordinarily be called swampy ground, perhaps because ground of this character in the section of England from which the colonists came had long been drained and cultivated when they migrated to America. They had the word *marsh* for extensive areas of wet land, applied especially to the salt marshes of the coast. But the word *swamp* first meant primarily thicket, land covered with undergrowth. It is still used in this sense by elderly persons in New England, though more generally the idea of wetness has become uppermost in the use of the word. The earlier sense is made certain by innumerable passages in seventeenth century records. In the *Dedham Records*, III, 33 (1637), when persons received lands for their houses, it was ordered that "their swamp lotts shall adioyne therunto." Thomas Jordan was granted, p. 61 (1639), "One Acre of Swamp to be layd out next his owne ground," and Edward Culver was granted, p. 96 (1642), "one smale parcell of upland and swampe nere his house lott." There is frequent reference to the clearing of "undergrowne stuffe" from the swamps, but nothing is said about draining or drying them. Swamps with large trees growing in them were distinguished from swamps only with undergrowth. The point here was that timber lands were held in common and the timber carefully guarded. But swamps were lotted out and clearing of them was encouraged in order that they might be brought under cultivation. This was done at least in the town of Dedham, and when the General Court at Boston ruled that large tracts of swamp should lie common, like the forests, the citizens of Dedham protested, "beinge we haue bin at charg to lay out the greatest part into proprieties and diuers have bin at charg in cleareing the same," *Dedham Records*, IV, 239 (1646). Jonathan Edwards, in his *Personal Narrative*, *Life*, by Dwight, p. 59, says that he, with some of his schoolmates, "joined together and built a booth in a swamp, in a very retired spot for a place of prayer." As Edwards was a native of Connecticut, near Hartford, his use of swamp in this passage to mean a place with thick undergrowth would be in keeping with local use. From this earlier sense of swamp apparently comes the colloquial phrase *to be swamped*, that is, to be lost in a multitude of tasks or duties. The phrase *to swamp out timber* is a current lumbering usage in Maine.

The undergrowth of the swamps is spoken of as *shruffe* in the *Dedham Records*, IV, 98 (1664), which also mentions *shruffey upland*, IV, 8 (1659), and *shruffey meadowe*, IV, 22 (1660), 98 (1664). An unusual use of the word *rubbish* occurs in *Southold Records*, I, 410 (1674), in the phrase *rubish land*, meaning land cumbered with undergrowth.

The *Plymouth Records*, I, 219 speak of "a little doak or valley." The word *doak*, *doke*, *dolk* occurs dialectally in England in the sense of a dint, a hollow, but has altogether passed out of American use.

Along the coast with its many indentations and peninsulas, the term *neck* came to be used almost in the sense of meadow. It is now known to many persons in the name of the Little Neck clam who have no notion that the historical meaning of the word is geographical, not anatomical. On Long Island, where the word *neck* still survives in many place names (also in Virginia in the Northern Neck), a controversy between Huntington and Oyster Bay arose over the question whether three necks or four necks of meadow belonged to Huntington, *Huntington Records*, p. 58 (1664). In a legal conveyance, p. 54 (1663), the phrase "my halfe neck of meddow excepted" apparently illustrates also the use of the word in the sense merely of section or strip of meadow. From this use of neck in neck of meadow may have come another Americanism, neck of woods, meaning region, section, settlement in the woods. The earliest example of this which Thornton has found is for 1851.

As the name for an island, *key*, adapted from Spanish *cayo*, "shoal, reef," has not been limited to American use, but the word has been much more commonly employed here than elsewhere, especially in the West Indies and Florida. Key West is the name of a city, but also now may be the name of a kind of cigar. An older spelling *kay* sometimes occurred.

The word *everglades* as used in Florida to designate the great swamps of that region is of unexplained etymological origin. The earliest occurrence cited by Thornton and by the *New English Dictionary* is for 1827. The word may be a corruption of some Indian word for the locality.

An interesting geographical word, records of which have been found only on Long Island, but of which several examples in England are cited by Wright, *English Dialect Dictionary*, is the word *bevel.* The quotations will illustrate its meaning. In *Hempstead Town Records*, I, 25 (1657) we read of a "parcell of Land Lying in ye Beavell plowed ye Last yeare." A place is named, I, 75 (1660), "ye hollowes lyeing in the beavell." In 1665, Adam Mott, I, 167, sells a "peace of Plaine Lande of mine Lieing in the Home Bevell." The phrase "home bavell" occurs again, I, 202 (1665). At another place, I, 234 (1668), we read of "the parsonage hous bevle." If one might hazard a guess at a slightly more precise meaning than the above quotations, and many like these, from the Hempstead Records justify, one might suppose that a bevel was a piece of level but sloping and well-drained ground. At I, 103 (1662), we read of "ye hollowes lying in ye Bevell," and at I, 90 (1660), of "ye hollos lieing in ye bevell"; and see above the quotation from I, 75 (1660). Evidently this was a well-known local name, and it is equally evident that a bevel was not as low as a hollow.

The word *hollow* as a geographical term is commonly used in these records, as at I, 107 (1659), "hollowes and Meadow Land," and apparently it meant ground lower than a meadow but not so low as a swamp. Though not now generally current in this sense, in the name of Sleepy Hollow the word has become forever established in American tradition. In *Hempstead Records*, I, 74 (1659), we read of "one hollow conteyning one and an halfe Accre." In the next year, p. 75, "the wallnut hollow" and "ye chery-tree hollow," in the plural designated as *hoolas*, were granted to a citizen of the town as a free gift "for his assistance, for ye help of him and his famely."

Another name for the tillable sections of New England which has not completely disappeared but is more familiar now in place names than as a common noun is the word *interval, intervale.* It occurs in the town records as early as the middle of the seventeenth century, but the term bottom-land, bottoms, has tended to displace it, and it is now archaic and poetic.

Peters, *General History of Connecticut* (1781), p. 110, preserves an Indian topographical word which is now known only as a proper name. Speaking of the Connecticut River, he says that "in its northern parts are three great bendings, called cohosses, about 100 miles asunder." From this word was derived the name of the present Coos County, in northern New Hampshire, still pronounced as a dissyllable and formerly sometimes written with an *h* between the two vowels, as in *Cohors*, Green, *Three Military Diaries*, p. 108. A tribe of Indians was known by the name of Coos, the name being, as frequently, merely the ascription of a geographical term to the Indians who happened to live in that locality. The Indian word is said to mean crooked, "which appropriately describes the channel of the Connecticut in the north," Sanborn, *History of New Hampshire*, 1875, p. 422. The same word probably appears in Cohoes, the name of a town on the Mohawk in Albany County, New York. Near

Cohoes is Boght, an old but small village, named from the Dutch word for bend, "in reference to a bend in the Mohawk," French, *Gazeteer of New York* (1860), p. 166. Apparently the Dutch word Boght is merely a translation of an older Indian name for the same locality.

The word *run* as a colloquial American word for a stream of water, as in Bull Run, etc., had an early origin in the phrase "a run of water," meaning a stream, *Huntington Records*, p. 86 (1666), and often. It occurs in the *Hempstead Records*, I, 314 (1679), "the run Called Jonsons run," also I, 167 (1665). The *New English Dictionary* gives two earlier citations, one for 1605 and another for 1652, and describes the word as American and northern British dialect. The earlier meaning of *creek* as a branch of the sea has been generally extended in America to mean a small fresh-water stream, though this use is not yet very common in New England, where such streams are usually called brooks. The popular pronunciation of the word is as though it were spelled crick. Early examples of the word in this sense are not found, but appear abundantly in the eighteenth century, Thornton's earliest being for 1674, and the next not until 1737. Webster, in the dictionary of 1828, says the word means "in some of the American States, a small river. This sense is not justified by etymology, but as streams often enter into creeks and small bays or form them, the name has been extended to small streams in general."

The method of portioning out the common lands to the townsmen of the first New England communities has led to the general American use of *lot* to designate a limited section of land. Ordinarily the word now means a portion of land facing a street and meant to be a site for a building. A fifty-foot lot means a lot with a street front fifty feet wide. Originally, however, lots were of various kinds, home lots, swamp lots, wood lots, pasture lots, etc. This usage still remains in New England where what would elsewhere be called fields are commonly called lots. From this usage was derived also the familiar popular saying, "to cut across lots," that is, to go over the fields instead of around by the road, or metaphorically, to follow economy rather than formality in any procedure. The practice of drawing lots was continued down into the eighteenth century. The town of Lunenburg, *Lunenburg Records*, p. 24 (1721), paid for "Travil and Expenc When The Lotts Were Drawn at Concord," and the records contain, p. 58, a list of all the lots in the town with "The names of those That first Drew them." References to the drawing of lots in the seventeenth century are numerous. At Dedham it was voted in 1669, *Dedham Records*, IV, 187, "that the proprietors at Pawcomptucke should draw Lotts in the first oportunitie, that it might be better knowen wher each mans propriety will lye." In the *Norwalk Records*, p. 60 (1671), the agreement is recorded that "all those men that now draw lots with their neighbors, shall stand to their lots that now they draw." If one is surprised that the Puritan fathers employed so worldly a method as drawing lots to decide important matters, it should be remembered that they had scripture authority in Acts I, 24–26, for so doing.

In connection with the lots of the colonial settlements a use of the word *frontier* occurs which shows interestingly the change in meaning of that word. In American history the frontier has been a moving border land between civilization and the desert. Perhaps its meaning in the following passage from the *Hempstead Records*, I, 37 (1658), is essentially the same: "it is ordered by the Townesmen of Hempsteede for this present yeare, That all ye fencis of ye frontiere lotts that runn into ye field shall bee substantially and suffissiently fenced by ye 25th day of this present monthe of Aprill," the penalty for neglect being five shillings, "unto ye use of ye towne."

A geographical word *folly* occurs in the *Hempstead Records*, I, 309 (1677), "there was given to Thomas sothard a small pese of land lying betwene his folly and the ould ox-paster"; also I, 320 (1678), "there was given to Nathaniell Pearsall . . . on the west side of his folly." In the *New English Dictionary* one finds the dialectal word *folly*, meaning a clump of trees on the top of a hill. The only two citations given are one for 1880, the other for 1888. Are these passages in the *Hempstead Records* early illustrations of the same word? The word is certainly topographical, but whether it means a hill or not, the context does not make evident. Near Wilmington, Delaware, is a place called Folly Woods. As a second guess one might derive the word from Dutch *vaalje,* a little valley, the valley of a brook, a word, however, not on record. The diminutive *-je* in Dutch words regularly becomes *-y,* and Dutch *aa* [ɑː] would be represented in English by *o* [ɔ]. The only modification would thus be the change of initial *v* to *f,* which might well take place through popular etymology.

Another word in the *Hempstead Records* which seems to be of geographical meaning has defied explanation. It occurs in the phrase "at the south sid of John Carmans tilsom," I, 291 (1672), a piece of land containing three acres being thus described. At a town meeting, I, 290 (1672), there was given "to John Pine a home lott by his fathers tilsom an privilig to kepe half a dusen Cattell in the sumer." Another piece of land is likewise described as "lying on the south sid of John Carmans toylsum the land Containing two or three eakers," I, 291 (1672). At an earlier town meeting, I, 98 (1661), the town gave to Thomas Jeacokex, that is Jaycocks, "three Acors of Land Liing att the South west Corner of John Carmons Tille sume, Provided itt be no hindernce to Any highway." The word occurs most frequently with reference to John Carman's land, but the reference to John Pine's tilsom seems to make it general.

Another unexplained word, though not geographical, in the *Hempstead Records,* I, 342 (1675), occurs in the phrase "to pine the earebred," this phrase being used in connection with a cart and wheels made by John Jennings. The purchaser agreed to pay for the "Cart and Whels" when Jennings should "pine the earebred." Perhaps *pine* is for *pin,* and *bred* probably means *board,* and if *eare* is the old-fashioned word for ploughing, the whole phrase might mean "to pin the plough-board." This meaning, however, does not fit well with the cart and wheels of which the *earebred* is apparently a part.

An unexplained bird name, *chirie birds,* occurs in the *Dedham Records,* III, 19 (1656), and so often. But perhaps this is merely *cherry birds.*

The verb *improve* and the noun *improvement* were in the early periods of colonial New England used in senses which are now no longer ordinarily attached to the words. As now used the words apply to buildings, fences, etc., constructed on land which by being placed there may be said to improve the land in the sense of making it more useful for man's purposes. One may even hear of improvements being made on a river, meaning the building of dams or bridges where they are necessary. This use of the word is directly derivable from the general value of the word in the sense to make better. The special American use of the word, often cited by critics as an illustration of Americanism, gave it the generalized meaning of to employ, use, occupy, without special reference to the notion of making better, though obviously this notion often lies very near. Thus we may improve the occasion to do something, or the busy bee improves each shining hour. As is pointed out by Logan Pearsall Smith, *The English Language*, p. 224, the generalized use is old, improve, improvement being terms of Law French "originally employed to describe the process of enclosing waste land and bringing it into cultivation." From this the transition to the meaning of making profitable use of anything is easy. Under *improve,* the *New English Dictionary* remarks that "the ancient sense, or something akin to it, was retained in the 17–18th century in the American colonies." But the fact is that the ancient senses were not all exactly alike. Thus in the *Plymouth Records*, I, 43 (1660), special provision is made for the disposition of trees which have been cut down and had the bark removed, if the person who cuts down the trees "shall . . . not Improve the bodyes of such trees soe peeled." But other uses are still more general. It was decreed, I, 54 (1663), that if any one cut wood at certain prohibited places, he should "forfeit all such wood to the townes use; to be Improved for the use of the minnester"; also that no one "under pretence of hiering of servants shall Improve and Imploy any man or boy that hath no Right to the Commons of the Towne," I, 72 (1664). The town agreed, I, 117 (1670), that the salary of "all such as are improved in any publicke place" should be "accoumpted as Ratable stocke." The earliest example of this American use of improve in Thornton and the *New English Dictionary* is from 1677, and no British occurrences are cited. It is almost certain, however, that the usage was brought to New England from England. It is found in the earliest of the town records, too early to have developed upon American soil.

Many other terms of varied meaning which arose in the process of occupying the land and which have in part or wholly passed out of use as the particular stage of civilization which brought them into being has been left behind, occur as one reads early American records. In the seventeenth and eighteenth centuries the word *yeoman* still survived as a designation for what has later come to be generally called a farmer. In the town records a tiller of the soil is occasionally designated as yeoman, just as a carpenter or mason would be given his distinctive trade name. The term was a favorite one with Noah Webster, who was fond of describing the landholders of Massachusetts and Connecticut as the yeomanry of New England. The word is now archaic and poetic in American use, except as it survives in the official terminology of the United States navy.

The words *settle, settler, settlement,* are self-explanatory and have had an obvious history. The associations of the word *planter* are now mainly with the plantations of the South, and the word has been immortalized, for St. Louis at least, by the name of the Planters Hotel. In earlier periods, however, both plantation and planter were used in the North also as equivalents of settlement, settler, or farmer. Governor Hutchinson, in the preface to his history of Massachusetts Bay, speaks of the "importation of planters" from England to that region. The patent of the Plymouth Company, 1620, was "for planting and governing that country called New England." In the *Huntington Records,* p. 403 (1684), p. 407 (1684), and often, planter means merely farmer or husbandman. The same use occurs in the *Hempstead Records,* as at I, 34 (1660), and often elsewhere. The older use survives in the last stanza of Woodworth's *Old Oaken Bucket,* "As fancy reverts to my father's plantation."

The word *homestead* has an interesting seventeenth-century variant in *homestall,* in *Watertown Records,* Land Grants, etc., p. 20, and often in these records. A variant of settle, settler which was formerly in use was *seat, seater,* for which a few citations are given by Thornton under *seat* and *unseated.* In the *Journal of the House of*

Burgesses, 1659–1693, p. 466, in Virginia, one finds the record of "a byll declareing wt Seating is," and on p. 468, another "giuing allowance to those yt by mistake Seat upon other mens lands."

The word *tarry* has now almost completely passed out of everyday use, though the word is quite familiarly known as a literary or somewhat poetic word. It was formerly, however, one of the common words of the New Englander's vocabulary, and is one of the words often met with in earlier realistic attempts to record rustic New England speech. Irving smiles at it in his *Knickerbocker History*, Book III, Chap. VIII, remarking that "a Yankee farmer is in a constant state of migration, tarrying occasionally here and there."

Other archaisms which persist in familiar speech are *carry*, in the sense of *conduct, escort*, as in the song, *Carry me back to old Virginia*, or *carry a horse to water*, Sherwood, *A Gazeteer* (1837), or in the phrase of rustic gallantry, *May I carry you home?* and the word *raise*, in the sense of to *rear* or *foster a person*. Both of these words are now more general in the South than elsewhere, but they seem merely to be local survivals there of formerly more general uses. In *Easthampton Records*, II, 452 (1699), a sum of money is paid "to Wm Rose for Carring Sarah whitehar [Whittier] away three dayes," and again, II, 458, advice is taken "about Carrying her to Docter Beateman." As for *raise* examples are found in the *New English Dictionary* as early as 1601, though the dictionary describes the usage as now chiefly found in the United States. Thornton's examples are abundant, though they do not distinguish between *raise* as applied to human beings and as applied to animals and plants. Webster, in the dictionary of 1828, says that "the English now use *grow* in regard to crops, as, to *grow* wheat. This verb intransitive has never been used in New England in a transitive sense, until recently some persons have adopted it from the English books. We always use *raise* [of crops], but in New England it is never applied to the breeding of the human race, as it is in the southern states." The polite equivalent for *raise* as applied to children is *to rear*.

The word *to girdle* as applied to trees, one of the methods by which trees were killed to aid in the more rapid clearing of the land, is mentioned by Webster in the dictionary of 1828 as an American use. The word has outlived pioneer days and is still in familiar use. When the trees were cut down and rolled together to be burnt, the neighbors came to assist in what was called a *log-rolling,* a social function that has passed out of existence, leaving the word, however, with a political metaphorical meaning.

The American *sidewalk,* in England *footway* or *pavement,* is an old word for which the earliest citation in the *New English Dictionary* is for 1739. This was then an English use of the word, but now the word has fallen out of favor in England, but has become the universal word in America. Thornton gives abundant examples from 1817 and later. A somewhat rare American word is *pave,* meaning sidewalk or pavement. A form *pavé* also occurs infrequently, being merely the French past participle. It is not clear whether *pave* arose as a transference of the verb *to pave* to a noun use, or as a contraction of *pavement.* It may have been, however, merely an Anglicization of French *pavé.* It occurs in Carlton, *The New Purchase* (1843), p. 65: "The *pave* [italicized by the author who commonly italicizes what he regards as Americanisms] was, of course, dust sometimes, sometimes mortar," and also p. 514: "This *pave* [a line of hewed logs] was used in miry times." Other examples are given in Thornton.

The good old-fashioned word *pillowbers* for pillow-cases occurs in *Southold Records,* II, 216 (1686), and a number of times elsewhere in the town records. This is the word Chaucer uses in the Prologue to the Canterbury Tales, line 694, when he describes the Pardoner as having a *pilwe-beer* which he tries to palm off as the Virgin's veil. A weakened form of the compound *household* was formerly widely current, as in *housel stuff, Southold Records,* II, 19 (1678), *housald stuff, Hempstead Records,* I, 120 (1662). This word has survived in the Georgia dialect of the nineteenth century, as recorded by R. M. Johnston, *Mr. Billingslea* (1888), p. 135, "in her housle an' kitchen furnicher."

Since agriculture and the crafts occupied so much of the attention of the early settlers in America, one naturally finds the language of the rustic and mechanical pursuits exceptionally rich in obsolete or partly obsolete terms. The use of *corn* in the general sense of grain, and more specifically of wheat was brought to America from England, and until Indian corn came to be the more prominent crop in the agriculture of the colonies, the word continued to be used in the English sense. To distinguish wheat from Indian corn, it was sometimes called *English corn*, *Watertown Records*, p. 23 (1651). The name *maize* for Indian corn has always been learned and literary in America. The first example of *breadstuff(s)* in the *New English Dictionary* is from Thomas Jefferson, 1793, and it is recorded by Pickering as an Americanism. It is still used, but not now so commonly as in the days of river freighting.

In the *Watertown Records*, p. 123 (1675), we read that the schoolmaster is to be allowed "a fortnites time in haysill," evidently for the purpose of getting in his hay. The word *haysill* means haying season, and is recorded in the *New English Dictionary* as dialectally peculiar in England to East Anglia. In connection with haying another obsolete word, *hurry*, occurs in the early records. In the *Dedham Records*, IV, 5 (1659), we read of a "load or hurry," and the word, spelled *hurie*, occurs again, IV, 47 (1662). The *New English Dictionary* records *hurry* as a verb, in the sense to transport or convey, but only in the northern dialect and with the earliest example for 1847. Nashe, however, in his *Lenten Stuffe*, in 1559, used the word *hurrie currie*, meaning a car, chariot, and *harry carry* is recorded for Yarmouth, the first citation in the *New English Dictionary* being for 1493, the next and only other one, for 1870. As Nashe wrote his *Lenten Stuffe* at Yarmouth in praise of the Yarmouth red herring, his use probably reflected a local custom, and the Dedham usage may also have been derived from the same locality. In the *Dedham Records* occurs another rustic archaism in the use of the word *dooled*, to dole, as in "all high wayes . . . to be well marked and dooled," III, 34 (1637), and also in reference to land granted to John Haward, "nere his house lott as it is marked and dooled out allready," III, 98 (1643). As the quotations indicate, the word means provided with posts or stones or similar marks to indicate the bounds of property. British examples will be found in the *New English Dictionary.* The injury done by cattle or swine not kept within bounds is frequently mentioned as *scathes,* as in *Dedham Records,* III, 43 (1638), "all scathes done by any Swyne shalbe satisfyed." On p. 47 (1638) the word is printed as *scares,* but this is probably an editorial error, since the connection of the word with standard scathe, scathing is obvious.

Another obsolete word for damage of this sort is the word variously spelled *stray, strey, stry.* In *Plymouth Records,* I, 114 (1670), complaint is made "of Great stray and wast of Timber"; and an order was passed, I, 273 (1699), "for the preventing the strey of timber," and at another time, I, 270 (1699), "to prevent further strey of the Comons." In the *Watertown Records,* p. 95 (1669), we read of "stry done in Corne." This word in its several forms is merely an aphetic modification of *destroy,* and examples of *stroy* occur in Bunyan and other authors cited in the *New English Dictionary.* The form *stry* is recorded in the *New English Dictionary* only for East Anglia, and first for 1825.

The harm done by straying cattle made the office of town pounder one of importance, and pounding regulations are fully specified in the early town records. In *Hempstead Records,* I, 27 (1657), mention is made of "Charges and powndeg," and I, 101 (1661), of *pounedge.* The *pener, penner* is mentioned, I, 300–301 (1661), and in the form *pinder,* I, 93 (1660). A noun formed from the verb *drive* was formerly used in senses now lost, as in *Watertown Records,* p. 85 (1665), "drifft of Cattell," meaning driving of cattle. In *Braintree Records,* p. 4 (1652), occurs the word *dwrift way,* drive way, and this word occurs in these records a century later, as in *drift way,* p. 164 (1731), p. 605 (1791), still in the sense of passage or driveway. It occurs also in the *Southold Records,* II, 485 (1719), "a drift way from the s^{d} open way going into ye s^{d} Little Neck." The word *drift way* still occurs in Connecticut legal phraseology.

The word *jade* for horse, now only an archaic or poetic word, was formerly commonly current, as in the *Hempstead Records,* I, 182

(1665), "Mary Willeses Reacord for gades"; I, 236 (1667), "Jadgs or Cattle or other Cretors." An officer mentioned in these records who perhaps has given the proper name Howard to the language, is the *hoaward*, I, 235 (1667), the hog warden, hired for "y'e Keeping y'e ffield for the preservation of the Corne."

The word *shoat*, a young pig, is frequently cited as a word which has passed out of use in England, but which persists in America. The earliest American citation in Thornton is for 1775, but the word occurs in the *Huntington Records*, p. 435 (1686), spelled *shots*, and in *Watertown Records*, p. 48 (1656), spelled *shoates*. It occurs in the *Southold Records*, I, 440 (1658). A similar American survival is the word *wilt*, to wither, the earliest occurrence of which in Thornton is for 1809. A rustic word is contained in the *Lunenburg Records*, p. 93 (1735), "Hifer-Hors, mare, or Colt," which has not survived. *Hoss-beast*, for horse, occurs in Carlton, *The New Purchase*, p. 119, and often. In giving the ages of horses, it was customary to give the number of full years of the horse's age and to speak of the uncompleted year as *the advantage*, as in *Southold Records*, I, 450 (1667), "a year and vantage colt," that is a colt something over a year old. An equivalent phrase, facetiously applied to a man, occurs in R. M. Johnston, *Mr. Billingslea*, p. 4, "forty three and the rise," meaning something over forty-three years old.

In the *Huntington Records*, p. 435 (1686), occurs the phrase, "Cart yoak and Cart clevey." The word *clevey* is manifestly the same as the word *clevis* now current. Other examples of a spelling without final *s* are recorded in the *New English Dictionary*, and the suggestion is made that *clevis* was felt to be a plural and thus a new singular, *clevy*, was formed. The popular form of the word, however, is still *clevis*, and moreover the nature of the object does not suggest a plural idea. The word *clevis* is also pronounced with final consonant voiceless, whereas if the word were felt to be a plural, the *s* would be voiced. The etymological origin of the word is unknown, though from the uses of the clevis to hold two things together, one thinks naturally of French *clef* as perhaps providing a clue to the logical content of the word. If the word was French in origin, the form *clevey* may be due merely to French pronunciation, as in the word *cherry* from Old Norman French *cherise.*

In connection with French it may be mentioned that the word *vendue,* common in earlier American usage in the meaning of public sale, for which the earliest citation in Thornton is for 1762, occurs also in the *Huntington Records,* as in "outcry or vandue," p. 467 (1686), and several other places. It occurs still earlier in the *Hempstead Records,* I, 341 (1681), *vandu;* the word *outcry* occurs in I, 27 (1657). Madam Knight, in her *Journal* (1704), pp. 52 ff., describes some vendues which she attended in New York and found entertaining.

Cooper, in his *Notions,* II, 116, speaks of the word *cradle,* an implement used in cutting grain, as a strange word, and he adds in a footnote that he "does not know whether this implement is an American invention or not." It was not an American invention, nor was the word peculiarly American. It occurs in this sense as early as the latter sixteenth century, and like many other words, it has become archaic only because modern machinery has done away with the kind of labor which it designated.

Two interesting words of the *New Haven Records* are *haunt* and *hanker.* On p. 62 (1641), an entry reads that "none shall hant their hoggs thatt way . . . but haunt them that way where their 2d division lyes." The word is here used in the causative sense of its primary meaning, cause their hogs to haunt, or frequent, a certain region. The interest of the word *hanker* lies in the fact that early records preserve a use of it in about the same sense as haunt, which was its original sense and the use from which the metaphorical meaning, to long for, was derived. The word occurs in an early Indian treaty, *New Haven Records,* p. 3 (1637), in which a certain sachem "his counsell and company doe hereby covenant . . . y^{t} none of them shall henceforth hanker about any of ye English 'houses.'" This is close to the meaning of the word in Milton, 1641, "But let us not . . . stand hankering and politizing," see the *New English Dictionary,* under *hanker.* From the meaning of merely standing idly about it was easy for this word to take on pejorative senses, an exactly similar process being illustrated in the modern uses of the word *loiter, loitering*.

The names of many plants and products have appeared in various modified forms in American usage. The word which now commonly takes the orthographic form *pumpkin* is occasionally met with in its earlier form, as in *pompions, New Haven Records*, p. 234 (1646). In the *Hempstead Records*, I, 304 (1676), however, it already appears in the form *pumpkins*. By origin the word comes from French *pompom*, which undergoes several phonetic modifications in English use. The early English forms are *pompeon, pompion, pumpion;* the ending was then assimilated to an English ending in *-kin*, giving pumpkin, examples of which are cited in the *New English Dictionary* from the middle of the seventeenth century. The vegetable itself has been so constantly one of the common products of the American garden that the name has readily taken on popular forms and uses and has thus come to be pronounced as though it were written *punkin*. Madam Knight in her *Journal* (1704), p. 37, describes a meeting of a court of justice in a field in Connecticut at which "the bench" for the justices consisted of *pompions;* but later, p. 47, she speaks of "Pumpkin and Indian mixt Bred" of awful aspect, and at Stonington, p. 67, she had "Rost Beef and pumpkin sause for supper." "The pumpkin, or pompion," says Peters, *General History of Connecticut* (1781), p. 186, "is one of the greatest blessings, and held very sacred in New England. . . . Of its meat are made beer, bread, custards, sauce, molasses, vinegar and, on thanksgiving days, pies, as a substitute for what the Blue Laws brand as antichristian minced pies." Peters also explains, p. 154, why New Englanders were called pumpkin heads. As every male was required to have his hair cut round by a cup, "when cups were not to be had, they substituted the hard shell of a pumpkin, which being put on the head every Saturday, the hair is cut by the shell all round the head." Thus early did the pumpkin engage the playful fancy of the American native. The pumpkin, or punkin, in "Peter, Peter, punkin eater," combined with the unmistakable echo of the rhythm of Yankee Doodle, is good circumstantial evidence that this rhyme is of American origin. The festivities of an American Halloween are not complete without a pumpkin, and Ichabod Crane also helps to keep interest alive in the pumpkin, even for those who have never eaten pumpkin pie or seen a pumpkin growing. The pumpkin, because of its habit of growing sometimes to prodigious size, has also given origin to the facetious phrase, *some pumpkins,* abundant examples of which are given in Thornton. The word has also been extended to name other objects, as in *punkin-seed,* a kind of fish, and also a kind of boat, the point of connection being similarity in shape. Punkin Hollow as a place name is perhaps reminiscent of Sleepy Hollow. The tale of the pumpkin vine that grew so fast that it wore the pumpkins out dragging them along the ground is a bit of characteristic American humor and folklore.

Another species of American "pie timber," the *huckleberry,* also started with a name that has been much obscured. The berry is the same as the whortleberry, or hurtleberry, as the word is spelled in *Plymouth Records,* I, 153. The transition from *hurtle-* to *huckle-* is easy, for the *r* before *t* being silent in New England pronunciation, one must only account for the change of *t* to *k,* and this is a frequently occurring phonetic process in naïve speech.

Along the coast, and especially on Long Island, the term *creek-thatch* as the name of salt water grass was very common, and is recorded by the *Century Dictionary* as still current. The *Southold Records,* I, 383 (1688), speak of "Seagrass or Kreekthatch lying at Southarbor," and I, 86 (1659), of "Creek thatch meadow." The first element of the word was sometimes *crick* and sometimes *creek,* both forms having been common since at least early in the seventeenth century. Both forms occur side by side, I, 168 (1681), "Krick thatch with the sunken grass at the mouth of Goose Kreek." In *Southold Records,* II, 50 (1685), we find *Crickthach,* spelled *Cricksach,* II, 364 (1697). It is spelled *creekthath,* II, 26 (1695), and probably as houses were then not thatched but shingled, the sense, and therefore the form of the second element was becoming obscured. In the latter entries of the *Southold Records,* a descriptive term often accompanies the word, as at II, 409 (1705), "Creekthatch or Salt Marsh," or II, 246 (1694), "krick thatch or sunken meadow." In 1656 a certain enterprising citizen was granted "the privilidge of having one half of all the Crickthatch or meadow which he shall make or cause to grow by art and industrie or shall be made to grow" within a specified area, II, 507.

The word *sauce* meaning vegetables has long been one of the stock words in literary versions of New England rustic dialects. It is recorded by Thornton under *sauce* and *long sauce*, though Thornton's earliest citation does not go back further than 1802. The word is mentioned by Webster in his Dissertations, 1789, but he mentions the word only to discuss its pronunciation, not its meaning. The pronunciation was frequently under fire, the debated point being whether the vowel should be [ɑː] or [ɔː]. In New England the preferred pronunciation was [ɑː], and writers of humorous dialect often indicate this sound by such spellings as *sarse, sarce, saace.* A still lower dialectal stage was reached when [sɑːs] became sass [sæs], just as the word *saucy* becomes *sassy* in dialect speech. It is extremely probable that this word in the sense of vegetables was current in New England use long before the earliest recorded instances, that it was in fact current throughout the whole of the American period and was brought over to this country from England. The citations in the *New English Dictionary* localize it in recent British use in East Anglia, and it is known also elsewhere in England. The citations also show how readily the transition from a piquant sauce to be eaten with meat to a vegetable or fruit sauce could be made. But the *New English Dictionary* goes much too far when it puts down as usage in the United States *long sauce,* meaning beets, carrots and parsnips, and *short sauce,* meaning potatoes, turnips, onions, pumpkins, etc. The word distinctly belongs to New England localities and to New England tradition, and may now be described as a New England archaism. In fact, it probably had a more vigorous life in New England humorous dialect writing than elsewhere, and this special emphasis has probably contributed to its almost complete disappearance even in New England. A typical literary use of the word is that by John Neal, in his novel *Randolph,* I, 279 (1823), where one of the characters, Sarah, a Southerner, writes to another, Juliet, explaining the diminishing ill-will between the South and the North. Speaking of herself and her community she says that "we are no longer in their [the Yankees] opinion, a people of billiard players, slave dealers and horse jockies; nor they in ours, a people made up of dealers in wooden ware, and 'long and short sarse,' as, it is said, they call vegetables, turnips, onions, potatoes being round sauce; which they pronounce *sarse,* and carrots, beats, parsnips, etc., long sauce." In all this it looks as though there were a distinct element of literary fancy. The legend indeed might have gone further than long, short and round sauce, except for the fact that these terms exhaust all the obvious geometrical forms of the vegetable world.

An interesting survival is the use of the word *walnut* occasionally in old-fashioned New England speech as the name for the fruit of the hickory tree. In general American usage of the present, walnut means only the fruit of the black walnut tree. But walnut in the seventeenth and eighteenth centuries in New England commonly meant the hickory tree. In the *Norwalk Records,* p. 94 (1699), "it was voted and agreed that all persons as carry fire wood to Mr. Buckingham, shall be allowed for each load of wallnut wood three shillings and six pence, and for each load of oake wood is allowed two shillings and six pence." In the *Lunenburg Records,* p. 40 (1727), walnut trees are mentioned several times, with others, as oaks of different kinds, "pople," birch, chestnut, maple, basswood, but no hickory. The word hickory was not in use in early New England, and it came into general American use through the South and Southwest, where it was necessary to have words to keep the black walnut and hickory distinct. The earliest citation for hickory, a word of ultimate Indian origin, in Thornton, is for 1705, in a Virginia book, and the only other two of the eighteenth century are also from the South. Several earlier citations are given in the *New English Dictionary,* also from the South. In New England, however, the black walnut did not exist, though hickories were common, and it is not now found in that region except here and there where specimens have been planted. When John Adams writes of being busy, *Works*, II, 201, "trimming the walnuts and oaks, and felling the pines and savins and hemlocks" on his farm, by walnuts we know he meant hickories, for when he made his first visit to the Middle States, he saw his first black walnut trees. "At Trenton ferry [in New Jersey]," he writes, *Works*, II, 357, "we saw four very large black walnut trees. . . . It seems that these trees are plenty in these southern Provinces; all the black walnut timber which is used by our cabinet makers in Boston is brought from the southern Provinces." A further extension of the use of walnut in America is that by which it has now come to mean primarily what is sometimes more specifically called the English walnut. The varied history and original meaning of walnut would carry one far beyond the limits of American usage, but they are fully illustrated by the comment and the citations in the *New English Dictionary*. The name of the *pecan*, a kind of hickory, is of Indian origin, through French, and came into American English, like hickory, from the South and Southwest. The first example of pecan in Thornton is for the year 1773. The pronunciation is variously [pɪkɑːn′], [pɪkæn′], or [′piːˋkɑːn].

The walnut appears in the *Hempstead Records*, I, 25 (1657), in the phrase "the wannute holow"; and in the *Southold Records*, II, 57 (1685), we read of "a wornutt tree that separates between Mr. Weles and myselfe."

The word *carf* is frequently used in the early records with reference to the cutting down of trees. In *Dedham Records*, III, 63 (1639), occurs mention of a tree twelve inches thick "at the Carfe." In the *New Haven Records*, p. 54 (1641), "a kerfe or planke of 2 inches thick" is mentioned. The word obviously is related to the word *carve*, to cut, and seems to have meant the butt end of a log, or even a thick board. The American citations supplement interestingly those contained in the *New English Dictionary*. Thornton has only one example of this word, for 1897, from W. D. Howells, *Landlord at Lion's Head*, Chap. VII: "He lifted his axe, and struck it into the carf on the tree." The scene of this story is laid in New England, and evidently Howells was repeating a word heard in that region.

It is, therefore, a remarkable instance of obscure survival and shows that from the early seventeenth to the end of the nineteenth century the word must have had an existence in oral tradition. The identity of the word is undoubted, though it is possible that Howells has not used it in a precisely idiomatic way.

An unexplained *odizar bush* is mentioned in *Plymouth Records*, I, 199.

Various manual activities called for a number of words which have passed out of use. The word *langle* in the sense of bind, hold together, occurs in *Watertown Records*, p. 95 (1669), in the phrase "side langueled with Iron Fetters." In the *Huntington Records*, p. 9 (1657), occurs the phrase "wampum y[t] is well strung or steaud." The verb *steeve* or *steave*, as used here, means evidently to put together in some kind of manageable or portable shape. It corresponds fairly closely therefore to a Scottish use of the word in the sense to make firm or stiff, or perhaps to a more general use of the word in the meaning *to pack*, for example, the hold of a ship. This latter is mainly an American use, and examples are cited in the *New English Dictionary*. Thornton gives examples of *stived up*, in the sense of crowded together, for 1851 and 1853. The passage in the *Huntington Records* seems to be an early example of the word in the sense of pack.

In *Dedham Records*, III, 48 (1638), occurs the word *brickstrieker*, one who strikes, that is molds or makes bricks. This particular use of the word is now obsolete both in England and America. The *New English Dictionary* has three examples of this use of striker, for 1585, 1610, 1703. But in an advertisement in *The Reportory*, Boston, Nov. 22, 1808 (see Thornton, under *stricken*), bricks not yet dried are called "newly stricken bricks." The archaic past participle *stricken* is apparently now much more widely used in America than in England. It is common newspaper English as an adjective in the phrase "the stricken family," and in courts of law, when a lawyer requests to have parts of the evidence removed from the record, he asks that it be "stricken out."

A kind of work akin to that of the brickstriker was that of the plasterer, or the *dauber*, as he was commonly called in the early records. In *Dedham Records*, III, 155 (1648), mention is made of "daubing work," and the word is often used in reference to the building of the meeting houses. Since the meeting houses were made of sawed boards, not of rough hewn logs, the dauber's task could not have been that of filling in the cracks between the logs with mud, as was commonly done with log cabins. Occasional references to the difficulty of getting a competent person to do daubing work show also that his was a recognized trade, calling for professional skill and experience.

In the phrase *widow's weeds* an old word *weed* still survives more or less in general comprehension. Originally the word, from Old English *wǣd*, meant equipment of various kinds, even a warrior's weapons. It has been gradually restricted in meaning until now it would be applied only to a widow's mourning garments. An earlier use in which the word seems to be restricted, on the contrary, to men's mourning garments is found in the *Lunenburg Records*. When the minister of the town died, the town voted, p. 191 (1761), that "they will Give the Late Rev^d^. M^r^. Stearns Brothers weed and Gloves and his Sisters Vails Handkerchiefs Gloves and Fans and his Sons in Law weeds and Gloves." When Samuel Payson, the successor of Mr. Stearns, died a few years later, the town voted, p. 202 (1763), to give "the Father and Brethren of the deceas'd Weeds, and Gloves, to the Mother of the deceas'd and to the ½ Sister Vails Handkerchiefs and Gloves." At the same time they voted "to give Mrs. Elizabeth Stearns a Neat handsome Suit of Mourning."

Longstreet, *Georgia Scenes*, p. 151, records a long forgotten military word, in the commands *Poise, foolk! Cock, foolk!* The word *foolk* he explains as "a contraction and corruption of 'Firelock.' Thus: 'Firelock,' 'f'lock,' 'foolk.'" The explanation does not make clear whether the *l* in *foolk* was pronounced or not, but probably it was silent. In Longstreet occurs another word which is now characteristically Southern but was formerly also current in New England. This is the word *hound dogs, Georgia Scenes*, p. 213, meaning hunting dogs. This occurs as early as 1649 in the *Dedham Records*, III, 162, where the town action is recorded that "care be taken that the young hound doggs be in time taught to hunt."

One of Webster's wild etymologies in the Dictionary of 1828 is registered under the word *nan*. This, he says, is "a Welsh word signifying *what*, used as an interrogative," and he adds that "it has been extensively used within my memory by the common people of New England." The meaning of the word Webster has defined correctly, and examples of it are met with not infrequently even in early nineteenth century literature. Cooper uses it, in the form *anan*, *The Pioneers*, Chap. XXVI, and elsewhere, as one of the picturesque features of Natty's dialect speech. In the form *nan* it occurs in Carlton, *The New Purchase*, p. 212. Some of the early grammarians mention it as a provincialism, and its literary occurrences are always in a popular dialect. In origin it is merely the older English *anon*, and the development in meaning is clearly indicated by the citations in the *New English Dictionary*.

Another archaic formula, one of polite greeting, is frequently illustrated in the dialect speech of Carlton's *New Purchase*, as in the following, p. 67: "Once in a domestic meeting, we were listening devoutly to the preacher, when a neighbor came . . . and after tying his horse, putting the stirrups over the saddle and pulling down his tow-linen trousers, he advanced to the house and startled both minister and people by administering a smart prefatory rap to the door cheek, and drawling out in a slow, but very loud tone, the usual formula— 'W-e-ll—who—keeps—house?' when he squeezed in among us and took a seat as innocent as a babe."

More interesting than those records of language which illustrate the disappearance of words from use are the indications of life and creative activity to be observed in the emergence of new words or of new meanings in old words to designate fresh experiences. In a new and rapidly developing country such experiences would naturally be varied and numerous, and the developments in vocabulary would more or less keep pace with the changing notions and adventures of the settlers in the new regions. First of all there was a whole new world of natural objects to be named when the Europeans landed in America. In many instances the objects to be named were so much like those already well known in the old world that the old names could simply be transferred without change. In others the native Indians had names that were learned at the time that the objects themselves entered the strangers' experience, and thus names like *opossum*, *raccoon*, *skunk*, *musquash* (Anglicized into *musk-rat*), *woodchuck*, probably with modifications through popular etymology, *moose*, *terrapin*, and others like these established themselves in the language as used in America. The name of the very American *buffalo*, however, is not of Indian, but apparently of ultimately Italian origin.

The *katydid* is American both in its name and in itself. The name is an echoic word made from the sound which the insect produces. Just what this sound is one could not precisely tell from the spellings of the name, since these vary more or less. The name first appeared in poetry in Freneau's *To a katydid.* Holmes has a poem on the katydid, entitled "To an Insect," *Works*, Cambridge edition, p. 7, and he appends a note, saying that he heard the insect at Providence, in Rhode Island, but does not remember hearing it at Cambridge, though it is well known in other towns in the neighborhood of Boston. Perhaps the sound of the insect was so familiar to Holmes at Cambridge that he never became conscious of it. Holmes spelled the word katydid, but Kennedy, *Swallow-Barn* (New York, 1852), p. 26, writing about 1830, speaks of "the little catadid," and the earliest citation of the word in Thornton, for 1800, gives it the form *kittydid.* When Frances Wright arrived in New York, one of the things that first caught her attention was the chorus of sound made in the dark by these insects. She asked her American friend what the sound was by which they were surrounded, but her friend answered, "I hear nothing, unless it be the cattydids?" "The catty-dids! And who, or what are they?"[1] Arthur Singleton,

[1] *Views of Society and Manners in America*, by Frances Wright D'Arusmont, New York, 1821, p. 10.

Letters from the South and West, p. 62, writing in 1816, says that the insects are called *katy dids* "because one seems to say Katy did, and the other to reply Katy didn't." Thornton, from whom the foregoing citation was taken, also records the form *Katydee* for 1818 in one of Woodworth's poems. The name of the *whippoorwill* is also of echoic origin and was spelled in a variety of ways. The whippoorwill shares with the katydid the honor of being among the first subjects for poetry taken from American nature. *A Sonnet to the Chick-Willow* by John Davis appeared in the *Monthly Magazine and American Review*, II (1800), 480. A correspondent added, Vol. III, p. 11, a bit of information about the name of the bird as *Whip-poor-Will*, and still another correspondent, W. D. (William Dunlap?), Vol. III, 256–257, made some suggestions as to the distribution of the various names of the bird, the "Goatsucker of Carolina, East-India Bat, Musqueto-Hawk, l'Engoulevent de la Caroline, Chick-Willow, Chuck-Will's-Widow, and Whip-poor-will." A satirical *Sonnet to John Davis*, by Chick-Willow, Vol. III, 79, is further evidence that the whippoorwill as poetical material had made some stir in the end of the century literary circles of America.

Other names of familiar American use are *lightning bug*, *bullfrog*, *hoptoad*, *bug*, a generic word for all insects, in England taken as referring only to the bedbug. The American vocabulary would not have been adequate without a word for the *mosquito*, and this name, through a variety of spellings, and amplified by a number of facetious additions, has definitely established itself. For mosquitoes of unusual size, the name *gallinipers* is illustrated by a number of examples in Thornton. The size of American mosquitoes has long been a matter of comment. In a review of Weld's *Travels*, the *Quarterly Review*, II, 334, note, says that the only exaggeration in Weld's book is the tale of a mosquito so big that it bit Washington through his leather boot. Facetious names for the mosquito, such as humming-bird, pile driver, etc., are numerous, and the mosquitoes of certain regions, especially New Jersey, are nationally famous for size and ferocity.

The names of American fishes, however, have in very few instances added new words to the vocabulary of the English language. The perch, bass, pike, pickerel, trout, and most other names of fishes, are old words in the English vocabulary. Both the delectable shad and the contemptible sculpin bear good old English names. Does this mean that American fishes do not differ from British fishes, or merely that the casual observer does not note any except the most striking differences among fishes? Undoubtedly the latter, for the silent, cold-blooded and unamusing fish cannot possibly make the same appeal to man's interest and sympathy as the furry creatures of field and forest. One of the kinds of fish first to interest the colonists in America were the *alewives*, which came up the salt water streams in great numbers at certain seasons of the year, and which furnished the colonists with an important part of their diet. The town records of the seventeenth century contain frequent regulations for building of weirs and methods of taking the alewives. The name took several forms, the oldest, 1678, being *aloofe*, of which *alewife, alewives* is probably a corruption. Thornton also gives a passage containing the spelling *old-wife*. The ultimate etymology of the word, perhaps Indian, is uncertain.

The American clam is sometimes referred to by its Indian name *quahaug*, also spelled *cohog*, but the common popular name has always been clam. The black-fish, also, is occasionally mentioned as the *tautaug*, but commonly it has had its English name. The *terrapin*, however, and the *muscalunge*, this latter word being spelled in various ways, both of Indian origin, have safely established themselves in American usage. The *gaspergou*, or *gaspergoo*, or *gasperoo* is a Southern river fish, the name probably being from French *gasparot*. Thornton gives two citations for a Lafayette fish, one for 1843, the other for 1859. According to Bartlett, this fish appears in great abundance in the summer on the Jersey coast, and it was given this name "on account of its appearance one summer coinciding with the last visit of General Lafayette to America." This sounds like an after the event explanation, though names undoubtedly are often given in just such casual fashion. Boys still fish for Lafayettes on the Jersey coast in the summer. Some years ago, when upper Riverside Drive in New York was known as Lafayette Boulevard, fishermen along the shores of the Hudson caught a small fish, the tom cod, which they called Lafayettes, and the name was commonly supposed to come from the name of the boulevard. In connection with fishes, it may be observed that the *chowder*, adapted from French *chaudière*, is mainly an American word, especially along the northern Atlantic coast, where the chowder chiefly flourishes. It may be noted also that the size of American fishes, as of other natives of the wild, must often have been the subject of complacent remark on the part of Americans to have made "a fish story" the American equivalent for drawing the long bow.

Some other words naming objects of the natural world characteristically American may be loosely grouped together. Among these are familiar names of birds, such as *blue jay, jay bird, bob-o-link, tanager, mocking bird, cat bird, bob-white.* The name robin, like lark and yellowhammer, is an old English word applied in America to a bird quite different from the bird of the same name in England. Some names of trees besides those already mentioned which are characteristically American are *butternut, buttonwood, sycamore, quaking asp, cottonwood, gum,* a *bee-gum* being a hollow gum in which wild bees have hived, *sumach, pawpaw, persimmon, tulip tree, dog-wood.* In the South the *china berry tree* is a familiar name and object. These words are not all strictly of American origin, but have become distinctive and familiar parts of the American vocabulary because the objects they name are such common features of the American landscape.

With the wild inhabitants of a whole continent to name, it is evident that a rich field for the roving imagination was opened to the American romancer and pseudo-scientist. This was especially true after the occupation of the western country towards the Mississippi. A poet of the early nineteenth century thus described the Mississippi Valley:

> "Where now the sylvan deserts wide expand,
> And spread a gloomy grandeur o'er the land;

> Where wild and huge amphibious monsters prowl,
> And bears and wolves and screaming panthers stroll;
> Beyond some years, not far remote the day,
> Children in crowds shall innocently play
> Along the streets, and o'er the village green
> Their balls rebound, and tow'ring kites be seen." [1]

This western world appeared to the poet at the time in which he wrote as "the abode of men and monsters, wild and rude," but he wisely does not attempt to designate any of his "huge amphibious monsters" by name. Others had not been so cautious and had made themselves targets for the shafts of the satirists. Brackenridge, in his *Modern Chivalry*, written during the latter eighteenth century, has a great deal to say about the Philosophical Society in Philadelphia and the absurdities of the natural scientists, culminating in the tale of the rascal Teague O'Regan, who had been tarred and feathered. Members of the Society were sent for to examine Teague, and they conclude, Vol. II, p. 136, that it, that is Teague, "is an animal of a species wholly new, and of a middle nature between a bird and a beast." The hoax is elaborately and amusingly carried out, and Teague finally comes out of it with a new name, Anthroposornis, or man-bird.

A few years earlier the authors of the *Anarchiad* had poked fun at the members of a fictitious society of antiquaries, especially at the scientist who had discovered "a monstrous new-invented animal" which had hitherto escaped the notice of every zoölogist, and at another who "regaled his readers with a most notable catfish," *Anarchiad*, ed. Riggs, p. 3. One section of the poem is also devoted to those Europeans who were "to invent so many curious theories, both in philosophy and history, for demonstrating the debility and diminution of nature in the western hemisphere, and for belittling the great objects on which they were to treat," until

> "Huge mammoth dwindle to a mouse's size—
> Columbia turkeys turn European flies:—
> Exotic birds, and foreign beasts, grow small,
> And man, the lordliest, shrink to least of all.'

[1] Charles Mead, *Mississippian Scenery*, Philadelphia, 1819, p. 18.

In this same vein of early nineteenth century humorous satire, Cooper devoted Chapter VI of his *Prairie* to an account of the scientific discoveries of Dr. Battius, a mild and harmless person at the worst. Cooper makes the doctor discover a new animal, the animal being really his own donkey which he has happened upon at night and taken for a monster which is learnedly and elaborately described. As this is an unknown genus, the discoverer names it after himself, Vespertilio Horribilis Americanus.

Another American monster, supposed not to be humorous but terrible, was the title character in Robert Montgomery Bird's *Nick of the Woods, or the Jibbenainosay*, published in 1837, though the scene of the story was set for Kentucky in 1782. The Jibbenainosay was a mysterious monster who killed Indians, always leaving upon their bodies a peculiar mark to show his work. "I never seed the crittur before," says one of the characters who has just discovered one of Nick's victims, "but I reckon it war he, for thar's nothing like him in natur'." When the hero finally did catch a glimpse of the Jibbenainosay, he "beheld with surprise, perhaps even for a moment with the stronger feelings of awe, a figure stalking through the woods at a distance, looking as tall and gigantic in the growing twilight, as the equally collossal spectress seen on the wild summits of the Peruvian Andes," Chapter XI. After all this one is not quite prepared to learn that the Jibbenainosay is human, and a particularly humble sort of human, being a Quaker whose wife and children had been massacred by the Indians and who had devoted his life to the secret killing of Indians, though outwardly and whenever he appeared among white men, as much a Quaker as ever.

A good deal of the natural lore, as well as the professed history, of the *General History of Connecticut*, by Samuel Peters, seems to be the product of the myth-making imagination. This history was first published in London in 1781, and an American edition, from which the citations here given have been taken, was published at New Haven in 1829. Apparently Peters was determined to be interesting, even to the extent of cracking credibility. He tells, p. 110, of a narrow place in the Connecticut river at which the water is so swift and dense that an iron crow-bar floats on top of it. He has a marvelous tale of an army of bullfrogs, p. 126, which appeared in the year 1758 in the town of Windham. The frogs "filled a road 40 yards wide for four miles in length, and were for several hours in passing through the town." This story is followed by a tale, p. 128, of an army of caterpillars which appeared in 1768, and which, after it had devoured every green thing for the space of a hundred miles, went down to the Connecticut River and drowned itself. In some instances the author's inventive genius led him to the actual creation of animals. Such seems to be the whapperknocker. He is described, p. 189, as "somewhat bigger than a weazel, and of a beautiful brown-red color." He lives in the woods on worms and birds, and is "so wild that no man can tame him; and, as he never quits his harbor in the daytime, is only to be taken by traps in the night." Of the fur of the whapperknocker are made muffs, "at the price of thirty or forty guineas apiece." The cuba, another of this historian's rarities, the size of a large cat, is interesting mainly on the female side. The male is a good warrior, p. 190, but "his lady is peaceable and harmless, and depends for protection upon her spouse; and as he has more courage than prudence, always attends him to moderate his temper. She sees danger, and he fears it not. She chatters at him while he is preparing for battle; and if she thinks the danger is too great, she runs to him, and clings about his neck, screaming her extreme distress—his wrath abates, and by her advice they fly to their caves." "When the male cuba is chained, and irritated into the greatest rage by an impertinent dog, his lady, who is never chained, will fly about his neck and kiss him, and in half a minute restore him to calmness."

Among the "feathered tribe" described by Peters as peculiar to America are mentioned together *humilitys*, *whipperwills*, and *dewminks*, p. 193. "The dewmink, so named from its articulating those syllables, is black and white, and of the size of an English robin. Its flesh is delicious." "The humility is so called, because it speaks the word humility, and seldom mounts high in the air. Its legs are long enough to enable it to outrun a dog for a little way;

its wings long and narrow, body maiger, and of the size of a blackbird's; plumage variegated with white, black, blue and red. It lives on tadpoles, spawn and worms; has an eye more piercing than the falcon, and the swiftness of the eagle. Hence it can never be shot: for it sees the sparks of fire even before they enkindle the powder, and, by the extreme rapidity of its flight, gets out of reach in an instant." As the name of a bird *humility*, with a variant *simplicity*, is cited twice in the *New English Dictionary* in American use before the passage just quoted, once for 1634 and again for 1678. It is probable that the name of the bird in the description given by Peters and in the passage of 1678 was derived from the earliest occurrence of it in the passage from 1634, but there is no further evidence that the word was used as a current name for a bird in New England. But if it was, certainly Peters did not describe the bird.

The third of his talking birds Peters calls the *whipperwill*, or *Whip-her-I-will*. This bird is also called the *pope*, "by reason of its darting with great swiftness, from the clouds to the ground, and bawling out Pope! which alarms young people and the fanatics very much, especially as they know it to be an ominous bird." It is also a weather prophet, always giving notice of an approaching storm. "If the tempest is to continue long, the augurs appear in flocks, and nothing can be heard but the word Pope! Pope!" Another marvel is the *bull-fly*, p. 195, "armed with a coat of mail, which it can move from one place to another, as sliders to a window are moved." The *glow-bug*, p. 195, is better known as the lightning bug. Rattlesnakes, large enough "to gorge a common cat," are called *belled snakes* because "before they bite, they rattle their bells three or four times." The *tree frog*, p. 197, is described with some fancy and is said to sing the word I—sa—ac all the night. "It is from the singing of the tree frog that the Americans have acquired the name Little Isaac."

This playful belief in impossible birds and beasts has left traces in American folklore. In that rustic and juvenile practical joke, known as holding the bag, the animal which is to be driven into the bag is called an *albotritch* or some other outlandish and made up name. Another animal of the fancy is the *prock*, mentioned by

Thornton, "which has two short legs on one side and two long on the other, to enable him to keep his perpendicular while browsing on the sides of steep mountains," *Knickerbocker Magazine*, XXXIII, 363. This animal is also known as the *side-winder* or side-hill badger, *Dialect Notes*, III, 249, from the peculiarity of his structure which permits him to feed only on a side hill. On the Texas range a pacing horse is called a side-winder. A side-hill gouger figures in popular Maine tradition, according to D. L. Sharpe, *The Woods of Maine*, *Harper's Monthly*, July, 1922, p. 188. The side-hill gouger is an animal who captures those inexpert woodsmen who lose their sense of direction and go astray in the woods. "I do not know," says Sharpe, "what sort of animal is Johnny's side-hill gouger; though I saw, far up on the side of the mountain, a big bare spot where he had been digging—according to the guide." A variant *bowger* is recorded for Maine in *Dialect Notes*, V, 188. Here also are mentioned *kickle snifters*, who live in old men's beards and in circular lakes; the *kankagee*, a word of undefined meaning from Maine; *lucives*, a kind of wild cat; *the mountain rabbit* and the *philamaloo bird;* the *screbouil*, a creature that steals chickens; the *swamp gahoon*, an animal that makes snowshoe tracks; the *swamp swiver;* the *treesqueak*, an animal that makes a noise like trees rubbing together in the wind; the *wampus cat*, a creature heard whining about camps at night; the *whiffenpuff*, a strange animal that ranges at night. The word *lucives* in this list, also recorded as *lucivee*, is evidently a corruption of Canadian French *loup cervier*. Popular tradition in some communities knows also of a *joint snake*, a snake which separates itself into numerous pieces when one attempts to catch it, assembling the pieces again when the danger is past. De Vere, *Americanisms*, p. 152, mentions a negro belief in a mythical animal called *moonack*, perhaps by some perversion of *arctomys monax*, the Latin name for the groundhog. In connection with these mythical animals may be mentioned the phrase *laros to catch meddlers*, also sometimes *lay ropes, lee ropes to catch medlarks*, as in Charles Egbert Craddock, *In the Clouds*, p. 406, "But when asked what she was talking about, she would reply in enigmatic phrase, 'Laros to ketch meddlers.'"

The origin and precise meaning of the phrase is not clear, though its obvious intent is to serve as a check to inquisitive curiosity.

The *plunkus,* also called the *ding-maul, Dialect Notes,* III, 248, is described as not very large in body, but as having a tail about six feet long, at the end of which is "a huge lump of bony gristle as large as an ordinary football." This is the chief weapon of defence of the plunkus.

Another creation of popular natural history is the *hoop-snake,* which puts its tail in its mouth and rolls incredibly fast, but which can be outrun if one will climb a fence, thereby causing the snake to unhoop before it can pass through. To the same region in the animal kingdom belongs the great *giastaticus,* a creature exceedingly large and exceedingly rare, but as to its other characteristics, exceedingly vague. This wonderful beast seems to have started with the name *gyanousa,* for which Thornton gives references for 1846, 1849 and 1862. In the reference for 1849 the guyanosa appears in company with four young wolves, one prock, and a young Penobscot ice-breaker, the last not being more specifically described. The name took also the form *gyastacutus,* and was applied to an instrument of noise used for charivaris. The *whifflepoof* is another animal which figures in American unnatural natural history; the name is widely distributed in popular tradition, but the characteristics of the creature it names are vague and varied. The *coach whip* is a kind of snake which looks like a braided whip; probably its name has given rise to the popular belief that it winds itself around people's legs and whips them to death with the end of its tail. The *wunk* is a strange animal that digs a hole and pulls the hole in after it. Hunting the wunk's hole is a child's adventure that may lead one far but in the nature of the thing is rarely successful. James Whitcomb Riley has a number of fictitious animals. There is of course the Gobble-uns of Little Orphant Annie, and in Dwainie, from *The Flying Islands of the Night,* "the lurloo ever sings," "the winno-welvers call," the teeper twitters, the tcheucker teeters, and the drowsy oovers drawl,

> But Dwainie hides in Spirkland
> And answers not at all.

Somewhat similar in spirit to these humorous names of impossible animals are the joke words for impossible objects, a number of which have been collected by O. F. Emerson, *Dialect Notes*, V, 93–97, under the heading Beguiling Words. Examples are black whitewash, a painter's joke; striped ink, a printing office joke; compass key; leather faced hammer, a machinist's joke; patent post hole; an italic period, a printer's joke, etc.

To these various popular fancies should be added the fictitious character Paul Bunyan, a Gargantuan backwoods hero. Everything relating to Paul Bunyan happens on a heroic scale. He combs his hair with a young pine tree. His feats of strength, his passions of rage are devastating. About him have gathered innumerable tales, a whole epic of the lumber camps, see Stevens, *Paul Bunyan*, New York, 1925, and Shephard, *Paul Bunyan*, Seattle, 1925.

The sportive imagination illustrated by these names of fictitious animals and objects is a native characteristic of American English. This kind of humorous fancy is always one of the essential elements in slang, which arises only among persons in groups whose social intercourse is playful and is carried on with some vivacity. Life of this kind has been perhaps peculiarly possible in America, where rapidly changing external conditions and also changes in social grouping have kept the mind alert and eager to express first impressions. American slang is thus often directly expressive of concrete experience, and in consequence vigorously picturesque. Perhaps the most striking difference between British and American popular slang is that the former is more largely merely a matter of the use of queer sounding words, like bally or swank, whereas American slang suggests vivid images and pictures.

The images which suggest slang are constantly changing, for nothing in language is so fugacious as slang. Consequently the slang phrase often completely disappears, or survives with only a weakened sense of its original picturesqueness. Thus one may now use the metaphorical phrases *to back and fill* or *to back water* without thinking of the river steamboat in connection with which the phrases arose. In some instances, as in *to acknowledge the corn,* no altogether satisfactory explanation of origins can be given. But one does not need antiquarian comment to perceive the meaning and the underlying story in phrases like *an Arkansas toothpick,* meaning a dagger, *to bark up the wrong tree, to make a bee line, a big bug, to cut across lots, the cap sheaf, to carry a chip on the shoulder, horse sense, to keep one's eye peeled, to face the music, to get on the band wagon, to keep a stiff upper lip, to get the grand bounce, to get one's walking papers, to settle one's hash.* This last phrase goes back to the eighteenth century, but apparently it became a part of familiar English only in the nineteenth century. The basis in fact upon which the metaphor rests in this instance is not altogether apparent. A hash is usually a mixture of minced meat and other things, and perhaps the phrase, to settle the hash, arose when the hash, which was one of the important features in the bill of fare of the barbecue, boiled over. As it was made over an open fire in a large kettle, it would be likely to boil over and need settling. But direct evidence confirming this explanation is lacking. A place in Kentucky is known as *Rabbit Hash.*

American facetious language is also rich in fantastically coined or combined words, as *absquatulate, bodacious,* perhaps made up from bold and audacious, but now rarely used, *bogus, bummer, caboodle, cahoot, cantankerous, catawampus, cavort, cohogle, conniption fit, contraption, dude, highfalutin, hornswoggle, jigger, jigmaree, rambunctious, rumpus, savagerous, savigrous, skedaddle, skeezicks, slantindicular, sockdologer, splurge, spondulicks* and many other words for money.

If one may judge from the character and variety of names for "the undesirable citizen" which have been present in the language, one would say that he has been both numerous and amusing. He may have been merely a poor cuss, or, more picturesquely, a bummer, hobo, or yegg, a hoodlum, a jayhawker, a plug ugly, a ring tail roarer, a rowdy, a scalawag, a soap lock, a rough neck, an ugly customer who shoots up the town or paints the town red, though with all this variety of nomenclature he was doubtless much the same under whatever name he was known. Like all highly specialized trades, the business of thieving[1] and swindling has developed a rich technical vocabulary, some of which, as in *confidence man, gold brick, frame up*, has come over into the general vocabulary, though in the main it has had only the limited circulation which the slang jargon of trade and technical vocabularies in general enjoy. The vocabulary of money is rich in facetious words, the exhilaration of having money putting one in a mood not to be satisfied by a literal name of the object. Thus the silver dollar became a cart wheel, or a plunk, and paper money a greenback, or a rag, see Paulding, *Letters from the South*, II, 122. The synonyms for money are infinite in number and fancy. Thornton, p. 971, quotes a set of verses in which the following occur: mopus, pewter, shiner, brad, dough, dollar, spoons, the bright and lively ready, the rowdy, the stumpy, the cash, the rhino, the tin, the dibs, the browns, the chips and dust and clinkers, dimes, horse-nails, the brass, the needful, spondulix, buttons, rocks, mint-drops.

The word *specie* now commonly means coin as contrasted with paper money, and in everyday use the word would be facetious. This meaning has been of gradual development, the stages of growth being well illustrated in the examples in the *New English Dictionary*. In the early town records occur many instances of the older meaning of the word, which is recorded in a variety of spellings, as merely kind or variety. In *Plymouth Records*, I, 143, the town agreed to see certain of its debts defrayed "in such specue as they shall agree with men for the doing it." One-half of certain charges the town agrees, I, 164, are to be "payed in Currant silver Mony of New England and the other halfe in Corne and provisions. . . . The one halfe of both specaes to payed by the first of October." Again the town decreed, I, 184, that "the Rates Both for Cuntrey and towne Charges should be made in one and the same speasey"; and also, I, 195, that "each person shall be payed both as to time and specey as Was Agreed on the last yeare."

[1] For an early American list of thieves' words, see *The Life and Adventure of Henry Tufts*, Dover, N. H., 1807, and T. W. Higginson, *Science*, V (1885), 380–382.

One form which the picturesque phrase sometimes took was that of abbreviation, as in O.K., which came in during the presidential campaign of 1828, and is commonly supposed to be from President Jackson's spelling of all correct as oll korrect. Other abbreviations are G.O.P., P.D.Q., G.B., "the grand bounce," the D.T.'s, etc., see also Long, Semi-Secret Abbreviations, *Dialect Notes,* IV, 245–246. Many modern trade names are a kind of abbreviation, being words built up from initial letters, as in the Reo automobile, made by the R. E. Olds Company. Trade names in general in America offer a rich field for study, inasmuch as the necessity of finding distinctive and taking names for objects has led advertisers and manufacturers to perform the most surprising feats of ingenious, sometimes of grotesque inventiveness. In a few instances, as in *kodak, victrola,* these trade names remain as probably permanent additions to the vocabulary, but in most cases they satisfy their fleeting purpose if they attract a moment's amused and interested attention, see Pound, Word-coinage and Modern Trade Names, *Dialect Notes,* IV, 29–41.

The social diversions of youth are always exceptionally vivacious and one is therefore not surprised to find an extraordinarily rich development of slang in these circles. An older generation finds itself often quite shut off from the younger generation because it has not acquired the newer language. This slang of social intercourse is as ephemeral as any other. Even its wit and picturesqueness rarely has virtue enough to save it. Who will know a generation hence that a snugglepup is a young man who attends petting parties, and that a petting party is a party devoted to hugging? Or that a crape-hanger is a reformer, or a lounge lizard one who suns himself eternally in good society, a cake eater being a harmless lounge lizard? A chaperone is a fire extinguisher, marriage is an eye-opener, dancing with a bashful partner is absent treatment. If there seems to be a vein of cynicism in this society cant, that also may be laid at the door of youth.

In the general class of humorous words belongs the long list of intensives or swear words which for many generations have given a distinctive flavor to the more excited moods, sometimes to the casual conversation, of the American speaker. A distinction must be made between cursing and swearing. The former is a serious matter, and the forms of cursing are likely to be established by venerable and inalterable custom. Swearing satisfies a less solemn need for expression and gives room for the play of fancy and imagination. It may range from a mild intensive or colorless expletive to the limits at which, by taking the name of God in vain, cursing begins. The swear word or phrase may be merely ordinary English of a rich and satisfying rhythm. "By Golding's bow key," says Quick, *Vandemark's Folly*, p. 304, the time and place being Iowa about 1850, "was a very solemn objurgation. It could be used by professors of religion, but under great provocation only. It harks back to the time when every man who had oxen named them Buck and Golding, and the bow-key held the yoke on."

Many mild expletives are merely weakened forms of original curses, and in this kind of swearing the American, especially the Yankee, has been considered to be particularly adept. Phrases like *I swan, I swow, I van, I vum, dad fetch it, to give a person Jesse,* or *particular Jesse, all fired, jo fired* are quite safe though they still bear enough of the marks of their origin upon them to satisfy the needs of Puritan imprecation. The word *eternal,* in the form *tarnal,* and in the composite *tarnation,* also extended its usefulness, and *tarnation* took on a contracted form *nation* which was formerly a necessary word in the stock in trade of any one who set about describing a rustic Yankee or telling a Yankee story.

Another originally Yankee word was *darn,* which may be said to be now the universal American expletive, and which has had so distinctive an American history that it must be examined in detail. The commonly accepted explanation of the word *darn* makes of it a euphemistic variant of *damn.* Thus the *Century Dictionary* speaks of darn as a "minced form of damn," and the same explanation is found regularly in the dictionaries of slang as well as in the dictionaries of the standard speech. *Darned* and *darnation* or *tarnation* are taken to be variant forms of *damned* and *damnation.* The linguistic process involved according to this explanation would be similar to that which has resulted in forms like *gad, gee whiz, gosh,* and various others. In present use there can be no question that *darn* and *damn* stand in intimate relation to each other. But there can also be no doubt that *darn* is historically of independent origin, that it is not a phonetic variant of *damn,* and that the contamination between the two words arose late and is one of meaning and not of form.

There are considerable phonetic difficulties in the way of assuming that *darn* is merely a euphemistic variant of *damn.* Jespersen, *Modern English Grammar,* I, 301, who seems to be familiar only with the verbal uses of *darn,* regards the participle *darned* as the original and characteristic form of the word. He cites one example of *darn* as an imperative, but this, he says, "is the only instance I remember of seeing this *r* outside of the participle." Americans who examine their memories will find no difficulty in adding many more instances to Professor Jespersen's single example, and will also readily recall adjective uses, as in *It's a darn shame,* and adverbial, as in *It's too darn heavy.* The phonetic form of the participle Professor Jespersen thinks has no *r* in it, though he adds on the authority of Professor Hempl, "that some Americans here really pronounce an *r,* in which case we may have one of those arbitrary sound substitutions that are so frequent in swearing." Not only some Americans but most Americans who freely use the word pronounce an *r,* both in *darned* and *darn.* The arbitrary substitution of an *r* to differentiate *darned* from *damned* is an extremely unlikely supposition. Moreover one must then suppose that the *n* of *darned* is also an arbitrary substitution, since the *n* of both *damned* and *damn* is silent. The vowel also would have been changed from the [æ] of *damned* to the [ɑ] of *darned, darn.* And finally this phonetic explanation of *darned, darn* takes no account of the very significant and widespread variant pronunciation *durned, durn.* Granting the need of a euphemistic variant for *damned, damn,* this word was scarcely bad enough as a swear word to occasion such thoroughgoing reconstruction as *darn* and *durn* imply. As a euphemistic variation of *damned, domd* or *demd,* both of which occur, would be more probable.

The right explanation of *darn, durn,* as verb, adjective and adverb, is that the word was originally a less highly colored element in the conventional vocabulary which later became corrupted through evil association with *damn.* The starting point is Old English *dierne,* common as an adjective but also present as adverb (cf. Beowulf, lines 150, 410), and as verb in the form *diernan.* The primary meaning of the adjective was "hidden," "secret," of the verb "to conceal." But already in Old English the substantive passed out of its primary meaning into related meanings which may be characterized as at least shady in general. Old English *dierne, diernan* became regularly Middle English *derne, dernen.* As the verb occurred infrequently in Old English and Middle English, and apparently disappeared from literary use in early Modern English, it may be dropped out of consideration. The point of departure in the extension of the use of the word in Modern English was evidently the adjective and adverb, not the verb. Assuming for a moment the identity of Modern English *darn, durn,* and Middle English *derne,* one may point out that the phonetic development is just what one might expect. The forms are exactly parallel to such doublets in pronunciation as one finds in *hearth,* pronounced to rime with garth and girth, *clerk,* riming with mark or mirk; in *parson, person; Hartford, Hertford; Barclay, Berkeley;* and in popular pronunciations like *sarvint* for *servant, larn* for *learn,* and a great many others. Of the two forms *darn* and *durn* in Modern English, the former seems to be the more common. The reverse is true of the greater number of *-er-* words with double pronunciation, the spelling with *-er-* perhaps tending to limit the number of *-ar-* pronunciations. In so popular a word as *darn, durn,* however, the spelling could have had but little influence either way, and for this reason one is not surprised to find both forms persisting in popular pronunciation.

The crucial point in this etymology of *darn, durn,* is obviously the change of meaning involved in the transition from a descriptive adjective or adverb to an imprecation. The general trend of the development which makes this supposition plausible is from a somewhat precise meaning towards a more general one, a development which ends in making the word an intensive of undifferentiated adverse significance, very much as words like awful, horrible, etc., have changed from specific to general intensive meanings. The process is already clearly indicated in Middle English, where *derne* occurs not only in its primary sense, but also in various secondary applications. Chaucer uses the word only three times, all in the Miller's Tale and all with reference to illicit love. Langland employs the word in the same connotation as Chaucer in the phrase "that deede derne," A. Passus, X, 299, B. Passus, IX, 189, C. Passus, XI, 295. But he speaks also of adultery, divorce, and "derne vsurye," B. Passus, II, 175, where the sense seems not to be secret usury but merely wicked usury. Another passage in Langland deserves to be quoted:

> "For out of reson thei ryde and rechelesliche taken on,
> As in durne dedes bothe drynkynge and elles."
> C. Passus. XIV, 154-155.

Two passages occur in Richard the Redeless, Passus, I, 42, 69, in which Skeat seems to hesitate between the readings *derue* and *derne*, but in the second at least, derne, meaning dreadful, wicked, seems necessary:

> "To deme youre dukys myssdedis so derne thei were."

Two further passages may be noted in the Bestiary. In one, Emerson, *Middle English Reader*, p. 14, lines 16–17, the devil is said to be unable to discover how the lord appeared on earth, though he be "derne hunte," though he be "a fierce hunter." In the other, p. 16, lines 13–14, man is said to be like the eagle, "Old in hise sinnes dern," "old in his dark or grievous sins," before he becomes Christian. But it is unnecessary to multiply examples of what is a clearly defined development of the word in Middle English.

In early Modern English the word appears not infrequently, both in its primary sense and in the generalized secondary senses. Levins, *Manipulus* (1576), defines *dearne* as *dirus*. The *New English Dictionary* cites an example from 1613 which reads, "Queene Elizabeth died, a dearne day to England," and another from 1650, "These derne, dreery, direful days." Examples are given also of uses of the word as an intensive in the sense of merely deep, intense, as in "Unable to restrain his derne desire" (1594). In the quarto edition of *Lear,* III, 7, 63, a form of the word occurs, though the folio here reads *stern,* which is the reading usually followed by the editors. But the phrase as it stands in the quartos, "that dearne time," need not be regarded with suspicion, since it is apparent from the examples already quoted that the adjective dern was not uncommonly joined to general terms like time and day. The only other occurrence of the word in the text of Shakspere is in *Pericles,* III, I, 15, where it is combined with "painful" in the phrase "dern and painful perch." The whole passage, presumably not by Shakspere, is consciously archaistic. In Spenser the word occurs only in the forms *dernly* and *dernful,* e.g., *Mourning Muse,* line 90, "dernfull noise," made by birds of "ill presage"; *Daphnaida,* 196, "thus dearnlie plained," thus grievously lamented; *Fairy Queen,* II, I, 35, 7, "a ruefull voice that dearnly cride"; also III, I, 14, 4, "Their puissaunce whylome full dernly tryde," very severely tried; and III, XII, 34, 4, "Dernly unto her called," earnestly unto her called. Its comparatively rare occurrence, however, and the character of the passages in which it is used, show that the word had already become more or less archaic by the beginning of the seventeenth century. After that it seems to have fallen almost completely out of literary use, and to have been restored to knowledge again only in modern times through the study of English rustic dialects. Wright, *English Dialect Dictionary,* finds the word widely distributed in modern English dialects, in meanings ranging from secret, obscure, through dark, dreary, lonely, hard, stern, determined, eager, earnest, careful, and even as applied to weather, raw, cold and generally disagreeable. Among a "List of words for the present kept back from the want of further information," Vol. I, p. v, he notes *dern,* as adjective or adverb in Scotland in the sense of daring, fierce, wild. If the examples and definitions which have been cited have shown, as they were intended to do, that *dern* developed into an intensive of broad general significance of an adverse kind, it is apparent that the word could be used in passages which would require a great variety of synonymous or approximately synonymous words, to express explicitly the senses intended.

It remains now to bridge the chasm between the use of *dern* as an intensive of general condemnatory significance and its use as an imprecation. No one familiar with the histories of popular words like oaths will expect to put his finger on the precise time and place when the change occurred. Evidence in such cases must be largely cumulative, though in this instance it seems that the conclusion can be placed beyond reasonable doubt. In the first place it should be noted that *damn* as a verb used profanely occurs early. The *New English Dictionary* records an instance as early as 1431, with others that follow consecutively. The participial adjective *damned* is recorded for 1596 and after. The first recorded instance of *damn* as a noun is for 1619, and of course later ones all along. But when we come to *darn, darnation*, we find the first instance in the *New English Dictionary* for 1837–40, in Haliburton's New England dialect sketches. This date may be carried back a few years, since the sketches appeared in journalistic form before they were published as a book. The *New English Dictionary* describes the word as occurring chiefly in the United States. The Century and the Standard have nothing to add to the *New English Dictionary*. Wright, *English Dialect Dictionary*, records the word as widely current in English and American use, but only very recent examples are given. When Dickens made his travels in America in 1842 he apparently met with the word for the first time when he heard an American say "darn my mother," *American Notes* (London, 1900), p. 150. Dickens did not connect the word with *damn* at all, as he remarks that he does not know "what the sensation of being darned may be, or whether a man's mother has a keener relish or disrelish of the process than anybody else." Dickens remembered the word, and in the first chapter of Martin Chuzzlewit in which Americans appear, Chapter XVI, he put it into the mouth of one of his American characters. Now if Dickens, familiar as he was with the popular life and language of his own country, had never heard *darn* in England, it is a pretty safe assumption that it was not there to be heard. Haliburton's use of it, however, establishes the word as current in New England by the first quarter of the nineteenth century. The most reasonable hypothesis seems to be that *darn, darned, darnation* and *tarnation*, as imprecations, are all of New England Puritan origin. All the early examples are localized in New England. Wherever the imprecation occurs in early Southern American English, it is always recorded as an outright *damn.*[1] In New England, however, one might expect the Puritan tradition against swearing to be sufficiently active to lead to the modification of swear words as a compromise, though certainly not strong enough to prevent their use.

As a further link in the argument for the New England origin of *darn*, one must note the important evidence of the survival of the older use of *darn* as a more or less colorless intensive in common New England usage. In one of the notes to his *Dissertations* (1789), p. 385, Noah Webster comments on the word, spelling it *dern*, and says that it "is in common use in New England and is pronounced *darn*." Webster was not often happy in his etymologies, but in this instance he correctly guessed the Middle English origin of the word. He adds, however, that the word does not have "the sense it had formerly; it is now used as an adverb to qualify an adjective, as darn sweet, denoting a great degree of the quality." Webster remarks further that for many years he "had supposed the word dern in the sense of *great* or *severe* was local in New England," and that "perhaps it may not now be used anywhere else." Apparently *darn* as imprecation was unknown to Webster, or else he would certainly have said something about it. But he did not record *dern* or *darn*

[1] A passage in Beveridge's *Life of John Marshall*, III, 205, illustrates the difference between New England and the South in the use of this word. The passage occurs in an account of the trial of Samuel Chase for impeachment before the Senate in February, 1805. Chase was charged with having used the word *damned* at an inappropriate moment, and in answer to this charge Luther Martin, attorney for Chase, replied as follows: "However it may sound elsewhere in the United States, I cannot apprehend it will be considered *very* offensive, *even* from the mouth of a judge on this side of the Susquehanna;—to the southward of that river it is in familiar use . . . supplying frequently the place of the word *very* . . . connected with subjects the most pleasing; thus we say indiscriminately a very good or a damned good bottle of wine, a damned good dinner, or a damned clever fellow."

in his dictionaries, probably regarding it as so distinctly a popular word as not to be deserving of dictionary record.

Some of the early American examples are interesting as showing the word in transition stages. Macintosh, *Essai Raisonné* (1797), p. 45, gives the word in two spellings, *dearn, darn,* and he seems to have regarded it as an ordinary conventional word. As a stronger intensive it already appears in *Jonathan Postfree* (1806), an American farce by L. Beach, in which the Yankee Jonathan says, "Came down [to New York from Connecticut] by land—drove down old Squire Herdy's cattle—darn'd ugly creatures to drive—almost pestered my heart out." In J. N. Barker's *Tears and Smiles* (1808), Nathan Yank speaks, Act I, "I'll be darned, sir, if I think this is the way, for I can't see a morsel of a church." In the preface to this play, the author speaks not impolitely but kindly of his "d——d good-natured friend." In *Love and Friendship* (1809), a comedy by A. B. Lindsley, a Yankee servant Jonathan says, "darn my skin 'f you wouldn't dewe it, clear as mud." In Woodworth's *Deed of Gift* (1822), p. 20, Dan'l, a Massachusetts village rustic, says to his mother, "But, darn it, mother, I don't want to get off," and to the maiden he is courting, p. 45, "I have taken a liking to you, 'cause you are so darn'd pretty." But the word could be used also as a much milder intensive. In Kendall's *Doleful Tragedy of the Raising of Jo. Burnham* (1832), Aunt Debby, an innocent New England dame, sitting by the fireside knitting, speaks of the night meetings of the Masons, Act II, Scene I, who "keep so darn'd sly about it." There was surely no off color in this use of the word, for when the swear word is used in this play, as it frequently is by men, the author writes it d——d. A similar use is that in *Haverhill*, by James A. Jones (1831), p. 253. This is a romance of the years just before the Revolution, in which there is a good deal of realistic description of New England. Aminidab, a rustic New Englander, speaks as New Englandly as the author can make him: "A tarnation big ship, too, and owned by Elder Pollard, he that built the block of housen where Elder Hillyard has his darned great bookstore, and owns that unimproved tract of brush on the road to Hingham." An earlier occurrence of *tarnation* is in Lambert's *Travels* in the years 1806, 1807 and 1808, Vol. II, p. 506, and Lambert also gives *nation* as a New England word, but he never puts *darn, darnation, tarnation* or *nation* in the mouth of a Southern speaker.

In J. Robinson's *Yorker's Stratagem,* New York, 1792, Act I, Sc. I, the phonetic variant form *dur* occurs. "I'll not put up with any of your half laughs," says Amant, who is "dressed like a Yankey clown" and tries to speak like one, "I'll be dur if I do, and that's point blank." The forms *tarnashon* and *tarnish* also occur in this play.

It should be noted that *darn* as an intensive has grown stronger with use. This is not the common fate, however, of intensives, which ordinarily by familiarity become weakened and must be replaced by fresher and stronger terms. If *darn* had become generalized in use as it was at first employed in New England and without association with *damn,* which in turn derived its strength by being frequently combined with the name of the Deity, it would probably long since have become as colorless as *awful, horrible, dreadful* and other similar commonplace intensive words. But when *darn* came to be regarded as a substitute for *damn,* it borrowed some of the powers of the latter word, though it never became its equal in intensive value.

In brief then the explanation of *darn, darned* is that the word was originally Old English *dierne,* which developed as an intensive adjective and adverb. As an adjective *darn* readily took on the form of a participial adjective, just as *addle,* originally an adjective, became also *addled,* a participial adjective. From *addled* a finite verb was then formed, as in "to addle one's head over accounts." So also from *darned* a verb *darn* was derived. As the New England social conscience was tender on this point of swearing, it was the most natural thing in the world for the New Englander to secure the necessary relief which an imprecation affords by substituting the already familiar and inoffensive *darn* for the bolder but unequivocally profane word of the vocabulary.

Another American intensive which calls for explanation is the phrase *torn down.* It occurs several times in Lindsley's *Love and*

Friendship (1809), as at p. 10, "Darnation! says 'e, in a torne down passion"; also on p. 57, "for we've put things all t' rights aboard in a torne down fine order," and again, "our capun . . . hopes you'll have a torne down agreeable night on 't." In Kennedy's *Swallow Barn*, p. 41, written about 1830, occurs the sentence, "His whole air is that of an untrimmed colt, torn down and disorderly." The word is recorded in present use, *Dialect Notes*, II, 334, for southwestern Missouri, the example cited being, "He is a torn-down fellow when he is drinking and everybody is afraid of him." The *New English Dictionary* gives this word as dialectal in England and as occurring in the United States, and takes it to be merely *torn* with the preposition *down*, comparing torn off, torn up, etc. The developments in meaning involved in this explanation are not clear, but the explanation may be correct. A not dissimilar use is that of *tear*, noun, as in "to go on a tear," or *tearing*, as in "to have a tearing time." A variant form of the phrase is employed by Charles Egbert Craddock, *Despot of Broomsedge Cove*, p, 140, in Tennessee mountain dialect: "Racin' an' bettin' air sinful," she declared, "an' that thar tearin'-down, good-lookin' Teck Jepson hev got mighty little religion ef he don't know it." Wright, *English Dialect Dictionary*, records *torn down* as current in the dialect speech of Scotland, Lancashire and Lincolnshire.

Another unexplained word is *jiffy*. It occurs in Kendall's *Doleful Tragedy* (1832), p. 23, in the form *giffin*, "cut his throat in a giffin." In Carlton's *New Purchase*, p. 38, the word is spelled as one would now expect it to be spelled—"we shall be off in what they call a jiffy—i.e., in a moment or two." The *New English Dictionary* has examples of *jiffy* beginning the latter part of the eighteenth century, and in the *English Dialect Dictionary*, both *jiff* and *jiffy* are recorded. No evidence, however, is available for the etymology of the word, and the form *giffin* is not listed.

Another expletive which occurs in two forms in Kendall and Carlton is the word *hooter, hait.* Kendall, p. 81, has "can't do a hooter," i.e., can do nothing. Carlton, p. 147, writes "they never did us harm—no, not a hait—(little bit)." Thornton gives examples of *hooter* down to 1862. That these two words are the same in origin is probable but not proved. The *New English Dictionary* under *hate, haet,* explains this word as from "Devil have it," in Scotch, "Deil hae't," in meaning equivalent to devil a bit. "Hence *haet,* with an ordinary negative, as *not a haet,* came sometimes to be understood as equivalent to 'whit,' 'atom,' or 'anything, the smallest thing that can be conceived' (Jamieson)." The Dictionary gives examples of *haet* from 1590 on, but does not record *hooter* in this sense. For the etymology given above a Scotch verdict of not proven must be rendered. In *Dialect Notes,* I, 389, "didn't get a hate," meaning "didn't get a thing" is recorded for Pennsylvania, Kentucky and Eastern Ohio.

Many other varieties of intensives are found on the more familiar levels of American speech. Universals and superlatives have often acquired intensive value, as in "like all creation," "all nature," "all wrath," "all possessed," indicating merely a high degree of the action expressed by a preceding verb, and *powerful, monstrous, universal, beatingest* have also acquired a similar generalized superlative meaning. The following sentence from Longstreet, *Georgia Scenes,* p. 22, "He's the best piece of hoss flesh in the thirteen united universal worlds," would seem really to have attained the superlative of eminence. Another American intensive is the word *tall,* as in *tall talk, tall swearing, tall shooting,* etc. This was good Elizabethan English, as in Sir Toby's remark, *Twelfth Night,* I, III, 18, "He's as tall a man as any's in Illyria." The word seems to have had a somewhat facetious color in Shakspere, and this it has retained in American speech. The use of *right* as an intensive, as in "right glad," is more characteristically Southern than general American use at present, and it is described in the *New English Dictionary* as archaic in England. In adverbial phrases like "right out," "right off," "right away," the use is general, and it is also recorded for England by the *New English Dictionary,* with the comment that it originated in America. But the proof of the correctness of this latter statement is lacking.

Emphasis by understatement is also not uncommon in American familiar speech, as when a person is said to be a caution or a case, or an action or object which is truly big is said not to be a circumstance to something else. The word *ordinary* in a colloquial form *ornery* has acquired general value as a strong term of disapproval. The word *common* has also tended to go the same way, but perhaps it is characteristic of the leveling forces in democracy that the word has also acquired in popular speech commendatory senses.

Picturesque and metaphorical intensives abound in the language, as in the negatives "not by a jugful," "not by a long sight," "no two ways about it," or when a person is said to be "some pumpkins," or the reverse, "small potatoes—and few in a hill." American popular speech especially is likely to be colored by striking but homely similes of this kind, as in "slow as molasses in January," "quick as greased lightning," "keen as a Philadelphia lawyer," "peanut politics." The earliest example of the hyperbolical phrase "to knock one into a cocked hat" in Thornton is for 1833, but as cocked hats had gone out of use by that time, the locution must have originated earlier. This rustic figurative style goes back to the beginning of the realization of a distinctive American Yankee language. It is ridiculed in the *Portfolio*, March 12, 1803, Vol. 3, No. 1, in the following verses and their introductory comment:

"Ever since the era of Dr. Franklin, the love of proverbs has waxed exceedingly fervent, among our countrymen. This debasement of the dignity and elegance of diction is not less justly than humorously ridiculed, by a Yankee bard [not named], who thus jeers the woeful insipidity of the simple style.

YANKEE PHRASES

As sound as a nut o'er the plain
I of late whistled, chock full of glee:
A stranger to sorrow and pain,
As happy as happy could be.

As plump as a partridge I grew,
My heart being lighter than cork:
My slumbers were calmer than dew!
My body was fatter than pork!

Thus happy I hop'd I should pass
Sleek as grease down the current of time,
But pleasures are brittle as glass,
Although, as a fiddle they're fine.

Jemima, the pride of the vale,
Like a top, nimbly danced o'er our plains:
With envy the lasses were pale—
With wonder stood gaping the swains.

She smiled like a basket of chips—
As tall as a hay pole her size—
As sweet as molasses her lips—
As bright as a button her eyes.

Admiring I gazed on each charm,
My peace that would trouble so soon,
And thought not of danger, nor harm,
Any more than the man in the moon.

But now to my sorrow I find
Her heart is as hard as a brick:
To my passion forever unkind,
Though of love I am full as a tick.

I sought her affection to win,
In hopes of obtaining relief,
Till I, like a hatchet, grew thin,
And she, like a haddock, grew deaf.

I late was as fat as a doe
And playful and spry as a cat:
But now I am dull as a hoe,
And lean and as weak as a rat.

Unless the unpitying fates
With passion as ardent shall cram her,
As certain as death or as rates,
I soon shall be dead as a hammer.

This poem was probably copied in the Portfolio from the *Federal Orrery,* where it appeared on May 11, 1795, Vol. 2, p. 230, under the title Cant Phrases, and signed Kadanda. A considerable fashion in the writing of such poems existed at the time.

Certain practical activities necessarily called for extensions of the English vocabulary in America. The Yankees being much given to bargain and exchange have accordingly enriched the vocabulary of the language in this direction. The verb *to trade,* amply illustrated in Thornton, has always had in it certain sporting implications which have saved it from degenerating into the same class as British *tradesman* or the phrase *in trade.* Another universal Americanism of the same kind is the word *swap,* for which the earliest American reference in Thornton is for 1782. It was current earlier, as we learn from *Suffield Records,* p. 308 (1748), the townsmen having voted "that the Sellect Men in the Spring by a good cow and Let Jeam Leraby have, to help him maintaine his child; and att ye fall of ye year if ye child Lives the Sellect men with Jeams swop the cow, or Do that thay shall think Best." Though apparently not originally facetious, the word later took on somewhat humorous color. It was included by Dr. Johnson in his dictionary, though it was there characterized as "a low word." This probably means nothing more, however, than that the word was known to Johnson only in provincial or local use.

Though not limited to American practice, the word *peddle* has taken on distinctively American significances from the earlier activities of the Yankee pedlar of Yankee notions. A *notion store* is still a small establishment where pins, needles, tape and a variety of similar articles are sold. Since the Yankee pedlar has passed out of existence the word has again tended to degenerate and to be applied to a poor creature with a pack on his back. In New England, however, the verb *peddle* still survives in the colorless meaning to sell at retail, especially to the selling of milk or meat or other household necessities from a wagon.

The American use of *store* is fully illustrated by Thornton's quotations. The earlier American word was *shop,* as now in England, and Thornton's first example of *store* is for 1773, where *store* and *shop* are used together as synonyms. Gradually *store* supplanted *shop,* until now in ordinary American use *store* means any place of some size where things are sold, and *shop* commonly means a smaller place where things are done or made. Thus one would speak of a *shoe store,* where shoes are sold, but of a *shoe shop,* where shoes are mended, of a *barber shop,* a *blacksmith shop,* a *machine shop,* but of a *drygoods store,* a *grocery store,* a *furniture store,* etc. The distinctions are not always clearly maintained, however, as in some communities one speaks of the *butcher shop,* the *meat shop,* the *bake shop,* and perhaps of other shops, in which the notion of doing something or making something is not strikingly prominent. And on the other hand the word *shop* has been extended to apply to factories in which things are made on a large scale, corresponding to the British use of *works.* Through British influence the use of *shop* for *store* has been extended here and there in self-conscious urban use, as in *boot shop, book shop* for the more customary *shoe store, book store.* In older American use the distinction between things bought at the store and things made at home gave rise to various locutions like *store clothes, store cloth, store tea, store cheese, storekeeper.* The terms *storekeeper, to keep store* were ordinarily used in older American communities in connection with the general store which supplied the community with all it wanted, *wet goods, dry goods* and *hardware.* A merchant was one who bought and sold on a larger scale, or when the dry goods part of selling became detached and specialized, the person who was called a *draper* in England came to be called a *merchant* in America, perhaps through the influence of *merchant taylor* or perhaps because the merchant dealt not in homely local produce, pork and flour and such other products as the farmer raised on his land, but in silks and satins and cloths from afar and thus became a more dignified person. Some tailors or taylors still describe themselves as *merchant tailors.* The earliest occurrence of *dry goods* in Thornton is for 1777, and early British travelers in America frequently noticed this use of the word as unfamiliar to them. Fearon, *Sketches of America* (1817), p. 10, remarked that the "linen and woolen drapers (dry goods stores, as they are denominated) leave quantities of their goods loose on boxes," and whenever he had occasion to use the word, Fearon always put it within quotation marks.

The word *lumber*, combined also with other words, as in *lumberman, lumber merchant*, has had a distinctive development in America. The starting place is the general sense of the word meaning a variety of discarded furniture, utensils, etc., as in *Huntington Records* (1686), p. 435, "a loume and weavers geer and other lumber." In the *Southold Records* (1658), I, 438, we read of "Iron, Cotton wool, a new beadtick, old caske, comes [combs], old sales, a malt mill and other lumber in the chambers." Sundries are grouped in this list under the heading "lumber omitted," p. 439. An equivalent term is found in the inventory of another estate in the same records, I, 443 (1658), where miscellaneous articles are described as "pewter, brasse, and other trumpery," words to make one's mouth water if one were a collector of antiques. But the word early came to be used in a more definite sense in the Colonies, and a surveyor of lumber was regularly appointed in the New England towns. In *Plymouth Records* II, 45 (1710), we read that "Sergant harlow and Jacob Mitchel are chosen to survey all sorts of lumber exposed to sale"; and elsewhere mention is made of "bords Timber and Lumber," II, 103 (1714), and of "Timber bords planks shingle and any other lumber," II, 202 (1720). In these quotations it is evident that the earlier meaning of lumber as signifying a variety of objects is still present, though the elements are also present which might lead to a narrowing of the content of the word. The line of transition is indicated by a remark of Cooper, in his *Notions of the Americans* (1828), I, 243, defining the word *lumber men*, which he had used in his text, as meaning those "who fell trees, and convert them into various objects of use, such as staves, shingles, etc." This is exactly what the early American woodsman did; he went into the woods, either alone or with one or two others, and having cut down his trees, he made them into shingles, staves, clapboards and other such "lumber." With the later arrival of the sawmill and the expansion of the business of converting trees into boards, the term lumber took on its now more generally current meaning of boards sawed and ready for building. Like other occupations, the business of lumbering has developed a highly technical vocabulary of its own.

The tree cut down and ready for the mill is a *log*, standing trees are *timber*, sawed beams for the framework of buildings are *timbers*. *To take to the tall timber* is a picturesque metaphor which explains itself as meaning to withdraw to a safe and secluded distance.

In the process of occupying the land, various new topographical terms acquired currency in American use, some becoming general, but many also establishing themselves only in the regions in which their use was a practical convenience or necessity. Among these may be mentioned *barrens, bayou, savannah* in the South, *bench* or *mesa, butte, chute, bluff, knob,* in western regions. The use of the word *prairie* became general in the early nineteenth century, with the beginning of the movement of the population westward. It took on various popular spellings and pronunciations, often becoming a trisyllable, as in *prararee*, Carlton, *New Purchase*, p. 135. The *licks* in various regions, to which deer and other animals resorted, have also made some characteristic additions to the American vocabulary. An *opening* or *oak opening*, utilized by Cooper in the title of one of his novels, was a natural park-like formation in the forest for which, the forests themselves having largely disappeared, a term is no longer needed. A new usage in the Far West is the application of the word *park* to those delightful meadowy valleys with trees scattered here and there which are found throughout the Rockies. Less agreeable are the *sinks, sink holes, sloughs, slews* and *swales* which occur in the level country. The aptly descriptive term *rolling land* is one which could have originated only where extensive stretches of territory appeared at a glance to the eye of the observer.

Not uninteresting are certain topographical terms which have acquired American flavor, though merely by custom and not because the words in themselves are unusual. Thus we speak of *down East* and *down South*, or *up North* and *out West*, and of the *Far West* and of the *Middle West*, though there is no Near West between which and the Far West the Middle West stands. The dividing line between the East and West is often made, however, when one speaks of *west of the Alleghanies*. The relativity of all geographical situations is well illustrated by the fact that though in the East one speaks of *out West,* on the Coast one frequently hears *out East,* though also often *back East,* perhaps with fond recollections of an old home. The *Eastern Shore,* a land if not of milk and honey at least of ducks and oysters, has become specifically the eastern shore of Maryland on the Chesapeake Bay. One speaks also of *tidewater Virginia,* meaning those lower sections of eastern Virginia reached by the James, Rappahannock and other tidal rivers, and also of regions further inland with the qualifying adjective freshwater, as in *freshwater towns* or *freshwater colleges,* the adjective carrying with it some implication of rusticity and provincialism. The higher and western regions of Virginia are known as *Piedmont Virginia.* The *Gulf States* are obviously those that touch the Gulf of Mexico. *The Coast* now commonly means the Pacific coast, especially California, but when one goes to the beach on the Atlantic side of the continent one speaks of *the Shore.*

The transportation system of a new country is almost certain to call for inventive modification of older traditional methods of locomotion, and thus for new terms in the vocabulary. In the first half of the nineteenth century when long distance traveling inland was done largely by water along the river courses, many new words or adaptations of words came into use, especially names of kinds of boats, such as *flat, flat boat, periogue, pirogue, keel boat, Kentucky boat, ark, batteau, broad-horn,* and a whole vocabulary of river travel which leads one back to a vanished but romantically interesting period of American history. Some of the words familiarized by river navigation have remained. Thus the noun *cut off,* meaning a way that shortens the distance between two points, first came into common use on the Mississippi, where a new and shorter channel sometimes makes itself at times of high water between two points on the main river. From the river it was extended to the railroad, any shortening of the line being called a cut off. Floating logs and trees in the channel of the river brought into use the terms *planter, sawyer,* and *snag,* but only the last of these three words appears to be a permanent addition to the American vocabulary. Their differences are described by Carlton, *New Purchase*, p. 43, as follows: "A planter is the trunk of a tree, perpendicular or inclined, with one end fixed or planted immoveable in the bottom of the river, and the other above or below the surface according to the state of the water. A snag is a miniature or youthful planter. . . . A sawyer is either a long trunk, or more commonly an entire tree, so fixed that its top plays up and down with the current and the wind."

The word *patron* as a nautical term, for which early citations will be found in the *New English Dictionary*, lingered in America in the sense of captain or steersman of a river boat, as in Brackenridge, *Journal*, p. 206, note, "The patron is the fresh water sailing master." This and other examples as late as 1850 will be found in Thornton.

With the application of steam to river navigation, both the character of river boats and those who ran them underwent a change. The romance of the river has now become a thing of the past, though not altogether unrecoverable in Hay's *Jim Bludsoe* and Mark Twain's *Life on the Mississippi*, and assuredly not lost in popular tradition and song. The steamboat still fills a large place in American boyish imagination, and though not what it used to be, wherever there is a river or lake large enough to float a steamboat, it still comes round the bend, still puffs black clouds from its smokestack, still whistles its invitation to holiday adventurers. According to the United States Official Postal Guide, three places in the United States have taken their name from the steamboat, one in Nevada, one in Colorado, and one in Iowa.

Characteristic parts of the American river and lake boats are the *pilot house* and the *hurricane deck*, and two others, *texas* and *stateroom*, are explained in the following words of an old river-boat man, given by Abdy, *On the Ohio* (1919), p. 246:

"You see, in the early days o' steam-boatin' all the cabins was named after States—that's where the name 'state-room' comes from, see? Well, there was a bright young feller in the Mississippi country who had designed some right speedy boats, so when he got a contract to build an extra smart and fancy packet—the 'Kate Barnsdale' was her name—he tried somethin' new. It was a little deck-house just behind the pilot—the idea being to provide more sleeping room for passengers. Well, he didn't know what to name the new contraption; but it so happened that the boat went into commission on the very day that the State of Texas was admitted into the Union; so the new cabin was named the 'texas.'" It has seemed worth while quoting this passage giving the origin of *stateroom* as used on American river-boats because it sounds so plausible, and yet is so probably not true. The explanation evidently grew from the name, and evidence that staterooms "in the early days o' steam-boatin'" were named after states is lacking. On the other hand, we find that stateroom, defined as "a captain's or superior officer's room on board ship," is recorded in the *New English Dictionary* for 1660, 1694, and at other times before any one ever dreamed of steamboats on American rivers. The American use seems merely to be an extension of the older use, and if there is anything American about it, perhaps it lies merely in the grandiloquent application of the term stateroom to all the cabins on a boat. That the *texas* took its name, however, from the State of Texas seems probable, and the details of the explanation given above may be correct. But as Texas was a lone star state, may not the texas have been thought of as a lone stateroom cabin?

It is not altogether clear whether the word *line* was first used of ships or of railways. Cooper, *Notions*, I, 293 (1828), speaks of "the steamboat lines, as they are called," and his words imply that this was a new usage. It is not probable that the newness consisted, however, in the transference of the word from railways to steamboats, for the railways at the time Cooper wrote were as new as the steamboats. The new use of the word apparently lay in the extension of it from the older notion of a succession, as in a line of kings, etc., to name a succession of steamboats arriving and departing at stated times. The first example of this use in the *New English Dictionary* is for 1848, twenty years later than the passage quoted from Cooper. The first example of *line* as applied to railways is for

1825. If the use originated in connection with railways, one may think of the parallel extended tracks as lines, or perhaps one may suppose that the term originated in the surveyor's line which was always run before the tracks could be laid. But it is possible that the word was first transferred from ocean to railway service, and the many uses of line in nautical senses, e.g., ships of the line, the lines of a ship, line meaning cord or rope, and various others defined in the *New English Dictionary*, support this conclusion. After the transference was made, meanings like those mentioned above attached themselves to the word in connection with the railways. In the history of very familiar words like this, evidence is frequently not available which would enable one to follow step by step the stages of development.

The vocabulary of railroading in America is in many respects characteristic of local usage. The differences between British and American railroad terminology have been frequently pointed out,[1] and a partial explanation offered to the effect that in England the railroads, when they were new, utilized coaching terms, such as *coach, driver, guard, booking-office,* whereas in America the vocabulary of steamboating was the familiar existent resource of the language which was transferred to the railroads. This would account for the American *all aboard* as a warning of departure, for *berth* as the name of the sleeping accommodation in a Pullman, and for *stateroom* as the name for a private room on a Pullman. The *caboose* on a freight train took its name from the older caboose on the deck of a ship. But manifestly it is easier to think of railroading terms which did not owe their origin to steamboating than to think of those that did. In most instances no simple principle appears, except the accident of convention, when the vocabulary of the American railroad is different from that of the British, as in American *conductor*, British *guard*, American *brakeman* or *trainman*, British *brakesman*, American *freight train*, British *goods train*, American

[1] See Matthews, *Parts of Speech*, pp. 114–115; Greenough and Kittredge, *Words and their Ways*, p. 271. For a list of American railroad terms, see *Dialect* Notes, IV, 335–357.

depot, largely giving way now to *station,* British *terminus,* American *baggage, baggage car,* British *luggage, luggage van.*

In some instances certain aspects of the American railway which are peculiar to America have in consequence given rise to words which have no counterparts in British usage. Thus the American *baggage check* has no equivalent in England, nor has *cowcatcher,* and the British have only their occasional *forwarding agencies* for the far-reaching American *express,* a word which has given rise to many characteristic American uses and combinations, such as *express office, express wagon, express man, expressage, express train,* and in the early days of Western life, *pony express.*

Suburban life in America has given rise to the peculiarly American words *commute, commuter, commutation.* Some American railway terms have passed into general and even metaphorical applications, as in *to side track, to sidewipe,* now also used of automobiles, *all aboard, to board,* meaning to ascend into anything, *cut rate, to switch, double track* and *single track,* etc. In the case of the word *sidewipe,* however, it is doubtful if the word arose in connection with the railways. There is a variant form *sideswipe,* and in the *New English Dictionary* the word is described as occurring in British dialects and in the United States. The dictionary gives an example for 1757 in the sense of indirect rebuke or censure, and records it as occurring in the dialect glossaries of the northern counties of England. In this word it seems probable that an older and dialectal British usage has been given a new lease of life in America.

The names of other forms of vehicular transportation are to some extent distinctive for American usage. The word *transportation* itself has a characteristic American meaning. "Have you bought your transportation?" merely means "Have you bought your railway ticket?" What is a *street car* in America is ordinarily a *tram* in England. The American street car is a much more important factor in American daily life than the tram is in England, and about it has consequently developed a rich and distinctive vocabulary. A *trolley car,* or merely a *trolley,* came in when electricity supplanted horses as a motive power. The trolley itself is now in danger of being supplanted by the automobile, the *jitney*, driven by a *jitneur*, and the *trollibus* being already well established in some communities. The term *jitneur* was obviously made on the model of chauffeur. The *trollibus*, or *trackless trolley*, combines the characteristics of the bus and the trolley, hence the compound.

Some few words associated with earlier methods of travel in America have now only a lingering or dictionary existence. The *prairie schooner* was the picturesque name for a covered wagon, the ship of the desert of the early western emigrant. The *Conestoga wagon* also figures largely in the early annals of emigration in America. These wagons were made at Conestoga, Lancaster County, Pennsylvania, whence their name. Similar wagons in other regions are known as *bolster wagons*, *Conklin wagons*, *boomer wagons*, etc. The Conestoga wagons were the freighters of the period before the railways, and from the name of the wagon in an abbreviated form the word *stogy* seems to have arisen, meaning goods, usually not of the highest quality, brought in the wagon, such as shoes and cigars, see *Dialect Notes*, I, 229, 237. In Texas inferior cattle are also called *stogies*.

In Peters, *General History of Connecticut*, p. 235, occurs the name *whiskey*, evidently as the name of a light vehicle: "There are few coaches in the colony, but many chaises and whiskeys." In country regions the name *dandy wagon* is still in current use for a light single-seated wagon, though the automobile, with a rich and distinctive vocabulary of its own, is rapidly crowding out all older vehicles like this, as well as the terminology that applied to them. A generation ago *a Studebaker* meant a kind of heavy farm wagon with high sides, but now the visions called forth by the word are not so humble. The *buckboard* and the *surrey* are also common American names for vehicles little used in England.

When travel was restricted largely to travel on horseback, certain uses were current which now are lost. One of these was the use of *oat* as a verb, meaning to give a feeding of oats. It occurs frequently in the diary of John Adams, II, 199 (1766), "we all oated at Martin's"; II, 276 (1771), "Took my departure from Middletown homeward the same way I went down; very hot; oated at Hartford." In Carlton's *New Purchase* instead of *tying* his horse to the hitching rack a rider usually *hangs* it to the hitching rack. This word occurs also in a realistic bit of dialogue in Stone's *Life and Times of Red Jacket* (1829), p. 29: "Suppose, now, a 'Riproarer' of Kentuck should ride up to the door of a 'young earthquake,' on the Red River—or, in other words, suppose, before Amos and Duff came to Washington to administer the government for General Jackson, that Amos should have called at the shanty of Duff in Missouri for a night's lodging:—Do you think there would have been any such palavering as—'Good evening, Mr. General Green: I am very happy to see you.' And:—'Why, how d'ye do, my dear Mr. Kendall?' Not at all. The dialogue . . . would have run thus:— *Amos.* 'Holloa, there. Can I *get* to stay with you to-night?' *Duff.* 'Well, I reckon.' *Amos.* 'Then, boy, *hang* my horse.' *Duff.* 'And give him a smart chance of roughness and toat in his plunder.' *Amos.* 'A smart chunk of a boy, that.' *Duff.* 'Well, I reckon; but here's the crack honeylove in the gum.' *Amos.* 'I don't quite let on to that.'" The "honeylove in the gum" is the baby, the gum being the hollow bee-gum tree from which the cradle was made.

To give a full list of distinctively American names of foods would take one a long though pleasant journey. Many of these names are now archaic or obsolete. The *hog and hominy* of the older dictionaries of Americanisms now suggests the days of Davy Crockett. Similarly archaic is the *chicken fixings* which appears so commonly in accounts of early frontier life. But many characteristic foods and their names survive, *hoe cake, johnny cake, pone, buckwheat cakes, flapjacks,* and to these have been added a recent vocabulary of breakfast foods and "cereals" that alone would fill a volume. Perhaps *roasting ears* and *sliced peaches* carry as full an American flavor as any two names of foods. The American climate is responsible for the popularity of ice cream and the soda fountain, about which no doubt as rich a technical vocabulary is collecting as formerly enriched the language of the American bar. One of these words, the *Sunday* or *sundae*, a combination of ice cream and sugar syrup of various flavors, is explained by Tucker, *American English*, p. 306, as having originated "about 1897, at Red Cross Pharmacy, State Street, Ithaca, N. Y., directly opposite to barroom of Ithaca Hotel, which was closed on Sunday, suggesting to the pharmacy people to offer a distinctively Sunday drink." The explanation is circumstantial but not convincing, being the kind of explanation which so readily appears after the event. Various newspaper correspondents have given practically the same explanation of the origin of the word, varying it however in the chronology and geography.

So also the term *porterhouse steak* has been attached to various different persons and places in the attempt to explain its origin. The New York *Times* for March 9, 1923, recorded the death of an aged woman who soon after the close of the Civil War "became cook at the Porter House in North Cambridge, Mass.," and who "developed such skill in carving steaks from the sides of heavy beef that the tender cuts she served became known as porterhouse steaks." Unfortunately for this explanation, Thornton gives citations for porterhouse steak in America as early as 1843. The term porterhouse is old, a porterhouse being a drinking place where steaks might be served, just as a chophouse is a place where drinks may be served. The early citations of porterhouse as an adjective applied to steak are all American, but according to the *New English Dictionary*, the term porterhouse steak is now also current in England.

On the other hand, there is little doubt that the *Parker House roll* took its name from Parker House in Boston. It may be pointed out, however, that Parker House roll is not an essential part of the daily vocabulary of Americans as are porterhouse steak and sundae.

Chewing-gum, popcorn and peanuts are words and things dear to the popular American fancy through many years of holiday association. Chewing-gum seems to have been a Yankee invention, the chewing of spruce gum being the Yankee maiden's substitute for the masculine tobacco. Thornton's first citation is for 1836. With the passing of tobacco as a polite masticatory and with the commercial manufacturing of chewing-gum from chicle, the habit has spread until it has become an almost universal popular American custom.

The mention of foods suggests the places in which foods are eaten, and an interesting study might be made of the vocabulary of public places of refreshment in America. The commonest name for these places is perhaps *café*, and from *café* has been derived a new word, *cafeteria*, not yet known to the dictionaries but familiar to every American. This word probably originated in California, perhaps in Los Angeles, where the cafeteria first flourished. There is no other English word like it on the analogy of which it could have been formed. There is of course *bacteria* and Latin words like *materia*, but these seem remote. The suggestion for the word was probably Spanish *cafetera*, "coffee-pot." The accent in *cafeteria* is sometimes on the penult, but the custom now seems to be establishing itself of stressing the antepenult. On the analogy of *cafeteria*, new words have been formed, designating places conducted on the principle of self service, such as *groceteria*, *caketeria*, *candyteria*, *pastreria*, a pastry shop, *drugeteria*. A somewhat similar development is that which started with *emporium*, the ambitious name for what was considered to be a big store, the word being then extended in the forms *suitorium*, *pantorium* to name a tailor's shop.

In Boston and New England a restaurant is often called a *spa*, this word being originally the name of a watering place in Belgium, then by extension in British use, any place of entertainment and refreshment. New England probably borrowed this use from England.

Words which pertain to the convivial life are likely to be numerous and distinctive in every language, and those of American English, especially names of American drinks, are particularly so. Mixed drinks were the special development of the American bar, and the American *bartender* was an artistic combiner as well as a mere dispenser of fluids. The jocose element naturally appears in many of these words, as in *cock-tail*, *colt's tail*, *corn juice*, *flip*, *fogcutter*, *anti-*

fogmatic, gin sling, hail storm, red eye, smile, for all of which, and for many more like these, citations will be found in Thornton. It is such words that make one realize the fleet-footedness of time.

The American saloon has been a special development of city life and the word has acquired certain ignoble connotations which arose from those conditions which have now brought about the almost complete extinction of the saloon by process of law. In earlier days, the drinking place was commonly called a *tavern,* and it provided, or was supposed to provide, all the entertainment that was required for man or beast. The number of taverns, however, soon tended to increase beyond the needs of the community, and one finds in the early colonial town records efforts to limit the number of places thus licensed. Among his many other activities, Noah Webster was an untiring advocate of limitation and economy in the use and sale of intoxicants. In the eighteenth and early nineteenth centuries, however, the number of places at which whisky and other alcoholic beverages were sold was very large, and many of them were not of highly reputable character. Such were the *doggeries, groggeries, grog shops, groceries, corner groceries,* at which the disorderly elements of a community tended to congregate. According to Summerfield, *Desperadoes of the Southwest,* New York, 1847, pp. 21–22, the word *doggery* had two pronunciations. "When they are speaking of a genteel doggery," says Summerfield, "they sound the last syllable like e—doggeree. But when they refer to one of a lower order, they give the last syllable the sound of i with a long accent, as doggeri." Summerfield quotes a song,

> "On the wings of love I'll fly
> From doggeree to doggery,"

And two other lines,

> "The stars shine in the hollow sky,
> But I shine in a doggery."

The saloon was a place of a higher type for which a finer and more ambitious word was necessary, for which, indeed, a finer word was sacrificed, since the word did not avail to save or elevate the saloon, and since now it has become practically impossible in America to use the word except in its degraded sense. The remark of Cooper, *Notions* (1828), I, 101, that "a man needs no small servitude in the more graceful schools of the Continent to figure to advantage in a saloon," has now a ludicrous color not at all in Cooper's mind when he wrote. Walt Whitman attempted to restore the word *saloon* to dignified use, but it is dignified in Whitman only by virtue of a poet's license. That the degrading of the word was not due entirely to American usage is evident from the British use of *hairdresser's saloon, billiard saloon,* see Hall, *Modern English,* p. 251, note.

Three words, *spree, spunk,* and *spry,* all of obscure origin, may be noted here. These words are found in British dialects, but have become much more general in American than in British usage. The same may be said of *spittoon,* first recorded for 1840, and *cuspidor(e),* an old word which gained currency when the object it named became an essential convenience in American society. The appearance of the cuspidor as an article of household furniture and its later disappearance might be made leading motives in two chapters of the history of American culture. The smoking and chewing of tobacco have been established customs almost from the beginning of the settlement of the country. The pleasant vice of the use of tobacco soon became international, however, and there is little about it now distinctively American, except perhaps chewing, now a disappearing habit. Madam Knight in her *Journal* (1704), p. 43, described a tobacco chewer of her day and in doing so used an unrecorded word. "Being at a merchant's house," she says, "in comes a tall country fellow, wth his alfogeos full of Tobacco; for they seldome Loose their Cudd, but keep Chewing and Spitting as long as they'r eyes are open." Madam Knight's name for the exudate is *Aromatick Tincture.* Examples of another term, *ambeer,* will be found by consulting the indexes to *Dialect Notes.* The word *alfogeos* is probably a corruption of Spanish *alforja,* saddle bag. It is recorded in the *New English Dictionary,* under the form of *alfoges,* as the name of the cheek pouch of the baboon.

The names of American sports, especially baseball and football, are in many instances characteristically American. The language of sport always tends to develop into a highly complicated slang or technical vocabulary, and this has been especially true of American baseball. Some of this vocabulary, however, has passed into general use, and every American knows what a *home run* is, what it is *to be off one's base, to strike out, to pound wind, to muff a fly, to make a foul, to get one's innings, to get on to one's curves.*

The game of poker has long been a popular American diversion, and from it and other games of cards, a number of words and phrases have passed into general use. Among these may be mentioned *to bluff, cash in, cash in one's chips, flush, four-flusher, square deal, trump.*

Certain features of the religious life have added to the picturesqueness of American life and the American vocabulary. The *camp-meeting,* as it flourished in the first half of the nineteenth century, was commented on by many travelers in America and elaborately described by some. From these phases of popular religious experience have come expressions like *to get religion, mourner's bench, the Amen corner, revival,* and other similar words. A synonym for revival which has now passed out of use is the word *attention,* or the phrase *period of attention.* "A Revival of Religion," says Dwight, *Life of Jonathan Edwards,* p. 126, "is nothing but the immediate result of an uncommon *Attention,* on the part of a church and congregation, to the Truth of God." Throughout Dwight's book, attention and period of attention are used in the established sense of revival of religion.

In America the word *church* has not the specialized meaning which permits it to be applied in England only to the established church. In American usage the difference between a church and a chapel, as the words are ordinarily used, is that a chapel is a smaller building than a church. The word *chapel* has of course technical ecclesiastical uses, but these have not colored the common understanding of the word. The *meeting house* of colonial times and the phrase "go to meeting" are now archaic terms, seldom used, except among the Quakers, even by old-fashioned persons. The lack of an established church in America has also occasioned a free and undiscriminated popular use of the terms minister, pastor, clergyman, preacher, parson. Ecclesiastics themselves may insist on certain proprieties in the use of these terms, the Presbyterians that minister belongs especially to them, the Episcopalians that clergyman is their appropriate word, but popular usage knows no such distinctions, except in the word *rector,* which is not, however, a popular word in America, and in *priest,* which is commonly limited in application to the Roman Catholic church. The *circuit rider* of an earlier period is no longer familiar as a person or a word. The word *dominie,* in the sense of minister or pastor, is still occasionally used as a somewhat facetious term. It came into American use, according to Thornton, through the Dutch settlements of New York and New Jersey.

The many varieties of religious experience in America have produced a number of words of more or less general and lasting character to name them, *Shakers, Hard Shell Baptists, Come Outers, Holy Rollers, Mormons, Danites,* and others.

The American college has developed various features peculiar to itself and also an appropriate vocabulary to accompany them. Most of these special words belong to the ephemeral vocabulary of student slang, of which various collections have been made.[1] The use of the words *college* and *hall* has varied a great deal at different times and places, the former sometimes meaning the institution as a whole, sometimes merely a building, sometimes the undergraduate part as distinguished from the graduate part of a university.[2]

The *campus* is distinctive for American college life, both the thing itself and the name for it. The first known occurrence of the word is in manuscript at Princeton in 1774, but after that it is not found

[1] See *Dialect Notes,* II, 3 ff., 135 ff., IV, 231 ff. Similar collections might be made for preparatory schools and for high schools, see *Dialect Notes,* V, 60 ff.

[2] Full illustrations are given by Albert Matthews, *Dialect Notes,* II, 91 ff.

until 1821 in an extract from the minutes of South Carolina College.[1] All the early records of the word seem to be localized at Princeton or in the South. In this connection it may be noted that Princeton in its early years maintained specially intimate connections with the South.[2] At Harvard and Yale the traditional word was the Yard or the Green. Within the last generation or two, however, the word has spread rapidly and now is in use at practically all American colleges, sometimes meaning the college grounds as a whole, sometimes a limited portion of the grounds. The question of the origin of the term is unsettled. Apparently no similar use has ever arisen in England and the word *campus* is not entered in the *New English Dictionary*. It is not probable that the word in American use originated in connection with college field sports, for these were not a prominent part of American college life until after the word had become established; neither does the word *campus* ordinarily mean the place where the young barbarians play, this being usually called a field, or athletic field. It is probable that the word arose from some connection with the Roman Campus Martius, and that even in early American college use, the militant significance of *campus* was uppermost. For if the college youth of America in the eighteenth and early nineteenth century were not much given to field sports, they were inclined to indulge in "riots" and college fights, the earlier equivalents of intercollegiate matches and games. Some of the earliest occurrences of the word clearly indicate a meaning "field of battle." Thus in Simms, *Guy Rivers*, I, 189 (1834), quoted in Thornton, we read: "He acted on the present occasion precisely as he might have done in the College Campus, with all the benefits of a fair field and a plentiful crowd of backers." In Longstreet, *Georgia Scenes*, p. 73 (1835), in a passage not in Thornton, the author satirically describes a performer on the piano in terms of the fray: "She brought her hands to the campus [the keyboard] this time in fine style, and they seemed now to be perfectly reconciled to each other." In another passage in

[1] See Matthews, The Term "Campus" in American Colleges, in *Transactions of the Colonial Society of Massachusetts*, III, 431–437 (1897).

[2] See Collins, *Princeton*, pp. 93–94.

Thornton for 1840, Mr. Colquitt of Georgia says: "We are told that the Abolition battle must be fought at the north; that we must deal kindly here, to afford a campus for their chivalry at home." These three illustrations establish an early southern use of the word *campus* in the sense of a place or field of combat, and it seems not improbable that it was with this sense that the college use of the word started on its career.

Perhaps the richest field for the invention of new words and new applications of words has been found in the world of politics. Since the establishment of the Union, politics has been the sole business of many and an engrossing pastime of almost all citizens of the republic. The full picturesqueness of American political discussion did not develop, however, until the opening up of the West, that is, the West of the Ohio valley, brought these regions into political importance. Then the Injin fighter was the popular presidential candidate, and Jeffersonian simplicity took on the more variegated hue of Jacksonian crudity and backwoods freedom in conduct and speech. The stump speaker was the appropriate orator to appear before frontier audiences, and the log rolling, which in the literal sense was a necessary part of the clearing of new land, readily suggested itself as a useful term, in a metaphorical sense, in the realm of politics. Another contribution from the frontier life of the second and third decades of the nineteenth century was the phrase "to row a man up Salt River," meaning to defeat him in politics. Salt River is a river in Kentucky which in the days of river travel was notorious for difficulty of navigation. The name suggested many fancies to the political humorist; according to Jack Downing, p. 319, "Salt River runs up stream," which supposedly would make it easy to navigate for any one who might be constrained to navigate it. The term with many others is passing out of use as American politics become more serious and matter of fact than they were in the old days of the picturesque politicians. In the meantime, however, the language has fortunately been enriched by the addition of a number of useful and concrete political expressions. Among these may be mentioned *barbecue* and *burgoo*, *to wave the bloody shirt*, *boodle*, *buncombe*, *on the fence*, *favorite son*, *filibuster*, *gerrymander*, *lobby*, *mugwump*, *pipe-laying*, *carpet bagger*, *wire puller*, *wire pulling*, *influence*, *rabble rouser*, *platform*, *caucus*, the *floor*, as in to speak on the floor, etc., *copperhead*, *boss*, *heeler*, *to cut a melon*, *pork*, *pork barrel*. If some of these terms seem to be of cynical significance, one may take comfort in the thought that they also convey valuable lessons. Most of them are discussed, with others, in Norton's *Political Americanisms*, but a rich field for historical study and illustration still remains unexplored. Some of them, for example, *buncombe*, *gerrymander*, *mugwump*, have become current also in England and must be counted as permanent and general additions to the English vocabulary. The etymology of *gerrymander*, from the proper name *Gerry*, combined with the last two syllables of *salamander*, now being forgotten, the initial consonant is sometimes mistakenly pronounced with a soft instead of a hard *g*.

The word *platform* had other established uses before it was employed as a political term. The Connecticut churches, at Saybrook, in 1708, agreed upon a set of principles, known as the Platform of the Connecticut Churches, Dwight, *Life of Jonathan Edwards*, p. 113. A still earlier use, showing that the word was a familiar village term, occurs in *Hempstead Records*, I, 175 (1665), "Alotment of land . . . lieing in or About Matenacoke so Commonly Called as will Apeare by the plott forme."

The terminology of the military life in the United States no doubt has many peculiar features on the popular and familiar sides, but in its organization the American army has always been practically the same as the British army, and so naturally the official vocabularies of the two armies have remained very similar. Some few differences, however, are noteworthy.

In England the official phrase for the person known in America as the Secretary of War is the Secretary for War, this being an abbreviation of the full title, the Secretary of State for War. The title *lieutenant* is ordinarily, and also in official circles, pronounced ['ɛftnænt] in England, but the *New English Dictionary* correctly states that [ljut′ɛnənt] is used exclusively in the United States. The word *doughboy*, meaning infantryman, is not official, but it has passed out of slang into general use. The *New English Dictionary* contains the word, defining it as nautical and as meaning a boiled dumpling of raised dough. The transition to the meaning infantryman has not been clearly traced. According to one explanation, given by Mrs. Custer, *Tenting on the Plains*, p. 516, it originated "early in the Civil War from the term doughboy being applied to the large globular brass buttons on the Infantry uniform and so passed by natural transition to the Infantrymen themselves." Various other origins for the word are offered by Moss, *Officers' Manual*, p. 295, but none seems convincing.

The American army toast is *How!*, a word of many explanations. The most reasonable, see Moss, *Officers' Manual*, p. 296, is that the word, spelled also *hough*, *hoo*, *ho* and *ehow*, was an Indian word, meaning perhaps Thanks, and that this Indian word was adopted by some regiment on frontier service, spreading thence through the whole army.

A uniform coat is called a *blouse* in the United States army, but a *tunic* in the British army. The barrack regulations require that a soldier's garments shall be arranged as follows: "Middle compartment: hung on hooks — overcoat, blouse, trousers, haversack . . ." etc. Other terms for parts of the American soldier's equipment are *campaign hat*, *shelter tent*, and *shelter half*.

The word *retreat* as the name of a bugle call is not given in the *New English Dictionary* and presumably is not in British use. In the *Manual of Guard Duty* by Andrews, *Fundamentals of Military Service*, p. 224, one of the directions reads "between reveille and retreat, to turn out the guard for all persons designated by the Commanding Officer." The name of another American bugle call is the *long roll*, and so also, in the plural form, *boots and saddles*, the signal to mounted troops that their formation is to be mounted. Corresponding to the British *last post*, every night at eleven o'clock in the American army, *taps* is sounded. Moss, *Officers' Manual*, p. 292, says that the custom of sounding taps over a soldier's grave was inaugurated at West Point in 1840, and became general during the Civil War, since which time it has been sounded at every military funeral.

In army transportation, the term *Dougherty wagon* is familiar and the thing itself is described by Farrow, *Dictionary of Military Terms.* The *New English Dictionary* notes that *police* in the military sense is peculiar to the United States. Police duty in the American army can include such domestic tasks as sweeping, scrubbing and cleaning up generally.

The term *canteen* as the name for a profit-sharing store to be used by the enlisted men was current in the United States, as in England, until Congress some twenty years ago was instigated to forbid the sale of beer and light wines in army canteens and also to change the name to *Post Exchange.*

The word *fogy, fogie, fogey* is an American colloquialism in the army and navy, meaning an increase in pay by reason of length of service. An officer's servant, called a *batman* in the English army, in the United States army is known as a *striker.*

Various occupational pursuits have added some of its individual characteristics to the American vocabulary. The language of speculation and the stock market has flourished so richly as to become in itself almost a special speech or dialect. Like most highly differentiated occupations it has developed a technical vocabulary of its own, special uses for example of ordinary words like *long* and *short, bull* and *bear,* and hundreds of metaphorical phrases such as *freeze out,* a *look in, gold brick, bucket shop.* Comparatively few of these words and phrases have passed out of the class of technical or trade vocabulary into general use.

The business of cattle raising has appealed to the American imagination and, as its more romantic aspects are passing away, it has left numerous vestiges in the American vocabulary. Every American lad aspires at some time to be a *cowboy,* to tighten the *cinch* on his pony, to take part in a *round up,* when the cattle are driven into a *corral*, or if they will not be driven, are *roped in* and *branded*, on which occasion they naturally *kick like a steer*. The cowboy also had his more specialized occupations and amusements, such as bronco busting, shooting up, and painting towns red. The word *stamping ground*, originally the place where cattle congregated and stamped to keep the flies off, has passed into general metaphorical use in the sense of a place of habitual resort. Like all highly developed businesses, cattle raising on the commercial side has acquired a large technical vocabulary of its own. A *canner*, for example, is an animal of not the best grade, but good enough for canning. As in *broiler*, the ending of the noun of agency in these words indicates not one who cans or broils, but that which is canned or broiled. Other similar terms are *stockers* and *feeders*.

A remarkably active world now is that of the moving picture and from it a number of new words have passed into general use. The exhibitions themselves are ordinarily referred to as the *movies*. From the methods of the actors in making moving picture films comes the verb *register*, meaning to express an emotion by an appropriate facial gesture. From the noun *film* a verb *to film* has been made, and dozens of other words, originally technical in this profession, have passed over into the general vocabulary of the language.

The American weather has not contributed any large number of words to the peculiar speech of the people. One thinks immediately of *blizzard*, *cold snap*, *hot wave*, *cyclone*, *hot spell*, and *cold spell*, of *muggy* as an indispensable word on the Atlantic seaboard, and of a few more like these. Each locality no doubt has its favorite weather words, dependent on the qualities of its climate. As a whole, however, the main characteristics of American climate are diversity and changeableness, qualities which do not readily lend themselves to description by epithet.

Every people must have its set of words or phrases which are used for the constantly recurring everyday situations of life, words and phrases of not very precise logical content, but satisfactory nevertheless because the situations in which they are used do not call for logical precision. These words are often merely words of approval or assent, or the reverse, and often they seem to be scarcely more than oratorical pauses, as it were, dropped in to fill space but not to express a great deal of thought. Thus the common expression of assent or approval in America is *All right.* As a phrase this is no better, and no worse, than the Britisher's *Very good.* In the interest of economy, some such phrase is necessary, and whatever phrase is used is bound to become stereotyped. Words employed for emphasis vary in strength all the way from slight metaphor, as in *fine* used as a general word of approval, through more violent stages of slang and imprecation. No emphasizing word in America, however, has aroused such bitter hostility as the word *bloody* in England, nor is it impossible in America as it would be in England to use the word *sick* in the sense of ill, or even in the general metaphorical sense of being tired or weary of a thing. For *Yes, Sir, No, Sir,* as emphatic affirmative and negative phrases, examples will be found in Thornton, where one can also examine uses of *nohow, no way you can fix it, no two ways about it, nary, that's so, most* (for almost), *eenamost,* and other phrases which now have the flavor of the rustic life of another generation. The intensive, *That's a fact,* may still be heard, however, in cultivated American speech. "I just don't know, Joe, that's a fact," says the heroine in Parrish, *My Lady of the South,* p. 21, a girl who supposedly represents the aristocracy of the South; but p. 22, a negro slave says, "Ye see, he never done treated dis nigger ver' nice, dat's a fact, fer shore." The use of *well* as a sentence beginner seems to be more deeply seated as a habit in America than in England. It has long been one of the marks of literary attempts to indicate the drawling rustic Yankee. So also has been the use of *guess* and *calculate* as constantly repeated words in the sense of think or suppose. The second of these has disappeared from present use, but *guess* is still universally heard in America as a somewhat colorless word implying merely intention. A synonym for American guess is *reckon,* freely used in Southern cultivated and popular speech.

As a general word for expressing mild surprise at meeting with something unexpected, American English has a variety of possibilities. The colorless literary words are *strange, remarkable, extraordinary,* besides phrases, as *Isn't that funny?* or *Isn't that queer? Isn't that the limit? Can you beat it? That beats the Dutch, That gets me, That gets my goat, Wouldn't that jar you?* and others like these, more or less colored by the ephemeral associations of slang. For an older generation in New England, characteristic phrases were *Do tell,* and *I want to know,* both now lost except as very provincial and archaic survivals. More recent than *well* are the words *say* and *listen* used as general introductions to sentences, more recent and perhaps on a lower cultural level. Words like these, however, are just the ones that give intimate colloquial color to the speech of a people. The use of *mad* as a frequent substitute for words of more precise meaning, such as vexed, annoyed, angry, must also be counted among characteristic American habits. As in the case of *guess, reckon* and other words of this type, it is easy to see how the American use has been derived, and good examples of the American use can doubtless be found in British English. What makes these words significant for American English is not the precise logical content given to them, but the fact that they are employed so continually as to make them parts of the convenient small change of social communication.

Despite the great mingling of races which has taken place in America, American English has been very slow to borrow new words from other languages. The main reason for this has already been given, that the foreign immigrant in America was almost always on a lower social level than the native population, that he strove therefore to acquire as many of the social habits and customs of the American as he could, and as rapidly as he could. In consequence his foreign speech was likely to become heavily charged with borrowed American words, though the American would feel no impulse to borrow from the foreigner's language, and the foreigner himself, when he spoke English, would try to keep it as free as possible of the words of his despised foreign idiom. Examples of foreign languages which have become more or less Anglicized through the incorporation of American words are the Pennsylvania German of Pennsylvania and the Valley of Virginia[1], Swedish, Italian, Polish, Yiddish, and various other languages, especially as they are spoken in crowded city communities. As most of these foreigners are directly engaged in manual occupations, as laborers, janitors, truckmen, through all stages to that of the skilled artisan, it is very natural that they should readily take over many of the concrete terms of their trades and surroundings. None of these mixed foreign languages, however, has shown any possibility of establishing itself as a reputable language, permanently utilizable for literature and cultivated intercourse. Pennsylvania German has a certain amount of literature of its own, and a kind of American Swedish is used in some of the Swedish newspapers printed in America. Italian, as modified by American English, appears in some interesting literary performances, conveniently reviewed by Livingston, *La Merica Sanemagogna*, *Romanic Review*, IX, 206–226.

As Americans have always been insulated from contact with foreign languages, from those which flourished about them because of social prejudice, and from the cultivated languages of other lands by ignorance of them, one would not expect to find in the American language any large number of foreign importations. More foreign words appear to have come in through Spanish and French than from any other source. Most of the Spanish words were first localized in the West and Southwest, and in these regions many more Spanish words are locally in use, through direct intercourse with the Mexicans and Greasers, than would be commonly known in other parts of the country. Among the Spanish words generally familiar may be mentioned *adobe*, *broncho*, *cafeteria*, *calaboose*, *chaparral*, *corral*, *coyote*, ultimately of Indian origin, and so also is *pirogue*, *placer*, as in *placer mining*, *pawpaw*, *potato*, *quirt*, probably from Spanish *corto*, extended to mean the short riding whip of the plainsman, *lariat*, *mustang*, *ranch*, *rodeo*, *sombrero*, *stampede*, *tobacco*, and *vamoose*,

[1] Perhaps the earliest literary example of German-English in America is to be found in *The Anglo-German: A Dialogue*, Philadelphia, Oct., 1800, in *The Monthly Mirror and American Review*, III (1800), pp. 327–328.

vamose. An abbreviated form of *chapparejos* appears as *chaps,* pronounced [ʃæps], a kind of riding trousers, and from Spanish *cincha,* girth, comes *cinch,* current in familiar colloquial speech in the sense of certainty of attainment, as the cowboy is certain when he has fastened the girths of his saddle. Several foods, especially *hot tamale* and *chili con carne,* have carried with them their Spanish names. Among words of French origin may be noted *bayou, butte, cache, caribou, coulee, crevasse, glacier, levee, plateau, portage, prairie,* all topographical words or words having to do with the life of the woods. In some regions of Canada and the northern United States a word which may be spelled *brooly* is in spoken use as the name for an open grassy place in the forest. This is from French *brulé,* and means ground burnt over upon which grass afterwards grows. Broolys were in effect incipient prairies. Several other words of French origin are *buccaneer, depot, mardi gras,* originally used only of a feast in New Orleans but later commonly used of town celebrations in general. The words *cent* and *dime* as names of pieces of money in America were derived from French. So also, apparently, was the word *picayune,* being originally the French name of a Spanish coin.

Literary words from German, such as *heimweh, wanderlust, weltschmertz, gemüthlichkeit, hinterland,* are not peculiar to America, nor can they be said to have become popularized. Popular German words are in the main words which have to do with eating or drinking, as in *rathskeller, stein, stube,* as in *wein stube, lager, bock, wiener wurst, pretzel, smear case, sauerkraut, zwieback, delicatessen.* In educational circles, *kindergarten* is now a current word. The word *standpoint* was formed after German *Standpunkt,* but apparently first in England, the *New English Dictionary* giving examples beginning with 1829.

Words derived from Dutch are more numerous and some of them have interesting histories. Contrary to the common opinion, however, it has been shown by Albert Matthews, *Dialect Notes,* II, 199–224, by abundant citation as early as 1638 in Virginia, that the word *state house* is not of Dutch origin, but an old native compound. The word *scup,* a children's swing, from Dutch *schop,* is still current in

New York. It is recorded in the *Century Dictionary*. The words *snoop* and *spook*, adopted from the Dutch and first used in America, have now passed also into British use. The same is true of the word *boss*. In New Amsterdam, the Dutch original of boss was an official title, and when the representatives from the United Colonies came to New Amsterdam to treat concerning the points at issue between the settlers of Connecticut and the Dutch, they signed their documents "From our Place of Residence at the Basses house in the Manhatoes," Hazard, *Historical Collections*, II, 236 (1653), and several other places. The later history of the word is illustrated by the citations in the dictionaries, and its phonetic history has been discussed in another connection. Cooper, in his *American Democrat* (1838), says that *boss* was taken from Dutch because white laborers objected to *master* as the term used by negro slaves. In *The Chainbearer* (1846) he speaks of *boss* as "that Manhattanese word."

It is possible that another Dutch officer has given his name to a phrase commonly current in America, though the chain of evidence to prove this is not complete. This is the phrase *a good scout*. When one speaks of a person as a good scout, one means that he is a good, reasonable fellow to live with, not precisely a hail fellow well met, but one who makes life comfortable for those with whom he associates. Now this meaning does not seem very similar to the ordinary meaning of scout as one who spies out the land. This latter sense of the word comes directly from the Old French original of the word as it appears in *escoute*, cognate to Latin *auscultare*. The Dutch word *schout* seems closer in meaning, and from the phonetic point of view gives just as regularly the English form scout. In New Amsterdam the schout was a town officer whose duties were a combination "of those pertaining now to the Mayor, Sheriff, and District Attorney," Earle, "The Stadthuys of New Amsterdam," in *Historic New York*, I, 50. "He also presided in the court . . . so it may be plainly seen that an offender could be arrested, prosecuted, and judged by one and the same person . . . but the bench of magistrates had one useful power—that of mitigating and altering the sentence demanded by the schout. And we frequently find in the records many changes of the sentences through this power. . . . I have not noted any cases where the schout's fine or sentence was increased by the magistrates"—though often it was mitigated. Irving, *Knickerbocker History,* Book III, Chap. II, uses the term bailiff as a synonym for the schout of New Amsterdam, whose office was similar to that of the schout in Holland. Mandeville, *Fable of the Bees,* Remark H, observes of the houses of pleasure at Amsterdam, where sailors resort in great numbers to be merry, that "the schout and his officers are always vexing, mulcting, and, upon the least complaint, removing the miserable keepers of them." From these accounts it would appear that a good scout in the days of New Amsterdam was notable chiefly because of his rarity, and the phrase may thus have persisted even after the schout, as a public officer, had passed into history. Further examples of the use of the word are needed, however, definitely to establish this line of development. At Oxford, a college servant who prepares and brings a student's meals to his rooms is called a scout. Hence apparently the phrase *to scout around,* meaning to hunt up food for a meal, or to hunt up any object needed for a practical purpose. Is this word Old French *escoute* or Dutch *schout?* It is quite probable that the two meanings have become more or less mingled in later use, but it remains probable also that we have in modern English *scout* two originally different words. That the word was commonly current in English use in America is evident from its presence in entries like the following in *Hempstead Records,* I, 295 (1674), "At a Jenerall townd Meting . . . Captin John semans was Elected . . . to kepe Cort with the scaut at Jemeco"; also I, 334 (1674), "at a Cort held in Hempsted by the scout and MaJestrats."

Another official title, apparently an abbreviated form of *fiskaal,* is preserved in the *Hempstead Records,* I, 345 (1675), "Peter Johnson scule"; also I, 395 (1682) "peter Jonson scol"; I, 440 (1684), "Pieter Johnson sckoll"; I, 483 (1684), "Petter Johnson Schol," these last two being signatures to documents. Peter Johnson is described, I, 482, as by trade a Cordwinder. He is often referred to merely as Peter Johnson, with no title added.

In the *Hempstead Records*, I, 43 (1658), occurs the phrase *one Hollands Accre or Morgen.* The Dutch word *morgen* was thus currently known on Long Island by the middle of the seventeenth century and it was frequently used, according to the *Century Dictionary*, "in old conveyances of property along the Hudson river." The word is recorded in the *New English Dictionary*, the earliest citation being for 1674 in New Jersey. An interesting example here given is that for 1868, in the *Report of the United States Commissioner of Agriculture*, 1869, p. 151: "connected with this department of forestry are six thousand morgen of forest." Examples are also given from South Africa, where the word is still current. Another Dutch word is preserved in the phrase, "one hundred schepells of wheate," *Hempstead Records*, I, 43 (1658), the Dutch word being *schepel*, a measure for dry wares, a bushel. The liquid measure *anker*, *ancker* is mentioned frequently in early American records, for example, *Hempstead Records*, I, 59 (1658). It is of Dutch origin, but was in use in England also in the Elizabethan period, as the citations in the *New English Dictionary* show. Another term of liquid measurement which appears to be of Dutch origin is the word *much*, as in *Hempstead Records*, I, 291 (1673), where it is ordered that those persons who fail to report for certain assigned duties in the town "shall pay six muches of Rume to them that gose"; in the same records, I, 349 (1676), we find a record of "five gallons and one quart an two muches of Rume." This word is probably Dutch *mutsje*, a liquid measure of small amount, about one-eighth of a pint. The derivation phonetically and logically is probable, the only doubt cast upon it being the presence in dialect English, as recorded in the *New English Dictionary*, of a word *mutch*, meaning a small cap. This word is not recorded in English as a term of measurement, but it is etymologically the same word as Dutch *mutsje*, this latter having a diminutive ending, and when one recalls the use of the word night cap, meaning a small drink, one would not be surprised to find the English *mutch*, *much* used as a term of liquid measure just as Dutch *mutsje* was used. If so, the word *much* in the *Hempstead Records* is of English origin.

The word *stoop* is of Dutch origin, but its use has been extended, especially in the phrase "the front stoop," to regions beyond those of Dutch influence. Cooper, *Notions* (1828), I, 149, remarks that "the New Yorkers (how much better is the word Manhattanese!) cherish the clumsy inconvenient entrances, I believe, as heirlooms of their Dutch progenitors. They are called 'stoops,' a word of whose derivation I am ignorant, though that may be of Holland too." Webster, in his dictionary of 1828, defines stoop as meaning in America "a kind of shed, generally open, but attached to a house, also, an open place for seats at a door." The latter was the common sense of the word, and Thornton gives examples in English as early as 1749. The stoop is defined by Irving, *Knickerbocker History*, as "the porch, commonly built in front of Dutch houses, with benches on each side." It was usually uncovered, and is well illustrated in the *Century Dictionary*, under *stoop*. One may note in passing that the varyingly proper use of *stoop, porch, piazza, gallery*, is only to be acquired by familiarity with local custom.

Several Dutch words of topographical meaning have survived in close connection with the landscape. One of these is *clove*, from Dutch kloof, current in the Catskills in the sense of a long, narrow valley in the mountains. The word *kill*, meaning creek, stream, of Dutch origin, appears in many proper nouns, as in *Catskill, Walkill, Sparkill*, the *Kill von Kull*, and in central New York in a word naming a bend, or eddy, or a branch of a stream, variantly spelled *binocle, binnacle, binnekill, bennakill, benderkill*, with a variant *binnewater*, see *Dialect Notes*, II, 131–4. The spelling *binnekill* is etymologically the most correct. The word *kill* doubtless underlies also the form *skell*, in *Easthampton Records*, II, 399 (1698), "they should be sett at y[e] end of bucks skell."

American words brought into the language through the negroes have been insignificant in number for the same reason that words were rarely borrowed from the language of the relatively uncultured foreign white immigrants. A few words like *juba*, a kind of dance, *banjo, hoodoo, voodoo, pickaninny,* exhaust the list of words of non-English origin that have been familiarized through their use by the negroes. The word *jazz,* naming a kind of dance and music made familiar and popular of recent years, is commonly said to be of negro, that is of African origin. But the chain of evidence is not complete, and it seems more probable that jazz is merely an old English dialectal word suddenly brought into prominence. Wright, *English Dialect Dictionary,* records *jass* in the sense of violent motion, also the sound produced by a heavy blow, meanings which sufficiently describe jazz music and dancing. Against the supposition of African origin is the further fact that jazz is not an old and familiar word in negro dialect use.

Scarcely longer than this list of supposedly non-English words from negro English is the number of English words that have special associations with negro life in America, such as *cake-walk, aunt* and *uncle, mammy, buck, colored, colored person, coon, darkey* and even of these some are facetious or now archaic. Negro sections of cities have sometimes received distinctive names, as *the Jungle, Africa, Egypt, the Levee,* by extension from the Levee at New Orleans where negroes congregate, *Frog Town, Frog Hollow.* The eponymous name for a negro Pullman porter is George. So far as language goes, however, there is very little evidence to show that the negroes are a special class in America, that they have developed a special idiom of their own or are addressed in a special idiom by their white fellow-citizens. The word *tote,* of unknown origin, has become characteristically Southern, by reason of its general use there, as in "I toted you (as they say in Virginia) up to Richmond," Paulding, *Letters from the South* (1817), I, 54, but there is no evidence that it is of negro origin. It is mentioned as early as 1781 by President Witherspoon as being a Southernism. Webster, in the dictionary of 1828, describes tote as "a word used in slaveholding countries; said to have been introduced by the blacks." The earliest citation in Thornton is for 1667, in a passage which localizes the word in Virginia, but does not use it in connection with negroes. His next citation is for 1816, after which examples are numerous. The word is probably a native dialect word, brought to the southern states by the earliest settlers, which has persisted only in the colloquial speech, but as Thornton's examples show, as abundantly in the speech of the whites as in that of the blacks. A noun *toat* occurs in Seba Smith's *My Thirty Years,* p. 158, "Mr. Van Buren would eat up the whole toat of 'em," apparently *the whole load of them.*

Words borrowed from the Indian languages of North America have usually been names of natural places or objects, such as *moccasin, tomahawk, wigwam, teepee, wickieup, succotash, hickory, squaw, squash, sachem, papoose, persimmon, wampum.* The word *Indian* appears in the names of a number of plants, though *Indian corn* has long since been known simply as *corn,* thus causing a sharper differentiation between corn and wheat in America than obtains in England. The same applies to the word *meal,* which in America means corn meal, but which may be used in England for flour and in the phrase wheat-meal. The use of the word Indian in connection with corn meal still survives in the name of Indian pudding, which is Indian only in the sense that it is made of corn meal. Other popular names of plants containing the adjective *Indian* are Indian turnip for the root of the Jack in the Pulpit, Indian hemp, Indian paint-pot, Indian tobacco. The association of tobacco and the smoking of tobacco with Indians is one of the disappearing traditions of American life. Formerly a cigar store, that is a place where cigars and tobacco were sold, was not complete without a big wooden Indian standing in front for a sign. Now the wooden Indian has gone the way of his human predecessor, has gone the way of the barber's pole, the tavern sign, and other symbols of an older civilization. The tradition still survives, however, in the phrase, *dumb as a wooden Indian.*

During the Great War, the word *napoo, napu* was current among the soldiers. It meant ended, finished, killed, as in "There's a pretty big crowd of ours still lying na-poo-ed out there," C. A. Smith, *New Words Self Defined,* p. 125, where other citations also are given. The explanation of this word usually given is that it is a corruption of French *Il n'y a plus.* It is possible, however, that the word may be

Indian in origin and that it was taken to Europe by the American army. "A man killed was nepoed," says Quick, *Vandemark's Folly*, p. 177, "a word which many new settlers in Wisconsin got from the Indians." This bit of "frontier argot," he adds, "was rather common in the West in the fifties. The reappearance in the same sense of napoo for death in the armies of the Allies in France is a little surprising." It is to be sure not proved that napoo is a reappearance, but this is as probable an explanation as that which derives the word from *Il n'y a plus*. The probable derivation of the United States army toast How! Here's how! from an Indian word has already been discussed. For *how* as an Indian greeting, see the *Century Dictionary* under this word.

An Indian word meaning *fitting*, *proper*, *good*, and in general having the sense of approval, seems formerly to have been current but is now lost. It occurs in the *New Haven Records*, p. 24 (1639), in the account of the trial of an Indian, named Nepaupuck. When he was asked "if he would nott confess y^{t} he deserved to dye, he answered, it is weregin." The word is used in an epitaph on the tombstone of an Indian named Uncas, printed in Barber, *Connecticut Historical Collections*, p. 298. According to Hodge, *Handbook of American Indians*, under *wauregan*, the author of this epitaph was Dr. Elisha Tracy. It is as follows:

> "For beauty, wit, for sterling sense,
> For temper mild, for eloquence,
> For courage bold, for things waureegan,
> He was the glory of Mohegan."

Another Indian epitaph is given by Thatcher, *Indian Biography*, (1832), I, 294:

> "Here lies the body of Sunseeto,
> Own son to Uncas, grandson to Oneko,
> Who were the famous sachems of Moheagan;
> But now they are all dead, I think it is Werheegen."

A footnote explains Werheegen as "the Mohegan term for All is well, or Good-news." The word survives as a place name in Wauregan, a village in Windham County, Conn.

More interesting than these concrete words are phrases of more general meaning which have been adopted into current English from certain features of Indian life. Among these are *on the warpath, the pipe of peace,* or *calumet of peace, to bury the hatchet, to hold a pow-wow, Indian summer, Indian yell, to yell like a wild Indian, mugwump, pale face, brave* (a noun), *firewater, run the gauntlet* (not originally Indian but now usually thought of as an Indian method of punishment and torture), *Indian file, Indian giving* (the giving of gifts afterwards recalled), *happy hunting grounds, Great Spirit, medicine man, war paint, war dance, to scalp* (figuratively), *to have a person's scalp, to be out for scalps, a ticket-scalper* (one who buys and sells tickets, especially railway tickets at less than the regular rates), *scalp locks, to sit around the council fire.*

The following is a list of all the words of Indian origin, exclusive of personal, place and other proper names, commented on in Hodge's *Handbook of American Indians,* that have had at some time or other greater or less currency as English words. Many of them are plant, fish and animal names, and though unknown to most persons, they frequently survive actively in limited localities. Some of the words have several different English forms.

achigan
angakok
apishamore
asimina
assapan
atamasco lily
babiche
baidarka
bayou
beshow
bogan
busk
camas
canoe
cantico
carcajou
caribou
cashaw
cassio berry
catalpa
catawba
caucus
cayuse
chautauqua
chebacco
chebog
chickwit
chinquapin
chipmunk
chunkey
cisco
cocash
cockarouse
cohosh
coon, raccoon
coonti
croton (bug)
cultus-cod
dahoon
dockmackie
eupishemo
eulachen
hens
hiaqua
hickory
hobnuts
hog, quahog
hominy
huddoh
humbo
huskanaw
husky
iglu
jackash
kaiak
killhog
kinnikinnick

kiskitomas
kiva
klondike
kooyah
kouse
logan
longe, lunge, mascalonge, etc.
maccarib
mahala mats
maize
maninose
manito
massassauga
maycock
maypop
menhaden
mescal
metate
methy
mingo
mishcup
moccasin
mocuck
moonack
moose
moosemise
muckawis
mugwump
mummychog
muskeg
musquash
nadowa
namaycush
nanticoke
neeskotting
neshannock
neshaw
netop
nikie name
nocake
nunkom
occow
opossum
otkon
ouananiche
oxidaddy
pappoose
parka
pauhagen
peag
pecan
pembina
pemmican
persimmon
peyote
piasa
pipsissewa
pishaug
plaquemine
pocan
pogamoggan
pogonip
pogy
poke
pokeloken
pone
pooquaw
pooseback
poquosin
porgy
potlatch
powitch
powow
puccoon
pung
punkie
quahog
quickhatch
quinnat
quoddy
raccoon
robbiboe
rockahominy
rokeag
runtee
sachem
sagakomi
sagamite
sagamore
salal
samp
saskatoon
savoyan
scuppaug
scuppernong
sego
senega
sequoia
sewan
shaganappi
shallon
Shawnee, haw, salad, etc.
shoepack
showtl
siskawet
skoka
skoke
skunk
slank
sockeye
sora
spanguliken
spatlum
squam
squantersquash
squantum
squash
squaw
squeteague
stogie
succotash
supawn
tamal
tarpon
tautog
tawkee
teepee
terrapin
texas
tipitiwicket
tipsinah
titymagg
tobacco
toboggan

togue
tomahawk
tom pung
tonkaway root
toopik
toshence
totem
touladi
towalt
tuckahoe
tuckernuck
tulibee
tump, tumpline
tweeg
tyee
wahoo
wampapen
wampee
wampoose
wampum
wanigan
wapacut
wapiti
wappatoo
watap
wauregan
wavey
weesick
wejack
wenona
whiggiggin
whipsiwog
whisky-john
wickakee
wickiup
wickup
wicopy
wigwam
wigwassing
wishtonwish
wokas
woodchuck
woolyneag
yampa
yokeag
yopon
yucca

A survey of vocabulary, such as has been attempted in this chapter, manifestly can accomplish only a relatively small number of the ends which it is desirable to attain in this field of study. In the first place, the limits of space make it impossible for such a discussion to become exhaustive. Complete inclusiveness would be possible only in a dictionary, and the provinces of the dictionary maker and the discursive historian are quite separate and distinct. Neither can such a discussion be exhaustive of all the main or the minor categories of words and shadings in the use of words, which have entered into the composition of the American vocabulary. What it can do, however, is to suggest some of the main lines of interest and of further investigation which may be carried along perhaps in the end to final conclusions. The greatest need in the study of American vocabulary is a more abundant collection of materials, not merely of words, but of words with an accompanying commentary of context or circumstance which makes their historical significance definitely determinable. This need can be satisfied only by systematic reading of the monuments of American literature. Casual jottings will not get one far, nor is the casual method an economical one of gathering the material. One has visions of a coöperative undertaking by which this task could be accomplished with no impracticable expense of labor. If the body of American literature which calls for examination could be gathered under one roof, a kind of Solomon's House, as indeed it is gathered under several roofs, and a body of industrious scholars and readers set to work on this literature, aiding and systematizing each other's work by mutual criticism, not many years would be required to finish the task in such way as to place it among the permanent achievements of human endeavor. When finished, the value of this work would consist in the light the history of the vocabulary throws on the development of ideas and culture in the life of the people who have used the language. That this light would illuminate all the dark places of American history could not be expected, but it would certainly aid in reading more clearly the hidden and unconscious thought of past generations, and would add many instructive and amusing moments to the life of our own.

PROPER NAMES

In many respects proper names occupy a special position in the historical study of language. The personal element enters into their formation and preservation more effectively than in common nouns, and individual volition, not to say whimsical volition, must often be taken into account in the endeavor to explain them. Proper names are also on the whole more conservative in form than common nouns, the reason being that there often collect about proper names certain legal, patriotic, pious and other sentiments which tend to give them a fixed form. The proper names with which an unlearned person is familiar are likely to be subjected to the crystallizing influences of written speech before the words of the ordinary language are reduced writing. One of the first things an illiterate person learns to write is his own name. Yet again proper names differ from common names in that they fall more readily into clearly defined logical categories. No great degree of generalizing power is required to divide proper names into place names and personal names, and then place names into mountain, river and city names, personal names into family and given names, and so on through a multitude of obvious classifications. This ease of classification tends to give proper names certain typical values and to cause them to be repeated in traditional associations.

The nomenclature of a civilized people is also likely to be much more variegated than its vocabulary of common nouns. All nations of the modern world are ethnologically mixed, and aliens when they enter a new community, if they carry not a stick of furniture with them, must at least enter with a name. Inferences as to race may be drawn from proper names, though even these may easily be mistaken, as Flom points out in detail in his discussion of Norwegian surnames, Scandinavian Studies, V, 130 ff., but inferences as to nationality cannot be derived securely from proper names. A person who comes from France may bear a German name and may be of German origin, but nevertheless may not be German.

The special interest of proper names in the history of the English language in America lies in the unparalleled opportunity afforded for the exercise of imagination, ingenuity, sentiment, in providing this virgin territory with the human associations of a local and personal nomenclature. Never before had a similar opportunity presented itself to a civilized people of the western world. With a whole continent at its disposal to name and to people, what use did the American colonists make of this privilege? Can we find in this situation a clear index of the powers of the American mind to rise or fail to rise to a great opportunity for the exercise of the creative imagination?

In fact, however, the opportunity was not as unhampered as it might seem to be. For the colonization of America was not an instantaneous process, but complicated and long continued. Nor is it conceivable that the colonists at any time thought of themselves as selected for the utilization of an unusual imaginative opportunity. When they came to settle in America they brought with them the same human impulses and associations as had colored their lives before migration. They came to America not to exemplify theories, but to live. It is therefore unfair to measure American nomenclature by any other tests than those of the practical circumstances under which the proper names of the country became established. These practical circumstances were very much the same as had determined the character of the names traditional in the old homes of the colonists. Fine names, even appropriate names, are not the exclusive possession of the old world, nor on the other hand are such crudities as Meadville or Jonesburg to be met with only in America. The esthetic distance between Jonesburg and Peterborough or Petrograd is not great, and it is true of all proper names that time and conventional association can make any name seem respectable or distinguished. If Pitt is a distinguished name, may not *Pittsburgh* be equally distinguished? May not the name also be as closely associated with its place, may it not be as "inevitable," as Edinburg, or Hamburg, or any *-ville* of France, or any *-by*, *-chester*, or *-ton* of England? "American local names lend themselves strangely little to retention," lamented Henry James, *Notes of a Son and Brother*, p. 309, "I find, if one has happened to deal for long years with almost any group of European designations—these latter springing, as it has almost always come to seem, straight from the soil where natural causes were anciently to root them, each with its rare identity. The bite into interest of the borrowed, the imposed, the 'faked' label, growing but as by a dab of glue on an article of trade, is inevitably much less sharp." All this because Henry James found it hard to remember after forty years the name of a convalescent camp for soldiers in Rhode Island which he had visited but once, though finally the name "figures" to his memory, "though with a certain vagueness," as Portsmouth Grove. It is difficult to see how at any time or in any country natural causes were able to "root" names. Names are applied only by agreement and convention, and though natural causes may suggest a name, proximity to a view, a mountain, a bay, or what not, yet only common acceptance of such a name can root it in common use. Names indeed always arise out of common human experiences, among which must be counted recollection and memory carrying over the name of an old and familiar place to a new and strange one. If this is borrowing or faking, mankind has been guilty of this misdemeanor in all ages and climes. If the glue which attaches a name to its place in America seems thin and lacking in adhesiveness, it can be so only because the human associations one has here with a place are thin and vague. But to assume that all local associations, all personal associations referable to names are dull and thin in America is to make one of those broad general charges against a race which are always rendered ineffective by their too indiscriminate inclusiveness.

No general or official method for establishing a fixed form for a name that varied in traditional use was available in the United States until the establishment of the United States Geographic Board in 1890. During the time it has existed this Board has made some fifteen thousand decisions. It has besides formulated a set of reasonable principles to govern its actions in determining names which should prove helpful to any one confronted with problems of nomenclature. The decisions of the Board must be accepted by the departments of the Government as finally authoritative, and though their acceptance otherwise is voluntary, the services which the Board can render are too manifestly useful to be disregarded. The Board has been especially helpful in establishing the names of rivers, mountains and similar features of the natural landscape. The names of such places have almost always become attached to them by more or less unanimous but uncritical social consent. Ordinarily the names of states or parts of states and towns have been determined by legislative enactment or by charter, and have thus by decree been fixed from the beginning. Where the fancy has had free play, however, in nomenclature, both variety and freakishness have entered, and it is much to be regretted that a Geographic Board has not been in existence from the beginning of American history.

Literally it is not true that the American colonists entered a country without a traditional nomenclature. The American Indians had a local terminology of their own which no doubt was richer in certain topographical respects of special importance to persons living their nomadic open-air life than was the terminology of their supplanters. In attempting to account for the motives and acts of the final name-givers on the American continent, one must therefore consider their attitude towards the names which they found in possession when they arrived, as well as towards the new material which they brought with them or gradually developed in the process of living.

In the earlier periods of American colonization, the attitude of the colonists towards Indian names seems to have been that such names might be retained as designations for natural features of the country, for rivers, hills, mountains, lakes and sometimes meadows, but that where the creative energy of the settlers themselves was prominent and when the name became a matter of official action and record, as in the organization of towns and counties, English names were much to be preferred. In this the colonists were following a reasonable desire. Their purpose in leaving England was not to make themselves over in the image of the American Indian, but rather to transfer to their new homes as much of the feeling and atmosphere of the old world as possible. The age of Rousseau and romanticism had not yet arrived, but even if it had, the joys of one compelled to dwell permanently in a wilderness are likely to contrast unfavorably with those of persons who dwell in an older and more humanly sanctified civilization. One is not surprised therefore to discover that in Massachusetts Colony, of the sixty towns named before 1690, not one retained an Indian name, Whitmore, p. 393. In Plymouth Colony, two Indian names, Scituate and Monomoy (now Chatham) date from this period. It is interesting to observe, however, that the Indian name Massachusetts survived, the reason being that it was primarily thought of as the name of Massachusetts Bay, a feature of the natural landscape. In the same way Connecticut became established as the name of a state because the river was so important an element in the experience of the early colonists of the state. Massachusetts and Connecticut are the only states on the Atlantic seaboard which bear Indian names.

After Monomoy, or Manamoyet, named in 1678, the next town in Massachusetts to be given an Indian name was Natick, in 1763, followed by Marshpee, 1763, and Cohasset, 1770. Some Indian town names of later origin may be added to these, the town name usually having been derived from a feature of the local landscape, but the number of such names in Massachusetts has remained surprisingly small. Sentimental feeling for Indian life has led in recent times to the naming of countless camps, cottages, and summer settlements by Indian names, but the romantic view of the Indian came too late to affect the naming of many towns in so old a community as Massachusetts. If one takes the United States Official Postal Guide and runs down the list of post offices in Massachusetts and a Western state like Washington, Idaho or Oregon, one will observe a much greater proportion of Indian names in the newer communities than in those longer settled. The settlement of the Western states was a more joyous adventure than the settlement of New England. The immigrant who went West did not go forth with dread into an altogether unknown region. Before he carried his family and his family belongings to a new home in the wilderness, he made a preliminary scouting expedition, or at least talked with those who had spied out the land. Migration westward also took place more rapidly, more dramatically and more sociably than the settlement of New England. All these circumstances permitted a play of fancy in light matters like finding and giving names such as the New Englander could not indulge in. Cooper and other writers of Indian romances likewise encouraged a sympathetic feeling towards Indian tradition just at the time when western migration was becoming extensive and was kindling the American imagination. In other words, the Indian became more interesting as he receded in the distance.

Old Indian town names are still less numerous in Connecticut than in Massachusetts. Norwalk, which dates from 1650, bears an Indian name. It has been Anglicized, however, in form, so that it looks like a compound of north and walk. Madam Knight, *Journals* (1704), speaks of Norowalk "from its halfe Indian name Northwalk," but it is difficult to see that either half of this compound, as thus given, is Indian. Barber, *Connecticut Historical Collections*, p. 392, says that "the name of Norwalk is derived from the above bargain, viz., the northern bounds of the lands purchased were to extend from the sea one day's 'north walk' into the country." This bargain is pure legend. Historically the place Norwalk has no connections which would justify such an interpretation as north-walk, and if the name were spelled Norwauk, in harmony with Winnipauk, Montauk, and other names of this phonetic form, current in the neighborhood, one would have no doubt of its pure Indian origin. Is Norridgewock of the same origin?

The next Indian town name in Connecticut does not appear until 1844, when Naugatuck was established, and became, according to Dexter, p. 442, "the only Indian name besides Norwalk borne by a Connecticut town." It should be remembered that a town in Connecticut is what would be elsewhere more commonly called a township. Indian names for lesser divisions than towns, for villages and cities, are more numerous, such as Willimantic, Niantic, Montowese, Cos Cob, Saugatuck, Pequot, but here also if one will consult the United States Official Postal Guide, one will probably find that such names are far less numerous in this state than one had expected.

One of the earliest commendatory references to Indian names was that of William Penn, who published in 1683 a general description of the province of Pennsylvania in the form of a letter to the Committee of the Free Society of Traders in London, reprinted in *Select Notes*, London, 1782, Vol. IV, pp. 299–317. Penn says in this letter, p. 305, that he understands the language of the Indians, and adds, "I know not a language spoken in Europe, that hath words of more sweetness or greatness, in accent or emphasis, than theirs: for instance, Octocockon, Rancocas, Oricton, Shak, Marian, Poquesien; all of which are names of places, and have grandeur in them." Perhaps one or two of these names may be traced in later periods, there is for example a stream in Pennsylvania called Poquessing, which may be Penn's Poquesien, and a town in New Jersey named Rancocas. None, however, has passed into familiar use, and Penn's commendation cannot be taken as indicating a general sympathetic interest which led to a custom of retaining Indian names in Pennsylvania. It is true, however, that a very large number of Indian names of rivers and other features of the landscape in Pennsylvania and along the shores of the Chesapeake have survived. The reason for this may be that these regions were not so rapidly or so thickly settled as were Connecticut and Massachusetts, and Indian traditions thus had an opportunity to establish themselves, perhaps first on printed maps or in printed descriptions of the regions, before they were crowded out by the white man's nomenclature. Certainly it is true to this day that mountainous regions, for example, the Adirondacks or the White Mountains, are likely to contain greater numbers of names of Indian origin than adjacent more level and fertile lands. Indian names on the whole have been only imperfectly domesticated. They still suggest something wild, romantic and grotesque, as they did to James K. Paulding, in his *Lay of the Scottish Fiddle*, published in 1814. In this poem a voyage up the Chesapeake Bay is thus described:

> "Steady the vessels held their way,
> Coasting along the spacious bay,
> By Hooper's Strait, Micomico,
> Nantikoke, Chickacomico,
> Dam-quarter, Chum, and Hiwassee,
> Cobequid, Shubamacoddie,
> Piankatank, and Pamunkey."

So the catalogue continues for a dozen or more lines, bringing in proper names from elsewhere in the United States — Chikago, Chickamoggaw and others—"high sounding and poetical names" . . . "certainly highly sonorous, and only to be paralleled by a catalogue of Russian generals, or Indian chiefs." The humorous connotation of certain Indian names has always been felt, and names like Hohokus, Hoboken, Kalamazoo, Keokuk, Oshkosh, Skaneateles, names of real places, have acquired more than local significance, as though they were grotesque creations of the fancy. There is, however, no post-office named Podunk in the United States Official Postal Guide. Just how this word came to be used as the designation for any small, out-of-the-way place is not known. It is an Indian word by origin, the name of a brook in Connecticut, and a pond in Massachusetts, occurring as early as 1687, Hodge, *Handbook*, II, 270. There is also a Potunk on Long Island.

In Virginia the county occupied a place similar in rank to that filled by the town in New England. Here also one notes a reluctance to give to the counties any other names than those with distinctively English associations, and this is especially true in tide-water Virginia. As one goes farther west one meets with a few Indian names, for example, Alleghany, Rappahannock, Shenandoah, names of wonderful resonance and of deep emotional content in American experience, but the number remains relatively small, and the associations that cluster around these names have little to do with the Indians.

An exhaustive study of Indian place names in all the states would carry one far into the details of local history. With the opening of

Kentucky and the Ohio valley to settlement, the new regions were entered by a race of frontiersmen with quite different interests and traditions from those of the earlier colonists. The hunting of the Indian by this time had come to be regarded with some of the sentiment which attaches to a sport. But whether the Indians were the hunted or the hunters they stirred the imagination and excited the spirit of adventure. It is not surprising therefore to find that the new states bore prevailingly Indian names, Kentucky, Ohio, Illinois, Tennessee, Michigan, Wisconsin, and of course, west of the Mississippi, names of this kind are quite as numerous. The name of Indiana is a still more direct evidence of sentimental interest in the disappearing native population. Towns, villages, counties, and townships in the western states also bear frequent witness by their names to a sympathetic interest in native Indian tradition. Regions in which Indians continued to dwell on their reservations after the main body of their tribes had gone West, literally or metaphorically, are likely to be rich in Indian nomenclature. So in central New York a large number of Indian place names, such as Onondaga, Canandaigua, Skaneateles, Schenectady, and hundreds like these, of romantic or grotesque association as one's mind inclines, are now in familiar use and have become so through direct contact with lingering tribes of Mohawks, Iroquois and Senecas. The same applies to the eastern end of Long Island, where Indians are still dwelling on their reservations. It must be acknowledged that these Indian names have been retained not usually from any realization of their appropriateness in meaning to the places they name, but merely because they had an imposing or quaint sound. As Beauchamp points out, p. 6, Indian place names are rarely poetical when one discovers their true etymology, which to be sure is not often known. Tradition in this matter, however, is seldom content to abide by the unromantic truth, for a high-sounding name with no clear meaning presents an irresistible appeal to the creative imagination. The island of Manhattan and the dwellers in it have had such diverse significations assigned to their names as "the island where we all became intoxicated," "the place where they gather wood to make bows," "the people of the whirlpool," referring to Hellgate, and perhaps most reasonably, see Tooker, p. 73, though less picturesquely, "the people of the island of hills." None of these meanings was in the mind of Irving or Cooper or Walt Whitman when they at different times registered their preference for Manhattan over commonplace New York. But now that the word Manhattan has been legalized as the name of the Borough of Manhattan, it is possible it may become colorlessly official and lose some of its romantic glamour. The form of the name of the city which Irving preferred and used in his Knickerbocker History was Mannahatta; the name of New York state he thought should be Ontario, of the Hudson, the Monhegan, and for the United States themselves he preferred Appalachia. Edgar Allan Poe also approved Appalachia as the name of the whole country, see Brander Matthews, *Poetry of Place Names*, in *Parts of Speech*, p. 290. Cooper, *Notions of the Americans* (1828), I, 111, regrets that the name Manhattan has not persisted. "It is a little surprising," he says, "that these republicans, who are not guiltless of sundry absurd changes in their nomenclature of streets, squares, counties, and towns, should have neglected the opportunity of the Revolution, not only to deprive the royal family of England of the honour of giving a name to both their principal state and principal town, but to restore a word so sonorous, and which admits of so many happy variations as the appellation of this island." Practical limits of convenience, however, count for a good deal in the matter of place names. It was comparatively easy to change King's College into Columbia College, for the name affected only scores, whereas the name of the city and state affected thousands.

Another example of the uncertainty of tradition in the meanings attached to the Indian names of places may be cited in the name Cohoes, see Masten, *History of Cohoes*, p. 1, Beauchamp, p. 19, 20, now a city of some importance in New York state, but undoubtedly the place was first thought to be worthy of a name because of the falls in the Mohawk river at that place. Tom Moore, who visited the place in 1804, wrote a poem which he called *Lines, Written at the Cohos, or Falls of the Mohawk River*. But it is not so certain that

Cohoes means falls, and various picturesque etymologies have been suggested. The name is now pronounced ['koː'hoːz] with about equal stress on the two syllables, but earlier spellings vary and some of them bring the word closer to what seems to have been at least a related form, the name Coos ['koːɔs], which now figures as the name of a county in northern New Hampshire, but which originally named a natural feature, a bend of the Connecticut river, and was thence transferred to the tribe of Indians who lived in that region and finally to the region itself. Does Cos Cob in Connecticut contain this same Indian word? And Cohasset in Massachusetts? And do we have the same word in Cohees, local name for the people who dwell in the Valley of Virginia, along the Shenandoah, the people who live in higher western Virginia being the Tuckahoes? The word Tuckahoe is said to be the name of a wild vegetable eaten by the Indians. But all these questions must be left to the scientific student of Indian dialects, for surface guessing at answers will not get one far. Douglas-Lithgow, in a list of Indian place names in New Hampshire, gives Coös as diminutive of Coa, meaning Pine Tree, being the "same as Coasset, Mass." Started on this career of wild surmise, the author then proceeds to connect Coos in New Hampshire, an Indian word, with a Coos in Asia Minor, mentioned in Acts, 21, 1, two words of the same form but inconceivably related to each other except by the coincidence of external similarity. The prime necessity before one can venture far in the explaining of Indian place names in America is a fuller and better knowledge of the phonology and etymology of the American Indian language than has been the possession of any of the investigators who have hitherto exercised themselves within this field.

Many Indian names first entered English through French, especially along the St. Lawrence and in the region of the Great Lakes. Old Kaskaskia also reflects French influence in some of the proper names of the region, and all through the northwest, along the Columbia river to the Pacific, one can still follow the trail of the French missionaries by the surviving French and Indian place names. As late as the first quarter of the nineteenth century, one still meets with cumbersome French spellings of Indian names in text books and books of travel written in English, spellings like Ouisconsin, Ouabasche, for Wisconsin, Wabash. This state of affairs was one among others that Noah Webster set himself to reform. "The advantage of familiarizing children to the spelling and pronunciation of American names is very obvious," he remarks, *American Spelling Book*, Boston, 1798, p. x, and the attention which he gave to the subject he thought must give to his own book "the preference to foreign Spelling Books." Foreign spelling books, in Webster's use of the term, meant merely British spelling books, which usually contained lists of the names of British towns, counties and market places, but none for America. This deficiency Webster endeavored to supply, and in preparing his lists of American place names he gave them in the main the simplified rational spellings which they still retain. "How does an unlettered American know," he asks, *American Spelling Book*, p. v, "the pronunciation of the names, *ouisconsin* or *quabasche*, in this French dress? Would he suspect the pronunciation to be Wisconsin and Wabosh?" In the Preface to his *Elements of Useful Knowledge* (1807), Vol. I, he commented again on the difficulty of finding out the true pronunciation of Indian names, and on the necessity of writing them according to ordinary English analogies after their pronunciations were determined. In the *American Spelling Book* (1803) most of the proper names appear in the forms which they now commonly have, exceptions being *Illenois, Kanhaway, Missorie, Mobill, Sagunau, Ashwelot, Chicopy, Lemington, Sunapy, Chicaugo, Shenango, Chatanuga.*

In some instances, the influence of French spelling and pronunciation is still observable in the American pronunciation of Indian names. Thus such pronunciations as that of Iroquois as [ˈɪrəˎkwɔː], of Illinois as [ɪləˈnɔɪ], of Arkansas as [ˈɑrkənˈsɔː], of Sioux as [suː] could have established themselves only on the basis of French, not of English pronunciation. So also the spelling *ch* following English associations would normally represent the sound [tʃ] as in *change, choose, chair*, etc. It is of course so pronounced in many Indian place names, as in Chicopee or Chatanooga, where, however, the analogy of the common English words *chick* and *chat* may have operated to produce the sound [tʃ]. More frequently *ch* in Indian names is pronounced [ʃ] as it would be in French. Thus the word *Chautauqua* has been normalized in this spelling, though the pronunciation varies somewhat between [tʃəˈtɔːkwə] and [ʃəˈtɔːkwə], with perhaps the latter as the more common. That this was the older pronunciation is made probable by many eighteenth century spellings; De Celoron spelled the word *Shatacoin* and *Chatakouin*, see Beauchamp, pp. 38-40. Other French spellings are *Chatacouit*, *Schatacoin*, *Chadakoins*. In Bonnecamp's journal, 1749, however, it is spelled *Tjadakoin* and another French spelling is *Tchadakoin*. These latter spellings may have been attempts to record the Indian pronunciation more exactly, but the sound ordinarily heard by the French for the letters now written *ch* in Indian words seems to have been unquestionably [ʃ]. English analogies would continually work to replace this by [tʃ], so that now Chicago is either [ʃɪˈkɔːgo] or [tʃɪˈkɔːgo], and when one comes across an unfamiliar name, as perhaps to some persons *Chenango* may be, one might hesitate whether to pronounce the word [ʃɪˈnæŋgo] or [tʃɪˈæŋgo]. The local pronunciation is of course the former of these, and generally as one gets closer to direct tradition Indian words spelled with *ch* will be pronounced [ʃ]. The name Ouachita [ˈwaʃɪˌtɔː] in Arkansas, name of a town and college, preserves three distinctly French features, *ou* for [w], *ch* for [ʃ], and *a* for [ɔː]. The name of a tribe of Montana Indians was Piegan, preserved as the name of a beautiful pass in the Glacier National Park. This name is pronounced [piːˈgæn], and both the value of the first vowel, [iː] for the spelling ie, and the stressing of the word on the second syllable are clear indications of French tradition. The natural English spelling would have been something like Peagann.

Another clear survival of French influence in Indian names is to be seen in the pronunciation of *a* as [ɔː]. Here again later usage varies somewhat between [ɔː] and [ɑː], the latter being in general the sound which *a* is now supposed to have when it has its Continental or Italian value, as contrasted with its ordinary English value, which would be [eː] or [æ]. Thus for Chicago one now hears both [ʃɪˈkɔːgo] and [ʃɪˈkɑːgo], for Omaha, one hears both [ˈoːməˌhɔː] and [ˈoːməˌhɑː], and the second is perhaps commonly regarded as the more refined pronunciation. But certainly the pronunciation with [ɔː] is the older and better tradition, and it appears in words with a variety of spellings besides *a*, for example *au* in Chautauqua, *aw* in Chickasaw, *as* in Arkansas, *augh* in Conemaugh.

In earlier periods of American history, before names had acquired fixed and conventional forms, established either by custom or by the decisions of the United States Geographic Board, the use of local Indian names was often embarrassed by the multitude of forms which an Indian name might take. As all Indian names when put down in writing were the attempts of the more or less sophisticated writer to record the natural sound of the name as he thought he heard it, different persons obviously might differ widely in their records. The United States Geographic Board, *Decisions*, 1916–1918, in authorizing *Egegik* as the name of a river in Alaska, rejected the variants Agouyak, Egegak, Igagik, Igiagik, Ougagouk, Ugagik, Ugaguk, and Ugiagik. The Cocheco, a river in New Hampshire, had the variants Cochechae, Cochechea, Cochecho, Cuttchecho, Kechceachy, Kecheachy, and Quochecho before the Board simplified matters by recognizing only Cocheco. For Milwaukee the following spellings are recorded by Legler:

Melleoki —Father Hennepin, 1679
Millioki —Father Zenobe Membre, 1679
Meleki —Old French map of 1684
Milwarik —John Buisson de St. Cosme, October 7, 1699
Milwacky —Lieut. James Gorrell, September, 1761
Milwakie —Col. Arent S. De Peyster, July 4, 1779
Millewackie—Samuel A. Storrow, September 29, 1817
Milwahkie —Dr. Jedediah Morse, 1820
Milwalky —Major Irwin, October 6, 1821
Milwaukie —The Sentinel, November 30, 1844
Milwaukee —November 30, 1844, to present time

These spellings all betray a family resemblance, and the differences of pronunciation which they seem to indicate probably lay as much in the ears of the white hearers as in the mouths of the Indian speakers of the name. For Iowa, Hodge's *Handbook of American Indians*, Bureau of American Ethnology, Bulletin 30, gives sixty-four spellings with citations for each. Names like Iowa and Ohio, made up chiefly of vowel sound, were particularly hard to reduce to the fixed forms of spelling.

A significant and commendable restraint has always been exercised in America in giving abstract and allegorical names to places. One might have expected names of this kind, so frequently found in personal names like Mercy, Charity, Comfort, Content, Hope, Faith, Tribulation, etc., to have been abundantly employed by the New England colonists in providing names for their new habitations. But in fact no such names appear, the name of Providence, in Rhode Island, being the exception to prove the rule. The first settlers at Dedham in Massachusetts petitioned the General Court that their settlement might be named Contentment, but the Court did not agree and gave the name Dedham, from a place of the same name in England, *Dedham Records*, III, p. v. In Connecticut likewise no abstract names appear until late, when, in 1708, Voluntown was manufactured "to denote the land granted by the Colony to the volunteer soldiers of New London County," Dexter, p. 440, and when in 1732, Union was so named. Neither of these inventions can be characterized as happy.

Elsewhere over the country one meets with a sprinkling of *Harmonies, Unions, Freedoms, Liberties*, and similar names. The name *Freedom* occurs in twelve different states, from New Hampshire to Wyoming. *Fredonia* occurs in eleven different states, as does also the name *Acme.* Still more numerous is the name *Alma,* which occurs twenty-one times in as many states. *Ira* occurs seven times, and *Amo* is the name of a town in Indiana, *Amor* of one in North Dakota, *Amoret* of one in Missouri, and *Amorita* of one in Oklahoma. An examination of the alphabetical list of post offices in the United States Official Postal Guide will reveal a great many similar curiosities, but on the whole among the thousands of names in this list these fanciful, sometimes pretentious, sometimes grotesque, symbolical names play a small part. They exhibit but little imaginative gift on the part of the inventors of them, and though they are usually names of Latin origin, it would not be safe to infer from them a high degree of interest in classical scholarship in American towns and villages thus designated. Latin seems often to have been used to produce that sense of slight removal from reality which satisfies in many people the feeling for refinement. There is only one *Saltville* in the United States, but a dozen or more Salines and Salinas. These Latinized names may be said to belong to the snobbery of nomenclature. Sometimes the learning displayed is made doubly attractive by being subtly veiled. Thus *Montville*, in Connecticut, was so named with "a covert reference to the family name of the first pastor of the flock, the Rev. James Hillhouse," Dexter, p. 442. The oil regions in New York and the Latin word *oleum* together explain the name *Olean*, in Cattaraugus County, the pronunciation of the word as a trisyllable with the stress on the last syllable pretty effectually removing the possibility of connecting it with oil. Several of the names of states exhale more or less of the flavor of classical scholarship, for example, *Vermont*, *Virginia*, the *Carolinas*, *Florida*, *Louisiana*, *Indiana*, and with a Spanish modification, *Nevada*, *Arizona*, and *California*, though the ultimate etymology of California is not clear.

If one descends still deeper into the turbid ocean of popular American nomenclature of minor features of the landscape, of streets, suburbs, and parlor cars, one finds inexhaustible illustrations of similar fancy and fantasy in proper names. Even here, however, it must be acknowledged that the taste for cheap refinement is exceptional. For the most part, people prefer as the names of places or objects which figure in their familiar lives what they would consider to be good substantial names, not too poetical or too literary. This feeling may indeed lead to the opposite extreme in the choice of names which make too little effort to escape the commonplace. So there are twenty-seven *Centervilles* in the United States. To these should be added twelve *Centrals*, five *Central Citys*, ten *Centralias*, a *Centra-*

homa in Oklahoma, a *Centropolis* in Kansas, and various other combinations of this overworked word in different localities. There are also sixteen *Enterprises* and twenty-five *Eurekas* in the United States. It seems, however, that symbolic allusions, unless they are perfectly obvious, as these are, soon tire the popular fancy. When Lewis and Clark were ascending the Missouri, it is recorded in their journals for Sunday, July 28, 1805, that the Missouri separating into three branches, they discontinued the name Missouri and named the three branches for President Jefferson, for Madison, then Secretary of State, and for Gallatin, then Secretary of the Treasury. Several days later they found the Jefferson branching again, and retaining Jefferson as the name of the main branch, they named one of the others Wisdom and the second branching of the Jefferson, Philanthropy river, these names being supposedly "attributes of that illustrious personage." A third branch was called Philosophy. This was a pleasant fancy, though of a kind in which these explorers seldom indulged. It is doubtful, however, if it should have been perpetuated in so permanent a form as nomenclature, and popular custom has registered against the names Wisdom, Philanthropy and Philosophy. The Wisdom is now known as the Big Hole, and this name was confirmed by the United States Geographic Board, by a decision of April 4, 1917. The Philanthropy had several names, Stinking Water, Passamari, and Ruby, the last of these being authorized by the United States Geographic Board in a decision of February 7, 1917. "Philosophy River," writes Mr. C. S. Sloane, secretary to the United States Geographic Board, "is now the modest Willow Creek, ten miles above Three Forks, Montana, on the south bank of Jefferson River. The United States Geographic Board has never rendered any decision in regard to the name for this stream." The name of the Wisdom River still survives as the name of a village, Wisdom, in Montana.

Somewhat similar to symbolical names are Scripture names which have acquired generalized abstract meanings. Here again, however, one is struck by the extreme restraint of the early American colonists in the employment of such names. One would expect Puritan settlements especially to be thickly sown with Bible names. In Massachusetts Colony, only one place, Salem, named in 1630, was given a Bible name before 1700, and Rehoboth, named in 1645, was the only place in Plymouth Colony. Massachusetts shows "in her entire history but three Biblical names in her list of towns," Dexter, p. 439, the third being Sharon, named in 1765. The list of Bible names is somewhat longer in Connecticut, among the older towns being Lebanon, Goshen, and Sharon. "Between 1697 and 1762, and chiefly towards the latter date, Connecticut named in this manner eight of her towns, besides several parts of towns or parishes. The fact accords with a certain devoutness of temperament and familiar recourse to Scripture, not out of place in a generation which was stirred to its depths by the revival preaching of Edwards and Whitefield," Dexter, p. 439. Even so the names were not usually given as the result of a popular demand but were assigned by the official action of the dignitaries. In the matter of Bible names as in that of symbolic names, perhaps the popular feeling is the same, the feeling that these names are a little hard to live up to. Many of the Bible names now found in various localities were doubtless often given with little realization that they were Bible names. Thus there are nineteen *Bethels*, twelve *Bethanys*, and about as many *Sharons* and *Shilohs* in the United States. These names must often be merely echoes of older American place names and not distinctly referable to the Bible. Names like *Gethsemane*, however, which has been given to two places in the United States, or *Jerusalem*, which also occurs twice, or *Ebenezer*, which occurs five times, seem to indicate a certain kind of acquaintance with the Bible. History sometimes plays ironically with these significant names. There are seven *Bethlehems* in the United States, but for none could the name be less appropriate than for the smoke-blackened town in Pennsylvania which shares it with the six others.

Absolute invention seems to have been as rare in proper names as in the common words of the language. Many place names can be found in the United States which defy explanation, but it will be difficult to find one that can be supposed to have been made out of whole cloth. Not infrequently names have been made by mechanically combining parts of other words. Thus *Saybrook*, in Connecticut, is a combination of the names of Viscount Say and Sele and Baron Brooke, the two foremost members in a company formed in 1632 to settle the valley of the Connecticut, Dexter, p. 423. The town was founded and the name given in 1634. The parish of Wintonbury in Windsor, Connecticut, "derived its name, it is said, from the circumstance of the parish being formed from three towns, viz., Windsor, Farmington, and Simsbury, the name Win-ton-bury being derived from a part of the name of each of these three towns," Barber, *Connecticut Historical Collections*, New Haven, 1836, p. 68. Almost any locality could offer further examples of this method of forming names. Thus *Penmar* in Pennsylvania is made up of the first syllable of Pennsylvania and Maryland. The place is at the boundary between the two states, a kind of location which explains a number of *State Lines* here and there. It explains also *Penn Line*, *Ohioville*, and *Linesville*, all towns in Pennsylvania on the boundary between Pennsylvania and Ohio. Other names of this kind are *Texhoma*, between Texas and Oklahoma, *Texarkana*, *Mondak*, between Montana and Dakota, *Mexicali* and *Calexico*, *Dalworth*, between Dallas and Ft. North in Texas, *Virgilina*, between Virginia and Carolina. *Elberon*, in New Jersey, is said to have been formed from the name L. B. Brown, who founded the place, and *Lake Carasaljo*, where Lakewood is situated, is said to have been made up from three names, Carrie, Sally and Joe, see Brander Matthews, *Parts of Speech*, p. 281. In the White Mountains, a ravine known as the *Jobildunk Ravine*, according to tradition, derived its name from three natives, Joe, Bill and Duncan, who were once lost in it. The village of *Penn Yan* in Gates County, New York, is said by French, *Gazeteer of New York*, p. 720, to have been made up of the first syllables of the words Pennsylvania and Yankee because a Pennsylvanian and a Yankee were rivals for the honor of naming the place, this composite name being accepted as a compromise. Slightly more plausible is the explanation given by Gannett, p. 241, that the name is a compound of the names of the two classes of settlers in the town, Pennsylvanians and Yankees. Names of this kind are likely to gather about them contradictory traditions, but fortunately such frivolities in the naming of places have never developed into general habits. The name *Yreka* in California is explained by Gannett, p. 333, as made by reading "bakery" backwards, yet he explains also that Yreka, a town in Siskiyou County, California, was named for an Indian tribe. The *b* in the first explanation seems to be brought down from heaven to satisfy the exigencies of the etymology. Both these explanations cannot be accepted, and one therefore hopes that the second is the right derivation of the name.

A classical instance of mechanical compounding should be noted in the name of Pennsylvania. The credit or blame for this name cannot, however, be assigned to William Penn. In a letter to his friend Robert Turner, dated the 5th of 1st mo., 1681, printed in Janney's *Life*, p. 165, Penn remarks that "this day my country was confirmed to me under the great seal of England, with large powers and privileges, by the name of Pennsylvania, a name the King would give it in honour of my father." Penn preferred the name New Wales, and when a request that it be so named was refused, he proposed Sylvania, "and they added Penn to it." "And though I opposed it," continues Penn, "and went to the King to have it struck out and altered, he said it was past, and would take it upon him; nor could twenty guineas move the under secretary to vary the name; for I feared lest it should be looked upon as a vanity in me, and not as a respect in the King, as it truly was, to my father, whom he often mentions with praise."

By far the greater number of place names in America have arisen either from an immediate circumstance attending the giving of the name, a happening, an object present, a natural feature of the landscape, or from memory association with other places or names. Names of the first kind may be described as casual or accidental. Speaking of Indiana about 1820, Carlton, *The New Purchase*, p. 86, says that, "out there a settlement usually takes its name from the person that first 'enters the land,' i.e. buys a tract at the land office. Often it takes the name from the family first actually settling or owning the largest number of acres; and very frequently from the person that established a ferry, a smithey, a mill, a tannery, and, above all, a Store." This statement summarizes some of the most simple and obvious ways of naming frontier places. Another would be the manufacture of names suggested by the natural situation of the place to be named. It is not safe to assume, however, that every Springfield, of which there are twenty-eight in the United States, or every Glenwood, of which there are just as many, or every Fairfield, of which there are twenty-five, was named as a result of fresh and accurate observation of natural surroundings, for these names also spread by imitative repetition. Still more common as a determining element in naming places has been the presence of some more or less striking object at the place and at the moment when it was necessary to provide the place with a name. Thus Horseheads, New York, a town in Chemung County, was so named because at this place "during the expedition against the Indians, General Sullivan caused his pack horses to be killed and the heads piled up," Gannett, p. 161. A post office in Virginia is also called Horse Head, and some score of places in the United States seem to have taken their names from the presence of horses. No other domestic animal has been so productive of proper names, though deer, buffalo, elk, moose, turkeys and other game animals have been the occasion of naming many more places than the horse. Other names, such as *Tomahawk*, the name of four post offices in the United States, *Wagon Wheel Gap* and *Picket Pin Park* in Colorado, various *Spades, Shoes, Blankets, Arrowheads, Grindstones, Flatirons, Fryingpans,* etc. are suggestive at least of an obvious explanation. There is, however, no post office named *Dead Man's Gulch* in the United States, and lurid names like this will be found more abundantly in fiction than in reality. The name Pipe Stave Neck, *Southold Records,* II, 154 (1712) brings before one the picture of a barrel stave on the Long Island beach as vividly as the image of the footprint of Friday on Robinson Crusoe's desert island. Trivial but real things like these have very commonly been the sources of names, as they have been obviously the normal experiences of mankind.

By far the most common source from which new place names have been derived has always been the recollection of the names of old places at home with which the settlers in the new regions were familiar. This has been true not only for later periods of American history, but for the Colonial period as well. Perhaps the most striking characteristic of New England place names is the fact that so many of them are taken from the names of small and obscure villages in England. Thus Haverhill, Hingham, Dedham, Groton, Dorchester, Hadley, Waltham, and dozens like these are names almost unknown to a Britisher, but of the very pith and marrow of American life and history. Each of these names probably "represents some local affection, some individual reason," and in most instances no doubt some original settler in the new town was an emigrant from the English village. In Connecticut as well as in Massachusetts, town names were freely imported from England. The first town names in Connecticut were Hartford, Windsor and Wethersfield, and "out of almost exactly one hundred names given public authority to prospective townships in this state before the Declaration of Independence," says Dexter, p. 423, "at least fifty seven were taken directly from British sources; if I have counted aright, seventeen of the remainder were owing to obvious peculiarities of natural location (as Waterbury, Middlefield), ten were variations or combinations of already existing names (as East Haddam, North Haven), eight were of Biblical origin, three were from names of Americans, founders or early settlers, two were borrowed from names in the Colony of Massachusetts Bay, and the remaining three can hardly be classified." In 1653, the oldest plantation east of the Connecticut river, hitherto known by the Indian name of *Pequot,* was re-named by Governor Winthrop as *New London,* his reason being the "commendable practice of all the Colonies of these parts, that as this Country hath its denomination from our dear Native Country of England, and thence is called New England, so the planters, in their first settling of most

new plantations, have given names to those plantations of some cities and towns in England, thereby intending to keep up and leave to posterity the memorial of several places of note there, as Boston, Hartford, Windsor," Dexter, p. 429. In the main, however, American town names derived from the names of the larger English cities, or from members of British noble families, or in honor of the king, as Lunenburg and Hanover in Massachusetts, will be found to have been given by various royal provincial governors and not by the people with the intent to memorialize English notabilities or great cities. Even in Virginia, where, as Paulding remarks, *Letters from the South*, I, 186, "among the high republican names of Jefferson, Madison, Monroe and Henry, we are amused to find Prince George and Prince Frederick, and innumerable other names that set forth the loyalty of the early settlers of Virginia," these names must be taken more as evidences of the interests of the gentry who organized and managed the Virginia Company than of the rank and file of the settlers who actually occupied the land.

The fond recollection of villages in Old England which is revealed by the names which the colonists gave to places in New England was duplicated when the New Englander of a later generation, leaving his rocky Massachusetts or Connecticut farm for more fertile regions in the West, carried with him as much of his native New England tradition as he could convey. Thus there are eight *Hatfields* in the United States, six *Grotons,* five *Haverhills,* ten *Hadleys,* four *Worcesters* and two *Woosters,* ten *Granvilles* besides several *Granville Centers* and a *Granville Summit,* nineteen *Hartfords* and twenty-five *Hanovers.* Practically none of these names occur in Southern states, and an interesting study of Western migratory movements could be made on the evidence of place names. It does not seem that Southern names of towns have been productive in the same way. There are seventeen *Petersburgs* in the United States and thirty-one *Richmonds* or combinations of Richmond with other words, but these names are so widely and variously distributed that the occurrence of them cannot be accounted for on the ground of interest in the two cities of Virginia of that name.

The occasions which led to the naming of countless places in the tumultuous expansion of the county westward were so varied that they cannot readily be reduced to systematic description. The great cities of the world suggested many place names, and Paris, London, Berlin, Dresden, Dublin, Rome, Pekin, Tokio, Madrid, and other names like these are widely distributed and often grotesquely attached to insignificant villages, to places containing only two cats and a chimney. Yet here again the more striking fact is that so many of American borrowed geographical names suggest intimate association with the place from which the borrowed name was taken. Thus there is a *Mora* in Idaho, Louisiana, Minnesota, Missouri, New Mexico, and Washington, and probably at each place a Swedish settler established the name in memory of his old home. In New York there is a *Dannemora* and in Nebraska a *Dannebrog*. Other Scandinavian names like *Nysted*, *Lund*, *Bergen*, etc., were doubtless given by persons with direct associations with the older places from which the names were taken. Of *Edinburghs* and *Glasgows* there are many in the United States, and these names may mean no more, so far as personal sentiment was concerned in the giving of them, than Delhi, or Pekin, or Cairo. But when one finds a place named Leith or Linlithgo, or Dumfries, one is justified in imagining a stray bit of genuine Scotch feeling.

The remote intellectual associations were also the occasion for naming many places in America. Probably no president of the United States has failed to have some place named in his honor, and of *Roosevelts*, there are fifteen. American generals, statesmen, and authors are also generously represented in American nomenclature, though perhaps not more so than European dignitaries. There are eight *Bismarcks* and fourteen *Gladstones* in the United States. There is, however, no *Wordsworth* or no *Shakspere* on the official list of post offices, though there is one Shelley, two Keats, and seventeen Byrons.

An early name of sentimental association was that given to the town of Wilkesbarre, in Pennsylvania. The name was made by combining the name of John Wilkes with that of Colonel Barre, two members of the British parliament who were American sympathizers at the time of the Revolution. The name was first proposed as the name of a Connecticut town in Windham County, but the petition was refused. Soon afterward, however, emigrants from Windham County to the Wyoming Valley in northeastern Pennsylvania, "planted there a living memorial to the incident, by naming, in 1775, the still flourishing town of Wilkes-Barre," Dexter, p. 434.

One of the most curious chapters in American place-naming is that which relates to the classical names of cities and townships in central New York. The names Troy, Rome, Ithaca, Utica and Syracuse are familiar to every one, but other less known fantastic names also occur—Lysander, Scipio, Sempronius, Ulysses, Ilion, Camillus, Manlius. These names were assigned to the places thus designated in the latter part of the eighteenth century, not all at one fell swoop, but over a period of years. On June 17, 1819, Halleck and Drake published in the Evening Post, as one of the *Croaker Papers*, An Ode to Simeon De Witt, Esquire, republished in the first complete edition, New York, 1860, pp. 69–72, with an editor's note on p. 163. In this poem DeWitt was ridiculed as the "God-father of the christn'd West" and as the originator of these fantastic names. De Witt was Surveyor General of the State of New York from 1784 to the year of his death, 1834. In a prefatory note, p. 69, the authors of the poem explain that "When the Western District was surveyed, the power of naming the townships was entrusted to the Surveyor-General. Finding the Indian appellations too sonorous and poetical, and that his own ear was not altogether adapted for the musical combination of syllables, this gentleman hit upon a plan, which for laughable absurdity has never been paralleled, except by the 'Philosophy' and 'Big Little Dry' system of Lewis and Clark. It was no other than selecting from Lemprière and the British Plutarch the great names which those works commemorate. This plan he executed with the most ridiculous fidelity, and reared for himself an everlasting monument of pedantry and folly." The editors of the complete edition of the Croakers, who are not named, added a note on p. 163, in which they remark that "allusion is made in this poem, to the names applied to the twenty-eight townships in the Military Tract of Central and Western New York," and that though De Witt has often been spoken of as entitled to the honor of giving these names, that honor, "such as it is, is believed to belong to Robert Harper, then Deputy Secretary of State." The note also quoted a direct statement from De Witt, in which he explains how the names were given. 'The names," he says, "were given by formal resolution of the Commissioners of the Land Office. The Board, consisting of the Governor, the Secretary of State, the Treasurer, the Auditor and the Attorney General, held its meetings in the city of New York. The Surveyor General had his office established by law in the city of Albany, and *knew nothing of these obnoxious names till they were officially communicated to him, nor had he even then*, any agency in *suggesting* them." A similar defense of the memory of De Witt is made in a Eulogium, Albany, 1835, delivered by T. Romeyn Beck, shortly after the death of the Surveyor General. "Let not then this charge be again brought against him," says Beck, "as through ignorance alone I have even heard it since his death." This makes too much of the matter. There may have been some question of the good taste of these names at the time they were given, but they were never disgraceful, and long use has made them less ridiculous than they may have seemed when they were new. One may even be grateful for this added touch of color upon the American map. The story of the origin of the names makes it clear, however, that they do not reflect an unusual interest in classical antiquity among the backwoodsmen of Central New York in the early nineteenth century. The settlers indeed were the victims, not the creators of the names. The names were evidently first applied on paper, and then later, when a group of settlers wished to incorporate, they found that they were already tagged with names, Cato or Camillus or Sempronius, names doubtless which seemed to them just like any other names.

The evidence fixing the personal responsibility for these names upon Robert Harper, Deputy Secretary of State, is lacking. He may indeed have been merely a scapegoat, and as one attempts to enter into the inner history of this matter, one realizes that a hundred years ago, even as now, public officials were skilled in that practice known as "passing the buck." A certain amount of information on the point is contained in the *Historical Magazine*, Vol. III, pp. 53–54, New York, 1859. The author of this article, whose name is not given, exonerates De Witt, and he cites the formal action of the Commissioners of the Land Office at the meeting in 1790 at which the townships already formed in the so-called Military Tract of the State were numbered and designated by the names Lysander, Hannibal, Cato, Brutus, Camillus, Cicero, Manlius, Aurelius, Marcellus, Pompey, Romulus, Scipio, Sempronius, Tully, Fabius, Ovid, Milton, Locke, Homer, Solon, Hector, Ulysses, Dryden, Virgil and Cincinnatus. The persons present at this meeting were Governor George Clinton, Secretary Lewis A. Scott, Treasurer Gerard Bancker, and Auditor Centenius. The name Centenius is corrected, p. 128, to Curtenius. At later meetings other townships were given similar names, the same commissioners being present. Just which one of the commissioners was responsible for the names is not apparent, though in the circumstances it is obvious that the finger of suspicion points steadily in the direction of one who bears so strange a Latinized name as Curtenius. The documentary information contained in this article from the *Historical Magazine* is confirmed by the later independent study of the records, published by Paltsits, state historian of New York, in the *Magazine of History*, XIII, 246–249, the only difference being that the name of the auditor as correctly given by Paltsits is Curtenius, not Centenius. Apparently the matter can be carried no farther, and the impelling motives in the mind of Curtenius or whoever it was who gave the names remain unknown.

It should be noted that *Seneca*, the name of a county and a village in Central New York, and by extension, of various other places in the United States, is not to be included among these names of classical origin. The word is a corruption of an Indian name, Sinnekaas, as it is given by Gannett, p. 279, but extant in various other forms in seventeenth-century records. In the Dutch maps of 1614 and 1616 the name already appears in the form Senecas, and the term seems first to have gained currency among the Dutch as an Indian tribal name, see Beauchamp, p. 204.

An interesting chapter in the consideration of American local names is that which treats of the obscurations which some of them have undergone. This obscuration may affect merely the spelling, as when Worcester in Massachusetts, derived from a British name of the same form, becomes Wooster in Arkansas and Ohio, or when Gloucester, which appears four or five times in the United States, becomes Gloster in Georgia, Louisiana, and Mississippi. On the other hand, change in place names may affect pronunciation, often radically, without affecting at least conventional spelling, as when in England Banff is pronounced as though it were written Bamf, and Tottenham as though there were no *e* and no *h* in the word. The causes of these obscurations, which probably are found in all languages, are not difficult to discover. Proper names by their nature are often the most intimate and common words that pass current in the life of a community. The name of the place one lives in is on one's tongue, at least in one's mind, more frequently than is any other word, more frequently than words applied to the weather. Thus communities frequently develop abbreviated or familiar pet names for their local habitation, speaking of it as the Burg, or the Old Town, or Little Old New York, or St. Joe instead of St. Joseph, or Schenec instead of Schenectady. In other words, proper names in common use belong to the very familiar vocabulary of the language. But they may also belong to the formal vocabulary, especially when they are used in official and documentary writings. One often finds, consequently, two forms of the same name, one colloquial, the other traditional and official. The conflict between these two names when it comes to a question of survival would naturally be decided by the particular circumstances, colloquial or official, which determine the associations of the name. It is obvious, however, that in the transmission of British names to America, colloquial interests must often have predominated, since the emigrants who settled villages frequently neither cared for nor were instructed in official literary traditions. A further occasion for colloquial perversions of proper names also arises when names originally of alien origin pass current in an English community. Examples of these are numerous French and Dutch names in common use in America. Doubtless the same obscuration and corruption has taken place in Indian names, though unfortunately no Indians are left to laugh at the ludicrous things which the English have done with their names. Numerous illustrations of the first of these processes can be found in the American vocabulary of proper names derived from English sources. When in 1677 the town of Burlington, in New Jersey, was founded, the settlers came in two bodies, one from London, the other from Yorkshire, forming, however, a united township, named after the Yorkshire town of Bridlington. The form which this name took, and which it has always maintained, was, however, the colloquial and not the official form of the name of the Yorkshire town, see Doyle, *English Colonies*, IV, 305. So in Connecticut the name *Killingworth* is by origin a colloquial form of Kenilworth, in Warwickshire, where the pronunciation Killingworth still survives, Dexter, p. 431. The original petition for the town in 1667 spells the name *Kenelmeworth*, but this petition was written by John Woodbridge, minister of the parish, who represented a learned minority, probably of one, in the community. *Pomfret* in Connecticut is likewise a colloquial form of *Pontefract*, in Yorkshire, *Windham* is from *Wymondham* on the east coast of England, and *Simsbury* from *Simondsbury* in Dorsetshire, see Dexter, pp. 432–3. The name of *Willington* in Connecticut was derived from a village in Somersetshire, preserved in its more official form in the title of the Duke of Wellington. There is also a *Willington* in South Carolina. Of course the popular pronunciations were not always the surviving forms of the names. Thus *Chelmsford*, in Massachusetts, was spelled, and doubtless at the time pronounced Chamesford, in the *Groton Records*, p. 117 (1697), and Jamestown in its first syllable was often spelled and pronounced *Jeames-*. Both of these popular forms have now disappeared.

Dutch proper names which have been transformed into something that looks like English are found at various places in New York and New Jersey. Thus Dutch *Zandt Hoek, Vlacht Bos* and *Helle Gat* have become *Sandy Hook, Flatbush,* and *Hell Gate.* Likewise *Beeren's Island* has become *Barren Island, Deutel Bay* has become *Turtle Bay,* and *Conyer's Island* has become *Coney Island,* Doyle, *English Colonies,* V, 24. The process of obscuration is well illustrated by a Dutch place name in lower New York. *Coenties Slip* was so named because the land in the vicinity was the property of Conraet Ten Eyck, nicknamed Coentje, or with *i* for *j*, Coentie. "This name, pronounced Coonty, was next called Coonchy, then Quinchy, and is now often called by dock-men, Quincey," Alice Morse Earle, "The Stadt Huys of New Amsterdam," in *Historic New York,* I, 45. Many other Dutch names underwent similar changes. *Brooklyn* is from *Breuckelen,* near Utrecht, and *Wallabout* in Brooklyn also illustrates the workings of popular etymology. Brooklyn in Connecticut is an entirely separate word, being originally *Brook-line,* like the town in Massachusetts, Dexter, p. 438. Stone Arabia, in Montgomery County, New York, is conjectured by Carpenter, p. 66, to be an anglicization of Dutch *steenraapje,* the first element of which means *stone,* the second element, *turnipfield.* Direct evidence is lacking, however, and the name Arabia Petrea, which would have been familiar to students of the Bible, suggests at least the possibility of a different explanation. Many Dutch names which were formerly current have now passed out of use. Thus Maiden Lane was formerly *Smit's V'lei,* or *Smith's Valley,* from a blacksmith's shop that stood there. This was shortened into *The V'lei,* and then corrupted into *Fly.* The first public market sheds were erected in New York at this place and were called *The Fly Market,* Hill and Waring, "Old Wells and Water Courses of the Island of Manhattan," in *Historic New York,* I, 202. The name persisted well into the nineteenth century, and Halleck, *Poems,* p. 271, says

> "No thief in Fly-Market, just caught in a robbery,
> Could raise such a clatter of blackguards and boys."

The word was used as an English word as early as 1675, for in *North and South Hempstead Town Records*, I, 301, we read of "the Lott of John Ellisons which Lys in the fly." It is given by Carpenter, p. 62, in the forms *vly, fly, vley, vlei, vlaie*, a swamp, a marsh, shallow pond, from Dutch, *vallei*, valley, but with no citations. A complete study of Dutch local terminology is much to be desired.

French names are found widely distributed throughout the States, though naturally they are more frequent in the neighborhood of older French settlements than elsewhere. They are found along the border between Canada and the United States, in Old Kaskaskia, and very abundantly in Louisiana. The obscurations which many of them have undergone are of the kind which would naturally affect all foreign words. Thus Bois Blanc, an island near Detroit, has become *Bob Low*, and *Terre Haute* in Indiana becomes Anglicized into ['tɛrɪhʌt] or ['tɛrə hʌt]; *Mount Desert* in Maine is pronounced like the English word *desert*, or with educated speakers who are aware of the French association of the name, it may retain a slight French quality and be pronounced with stress on the final syllable, like *dessert*. Translation and popular etymology sometimes work together to produce strange modifications of foreign names. Thus *Burnt Coat*, a name traditional on Swan's Island, Maine, is French *Côte Brulé*, or *Burnt Coast*. The word *brulé* with the Anglicized pronunciation *brooly* is still commonly current in Canada and on the border in the sense of a grassy meadow in the woods, these meadows having been made by the Indians who burnt them over regularly to keep the forest from crowding out the grass and blueberry bushes.

In passing it may be noted that a river and place in Oregon bearing the name *Willamette* do not, as the appearance of the name indicates, owe their name to a French model. The word is stressed on the second and not on the third syllable and is said to be of Indian origin, see Gannett, p. 325. In spelling, however, it seems to have come under the influence of French. The United States Geographic Board, Fourth Report, p. 282, passed upon this name, establishing *Willamette* as the authorized form and rejecting the variants *Ouallamet, Wahlahmath, Williamette*. No tears need be shed over the disappearance of the last of the variants, but one may regret that the first two must be rejected. The spelling *ou* is of course merely the traditional French spelling for *w* in Indian names. The Board in authorizing Willamette and rejecting the other forms of the name was no doubt following its general principle of accepting established local custom, when custom was established, even if the custom was contrary to etymology. Following this principle, the Board has refrained from restoring *Pysht,* village and river in Washington, to *Pysche,* rejecting also the variants *Fish, Pisht,* and *Pyscht;* or *Ozan* in Arkansas to *Aux ânes;* or *Low Freight* to *L'eau frais.* The principle is sound, though one may regret the loss of the historical forms of the names. The character of a name is not to be determined by its etymological origin, however, but by the form which it takes in actual use.

This process of obscuration which has been illustrated in place names is exemplified still more abundantly in personal names. If familiarity does not breed contempt in the use of personal names, it certainly leads to the neglect of niceties of pronunciation which formal style would more fully preserve. Here again British family names, like *Cholmondeley* [ˈtʃʌmlɪ], *Marjoribanks* [ˈmɑːtʃˋbæŋks], etc., have often been cited to arouse an American smile over the grotesque contrast between the aural and the visual forms of the names. Manifestly such a pronunciation as Chumley for Cholmondeley could only become established in a community use of the name on a level in which the spoken associations of language were much more numerous and important than the printed or written associations. If one has never signed one's name and has no notions how it should appear to the eye, one is not likely to be much troubled by any pronunciation of it, or to make any effort to restrain changes in the pronunciation of it. As one becomes more learned, however, one may appeal to tradition to establish the historical form of one's name, or what is more commonly the case, having arrived at a literary stage of culture, one merely gives literary form to one's name in such fashion as will echo the auditory form which the name has at that moment. These processes are abundantly illustrated in the records of American personal names. In the *Plymouth Records*, I, 18, occurs the name *Southwood*, though the usual spelling of the name of the person here referred to is *Southworth:* but the editor of these records remarks, p. xi, that "the pronunciation of Southworth at the present day as a Christian name is almost always in accordance with the Southwood spelling, which disappeared from the records at a very early date." In these records one also finds the name *Murdock* written *Murdow, Mordow, Murdo*, see I, 201. The name *Shurtleff* is *Shirtley*, I, 33, and *Shurtley*, I, 178. For *Brinsmead*, the form *Brinsme* occurs, I, 77, and so frequently elsewhere that there can be no doubt that the final consonant was ordinarily omitted in conversational use in the seventeenth century. The spelling *Holums* for *Holmes*, I, 20, indicates clearly enough a dissyllabic pronunciation of the name. In the *Dedham Records, Everett* and *Prescott* are often spelled *Euered* and *Prescod*, the final consonant being voiced in a relaxed pronunciation.

The proper name which now commonly appears in the forms *Briscoe, Briscow, Bristow*, had a great variety of spellings in the *Watertown Records*, all showing that the *r* was not pronounced, e.g. *Bisco*, p. 12 (1647), and also *Biscoo, Bysco, Bisko*, and occasionally with *r*, as in *Brysko*, p. 21 (1650). In the same records *Parson* appears as *Passen*, p. 19 (1649), and also as *Passam, Passon*. For *Parkhurst* one finds *Parkhust*, p. 44 (1655), and *Parkis*, p. 136 (1678). For *Barsham* occurs *Bassum*, p. 45 (1655), also *Barsum, Bersham*. For *Barnard* occurs *Barnad*, p. 87 (1666), and so often. Final consonants are frequently omitted in these records, as in *Arnall*, p. 11 (1647), and often, for *Arnold; Line*, p. 77 (1663), for *Lynde?; Hollon*, p. 113 (1672), for *Holland; Garfill*, p. 128 (1676), and often, for *Garfield; Townsin*, p. 118 (1673), for *Townsend*. For *Pickering* occurs the spelling *Pickram*, p. 79 (1663). The development of *Pickering* into *Pickram*, which probably is the same name as *Pegram*, a present Virginian family name and current also in other communities, would be similar to that which gives *grogram* from *gros grain*, and *megrim* from *migraine*. The pronunciation *Pickerin* would of course be common in colloquial use. The change of a final *n* to *m* is also illustrated in the common popular pronunciation of *rosin* as *rozum*, as in R. M. Johnston's *Mr. Billingslea*, p. 136 and elsewhere, where the word is spelled *rawsom*.

For *Pendleton*, *Pembleton* occurs in the Watertown Records, p. 1 (1634), and though no example of this change has been observed, the form *Pemberton* is probably a still further modification of *Pembleton*. In the Watertown Records one finds a great variety of spellings for *Chenery*, e.g., *Ginnery*, *Ginnrie*, *Gennry*, and others recorded in the index to these records. For *Simon*, a form with final *t*, *Simont*, occurs, p. 22 (1651), and often. A final *t* is added after *f* in *proft* for proof, p. 83 (1664), in these records by a similar phonetic process.

In the *Norwalk Records* occur a number of interesting variants of proper names. For *St. John* occurs *Sention*, p. 17 (1655), *Senchion*, p. 20 (1656), and *Sension*, p. 55 (1668). Undoubtedly the name was pronounced at this time as if written Senchion. This pronunciation persists as the name of a street in Norwalk. Longstreet, *Georgia Scenes*, p. 85, says that the name St. John "was always pronounced 'Sinjin' by the common people" about the year 1790 in Georgia. The pronunciation of this name in America has now been completely normalized by the spelling, though the older popular pronunciation still persists in England. Similar to this word is the name *St. Clair*, now widely distributed in the form *Sinclair*, and current in the Kentucky mountains in a further corruption giving *Slinker*. In the *Norwalk Records* occurs also *Seamer*, p. 17 (1655), for *Seymour; Raiment*, p. 18 (1655), for *Raymond; Rithard*, p. 32 (1650), and so often, for *Richard; Haite*, p. 45 (1655), for *Hoyt; Beldin*, p. 86 (1694), and also often *Belden*, for *Belding; Griggorie*, p. 17 (1655), and often for *Gregory*. *Grenwich* is given as *Grenwig*, p. 58 (1670), meaning ['grɛn'wɪdʒ], but the name of the place is now uniformly ['griːn'wɪtʃ]. The place now known as *Rowayton* [ro'eːtən] is spelled *Rowerton*, p. 93 (697).

A proper name now spelled *Hough* is sometimes pronounced as though spelled *Hoff* and sometimes as though spelled *Howe*. Both pronunciations are historical and are recorded in early spellings.

Thus in the *New Haven Records*, p. 33 (1639), the name is spelled both *Hoff* and *Hough*. In the *Hanover Records*, p. 151 (1797), it is spelled *Houghf*. A word of parallel phonetic form is the poetic and archaic *enow*, a variant of the standard *enough*. In the *New Haven Records*, p. 97 (1643), one finds *Wintrop* for *Winthrop*, the exchange of [t] for [θ] being not uncommon in the seventeenth century. The given name *Arthur* is *Arter* in the *Huntington Records*, p. 206.

Another name formerly spelled in a variety of ways which have now come to be regarded as altogether different names is the name variously spelled as *Hobart*, *Huburt*, *Hubord*, *Hubbard*, and other forms to be found in the index of the *Groton Records*. So also one finds in the *Huntington Records*, *Ingersoll*, *Inkersol*, *Inkerson* as variants of the name now most commonly *Ingersoll*. In these records one also finds *Wickes*, *Weeks*, *Weicks* and similar variant spellings for the name which has now settled down into two names, *Wickes* and *Weeks*. The same variants in spelling occur in the *North and South Hempstead Records*. In the *Huntington Records*, *Conklin* and *Conkling* are used interchangeably, *Sticklen*, *Sticklan* and *Strickland*, *Kecham* and *Kicham*, for numerous examples of all of which, consult the index to the records. Is the name, *Kecham*, *Kicham* merely a variant form of Kitchen, like Pickering, Pickerin becoming *Pickram*, *Pegram*?

In the *North and South Hempstead Records* a large number of old forms of proper names are recorded. For *Valentine* occurs *Vallingtyne*, I, 16 (1657), and elsewhere often; a rounded form of the vowel, spelled *Vol—*, also occurs, see index, an example of which in London English of the latter fifteenth century is cited by Wyld, *History of Modern Colloquial English*, p. 94. The proper name *Weeks*, *Wickes* is variously spelled, and the common noun also appears as *weeckes*, I, 22 (1657), or *weaike*, I, 23 (1657), or *weacke*, I, 24 (1657). *Strickline* appears as *Stickline*, I, 21 (1657), and *Stickling*, I, 22 (1657). *Brutnall* appears often as *Brudnell*, I, 24 (1657), or *Brudnill*, I, 53 (1658). *Chadderton* appears as *Charterton*, I, 18 (1657), and *Carterton*, I, 25 (1657). The name De Mott occurs in a curious variety of forms, *Dement*, *Dremant*, *Demont* and *Demynt*, see index under De Mott.

The name *Scadding* appears as *Scadden, Scaddin,* and various other similar spellings, but also as *Schadden,* I, 54 (1658), where the *sch* is merely a Dutch spelling for *sc, sk,* as in *Schuylkill,* etc. So also the name *Scott* appears as *Schott,* I, 63 (1658). For *Champion* various spellings occur, *Champin, Champean, Champien,* and once *Chamin,* I, 171 (1665), and it is probable that these names indicate a pronunciation with stress on the last syllable [tʃæm'piːn], which persists in popular speech as a pronunciation for the common noun *champion.* The ending *-ing* appears in the weakened form in a great many names, e.g., *Seryin, Serrin,* etc., for *Searing; Genen, Jennens,* etc., for *Jennings; Burlin* for *Burling, Lattin* for *Latting* (or is this the reverse process?), *Linenton* for *Linnington,* etc. In 1666 Mrs. Washburn sold to Rope Warnull, I, 227, a bay horse; Rope Warnull seems to be of the same family as one who signed himself *Wandell* in a document of 1659, and the pronunciation of this name to which the spelling *Warnull* points, is simply ['wɑːnəl]. As for the given name Rope one wonders whether the editor has not misread this for *Rafe,* a form of *Ralph* which occurs, I, 334 (1674), and in the spelling *Reaph,* I, 241 (1667). The family name *Rope* or *Ropes* does not occur in these records. The spelling *Rafe* appears a number of times in the records, and *Rafe Shepherd* figures in the *Dedham Records,* III, 22 (1636). In *Hempstead Records,* I, 241 (1667), *Reaph Hall* is mentioned and I, 334 (1674), occurs the name *Rafe Keler.* In these records, I, 93 (1660), *Walter* is spelled *Water,* a form of Walter from which the abbreviation *Wat* would be derived. The name of *Nathan Birdsall* appears in the possessive form as *Berdshals, North and South Hempstead Records,* I, 205 (1679), and this spelling makes it probable that Benjamin Berchsell and Stephen Birchsell were members of the same family. The change of *s* to *sh* is also illustrated in *Mashinger,* I, 192 (1665), a name more commonly spelled *Messenger.* In other words the change occurs in *witneshth,* I, 167 (1665), *wittnesh,* I, 172 (1665), for witnesseth, witness, in *parshall,* I, 249 (1668), for *parcel,* a general sound change discussed in the chapter on pronunciation under [s]. The name *Cornwall* appears commonly either in this form or as *Cornwell,* but also as *Cornell,* the several forms sometimes being written in the same page, as on I, 214 (1665). The full form of a name spelled *Minthorne* also appears as *Minttorne* or *Mentorne*, from which it would be but a short step to the commonly current form *Minturn*. The name *Ogden* is written *Ocktdin*, I, 176 (1665), though on the same page it is also written *Ogden*. On p. 263 (1669), one finds *Osbond* and *Osbon* for the name more conventionally spelled *Osborn* or *Osburn*. When two spellings like these stand side by side, obviously the less formal spelling is more significant for pronunciation than the official spelling. Many other interesting variants of proper names could be cited from these records, but perhaps enough have been mentioned to show that a genealogist must also be a linguist and phonetician.

Most of the examples cited above have been taken from New England town records, but similar modifications of proper names took place in other regions. Green, *Word Book*, pp. 13–16, gives a long list of Virginia names spelled one way and pronounced another. Among these may be noted *Armistead*, pronounced *Umsted*, *Boswell* pronounced *Bosell*, *Boulward* pronounced *Boler*, *Burwell* pronounced *Burel*, *Callowhill* pronounced *Carroll*, *Crenshaw* pronounced *Granger*, *Gawin* pronounced *Goin*, *Higginson* pronounced *Hickersom*, *Jenkins* pronounced *Jinkins*, *Norsworthy* pronounced *Nazary*, *Sinclair* pronounced *Sinkler*, *Wyatt* pronounced *Wait*, and many others.

A few given names may be noted as they are given in the *North and South Hempstead Records*. For *Robert* occurs *Robord*, I, 16 (1657), and frequently. For *Henry* a trisyllabic pronunciation was popular, as in the spelling *Hinery*, I, 18 (1657), and often. For *Benjamin* the spelling *Beniamyne*, I, 21 (1657), indicates a final syllable with a long vowel. For *James*, *Jeames* is common. For *Samuel* the spelling *Samivell*, I, 21 (1657), I, 31 (1658), indicates a pronunciation which later generations were to know only as a humorous one. The name is spelled *Samiwell* in the *Groton Records*, p. 70 (1680), and so often. *Daniel* is very frequently *Dannel* throughout the seventeenth and eighteenth centuries. *Walter* in the form *Water*, *North and South Hempstead Records*, I, 93 (1660), was of course the necessary antecedent to the abbreviation *Wat*. *Rafe* for *Ralph* has already been mentioned; the given names *Repe*, I, 183, and *Rope*, I, 227, in these records one is inclined to take as misreadings of the manuscript for Rafe. A strange name is that of *After Albertus*, mentioned twice, I, 118 (1659), and I, 453 (1683).

The word *goody* as a title of address, said to survive in America only as applied to a caretaker in Harvard dormitories, is used not infrequently in the records, as when, in 1682, the town of Hempstead voted, I, 411, "that the towne will satisfie the docter coper for the cuer he did for gooddy bats of our town which is thre pound and har diat while she was at oyster bay which is five and thirty shilins." The corresponding *goodman* is also used, though neither is general, and apparently the terms were not considered highly honorable in the usage of the community, perhaps connoting age and indigence. The meaning of forms of address in general during the American colonial period call for much more detailed study than they have received. It is not quite clear on what grounds the title *Master*, or *Mr.*, *Mistress* or *Mrs.* was given to some persons and withheld from others in the early town records. Both were evidently titles of distinction, since they were not freely applied. Very commonly a descriptive appellation is put down after a man's name, and when this appellation is flax-dresser, or cordwainer, or carpenter, or mariner, or some similar trade name, its meaning is clear. Some uncertainty attaches, however, to the names for the most common of the occupations of colonial America, that of tilling the land. The term *yeoman* is frequently found in town records down into the eighteenth century. Yet beside it will also be found the terms *planter* and *farmer*, the three differentiated in a way which perhaps was vitally important in the social communities in which the term passes current but which now escapes us.

The distinction between *Miss* and *Mrs.* was formerly not so clearly established as it now is. In the *Hanover Records*, p. 66 (1786), and elsewhere several times a widow is referred to as *Miss Cleavland*, though she is usually designated as *Mrs. Cleavland*, as at p. 48 (1785). Noah Webster, writing in 1790, found it necessary to warn his fellow

Americans that "the use of Miss for Mistress in this country is a gross impropriety. The word Mistress (or Madam to an old lady) should always be applied to a married lady, and Miss to one who has never been married," see Thornton, under *Miss*. Cooper, *Pioneers*, Chap. X, satirizes this use in the character of Remarkable Pettibone, a transplanted New England woman in Central New York, who would call all unmarried women only by their first names, even the daughter of the magnificent Marmaduke Temple. For this Marmaduke rebukes her sternly. "Do tell!" exclaimed Remarkable, a little aghast, "well, who ever heerd of a young woman's being called Miss? If the Judge had a wife now, I shouldn't think of calling her anything but Miss Temple; but——" "Having nothing but a daughter, you will observe that style to her, if you please, in future," interrupted Marmaduke. But the custom was not merely a down-east peculiarity. Thornton gives an example from Georgia, 1840, and *Miss* for *Mrs.*, or in the South *Miz* for *Mrs.*, can still be heard in popular English almost anywhere.

Somewhat similar to these popular obscurations of native names are those modifications which foreign personal names are likely to undergo when they pass current in American communities. In these circumstances, however, the social disconnection between foreigner and native is greater than it is among the members of an unmixed community, and occasion is thus offered for the operation of more thoroughgoing changes and also for the exercise of conscious intention in bringing about change in a way which would scarcely arise in a homogeneous native community. Before the period of immigration in the nineteenth century, the chief mixed communities in the country were those made up of French and English elements, of Dutch and English in the Central States, of German and English in Central New York, in Pennsylvania, Virginia, and North and South Carolina. Interesting studies could and should be made of the family and given names which passed current in these several groups. It is true that these studies would be concerned primarily with what has happened to French and German and Dutch names. But in fact most of these older foreign names no longer seem foreign. They have been as thoroughly incorporated into the American consciousness as were the numerous French names which entered English after the Norman Conquest. Even the persons who bear the names, unless they are genealogists or etymologists, often cannot tell, after a period of several generations, whether their names are native or foreign. Could one guess, for example, that Krehbiel and Graybill are the same name, that Kühle and Keeley are the same, Stehli and Staley, Lehn and Lane, Vögelin and Fagley, and dozens of others which have undergone a sea change, perhaps slight in form but great in social significance.

In general, there are three ways, as is pointed out by Kuhns, *German and Swiss Settlements of Colonial Pennsylvania*, p. 242, in which these foreign names may change. For one, they may be merely translated, as when *Lebengut* becomes *Livingood*, *Zimmermann* becomes *Carpenter*, *Fuchs* becomes *Fox*, *Schmidt* becomes *Smith*. Sometimes only part of a name may be translated, as in *Wannemacher* becoming *Wanamaker*. The second kind of change is that which may be described as transliteration. This change may not be very great so far as the sound of the name is concerned, but the difference in the appeal to the eye apparently connotes a very great difference in feeling with respect to the name. Thus *Rice* and *Reis* would be pronounced alike, but they look different and are felt to be different. The same applies to *Staley* and *Stehli*, *Amwake* and *Amweg*, *Coon* and *Kuhn*, *Keeney* and *Kuehne*, *Keeley* and *Kuehle*, *Miller* and *Mueller*, and many similar names. A third kind of change is that in which a general similarity to an English name tends to bring the foreign name to the same form as the English by analogical imitation. Examples of this cited by Kuhns, p. 246, are *Roesch* becoming *Rush*, *Roth* becoming *Rhoades*, *Reichert* becoming *Richards*. Many other examples are given by Kuhns, *Studies in Pennsylvania German Family Names*, *Americana Germanica*, IV, 299–341 (1902).

The examples cited above have all been taken from Pennsylvania German, but various other communities would offer many similar illustrations. Dutch, French and Flemish names have been studied by Dunlap, *A Tragedy of Surnames,* in *Dialect Notes,* IV, 7–8, as they now appear in a rural region of Southern Kentucky. Here we find that *Guizot* has become *Cossett, Gossett, Cozart,* and *Cozatt; Vermilyea* has become *Vermillion; Petit* has become *Poteet; Des Champs* is *Scomp, De La Haye* is *Dillehay.* Examples of Teutonic names are *Van Huys* becoming *Vannice, Zinkern* becoming *Sinkhorn, Van Arsdale* becoming *Vanarsdell, Vanasdell, Vanarsdall, Vanarsdill, Vannersdale,* and *Wittnacht* becoming *Whiteneck.* The stages through which French *Petit* passed until it reached American *Poteet* are given by Joel Chandler Harris, *Mingo* (1884), p. 40. The name started, declares Harris, with the landing of Gérard Petit on the coast of South Carolina. But Gérard soon migrated to the mountains of north Georgia, where his name became Jerd Poteet. "He made such protest as he might. He brought his patriotism to bear upon the emergency, and named his eldest son Huguenin Petit. How long this contest between hospitality on the one hand and family pride and patriotism on the other was kept up, it is unnecessary to inquire. It is enough to say that the Huguenin of one generation left Hugue Poteet as his son and heir; Hugue left Hague, and this Hague, or a succeeding one, by some mysterious development of fate, left Teague Poteet." Meanwhile members of the family had been carried along by a stream of migration into Alabama, where some of the *Petits* became *Pettys* and *Pettises.*

Two Frenchmen, Pierre Lacroix and Napoleon B. Bouchard, settled in Iowa about 1850, Quick, *Vandemark's Folly,* p. 371, and the American natives "called the one Pete Lackwire and the other Poly Busher. They were the only French people who came into the township." The changes here illustrated took place in the main on distinctly popular levels of speech, with very little or no interference on the part of the persons to whom the names intimately belonged. Manifestly, however, when two social groups, one relatively high, the other relatively low, dwell in more or less harmony, the matter of personal names is likely to occasion some conscious reflection, some heartburning, and some more or less ingenious manipulation. The change of *Klein* to *Small* or *Little* could scarcely take place without some assistance on the part of the persons who possessed the name. Attempts to Americanize names are continually taking place in polyglot communities, and a useful study might be made of all cases of this kind which have come up for legal decision. Frequently the change is merely for convenience to reduce a long name to a shorter form, as when the Finn drops off an *-ainen* ending, or a Russian amputates a *-wich* or a *-witz*. Difficult sound combinations are also frequently simplified, especially in Polish and Slavonic names. Or again, the name may be altered to evade too intimate association with a contemned social order, as when the Jewish *Ginsburg* becomes the more distinguished *Gainsburgh*, perhaps preparatory to a further flight into *Gainsborough*, or *Grünthal* becomes *Gruntle*, or *Steinfeld* becomes *Stonefield*. Sometimes distinction is made to reside merely in the change of quality in a sound, as when the frequent ending *-stein* is pronounced *-steen*, or *Reis* becomes not simply *Rice*, but *Rees*, *Reece*, *Reese*. The study of similar Jewish proper names is carried further by Mencken, pp. 268–300. The question whether one shall approve or disapprove personal interference with the forms of proper names is complicated by the mingling of social with linguistic considerations. In the main, the linguist could scarcely look with favor upon individual tampering with elements in the language which are the common social possession of all. Proper names, however, are in a peculiar sense the possession of the persons who must bear them from their cradles to their graves. No one is more intimately concerned in the form of a proper name than the person whom it designates. It would seem, therefore, that the owner of a name might be thought to have peculiar privileges with respect to it, even perhaps to the extent of making himself an absurdity by foolishly altering it. If on the other hand an alteration results in a positive gain, in social comfort, in social sympathy and intelligibility, it is difficult to see how such a change can be regarded otherwise than as commendable.

A modification of traditional pronunciation which in certain instances has taken on conscious aristocratic coloring is the stressing of the final syllable in dissyllabic names which ordinarily and historically should have initial stress. A good example of this is *Littell*, a form of *Little*. The pronunciation *Littell* has now been so long established in the language that it can scarcely be said to be an affectation, and in origin it is not probable that it was an affectation at all. It probably arose through a fairly heavy stressing of the final syllable in *little*, i.e. [ˈlɪˎtɛl] becoming [lɪˈtɛl]. One may still hear a similar pronunciation in New England, *towel*, *Lowell*, for example, being pronounced [ˈtaʊˎɛl], [ˈloːˎɛl]. And it should not be forgotten that if *Littell* is an occasionally surviving dialectal pronunciation of *little*, the ordinary standard pronunciation is much more frequently represented in the proper name *Little*. Many early spellings make this explanation of the origin of proper names with stress on the second syllable seem altogether probable. Thus in the *Southold Records* one of the names occurring most frequently is *Tuthill*. Only a fairly heavy stress on the second element of this name could prevent it from becoming *Tuttle*, a form which it no doubt often took. So also we find in the records the name *Dibell*, II, 431 (1707), *Debell*, II, 219 (1710), which perhaps may look more familiar in the form *Dibble*. One finds also *Terrell*, besides *Turril*, *Turrel*, II, 164 (1699), and II, 93 (1700), *Fawsett*. In the *Hempstead Records*, the name of *Robert Beadle* appears in a variety of forms, such as *robord beadille*, I, 16 (1657), *robord Bedell*, I, 19 (1657). In these records, I, 366 (1670) we find a reference to *Mr. oDle*, who is elsewhere more recognizably mentioned as *Mr. Odell*, I, 16 (1659). The author has found no evidence to indicate that *Odell* is a corruption of *Woodhull*, as it is frequently said to be. Perhaps it is the same as *Udall* which in turn is a corruption of *Uvedale*. One cannot be quite sure how heavy a stress names like *Odell*, *Bedell*, *Dibell*, etc. had in the seventeenth century. It is quite probable that pronunciations with stress on the first or on the second syllable existed side by side, perhaps at the same time and in the same community. As spelling and social custom in these respects became more conventionally established, however, the names probably separated into what were felt to be two quite distinct names, for example, *Beadle* and *Bedell*, *Dibble* and *Dibell*, or *Dobell*. So far as the writer is aware, the pronunciation *Odell* is the only one that survives for that name, but a pronunciation with stress on the first syllable is remembered historically in some families bearing the name. Spelling undoubtedly has greatly assisted the tendency towards heavy stressing of the final syllable when it ended in two consonants, as now in *Birrell,* often pronounced with final stress in America, but with initial stress in England. So also *Burnett* is more likely to have final stress than *Burnet*, *Bennett* than *Bennet*, *Gillett* than *Gillet*. In *Furness* a stress on the final syllable may differentiate the word from *furnace*, and in *Bottome* from *bottom*. *In Cornell, Purcell, Purnell* the same tendency would be present as in *Birrell*. In *Farrar*, *Gerard*, *Millard* and many similar names with unexpected stress on the second syllable a certain amount of conscious direction has probably been present.

Fashion has changed also in the matter of the number of given names which a well-provided person ought to have. Nowadays practically all persons in America have two given names. In a total of six hundred names taken distributively from four different letters of *Who's Who in America*, 1920, 80+ per cent have two given names, 17+ per cent have only one given name, and 2+ per cent carry three or more names before their family names. In the last group, however, a number are married women who thus preserve their maiden names after marriage. The proportions according to British custom are different, but probably not as widely different as one would expect. In the British *Who's Who*, 1920, excluding members of the nobility who commonly have numerous names, and excluding also foreigners, but otherwise covering a body of detail equivalent to that examined in *Who's Who in America*, 63+ per cent have two given names, 22+ per cent have one given name, and 13+ per cent have three or more given names, though rarely more than three. Of course, no private citizen among the names examined can equal the present Prince of Wales, whose names in full are Edward Albert Christian George Andrew Patrick David.

All this wealth of display in personal terminology contrasts sharply with the simplicity of an earlier day. Throughout the seventeenth and eighteenth centuries it was extremely rare for a person to bear more than one given name. Among the early American presidents, John Quincy Adams obviously acquired his middle name to distinguish him from the second president, but otherwise the early presidents were all commonly designated with only one name. Bowditch, *Suffolk Surnames*, p. 11, quotes from *Britaine's Remaines*, of the date 1614, the remark that "two Christian names are rare in England: and I only remember now his majesty, who was named Charles James; as the prince, his sonne, Henry Frederic; and among private men, Thomas Maria Wingfield and Sir Thomas Posthumus Hobby." But Maria and Posthumus as names of men are manifestly freakish, as the giving of two names at this time would be in any case. In the colonial records in America a single Christian name is universal in communities of English origin. In the Hempstead *Records*, I, 410 (1682), the two names of Matthias Johnson Boockout, by their number as well as their character, prove him to have been a Dutchman. The difficulties sometimes occasioned by this custom of giving only one name are well illustrated in the North and South Hempstead *Town Records*, in which the name of John Smith appears very frequently, the Smith family being large in this community and having an unfortunate fondness for the name John. Some relief was afforded by amplifying John into Jonathan, and by adding Junior or Senior to the son's or to the father's name, but these devices were inadequate to care for all the John Smiths. In this pressing difficulty alone, in these records, middle names appear, and one reads of John Nan Smith, John Rock Smith, John Blue Smith. Neither the name Rock nor the name Blue occurs as a family name in these records, and doubtless the common nouns rock and blue were used as proper names through some locally intelligible association. John Nan Smith probably derived his middle name from his mother. He is frequently referred to as John Smith Nan's, and generally some uncertainty seems to have been felt where to place the second given name of a man who was blessed with such an abundance. The particular Nan who may have been the mother of John Nan Smith is not explicitly on record, but not improbably it was that Nan who was sufficiently known in seventeenth-century Hempstead circles to give its name to Mad Nan's Neck.

The time at which the fashion of giving two names became prevalent in America can be determined, though the causes of this change in fashion are not so clear. "From the catalogue of Harvard," says Bowditch, *Suffolk Surnames*, p. 11, "it will be found, that, during more than one hundred years, there were but six graduates who had two Christian names. By the catalogue of 1859–60, it appears, that, of 431 students, 77 have one name, while 354 have two or more. The catalogue of Williams College gives a similar result; viz., of 240 students, 37 have one name, while 203 have two or more." The six persons with two given names mentioned above and their dates are Ammi Ruhamel Corlet, 1670, Brocklebank Samuel Coffin, 1718, Ammi Ruhamel Cutter, 1725, Robert Eliot Gerrish, 1730, William Blair Townsend, 1741, and Edward Augustus Holyoke, 1746. The first three of these seem to have owed their names to something special and perhaps fantastic. Between 1746 and 1859, however, the fashion of giving two names was definitely established. The middle stage of the development may be inferred from the statistics derivable from the catalogue of Bristol College, 1834–5, in Bucks County, Pennsylvania. In this catalogue 99 students are listed, 70 with more than one given name, 29 with only one name. Among the students, the new generation, the fashion by 1834 had overwhelmingly established itself. The list of trustees and professors contains 41 names, of which 22 had only one given name, and 19 had more than one, the older generation thus looking back as one might expect, to the disappearing fashion of an earlier day.

The roll of the presidents of the United States is illustrative of these changes in fashion. The first president to bear two names was the second Adams, and the next was William Henry Harrison. Following Harrison came John Tyler, and after Tyler, James K. Polk, who was inaugurated in 1845. Polk's middle name seems to have been commonly indicated merely by the letter K., as it still is in the traditional way of reciting the list of the presidents. One says John Quincy Adams and William Henry Harrison, but

James K. Polk. This gave rise to the opinion that the K. in this name was not an abbreviation, but merely the letter of the alphabet, mechanically inserted to distinguish one James Polk from another. This statement was made in the Historical Magazine (1857), I, 25, and other examples are given, I, 51, II, 364, III, 91, of middle names which were supposedly merely letters of the alphabet or initials. In actual fact Polk's middle name was Knox and the opinion that K. was merely a letter of the alphabet seemed credible only because middle names were relatively uncommon, and middle initials still less common. British critics of America have not infrequently called attention to initial names in America as one of the evidences of a crude and mechanical social life, like the naming of streets by means of letters of the alphabet or numbers. By origin the custom probably was mechanical, the abbreviated name being intended mainly for the eye and not for the ear. Long use has made of it, however, a familiar spoken practice in the United States, and many persons are known to fame only by the initials of their given names. After James K. Polk, came Taylor, Fillmore, Pearce, Buchanan, Lincoln and Johnson, all with only one given name. The next four, however, Grant, Hayes, Garfield and Arthur, all had two names, the second being customarily indicated only by an initial. Among the remaining presidents only Taft and Harding have made use of a middle name and perhaps one may infer from this fact that preference is again veering in favor of but one given name.

The statistics to be derived from the *Catalogue of the Officers and Graduates of Yale University* present a similar picture in fuller detail. In the years 1702–1720, eighty-eight students were graduated, but none of them had middle names. In the years 1721–1775 the total number of graduates with more than one given name is forty-nine, an average of less than one for each class. Of these forty-nine, thirty-seven have family names for middle names, the others have the ordinary names, John, Samuel, Abraham, Andrew, Henry, etc. Several are Dutch names, like Hendrick Hans Hansen (1742), Peter Van Brugh Livingston (1731), John Cornelius Cuyler (1748), and several must reflect unusual family traditions, like Ammi Ruhamel

Robbins (1760) and Samuel Still Augustus Baker (1772). The statistics for the years 1776–1800 can best be given in tabular form.

Class year	*With middle name*	*Total in the class*
1776	2	33
1777	6	56
1778	1	40
1779	4	34
1780	3	27
1781	3	27
1782	4	26
1783	7	42
1784	6	52
1785	13	70
1786	13	51
1787	6	58
1788	5	34
1789	6	30
1790	8	24
1791	3	27
1792	6	34
1793	10	38
1794	8	22
1795	6	33
1796	6	34
1797	5	37
1798	4	21
1799	6	26
1800	4	36

From 1800 on the number of graduates with middle names increases rapidly, and for the year 1830, of a total of seventy, forty-eight, or 68.5 per cent have middle names. The class of 1900 numbered 316, of which 273, or 86.5 per cent had middle names, and the same proportions hold for later classes. Of the forty-eight with middle names in the class of 1830, seven have middle names like John, William, etc., the middle names of the others are family names. Of the 273 in the class of 1900 with middle names, 70 have middle names like John, William, etc., and 203 have middle names that are the names of families. Of course a general name like John, William, etc., may be in effect a family name, being given to a child to establish or to continue a tradition in relation to some other member of the family.

The reasons for these changes of fashion do not lie on the surface. It is true that Continental Europeans had the custom of giving two or more Christian names long before the English. In Catholic countries this custom reflected the desire to honor several saints at one time, or perhaps to secure their favor. It does not appear, however, that either the English or Americans were under foreign influence when at the end of the eighteenth century and the beginning of the nineteenth century the custom of giving two names became prevalent. In the early records one finds that persons of Dutch origin in America occasionally have two names. In the *Names of Foreigners who took the Oath of Allegiance to the Province and State of Pennsylvania, 1727–1775*, edited by Egle, Harrisburg, 1892, a list of over twenty thousand names, mostly German and Swiss, one again finds a considerable number of persons who had two given names. These however are but echoes of the Continental custom and cannot be shown to have influenced American social conventions. Much more probably the introduction of the custom of giving two names was a part of the general expansion of social activity which characterized the latter eighteenth century and the early nineteenth century. The social world then became larger, more varied, more flamboyant than it had been before. The emergence of new families through increased commercial and political opportunity was one of the striking features of the new life. It is not improbable that the custom of giving two names instead of the simpler village custom of giving only one was a part of this new worldliness, of a new pride of family. To some extent the circle has now been completed, and double names being the almost universal custom, distinction is now sometimes supposed to reside in the older simplicity. But in the early nineteenth century in America, grandiosity was in the air. In *Home as Found*, 1838, Cooper has an American character named Bragg, whom he treats with scant sympathy. This youth called upon a lady, and "when Eve received the card from Pierre and read aloud, with the tone of surprise that the name would be apt to excite in a novice in the art of American nomenclature, the words 'Aristabulus Bragg,' her cousin began to laugh," Chap. I. But Cooper's own preferences seem a little amusing now. For him Pierre was a perfectly good name for an American hero, and his finest gentleman must be feathered with so fine a name as Marmaduke Temple.

Certain elements of playfulness and fancy have entered into the spirit of American nomenclature. A nickname is etymologically an eke-name, that is an also-name or additional name. It is not merely a diminutive, as when John becomes Jack. When Jack becomes Jack the Giant-killer we have the addition of a real nickname. In certain uses the nickname might supplant the real name, and Jack might be called simply Giant-killer. Americans have been particularly fond of giving names of this type, especially to their political heroes. Sometimes the names were affectionate and familiar, as in Old Hickory or the Old Roman for Jackson, Old Rough and Ready or Old Zack for Zachary Taylor, Old Tip for General Harrison, of Tippecanoe fame, Old Abe and Honest Old Abe for Lincoln, Old Buck for Buchanan, Old Chapultepec for General Winfield Scott, see Thornton, II, 622 ff. Names of this kind readily pass into oblivion, and perhaps one needs a note, which Thornton provides, to remind one that the Ashland Dictator, the Sage of Ashland, was Henry Clay, that the Little Giant was Stephen A. Douglas, that the Plumed Knight was James G. Blaine. Research in the campaign literature of earlier days reveals many similar nicknames, for example, those centering about the War of 1812, which have been collected by Albert Matthews, *American Antiquarian Society*, XIX, pp. 23 ff., and it would also emphasize the fact that this fashion seems to have gone the way of torchlight processions and barbecues and the other picturesque features of older political campaigning. Even the tradition of the great Roosevelt, a popular idol if there ever was one, has not crystallized in a popular synonym, and during the past few years Wilson and Harding and Coolidge, the three political figures most prominently before the public eye, have been merely Wilson, Harding, and Coolidge and nothing more.

As eponyms for the American people as a whole various imaginative figures have from time to time remained permanently and universally known, *Brother Jonathan, Uncle Sam,* and the dubious term *Yankee.* The ultimate origin of the name Jonathan in this kind of familiar symbolic application has been commonly supposed to be 2 Samuel, I, 26, in the lamentation of David for Saul and Jonathan: "I am distressed for thee, my brother Jonathan: very pleasant hast thou been unto me: thy love to me was wonderful, passing the love of women." It is assumed that the name Jonathan first passed into rather frequent use as a familiar and friendly term of address between persons. Washington is thus supposed to have addressed Jonathan Trumbull, governor of Connecticut, to whom he frequently applied for advice, as Brother Jonathan. The name then came to be used to designate specifically a New Englander, and finally, like Yankee, a citizen of the United States. The progression here indicated is not improbable, although in this as in most instances of folklore, one cannot point one's finger to a decisive and dramatic moment when the tradition became established. Certainly the name Jonathan was very common in eighteenth-century New England, and Jonathan Postfree, a character in a comedy of 1806, occupies a typical position. Yet perhaps after all too much has been made of the Biblical associations of Jonathan. The obvious fact is that the name Brother Jonathan is a necessary complement to John Bull. Now if one seeks a name to put beside John Bull, would any name suggest itself more readily than Jonathan? The earliest example of Jonathan meaning explicitly a citizen of the United States in the *New English Dictionary* is for the year 1816. The earliest example of Brother Jonathan in this sense in Thornton is for 1815, of Jonathan without the brother is for 1816. The most plausible supposition is that the term Brother Jonathan or Jonathan came into popular use during the period of strong feeling and excitement of the War of 1812, and that Brother Jonathan was created merely as an antagonist to John Bull, the central figure on the stage.

The genealogy of Uncle Sam is involved in as much obscurity as that of Brother Jonathan. It is commonly said that the name was derived from a facetious and familiar manner of alluding to Samuel Wilson, an army contractor and inspector who lived at Troy at the time of the War of 1812. In an admirable article, entitled *Uncle Sam,* in the *Proceedings of the American Antiquarian Society,* New Series, XIX, 21–65, also pp. 250–252 (1908), Albert Matthews has proved as positively as one can hope ever to prove such things, that the name had nothing to do with Samuel Wilson, and that it was merely a jocular, and at first perhaps derisive, expansion of U. S., the abbreviation for United States, which was stamped on articles and supplies for use in the army, that it arose during the War of 1812, and as one would expect, along the Canadian border where the war was most actively fought.

For the name *Yankee,* no conclusive etymology has been discovered, though many have been suggested and have been summarized by Sonneck, pp. 83–95. It is often said to have been derived from Dutch *Jancke,* or *Jankin,* but the chain of evidence is incomplete. The same must be said of the derivation from an Indian pronunciation of the name of the English, generally represented as *Yengeese.* Whatever its origin, the name was already current, as Thornton's citations show, at the beginning of the American Revolution. It meant, as it still does in American use, primarily a native of New England. The meaning has been extended, however, so that it often means merely northern as contrasted with southern. But as the terms northern and southern are not precise but vague geographical terms, so one finds the term Yankee used with varying local significance. No one knows where the West begins, neither does any one know where the North or the South begins. Relative to Richmond, New Yorkers are Yankees, but relative to Hartford, they are not. And if one gets far enough away to reduce in the perspective of distance all American distinctions to insignificance, as the Englishman often succeeds in doing, then Americans of both North and South, of East and West are Yankees. A study of the three score citations illustrating the use of this word which have been collected by Thornton, will show further that the term has not only geographical but also moral significance. A Yankee trick need not necessarily be the act of one who comes from New England, nor are all New Englanders, as one need scarcely add, capable of Yankee tricks.

A term of less extended geographical application than Yankee but not of less fervid emotional content is *Dixie*. Commonly now it is taken to mean the South in general, and is supposed to have some connection with Mason and Dixon's Line. A more probable explanation, see *Century Cyclopedia of Names*, under Dixie, Dixie's Land, is that which derives it from a man named Dixie. In the phrase Dixie's Land, meaning a kind of lost earthly paradise, the name is said to have passed current among the negroes, and gradually to have been accepted generally in southern song and verse as the poetical or affectionate name for that region. Much of the success of the term is obviously due to the stirring melody to which the song Dixie is sung. It is interesting to note that the word did not become widely current until the time of the Civil War, Thornton's first citation being for 1863, and that like other similar terms, it owed its extended use to the passions and excitements of a great national upheaval.

The South is not the only section of the country which rejoices in the possession of a poetical and affectionate name to supplement its literal name. Probably every state in the Union has its second name, always useful in song and oratory, and sometimes popularly familiar. Sometimes the name is derived from a natural feature, as in the pseudonym Granite State for New Hampshire, or Bay State for Massachusetts, or Prairie State for Illinois. Sometimes it is merely an affectionate diminutive, as in Little Rhody, or Kentuck, Old Kentuck, or merely Jersey for New Jersey. Keystone State as applied to Pennsylvania arose from the fact that Pennsylvania was the seventh among the thirteen original colonies, the key-stone of the Union. Perhaps New York may be said to have chosen the name Empire State by right of eminent domain. Its characteristic, or supposedly characteristic, natural product sometimes gives a nickname to a state, as in Palmetto State for South Carolina, Sunflower State for Kansas, Buckeye State for Ohio. A number of second names of states are apparently of zoölogical origin, as in Badger for Wisconsin, Wolverine for Michigan, Sucker for Illinois, Gopher for Minnesota, Hawkeye for Iowa, Buckskin for a Virginian. The explanation of the origins of these names, however, does not lie on the surface. With respect to Badger, Quick, *Vandemark's Folly*, p. 105, remarks that it came from a mining region, "where lead had been dug for many years, and where the men lived who dug the holes and were called Badgers, thus giving the people of Wisconsin their nickname, as distinguished from the Illinois people, who came up the rivers to work in the spring, and went back in the fall, and were therefore named after a migratory fish and called Suckers." Some of these names have now only an historical interest and have passed out of popular use. Many of them seem to have arisen during the time of western expansion in the middle decades of the nineteenth century, and they were thus a part of the general picturesque and humorous turmoil of that period. A Kentuckian today would not appropriately be called a Corn Cracker or a Red Horse, or a Missourian a Puke. The Hoosiers of Indiana, however, have retained their name and made it a badge of distinction. Despite much ingenious speculation, this name still defies precise explanation. Thornton's earliest example is for 1833, when it appears full fledged, doubtless having come into general use during the western migration of that period. It is probably an old British dialectal word which has received special applications in America, see *Publications of the Indiana Historical Society*, Vol. IV, No. 2, and the *Indiana Quarterly Magazine of History* for June, 1911.

The names of some states recall interesting chapters in American history. Thus Kentucky, which possesses an unusual share of nicknames, is called the Dark and Bloody Ground, because within that state many tribal hostilities among northern and southern American Indians were fought out. Texas is the Lone Star State still in spite of the fact that she has been annexed to the other states. Virginia has been the Mother of Presidents, though this term also is probably doomed since it seems to take away honor from Ohio. Another name for Virginia is the Old Dominion. As applied to Virginia, the word dominion is a survival from an earlier and more general use. In Canada the name Dominion of Canada is of recent origin, the country having been thus legally named and constructed out of several provinces by an act of 1867. During the colonial period of American history, however, the term dominion passed generally current. "Dominion in New England," says Peters, *General History of Connecticut*, p. 41, note, "signifies a sovereign, independent state, uncontrollable by any other earthly power." Peters speaks of the dominion of New Haven, of Hartford, etc., and the Old Dominion for Virginia would apparently thus be merely an affectionate appropriation of a general and now archaic term for special uses.

Various other geographical terms have acquired a richer emotional significance than the official names of the places in these regions convey. Thus The East and The West, The North and The South mean vastly more than directions on a map. The Middle West and The Far West raise visions, the one perhaps of comfort, the other of romance. Down East to the average American probably connotes doughnuts and pie and farmyard drama, and similar idyllic visions. The Western Reserve of Ohio and the Blue Grass of Kentucky define minor but important distinctions in the life of the Middle West. In Virginia, Tidewater Virginia, The Valley of Virginia, and Piedmont Virginia are terms fraught with the deepest social, even though local significance. Of broader meaning in the South is the term The Cotton Belt. The Coast, of course, means the Pacific coast. The Shore means the Atlantic littoral. This sort of terminology could be followed far into the finest minutiae of the intimate vocabulary of localities. Every town or community has its West Sides and East Sides, its North Ends and South Ends, its Upper Parishes and its Lower Parishes, its Heights or its Flats, words which to the local sense often convey a meaning not on the surface and in fact beyond the power of mere words to express.

Like the States, American cities also cultivate poetic and oratorical second designations—or sometimes have such designations thrust upon them. Thus Boston is in name at least The Hub of the Universe. New York is Gotham, or preëminently The Metropolis, though this latter name is likely to be assumed by any city which is larger than some other city in the vicinity. Philadelphia is the City of Brotherly Love or the Quaker City. Chicago is the Windy City. Cincinnati is the Queen City of the West, though in the middle decades of the nineteenth century, before Chicago took this particular kind of distinction away from it, the city was also known as Porkopolis. Cleveland is the Forest City. Washington is the City of Magnificent Distances, Baltimore is the City of Monuments, or the Monumental City, a designation cheaply won by the fact that the Washington Monument in Baltimore was one of the first to be erected in America. To exhaust this list would be practically to make a catalogue of all village, town and city names in the United States, and for the beginnings of such a catalogue one may consult the list in the World Almanac. A self-respecting, progressive American town feels it must have its poetic name, and also its slogan, before it is adequately equipped for rivalry with its neighboring towns. It is all a part of "boosting" the town, live American towns being constantly in a state of being built and rebuilt, and all live citizens being very active participants in this process, in the building of names as well as avenues and factories.

At the conclusion of the preceding chapter, attention was called to the need for a comprehensive dictionary of American English. Two further desiderata now suggest themselves. The work of providing gazetteers for the United States has scarcely begun. Occasional local studies have been made, but many more are needed, all looking towards a final and comprehensive geographical dictionary. The second need is for a dictionary of proper names. Genealogists have entered this field scatteringly, but the great body of the material remains hidden and untouched.

LITERARY DIALECTS

Literary dialects are popular dialects which have been employed as forms of literary expression. The relations of literary dialects to "real" dialects are not easily explicable, mainly because "real" dialects themselves are elusive and hard to define. Literary dialects, on the other hand, depend for their success upon being positive and readily recognizable.

Literature written in dialect has been present at all times among highly civilized peoples, but probably more abundant when social life has been variegated and social standards still in process of formation than when the community life of a people has been established by long tradition. This may account for the fact that dialect literature has been, during the past one hundred years, an exceptionally favored form of literary composition in America. The contrast between a desiderated refined literary style and an actually present and respected native colloquial style must always be stimulating. Perhaps, also, in America, since the period of national independence, there has always been in the literary consciousness a background of hope that the popular native style might turn out to be the prince in disguise after all, that America might have in its immediate possession an original and unique literary medium of expression which when illustrated by the writings of genius would take its place among the perfected literary languages of the world. Certain it is that few American authors have been able to resist the temptation to experiment in the literary possibilities of the popular speech.

The discussion of dialect always raises complicated questions of theoretical definition. In the common understanding of the term, a dialect is an irregular type of speech, estimated and in greater or less degree condemned, by comparison with what is assumed to be a normal and approved set of speech habits. In this conception, a dialect is a limited modification of "the language," limited either by local or by cultural considerations, whereas the standard speech is the thing itself. The language itself and a dialect are also conceived as each having a separate and distinctive existence, the dialect being a species of "the language," as the russet or the pippin are species of the apple. It is apparent on reflection, however, that genetically there is very little difference between an approved set of customs in speech, that is "the language," and a contemned set, that is, "a dialect." As there is no apple, but only varieties of apple exist, so there is no essential language, but only varieties of languages. Both the terms "the language" and "a dialect" designate merely the peculiar body of linguistic detail which the speakers of a particular group under observation at a given moment are seen to have in common. The question of approval or disapproval, that is of standard language or dialect, arises only after the event, only after the habits of the group have established themselves, and this question is answerable only on the basis of considerations different from those which were effective in establishing the customs of the group in the process of their formation.

It thus appears that in a true sense the standard speech also is a dialect. Moreover it is apparent that such generalizations made with respect to language are merely the convenient summaries of systematizers and theorizers, that a popular or local dialect becomes such in relation to the central language not at an absolutely fixed point, but at a point where in the opinion of some observer it becomes sufficiently different from his conception of "the language" to justify him in regarding it as a distinct modification of the real language. It is often said that there are no true dialects in America, but if by true, one means truth to an objective reality, the question raised by this statement is futile, since there is no such thing as an absolute dialect, literary or colloquial. Dialects of all kinds are merely the convenient summaries of observers who bring together certain homogeneities in the speech habits of a group and thus secure for themselves an impression of unity. Other observers might secure different impressions by assembling different habits of the same groups, and it is true of course that in this matter of dialectal variations, final analysis brings one down to the individual speaker or writer as the ultimate "group." No two speakers ever speak exactly alike. We may agree by convention to think that they do, but as soon as the bond of sympathy uniting two or more persons is broken, unexpected differences appear and become important.

These theoretical aspects of a dialect have been thus briefly debated merely to prepare the way to answer the question whether American dialect writers have been true to reality, or perhaps the question may be better phrased, whether there has been an obvious reality, discovered by the scientific student, to which a writer of dialect was under obligation to conform. The answer to this latter question must be negative. The literary dialect and the scientific dialect are both merely summaries of detail which produce a sense of unity, of separateness and completeness, only in the mind of the person who constructs for himself from this detail a sense of unity and homogeneity. The difference between the literary and the scientific student of dialect is mainly one of degree. The latter at least attempts to exhaust all the details of dialect speech which can come under his observation, thus arriving at a finality of some kind, whereas the former utilizes only as much of his material as he thinks he needs for his special literary purposes. The literary artist attempts by occasional suggestion to produce the illusion of a distinct and "real" dialect speech, but the scientist endeavors to attain a different conception of reality with an analytic method and an exhaustive examination of the material open to him for observation. Sometimes, however, writers of literary dialects have become so interested in their dialect observations as to forget their literary purposes. They have often recorded dialect detail when it was not necessary or useful in suggesting an impression of dialect speech, carrying dialect thus beyond the literary into the scientific field. The purpose of this chapter will not be, however, to criticize American literary dialects from the point of view of their faithfulness to any supposed norms of dialect speech, but merely to indicate the character of the dialects chosen for literary purposes by examining the details of speech utilized to produce the impression of dialect.

When it is said that there are no true dialects in America, the meaning plainly intended is that the characteristics of American speech are in no region or on no social level so obviously distinguished from those of the customary standard speech that they make of the dialect speech an easily recognizable kind of language in itself, perhaps intelligible only to those who are instructed in its peculiarities. Dialects of this kind have certainly not appeared in American literature. There is, for example, no American dialect literature, representing native English speech, as different from classic American literature as broad Scots or the Somerset dialect of the poet Barnes is different from classic British literature. Such dialects as have been used for literary purposes in America represent on the whole relatively slight departures from the forms of standard speech, and they always imply the standard speech as the background against which the dialect speech is contrasted. Nevertheless Americans themselves for the past century at least have been keenly aware of what they have felt to be dialectal differences, and variations which might seem slight to others, may be momentous in significance to the highly socialized American.

Of the dialect material employed in American literature, several clear kinds may be distinguished. First and most extensive in use is the class dialect which distinguishes between popular and cultivated or standard speech. This calls for no detailed discussion. The impression of popular speech is easily produced by a sprinkling of such forms as *aint*, for *isn't, done* for *did, them* for *those*, and similar grammatical improprieties. This impression is often assisted by what may be termed "eye dialect," in which the convention violated is one of the eye, not of the ear. Thus a dialect writer often spells a word like *front* as *frunt*, or *face* as *fase*, or *picture* as *pictsher*, not because he intends to indicate here a genuine difference of pronunciation, but the spelling is merely a friendly nudge to the reader, a knowing look which establishes a sympathetic sense of superiority between the author and reader as contrasted with the humble speaker of dialect.

Another kind of class dialect is that which occurs in mixed speech, and racial conditions in America have likewise been favorable to an abundant use of this type of dialect expression. None of it, however, has been of much literary significance, the mixture of German and English, Italian and English, Swedish and English, Polish and English, Yiddish and English, and a great variety of possible and actually occurring combinations having been of interest mainly in the humorous sketch of the vaudeville stage or for occasional comic relief in narrative. In all use of dialect there is probably present some sense of amused superiority on the part of the conventional speaker as he views the forms of the dialect speech, but in his attitude towards mixed foreign dialects the American seems always to have experienced an unusual degree of exaltation and self-satisfaction. That is, the contrasts implied have been so violent that foreign mixed dialects have been available only for farce or very broad comedy.

Besides the various kinds of class dialect, several forms of local dialect have also established themselves as recognizable types in American literary practice, and it is these indeed that one usually thinks of when one speaks of dialect literature. Just when a dialect may be said to have acquired position as a literary dialect, it is not always easy to say. The mountain speech of the Tennessee and Kentucky highlands, for example, has certain somewhat familiar and picturesque characteristics of its own and it has been used to some extent in literature, notably in the novels of Charles Egbert Craddock. It is a mixed dialect, containing numerous archaisms of speech which might appear in any American popular dialect, combined with other elements usually supposed to be characteristic of Southern speech. More to the point, however, is the fact that it has not been used in such a way in literature as to lead to literary imitations of it. Persons who have written the mountain dialect have usually stood in some first-hand relation to it, have in fact reported their observations in the spirit of the student of folklore. Perhaps the dialect has been too remote, too much the speech of a limited and uncouth people to serve as a general form of literary expression.

American literary dialects which have been imitatively cultivated in any considerable body of literature are indeed not numerous and are readily recognizable as such from the literary monuments in which they appear. Of these the most familiar are the New England dialect, the Pike County or Southwestern dialect of John Hay, Bret Harte, Mark Twain, and others, the Southern dialect, and the negro dialect. All of these dialects have been used sympathetically. The distinction between standard and dialect speech has always been very clearly present in the use of them by various writers, but the attitude both towards the life depicted in dialect literature and toward the language in which the pictures of life have been written, has been interested and kindly. This has permitted the utilization of a rich dialect material, the writer being unhampered by a timid respect for the conventionalities and respectabilities of the standard speech. Least free and least expressive in this respect has been the dialect literature of the Southern whites. The tradition of dialect writing has not had as favorable a field for development in the South as it has had in the North or the West, or in negro literature, the reason probably being that unconventional Southern speech suggested to the Southern writer or reader, on the one hand, the speech of the despised poor white, whom the South has rarely treated sympathetically, and, on the other hand, the speech of the negro, whom the South was willing to treat sympathetically as long as such treatment did not imply the inclusion of white and black within the same group.

One would not expect writers even of what is presumably the same dialect to use the same forms. Since a dialect is merely the sum of the particulars which a given observer synthesizes into an impression of a homogeneous speech, it may well happen that two different persons observing the speech of the same group, will base their impressions of unity upon widely differing details. One person will regard one feature of speech as quintessentially the mark of a certain dialect and another will choose quite a different feature or set of features. This merely means that each groups his associations around what for him have become distinguishing marks, what indeed with many dialect writers become distinguishing tricks. These marks may be called centers of association. Since it is impossible for the dialect writer to exhaust all the material, a selection he must make, and the selected details must be given a sort of arbitrary value as standing for the dialect as a whole. The interest in the examination of literary dialects lies in seeing just what the details selected are and what the reasons were which determined the choice of them.

The humorous dialect character exemplified in the rustic but shrewd Yankee has had a long genealogy. He made his first appearance in drama, and Jonathan in Royall Tyler's *The Contrast* (1787) began a stage tradition which has not yet expired. A good early example of rustic Yankee character in drama is Jonathan Postfree, in the comedy of that name (1806), by L. Beach. The type of character, however, did not become widely known and popular as a literary device until the publication of the Jack Downing letters of Seba Smith, which first began to appear in the *Daily Courier* at Portland, Maine, in 1830. After that the character became a common possession, a familiar citizen, one may say, in the world of popular imagination. The fullest and most important realization of this literary figure was in the character of Hosea Biglow, in Lowell's *Biglow Papers*, the First Series of which appeared in a published volume in 1848, the Second Series, in 1866. In the third quarter of the century the local sketch and story engaged the interest of many writers in America, and numerous dialect studies of New England life and character gave evidence of study of local speech which was often minute and painstaking. There have thus been many literary transcriptions of rustic New England speech, differing as one would expect according to the powers of observation of the various recorders and the different speech habits examined by them. Obviously no one of these many literary transcriptions of New England rustic speech can lay claim to being the only true and right record, since there never has existed a single "true" dialect in New England. In choosing a literary dialect for exemplification, therefore, one must make a decision more or less arbitrary. But perhaps no New England dialect literature has been more generally or more readily recognized as such than the *Biglow Papers*. Lowell himself insisted that his dialect transcriptions were very accurate, that he recorded nothing which he had not himself heard. But whether they were accurate or not, it is true that to the American reader they have stood as typically representative of Yankee dialect speech and have thus, one may say, made the speech for literary purposes. It will be not uninstructive to examine the *Biglow Papers* to see just what ingredients entered into the composition of this recognizable American dialect.

Lowell himself in the introduction to the First Series of the *Biglow Papers* has given a prescription for the compounding of Yankee dialect. The directions are as follows:

1. "The genuine Yankee never gives the rough sound to the *r* when he can help it, and often displays considerable ingenuity in avoiding it even before a vowel." This rule covers the well-known fact of the tendency of all Eastern and Southern speech not to pronounce *r* finally and before consonants.

2. "He seldom sounds the final *g*, a piece of self-denial, if we consider his partiality for nasals. The same of the final *d*, as *han'* and *stan'* for *hand* and *stand*." The unsounded final *g* here referred to is the letter as it appears in *writing*, etc., pronounced in all popular speech with final [n] instead of [ŋ]. The pronunciation of *han'* for *hand*, etc., is a lax articulation also found in all forms of popular speech.

3. "The *h* in such words as *while, when, where,* he omits altogether." This also is a characteristic of speech widely distributed and found in other regions than in New England.

4. "In regard to *a*, he shows some inconsistency, sometimes giving a close and obscure sound, as *hev* for *have, hendy* for *handy, ez* for *as, thet* for *that,* and again giving it the broad sound it has in *father*, as *hânsome* for *handsome*." These are two quite different things, one being [ɛ] where standard speech has [æ], the other being [ɑː] where standard speech has [æ]. Of these two the latter is much more distinctive as a characteristic of dialect, though it appeared in relatively only a small number of words.

5. "To the sound *ou* he prefixes an *e* (hard to exemplify otherwise than orally)." This sound Lowell does try to indicate by the spelling *neow* for *now, heouse* for *house*, etc., in a sample pas-

sage of New England dialect. Pronounced literally as Lowell spelled them, one would get in these words a pronunciation which Lowell pretty certainly did not have in mind. What he had in mind was the pronunciation of a diphthong for *ou*, the first element of which was approximately the vowel of *mat* or of *met*, a pronunciation found not only in New England but also in the South.

6. "*Au*, in such words as *daughter* and *slaughter*, he pronounces *ah*," that is with the vowel of *father*.

7. "To the dish thus seasoned add a drawl *ad libitum*"—though unfortunately Lowell does not say what he means by the word drawl.

When one looks at these rules from the point of view of general American speech, one finds that only the fourth and the sixth may be said to be in any high degree characteristic of New England. The first and the fourth New England shares with the South, and the second and third are common to all popular English speech. The seventh may designate something peculiar to New England, but Lowell's statement gives no clue as to what it is. Since five and seven can be exemplified only orally, and since one, two and three are common to all popular speech and six would apply at the most only to a few words, if one were to write dialect according to Lowell's rules, the only features of speech which might be regarded as characteristic of New England speech would be those of four, that is *hev* for *have*, etc., and an occasional *a* of *father* for the first vowel in *handsome* and a few other words. Manifestly one would need ampler and clearer directions than these to write what would be recognized as a New England dialect.

When one examines Lowell's practice in the writing of his New England dialect, one observes that even his own few rules are not adequately exemplified in his spellings. He did not omit *r* finally or before consonants, nor did he spell words like *while, when, where,* as *w'ile, w'en, w'ere.* He made no attempt in the *Papers* to reduce to spelling the pronunciation of *ou* mentioned in his fifth rule, or of *au* in his sixth, or of broad *a* in *handsome* in the second half of his fourth, and of course the drawl of the seventh went unrecorded. With these exclusions what would be left of Lowell's rules would be very little, not enough to establish the impression of a dialect style, except merely the style of general low colloquial speech. Lowell's practice, however, was much more complicated than his precept, and it is only by turning to the poems themselves that one can examine the various devices by means of which Lowell produced the impression of dialect.

For the purpose of making such an examination, it seems fair to take a passage from *The Courtin'*, a poem which Lowell himself selected as representative. Such dialect color as the *Biglow Papers* have is illustrated in the following stanzas:

An' yit she gin her cheer a jerk
  Ez though she wished him furder,
An' on her apples kep' to work,
  Parin' away like murder.

"You want to see my Pa, I s'pose?"
  "Wal . . . no . . . I come dasignin'—"
"To see my Ma? She's sprinklin' clo'es
  Agin to-morrer's i'nin'."

To say why gals acts so or so,
  Or don't, 'ould be presumin';
Mebby to mean *yes* an' say *no*
  Comes nateral to women.

He stood a spell on one foot fust,
  Then stood a spell on t'other,
An' on which one he felt the wust
  He couldn't ha' told ye nuther.

Says he, "I'd better call agin,"
  Says she, "Think likely, Mister:"
Thet last word pricked him like a pin,
  An' . . . Wal, he up an' kist her.

When Ma bimeby upon 'em slips,
  Huldy sot pale ez ashes,
All kin' o' smily roun' the lips
  An' teary roun' the lashes.

Even a cursory analysis of this passage shows that the departures from the customary uncolored style of literary English are not all on the same level. Some of them are merely phonetic spellings of pronunciations that might occur in any speech except the most formal. Such are *an'* for *and* and *ez* for unstressed *as*, which in such a position would ordinarily be pronounced [əz]. Others belong to the speech of the careless or uneducated English speaker everywhere, and these may be designated merely as General Low Colloquial, pronunciations like *an'* and *ez* being designated as General Colloquial. There remain then certain forms possibly peculiar to New England, or at least commonly felt to be characteristic of New England speech, and these may be described as Local Dialect. All the details in the passage quoted above which differ from conventional literary English might then be grouped under these three heads as follows:

General Colloquial	*General Low Colloquial*	*Local Dialect*
an'	yit	wal
ez	gin	nateral
Pa	cheer	fust
s'pose	furder	wust
Ma	kep'	thet
clo'es	parin'	sot
don't	dasignin'	
couldn't	sprinklin'	
ye	agin	
kist	tomorrer's	
'em	i'nin'	
	gals	
	'ould	
	presumin'	
	mebby	
	t'other	
	ha'	
	nuther	
	bimeby	
	Huldy	
	kin'	
	o'	
	roun'	

From this tabulation one must conclude that Lowell's New England dialect is merely the speech of ordinary low colloquial American discourse with a relatively slight addition of dialect detail more or less peculiar to New England. Further analysis of Lowell's dialect writing and of those of others who have written in the New England dialect would confirm this conclusion. The New England dialect as a literary form is mainly popular or illiterate American English with a very occasional splash of genuine local color. The intimate association of New England dialect literature with New England life was not made through language but through content, through setting, characterization, incident and sentiment. In this poem, for example, the New England feeling is given more by the rustic simplicity of the content of the poem than by the language of it, and the same observation could be made of a surprisingly large part of American dialect literature. Lowell's dialect in a story of the California gold fields would pass as a Western dialect, and would seem not widely out of place on a cotton plantation in the South. An idyllic rustic situation of apple paring and kissing, however, localizes the poem as at least in the spirit of New England dialect literature.

The same method of analysis as that employed in *The Courtin'* when applied to a typical specimen of Southwestern literary dialect will yield a similar result. For the purpose of illustration, John Hay's *Little Breeches*, in *Pike County Ballads* (1871), may be chosen:

General Colloquial	*Low Colloquial*	*Local Dialect*
I'd	I never ain't had no show	larnt
	sence = since	hell-to-split
	peart and chipper and sassy	sarched
	chaw = chew	hosses
	terbacker	upsot
	skeer	critter's
	rousted up	somewhar
	jest = just	thar
	crotch-deep	sot
	Isrul = Israel	toted
	git	fotching
	derned	

Here again the basis of John Hay's Southwestern dialect is seen to be ordinary uncultivated American speech with some specifically local characteristics added. But when one looks more closely at the local dialect words in this poem one finds few of them that may be regarded as peculiar to a Southwestern or Pike County dialect, for *larnt, sarched, hosses, upsot, critter's, sot* might all be taken as marks of New England dialect, and *somewhar, thar, toted,* and *fotching* are of course familiar in all Southern dialect. The so-called Southwestern dialect as it has existed in literature has been in reality merely low colloquial speech with an addition of certain details from New England and from Southern dialect speech. Occasionally, as in Bret Harte, some local terms of the mining camps and the gambling table found their way into Southwestern literature, but these words came because of the subject matter and were not essential to the dialect, except indeed as subject matter gave to this literature its peculiar color and quality. The content of the New England dialect literature has been rustic, simple, worldly-wise beneath a surface covering of seeming guilelessness. Southwestern literature has been free and easy, with a careless largeness both of sentiment and expression. In *Little Breeches, hell-to-split* is a characteristically unrestrained Southwestern intensive. Western picturesqueness and magnanimity appear in Jim Bludso's promise and deed as the fire swept over his burning vessel:

> "I'll hold her nozzle agin the bank
> Till the last galoot's ashore."

Or in the concluding words of Banty Tim, in another of the *Pike County Ballads:*

> "You may rezoloot till the cows come home,
> But ef one of you tetches the boy,
> He'll wrastle his hash tonight in hell,
> Or my name's not Tilman Joy."

The figurative picturesqueness of writing like this, however, is not fairly to be described as dialectal. It belongs to the realm of imagination, of thought or content, whereas dialect more properly is a matter of the forms of language. So far as the mere forms of language are concerned, there is little in the *Pike County Ballads* or in the writings of Bret Harte or any other Southwestern writer which could not be found in almost any dialect community in America. Content, on the other hand, is extremely highly colored in this literature and in the main unmistakably indicative of a clearly defined local type of American life. One readily transfers the feeling for distinctive locality and action to language, for language, like the chameleon, takes color to accord with surroundings.

When one comes to the selection of a passage illustrating Southern literary dialect one is embarrassed by the fact that there are no Southern writings which may be said to stand as typically representative of Southern white dialect in the way that Lowell is representative of New England dialect and Bret Harte or John Hay is representative of Pike County dialect. When one thinks of the South in a literary way, ordinarily one thinks of Virginia, but the Virginian as he figures in literature speaks usually as a conventional gentleman, with slight touches of local color indicated by the occasional omission of *r*, as in *suh* for *sir*, or by such pronunciations as *gya'dn* for *garden*, *Cya'ter* for *Carter*, etc. But writers who have attempted to depict what may be called reputable Southern persons on the whole have sedulously avoided the deviations from standard grammar and standard pronunciation common to most forms of familiar American English. That the "Southern gentleman" always spoke with strict grammatical propriety and with nice precision in enunciation, one may doubt. If he seems to have been much more a man of the conventional world than local characters elsewhere in America, this is probably an illusion cherished by the transcribers of Southern life, who perhaps have been willing to sacrifice certain elements of realism and truthfulness in order not to seem to imperil the dignity of the accredited conservers of the social tradition of the Southern community.

Parallel to the seven rules for writing the New England dialect which Lowell gave, a Southern scholar and historian has given seven rules for writing the Southern literary dialect, see C. Alphonso Smith, *A History of American Literature*, ed. Trent, II, 365. These rules are as follows:

1. "*Like* does duty for *as if* in such sentences as 'He looks like he was sick.' This construction, says Lowell, is 'never found in New England.'"

2. "'*Low* (allow), meaning *think* and *say*, though 'never heard in New England' (Lowell), is very common among white and black illiterates, as it is in the pages of Bret Harte. *Guess* in the New England sense is also used, but New England *cal'late* (*calculate*) is unknown."

3. "Such words as *tune, news, duty* (but not *true, rule, sue, dude*) have the vanishing *y*-sound heard in *few*. This pronunciation, like the retention of broad *a*, can hardly be called dialect, but it is almost a shibboleth of the Southerner to the manner born, and helps to differentiate him from the Westerner and Northerner."

4. "The vanishing *y*-sound heard in *gyarden, cyards, Cyarter, Gyarfield*, is common in Virginia but less so in other parts of the South."

5. "The same may be said of broad *a*, intermediate *a* (halfway between *father* and *fat*) being distinctively academic and acquired."

6. "*More, store, floor, four, door*, and similar words are usually pronounced *mo, sto, flo, fo, do*, by negroes. Among the white population the *r* is not pronounced, but these words have two distinct syllables, the last syllable having the obscure *uh* sound heard in *mower, stower*. The tendency in the North and West to pronounce long *o* as *au* (in *autumnal* rather than in *autumn*) is not observable in the South."

7. "The most distinctive idiom in the South is the use of *you all*, meaning not *all of you* but *you folks, you people, you boys, you girls*. It may be addressed to one person but always implies more than one. If a Southerner says to a clerk in a store, 'Do you all keep shoes here?' he means by 'you all' not the single clerk but the entire firm or force that owns or operates the store."

The rules in this list for writing Southern dialect have to do both with words or constructions and with pronunciations. The first two are dubious as local tests. The *Century Dictionary* points out that *like* as a conjunction, though ordinarily condemned or unrecorded in the dictionaries, occurs "several times in Shakespeare," "not unfrequently in modern writers," and is "common in colloquial and provincial English." Lowell's statement that *like* as a conjunction is "never found in New England" is one of those universal negatives that invite disbelief. The construction indeed is so common in popular American English that it has no distinctive local associations, and so general that all purists and rhetoricians unite in condemning it. The use of *'low, allow*, in the sense of *think* or *say*, Lowell again declared was "never heard in New England." Thornton queries this statement, and under *allow* gives American examples beginning with 1801, some of which belong to New England. The fact that this use of *allow* existed in New England does not, however, altogether destroy its value as a test of Southern speech, since undoubtedly it was and still is much more commonly used in the South than elsewhere. The pronunciation mentioned in the third rule is again so general as to have little value as a mark of local dialect, especially literary dialect, for dialect writers have rarely made any effort to distinguish by spelling or otherwise between the pronunciation of *tune* with the vowel of *boot* and with the vowel of *mute*. Rules four and five apply only to Virginia, and even there only to certain types of Virginian speech. Rules six and seven remain as describing fairly definite characteristics of Southern dialect speech. It is apparent, however, that these two rules, or the whole set of seven rules, are altogether inadequate as directions for writing a satisfactory and recognizable Southern dialect. As Lowell's own practice was better than the precepts laid down in his rules, so any literary transcription of Southern speech by a fairly competent observer will give a more convincing impression of Southern dialect speech than a set of rules like that which has just been analyzed.

No more skilful literary transcriptions of Southern speech, both the speech of whites and of negroes, have been made than those of Joel Chandler Harris. The following passage is taken from *Mingo* (1884), and from the title story of the volume, described as a sketch not of a "poor white," but of a self-respecting well-to-do woman of democratical central Georgia, a woman who hates "Virginia ways" and "quality idees," but is not lacking in pride of her own:

"When I seen her a-kneelin' thar, with 'er year-rings a-danglin' an' 'er fine feathers a-tossin' an' a-trimblin', leetle more an' my thoughts would 'a' sot me afire. I riz an' I stood over her, an' I says, says I,—

"'Emily Wornum, whar you er huntin' the dead you oughter hunted the livin'. What's betwix' you an' your Maker I can't tell,' says I, 'but if you git down on your face an' lick the dirt what Deely Bivins walked on, still you won't be humble enough to go whar *she's* gone, nor good enough nuther. She died right yer while you was a-traipsin' an' a-trollopin' roun' frum pos' to pillar a-upholdin' your quality idees. These arms helt 'er,' says I, 'an' ef hit hadn't but 'a' bin for *her*, Emily Wornum,' says I, 'I'd 'a' strangled the life out'n you time your shadder darkened my door. An' what's more,' says I, 'ef you er come to bother airter Pud, *thes make the trial of it. Thes so much as lay the weight er your little finger on 'er,'* says I, 'an' I'll grab you by the goozle an' t'ar your haslet out,' says I."

Applying the same method of analysis to this piece of admirable writing as to the passage of New England and Southwestern dialect, one has the following tables as the result:

General Colloquial	*Low Colloquial*	*Local Dialect*
an'	seen = saw	thar
er = are	a-kneelin'	year-rings = ear-rings
what's = what is	'er = her	sot = set
can't	a-danglin'	riz = rose
won't	a-tossin'	whar
frum = from	a-trimblin'	yer
hadn't	leetle	helt
bin = been	'a' = have	airter = after
I'd	I says	thes = just
what's	huntin'	goozle = throat
er = of	oughter = ought to have	t'ar = tear
I'll	livin'	haslet = inwards
	betwix'	
	git	
	Deely = Delia	

Low Colloquial

for to go
nuther
you was
a-traipsin'
a-trollopin'
roun'
pos'
a-upholdin'
idees
ef = if
out'n = out of
shadder

Of the details listed under the head of General Colloquial, some are merely the ordinary abbreviations of all colloquial speech, like *can't, won't, what's,* others are pure eye dialect, like *frum* and *bin,* which everybody pronounces in this way, and the spelling *er* is used to represent an unstressed form of *are* and *of,* both of which would take weakened forms in the unstressed position in all colloquial speech. In the third column, it is doubtful if such variant preterite forms as *sot, riz,* and *helt* should be included and should not rather be placed in the second column. This would leave as the characteristic marks of this local dialect a pronunciation of *where, there,* and *tear* with the vowel of *far,* of the initial sound of *ear, hear* as though a *y* preceded, of *just* as *thes,* of *after* as *airter,* though this might also go into the second column, and finally the two words *goozle* and *haslet.* Of these the most characteristic are the pronunciations *thar, whar* and *t'ar,* fairly constant marks of literary transcriptions of Southern dialect.

The main conclusion to be drawn from this analysis of passages from American dialect literature is that all local dialects of this kind are at bottom merely general colloquial or low colloquial American English, with a slight sprinkling of more characteristic words or pronunciations, some of which suggest fairly definite local associations, often in the case of words by connection with some peculiar local occupation or activity. A person who speaks a low colloquial English in plantation surroundings is readily interpreted to be a Southerner of some degree, but essentially the same language spoken on the range would establish the speaker as a cowboy, or in the gold region as a miner. The statement quoted earlier in this chapter, that there are no true dialects in America, is thus seen to be in the main defensible, so far as dialects have been utilized for literary purposes. One may say that there have been only two forms of speech in America, the more or less formal standard and the more or less informal colloquial. American dialect literature rests upon a foundation of general informal colloquial speech, locally established by action and setting with its local character confirmed by a slight addition of local practices in speech.

According to a prevalent and traditional opinion, Bret Harte wrote bad dialect, bad in the sense that it was not true to the speech of the kinds of persons who figured in his stories. Brander Matthews, *Essays on English*, Chapter XIII, quotes Mark Twain as saying that he had to go over a piece written in collaboration by Twain and Harte "and get the dialect right," that Harte "never did know anything about dialect." Whether Bret Harte's dialect was true or not is a question which obviously cannot now be answered, for there is no more authentic record of the speech of the mining camps now available than that which Bret Harte himself has given. But even at the time the stories and poems were written, it would have been difficult to tell whether or not Bret Harte had actually heard and observed the forms of speech which he utilized for dialect color. One could tell this only if one had present for examination the very same persons that Bret Harte used as his models. But if one examines Bret Harte's dialect from the point of view of its historical plausibility, there appears to be no reason why it should not have existed in California, since the elements of it all have a reputable dialect history. The ingredients of Bret Harte's dialect are historically good, but whether or not these ingredients were judiciously mixed could be determined only by knowing how the persons actually spoke whom Bret Harte heard—a knowledge now past finding out. If one takes a poem like *Penelope* (*Simpson's Bar, 1885*), as abundantly and strikingly dialectal as any of Bret Harte's writings, and if one classifies all the dialect detail in the poem as was done with other dialect passages, one finds little that is not perfectly familiar:

General Colloquial	*Low Colloquial*	*Southern Low Colloquial*
you've	kem = come	'yer = here
agen = again	derned	'yer's = here is
won't	cavortin'	thar = there
I've	ef = if	
can't	cheer = chair	
don't	them (demonstrative adjective)	
you'd	theer = there	
	cushings = cushions	
	jest = just	
	a courtin'	
	widder = widow	
	critter	
	baird = beard	
	nary = not any	
	foolin'	
	sartain	
	gal = girl	
	anywheer = any where	

The most interesting result of such an analysis is that it shows nothing in this poem distinctive for a Western or California dialect, and the result would be the same if one included other dialect writings of Bret Harte. Aside from a few Spanish words or phrases and some locutions peculiar to the life of the mining camps, all of Bret Harte's local color in speech is a mixture of familiar New England and general low colloquialisms with some more definitely Southern low colloquialisms. The use of *kem* for *come* is not frequently recorded, but it is common in the Indiana dialect of the second quarter of the nineteenth century as it appears in Carlton's *New Purchase* and is used in the Tennessee mountain dialect of Charles Egbert Craddock. Other forms like *cheer* for *chair, theer* for *there, baird* for *beard, nary* for *not any, sartain* for *certain,* are good old New Englandisms. The common statement that Bret Harte got his dialect from Dickens is not supported by an examination of the actual details of his practice. All his dialect material was good American. Even his use of *which* as a kind of demonstrative or coördinating conjunction is supported by other local American use. A typical instance of this use is found in the opening stanza of Truthful James:

> "Which I wish to remark
> And my language is plain,
> That for ways that are dark
> And for tricks that are vain,
> The heathen Chinee is peculiar,
> Which the same I would rise to explain."

Similar constructions are cited by Merwin, *Life of Bret Harte*, p. 326, for Kentucky, Virginia, Georgia and Arkansas. It seems not to have been recorded for New England, but the evidence for its existence as a Southern low colloquialism is too conclusive to be doubted. To the authorities cited by Merwin may be added two other competent observers. In *Mingo*, p. 22, Joel Chandler Harris wrote: " 'an how she cast off her own daughter, which Deely was as good a girl as ever draw'd the breath er life." The dialect poems of Sidney Lanier, which also record Middle Georgia speech, contain numerous examples, the following being representative: "This man—which his name it was also Jones" (1869), *Poems*, p. 180; "But Jones (which he had tuck a tod)" (1870), p. 184; "Five years glid by, and Brown, one day (which he'd got so fat, that he wouldn't weigh)" (1869), p. 181.

Probably the best known and best loved of all dialect writers in America has been James Whitcomb Riley. The dialect he supposedly used was the Hoosier dialect of Indiana. Analysis again shows, however, that this dialect is made up of an abundance of ordinary colloquialisms, including much eye dialect, with some archaisms of speech which survive as low colloquialisms. The following tabulation of all the dialect detail in *The Old Man and Jim* shows nothing that would not seem natural anywhere in America:

General Colloquial	*Low Colloquial*
er = unstressed *or*	'ceptin' = excepting
fer = for	jes' = just
deepot = depot	heerd = heard
ust to = used to	backin'

General Colloquial	*Low Colloquial*
he'd = he would	'at = that
he'd = he had	keer = care
instunce = instance	yourse'f
'em = them	'peared = appeared
plum' = plumb	lookin'
hadn't	likin'
	hisse'f-like
	'cause = because
	drillin'
	a-watchin'
	a-heerin'
	nothin'
	disting'ished
	writ = wrote
	dern
	rigiment
	fightin'
	farmin'
	seen = saw
	calvery = cavalry
	'lowed
	sich
	afore
	follered
	'tel = until
	rid = rode
	tuk = took
	believin'
	'ud = would
	p'inted = pointed
	t'other
	clumb = climbed
	a-laughin'
	bendin'
	turnin'
	dyin'

A typical passage of Southern negro dialect is almost as difficult to discover as one for Southern white popular dialect. "The dialect of the negroes of Eastern Virginia," says Thomas Nelson Page, in a note prefixed to *In Ole Virginia,* "differs totally from that of the Southern negroes, and in some material points from that of those located farther west." The dialect of the Southern negroes here referred to is presumably the Gullah dialect of the rice fields of South Carolina and Georgia. This is indeed a very individual negro dialect, but it has not of recent years been utilized to any great extent in literature. The two remaining dialects are the dialect of Eastern Virginia and the dialect of the inland regions of Virginia and Georgia. The first of these latter two types has been most skilfully utilized in the Virginia tales and sketches of Thomas Nelson Page, the second in the plantation legends of Joel Chandler Harris. Remarking that it is "impossible to reproduce the exact sound" and that he has found it "necessary to subordinate the phonetic arrangement to intelligibility," Page gives the following rules as of aid in representing the negro dialect of Eastern Virginia:

"The final consonant is rarely sounded. Adverbs, prepositions and short words are frequently slighted, as is the possessive. The letter *r* is not usually rolled except when used as a substitute for *th*, but is pronounced *ah*. For instance the following is a fair representation of the peculiarities cited: The sentence, 'It was curious, he said, he wanted to go into the other army' would sound: ' 'Twuz cu-yus, he say, he wan(t) (to) go in (to) turr ah-my.' "

English thus transcribed looks markedly different from other forms of literary dialect. But it is a legitimate inquiry how far this difference is due merely to a completer carrying out of a phonetic method than is customary in transcriptions of the dialect of whites. Thus *'Twuz* for *It was* might be observed in any rapid colloquial speech, and *ah-my* for *army* would be general Southern or New England usage. Even *cu-yus* for *curious* one would not be surprised to hear generally in the South, since *r* is ordinarily omitted in final position in this type of speech, and the first syllable of *curious* may be treated as independent. In the transcription, *wan go* for *want to go*, the record is certainly not adequate. The negro pronunciation *he wan go* is not merely equivalent rhythmically to *a man go*, but *wan* is followed by a pause, the stop position for *t* being formed but no explosion made, which separates the word *want* from *go*. The final *n* of *wan* may thus be said to be long. In colloquial English the phrase *want to go* would be pronounced in any case only with one *t* and in rapid speech it would be [wɑn tə goː] or even [wɑn t goː]. The difference between [wɑnː goː] and [wɑn t goː] is thus seen to be much less than the apparent difference between *want to go* and *wan go*. In other words, literary transcriptions of negro dialect are likely to approach more nearly to scientific exactness in the recording of the minuter details of the phonetic side of speech than other literary transcriptions of dialect ordinarily do, and thus to seem further removed from the familiar forms of standard speech. One hears the illiterate speech of negroes more illiterately than one hears the illiterate speech of one's fellow-whites.

In the recording of the best known negro dialect, that of Uncle Remus, Joel Chandler Harris definitely avowed a scientific intention. He declared that the language of his negro legends was "phonetically genuine," *Uncle Remus*, p. 4, and that his book, though included by the publishers in the list of their humorous publications, was in intention perfectly serious. When the book was issued, however, the interest of the public soon made it apparent that the plantation legends it contained and the language in which they were related were much more important as literature than as folk-lore. If there is such a thing as classic negro literary dialect, it is to be found in the speech of Uncle Remus. The following passage from the conclusion of the story of the Tar-Baby is typical and may be made the basis of analysis:

" 'Skin me, Brer Fox,' sez Brer Rabbit, sezee, 'snatch out my eyeballs, t'ar out my years by de roots, en cut off my legs,' sezee, 'but do please, Brer Fox, don't fling me in dat brier-patch,' sezee.

"Co'se Brer Fox wanter hurt Brer Rabbit bad ez he kin, so he cotch 'im by de behime legs en slung 'im right in de middle er de brier-patch. Dar wuz a considerbul flutter whar Brer Rabbit struck the bushes, en Brer Fox sorter hang 'roun' fer to see w'at wuz gwineter happen. Bimeby he hear somebody call 'im, en way up de hill he see Brer Rabbit settin' cross-legged on a chinkapin log koamin' de pitch outen his har wid a chip. Den Brer Fox know dat he bin swop off mighty bad. Brer Rabbit wuz bleedzed fer ter fling back some er his sass, en he holler out:

"'Bred en bawn in a brier-patch, Brer Fox—bred en bawn in a brier-patch!' en wid dat he skip out des ez lively ez a cricket in de embers."

Like most semi-scientific phonetic transcriptions, this passage calls for some explanation. For the first thing, it is not altogether clear what Harris meant by the spelling *Brer* for *brother*, *er* for *of*, *sorter* for *sort of*, *ter* for *to*, *wanter* for *want to*, *gwineter* for *going to*, but the probabilities are that he meant to indicate by the spelling *er* in *Brer* not [brɛr], but a vowel sound similar to the vowel of *brother* with its ordinary pronunciation, though with the *th* lost in the negro dialect of Uncle Remus; *er* for *of* would be the sound of the word as it appears in the phrase four o'clock, and *ter* for *to* would be the pronunciation which this word would have in unstressed position in any colloquial speech.

The value of the consonant represented by *d* in spelling like *de* for *the*, *dar* for *there*, *wid* for *with*, that is for voiced *th* in unstressed position, seems also not certain. Was the *d* intended to represent a genuine explosive [d], or merely a very much voiced [ð], a sound which could only be represented in the conventional alphabet by *d*? The latter is the more probable supposition. It will be observed also that Harris made frequent use of eye dialect, as in *sez* for *says*, and that on the other hand he did not systematically indicate the loss of *r* finally or before consonants, as in *hurt*, *hear*, but did write *co'se* for *course* and *bawn* for *born*, an inconsistency probably resulting from a disinclination to load the page too heavily with unconventional spellings. The general effect produced by the Uncle Remus stories is strongly dialectal, but on examination relatively little in them is found to be dialectally peculiar. Classifying the dialect details of this passage under the four heads, *General Colloquial*, *General Low Colloquial*, *Southern Low Colloquial*, and *Negro Dialect*, *General Colloquial* including eye dialect, one has the following result:

General Colloquial	*General Low Colloquial*	*Southern Low Colloquial*	*Negro Dialect*
sez	sezee = says he	t'ar = tear	Brer
en = and	wanter = want to	years = ears	de = the
'im	ez = as	co'se = course	dat = that
wuz = was	kin = can	whar = where	behime = behind
considerbul	cotch	gwineter = going to	dar = there
koam(in') = comb(ing)	er = of	har = hair	bimeby = by and by
bin = been	sorter = sort of	bleedzed = obliged	wid = with
	'roun' = around	bawn	den = then
	fer = for		des = just
	ter = to		
	w'at = what		
	settin' = sitting		
	koamin' = combing		
	outen = out of		
	swop		
	sass		
	holler		

To the fourth column should be added certain characteristic tense formations. As a preterite of *catch, cotch* historically belongs to general colloquial American speech, but lingers now chiefly in negro English. The emphatic negative *do don't* is not current as a general low colloquialism, and the persistent use of present forms, as *hang, hear, see, know, skip,* and *bin* (*been*) for *had been* is also not found in general low colloquial use. If to these one adds the spelling *d* for voiced *th,* one exhausts all the possible distinctive marks of negro dialect in this passage. That the speech of Uncle Remus as Joel Chandler Harris heard it differed markedly even from Southern low colloquial is possible, but if so, his literary transcription of the dialect of Uncle Remus gives remarkably few clues which will enable one to realize this difference. The speech of Uncle Remus and the speech of rustic whites as Harris records it are so much alike that if one did not know which character was speaking, one might often be unable to tell whether the words were those of a white man or of a negro. A similar statement has been made by a competent Southern observer. "If one happened to be talking to a native with one's eyes shut," says Harrison, *Negro English,* p. 232, "it would be impossible to tell whether a negro or a white person were responding."

However this may be in actual speech, certainly in literary transcriptions of negro speech there is very little that might be regarded as making a specifically negro dialect. There are no African elements, in these transcriptions, no survivals of an original speech which make the English of negroes seem like the speech of foreigners who have imperfectly assimilated English. Negro English as written by such representative authors as Thomas Nelson Page and Joel Chandler Harris is in fact not different from any other dialectal form of American English, that is, it is merely general low colloquial English with a light sprinkling of words or phrases which by custom have come to have closer associations with negro speech. Whether these literary transcriptions are true to the "real" negro dialect is one of those questions impossible to answer in the lack of any accepted definition of the essential elements of negro English. One cannot suppose, however, that writers like Page and Harris have intentionally misrepresented the facts, and moreover the historical examination of the characteristics of American dialect speech makes it plain that the details of American dialect speech, both of negro and white, are for the most part survivals of older and native English elements in the language.

The several attempts that have been made to record Gullah dialect differ considerably from each other, but the following passage is as fully dialectal as any. It is taken from *The Black Border, Gullah Stories of the Carolina Coast*, by Ambrose E. Gonzales, Columbia, S. C., 1922. In the foreword to this book, the author gives the titles of several other works in Gullah dialect, though none of these employ as thoroughgoing, realistic and phonetic method of transcription. The following passage occurs on p. 207:

"Maussuh, uh binnuh stan' een Willtown road close to Mas' Edwu'd Baa'nwell' Clifton place, w'en uh yeddy de dog duh comin' fuh me, en' uh stop fuh liss'n. Bimeby, uh see de mukkle [myrtle] duh shake, en', fus' t'ing uh know, de deer jump out de t'icket en' light een de big road en' look 'puntop me! 'E foot fall saaf'ly 'pun de groun' same lukkuh cat duh sneak 'puntop 'uh bu'd. 'E tu'n 'e head en' 'e look 'puntop me lukkuh somebody, 'cep'n suh [that] 'e yeye big lukkuh hawn owl' eye. 'E look at me so posittubble, uh t'ink mus' be 'e duh haant, en' uh dat 'f'aid 'e gwine t'row one spell 'puntop me, uh tu'n 'way me head. W'en uh look roun' 'gen, 'e gone! Yuh come de dog'! Uh nebbuh see summuch dog! Dem full' de road, en' dem woice' roll 'tell you nebbuh yeddy shishuh music. Dem cross' de road, en' dem gone! Attuh leetle w'ile, uh yeddy 'um duh giv dem toung een de gyaa'd'n uh ole Maussuh' Clifton house wuh dem Nyankee bu'n down eenjurin' uh de wah. De gyaa'd'n big ez uh cawnfiel', en' 'e full' uh high rose bush duh climb up 'pun de tree, en' all kind'uh briah en' t'icket dey dey. Uh yeddy de dog' mek uh sukkle roun' de gyaa'd'n, den dem stop. Bimeby, yuh come de ole buck duh run puhzackly 'pun 'e back track, en', w'en 'e git to de big road weh him lef' me duh stan'up, uh t'awt at de fus' 'e bin gwine jump 'puntop me, but 'e tu'n shaa'p roun' en' light down de road gwine Paa'kuh' Ferry Cross-Road' . . . Da' duh de las' uh shum, en' uh nebbuh yeddy 'um no mo' attuh 'e done gone."

A patient phonetic analysis of this transcription will reveal all its mysteries, and hidden beneath the author's spellings will be found regular phonetic developments of ordinary English words. The dialect has, however, an unusually outlandish appearance, and in many respects it is different from the more familiar negro speech of Harris and Page. The name Gullah which has been applied to it and to the people who speak it, is a word of unknown etymological origin, nor are the racial origins of the Gullah negroes discoverable with reference to the particular regions of Africa from which they may have come. The question of African origins is of very little importance, however, since there is practically nothing in the recorded forms of Gullah speech which cannot be derived from English. Like the negro English of Harris and Page, Gullah speech is merely a debased dialect of English, learned by the negroes from the whites. The English speech which the whites probably used in addressing their savage slave captives was the much simplified, infantile English which superiors sometimes assume in addressing inferiors, or which with repetition and vociferation is used in trying to communicate with people who do not know the language. The English which lies at the basis of the Gullah dialect must have been something like the English of an Irish labor boss directing a gang of Italian workmen. Similar forms of English appear in Beach-la-Mar and Pidgin English. It is not improbable that the English of the original Gullah negroes was a kind of Pan-African English, used all along the slave coast, by Portuguese, Italian and other slave drivers as well as native Englishmen.

The geographical limits of Gullah English among the negroes of the South have not been very definitely determined. It has been usually placed in the lower regions of Georgia and South Carolina, especially on the rice plantations of the coast. The culture of the Gullah negroes is in general very low, and probably their speech has not more fully conformed to the white man's conventionally correct English because these negroes have always been field hands, low-class working people with few domestic contacts with the white population. It is not likely that the native African characteristics of these negroes have stood in the way of their acquiring a better English, but rather that they have learned as much from the white man as he gave them opportunity to learn. The Gullah dialect, therefore, has not taken on the character of conventional English speech so extensively as the Virginia negro dialect. "It recognizes no gender," says Harris, *Nights With Uncle Remus* (1881), p. xxxiii, "and scorns the use of the plural number except accidentally. 'E' stands for 'he,' 'she,' 'it,' and 'dem' may allude to one thing, or may include a thousand." A characteristic feature of the Gullah dialect is the adding of a vowel at the end of a word with final consonant, as in "I bin-a wait fer you; come-a ring-a dem bell. Wut mek-a (or mekky) you stay so?" "In such words as 'back,' 'ax,' *a* has the sound of *ah*," and in vocabulary also the dialect is markedly individual. The consonant *v* becomes *b* in Gullah. Harris has illustrated Gullah talk in the speech of Daddy Jack, who says *berry* for *very*, *hab* for *have*, and who exhibits numerous other traits of speech not found in the dialect of Uncle Remus and other upland negroes. Certain words in Gullah speech have developed an initial *y*, as for example, *yeddy* for *heard*, *year* for *ear*. A peculiar feature in syntax is the use of a word which originally was presumably the verb *do* as the general sign of verbal action, *do thief* meaning to steal, *do stand up* meaning standing up. In general the verb pays little attention to distinctions of person, tense and number. An unemphatic form of the demonstrative *that* takes a form variously recorded by different transcribers as *suh* [sə] or *say*, the emphatic form being *dat*. "*Wunnuh, yunnuh, oonuh, unnuh*, occasionally *hoonuh*, probably from one and another, is used for *you* and *ye*, usually in addressing more than one, though sometimes also in the singular," Gonzales, p. 283. The word *nyam* means to eat, in various tense applications, and it is explained by J. G. Williams, *De Ole Plantation* (1895), p. vi, as being the same word as the noun yam, meaning sweet potato, the verb developing from the name of the common article of diet among the negroes. It is more probable, however, that the verb is a sort of sound imitation word, like present infantile yum-yum, meaning something good. These are only a few of a considerable number of Gullah characteristics that may be assembled from different literary transcriptions. When they are all used together, as in *The Black Border*, by Gonzales, the effect is extraordinary and perhaps somewhat artificial. According to Williams, *De Ole Plantation*, p. v, Mr. Gonzales's Gullah is as "perfect as it can be written," but he adds that "the negro's description of a jackass to a negro who had never seen a jackass: 'E look same like mule, only mo so,' is almost true of Mr. Gonzales's Gullah."

That the Gullah dialect has not become the conventional literary negro dialect seems to be owing to the fact that Virginia plantation life has appealed more to the interest and sympathy of readers, therefore has provided more useful literary material, than the life of the rice fields along the coast. In the earlier literary examples of negro dialect, however, this was not the case, and the barbarous Gullah was the customary form of negro dialect for use in literature until after the middle of the nineteenth century. Virginia life in the period following was more skilfully exploited in literature than the life of any other region in the South and thus has come to seem most typically Southern.

The older type of negro speech appears in the earliest American plays, one of the first negro characters in literature being Cudjo, in John Leacock's *Fall of British Tyranny,* Philadelphia, 1776. Act IV, Scene iv, takes place on a British man-of-war, near Norfolk, Virginia, and Lord Kidnapper converses with Cudjo as follows:

Kidnapper. Well, my brave blacks, are you come to list?
Cudjo. Eas, massa Lord, you preazee.
Kidnapper. How many are there of you?
Cudjo. Twenty-two, massa.
Kidnapper. Very well, did you all run away from your masters?
Cudjo. Eas, massa Lord, eb'ry one, me too.
Kidnapper. That's clever; they have no right to make you slaves. I wish all the Negroes wou'd do the same. I'll make 'em free—what part did you come from?
Cudjo. Disse brack man, disse one, disse one, disse one, come from Hamton, disse one, disse one, come from Nawfok, me come from Nawfok too.
Kidnapper. Very well, what was your master's name?
Cudjo. Me massa name Cunney Tomsee.
Kidnapper. Colonel Thompson—eigh?
Cudjo. Eas, massa, Cunney Tomsee.
Kidnapper. Well then I'll make you a major—and what's your name?
Cudjo. Me massa cawra me Cudjo.
Kidnapper. Cudjo?—very good—was you ever Christened, Cudjo?
Cudjo. No, massa, me no crissen.
Kidnapper. Well then I'll christen you—you shall be called major Cudjo Thompson. . . .
Cudjo. Tankee, massa, gaw bresse, massa Kidnap.

In another early American play, Murdock's *Triumphs of Love,* Philadelphia, 1775, a character Sambo speaks a negro dialect with clear traces of Gullah talk in it. Looking at himself in the glass, he monologizes as follows, Reed, *Realistic Characters*, p. 56: "Sambo, what a gall call a pretty fellow. Dis wool of mine will curlee up so, can't get him straight—dat all de fashion emong gemmen. Sambo tinks handsome. He berry 'complish'd too: he sing well; he dance well; he play fiddle well. He tink—he berry often tink why he slave to white man; why black folke sold like cow or horse. He tink de Great Somebody above no order tings so."

Samuel Low's *Politician Outwitted*, New York, 1789, has a character Cuffy, who speaks some short passages of negro dialect which have the common marks of Gullah speech. "Tankee, massa buckaraw," he says, Act V, Sc. i, "you gi me lilly lif [lift] me bery glad; —disa ting damma' heby. [Puts down the trunk]—An de debelis crooka tone in a treet [crooked stones in the street] more worsa naw prickapear for poor son a bitch foot; and de cole pinch um so too." The name Cuffy is recorded in the *Century Dictionary* as a general name for a negro in the South. It is said to be derived from Dutch Koffi, in Guiana a common name for negroes and by custom applies to any one born on Friday. It is this name probably which has given rise to the phrase "proud as Cuffy," that is, proud as a negro tricked out in gaudy splendor.

Benjamin Franklin has a short passage of negro dialect, which is of the Gullah variety, in his "Information to those who would remove to America," *Writings*, Ed. Smythe, VIII, 606, probably written in 1782. "They are pleased," the passage runs, "with the observation of a Negro, and frequently mention it, that *Boccarorra* (meaning the white man) *make de black man workee, make de Horse workee, make de Ox workee, make ebery thing workee; only de Hog. He, de hog, no workee; he eat, he drink, he walk about, he go to sleep when he please, he libb like a Gentleman.*"

Excellent negro characterization appears in J. Robinson's *The Yorker's Stratagem*, New York, 1792. In this play, the action of which takes place in the West Indies, Banana's mother wants her son Banana to desert his wife Priscilla and marry a rich white girl.

Mrs. Banana. What is here fur do? You, Priscilla, you no hab de impurence of de debil, to make such a noise in a my house?

Priscilla. I no hab right for come see my husband?

Mrs. Banana. Who da you husband?

Priscilla. Banana da my husband.

Mrs. Banana. Who tell you so?

Priscilla. Da, me tell myself so.

Mrs. Banana. Who you, you?

Priscilla. Me, me, me, me, Priscilla.

Mrs. Banana. You mulatto Seasor, go tell de obaseer for come turn dis imperence hussy out of doors.

Priscilla. Lord a mighty in a tap, me poor one in a buckra country; you eber been hear de like of dat—me da imperence hussy—eh—who da you?

Mrs. Banana. Me da lady.

Priscilla. You da deble, look a like a lady; tigh, dirty no come dab me.

Mrs. Banana. Me hab plantation.

Priscilla. You, ye lookee like a mumu; you mout like a bull-frog.

Mrs. Banana. Me hab nega like a you.

Priscilla. You lye, you sesy yi, you mumu nose, you daddy mout chew tobacco, fire gun beem; me no care dat for you.

The following verses, entitled "True African Wit," occur in the *New Hampshire and Vermont Journal:* or *The Farmer's Weekly Museum* [Walpole, N. H.], July 26, 1796.

"Old Cato, on his death bed lying,
Worn out with work and almost dying,
With patience heard his friend propose
What bearers for him they had chose—
There's Cuff and Cæsar, Pomp and Plato,
'Dey will do bery well,' quoth Cato,
And Bantam Philips—now for t'other
We must take Scipio, Bantam's brother.

'I no like Scip,' old Cato cries,
'Scip rascal, tell about me lies,
And get me whip'd,' ki, 'tis all one,
Scip shall be bearer, Scip or none.
'Mind me,' quoth Cato, 'if dat cur,
Dat Scip, come bearer, I wont tir!' "[1]

A poem, "A Negro's Lamentation," written at Charleston, *Monthly Mirror*, III (1800), p. 398, contains only one or two words of negro speech, though it has several descriptive touches of negro life in Charleston.

In *Jonathan Postfree*, by L. Beach, New York, 1807, Cesar in Act I, Sc. i, also speaks a Gullah type of negro dialect: "I no likee this massa Fopling—I don't know what ole missee can see in him to make her likee him so much:—he no half so good as Jemmy Seamore;—and younga missee Maria she know it;—she love one little finger of Jemmy more better than Fopling's whole body—but I must holee my tongue—here he come— . . . Me no muchee fear the weight of your cane, massa, such a little tick [stick] no hurtee me much—." The dialect is not very consistently maintained in this character, the most regular features being the addition of a vowel after words ending in a consonant, as in *younga*, *workee*, *teachee*, *likee*, and the change of *v* to *b*, as in *lobe* for *love*, *libe* for *live*. The scene of this play is New York, and Cesar is servant to an old Mr. Ledger, a man of business in that city. The crude and childlike syntax and pronunciation of this negro dialect are indicative of a very different conception of the negro body servant from that which came to prevail later. It is now in the tradition of this type of character that he should exhibit even marks of courtliness and distinction in manner, should reflect some of the polish of the gentlemen of the old school in the service of whom his conduct was formed.

The scene of A. B. Lindsley's *Love and Friendship*, New York, 1807, is laid in Charleston, South Carolina, where Gullah dialect would be appropriate to the locality. Among the characters are Harry, a black boy, and Phillis, a black woman. The following speech

[1] Through the courtesy of Mr. Clarence S. Brigham, Librarian of the American Antiquarian Society.

of Harry's, Act I, Sc. i, shows clearly enough the type of dialect which they speak: "Oh massa, you de terrible young man for true—you bin de bery debil wid de gal; dey often axa me how you do, and say you bin de man for dem; you no hab bashful like some younga buckrah, you pull dere cap and hug 'em, so dey feel it tickle like all over, from de knee way long up to de head; and, for true, I tink dey bin like sich man de bess, for dey like for be tumel bout."

In Tabitha Tenney's *Female Quixotism*, the first edition of which appeared about 1808, appears Scipio, who seems to be the first negro character developed at length in fiction. The scene of this novel is the neighborhood of Philadelphia. Several samples of Scipio's speech are the following:

"But what devil put him in your head, Betty, to dress in masser croase, and go in de grobe?" Vol. I, Chap. XIV. "Gor bressa my soul' where you gown, you cap, you hanker, you every ting?" Vol I, Chap. XV. "Yes he be, Betty—he wife die, two tree year ago, and he darter all marry. Pose he want somebody wass he sirt, cook he vittles, make he bed; and so come gette you."[1]

Among the various dialect experiments in Cooper's *Pioneers* (1823), German English, French English, Irish English, British English and American English, occur samples also of negro English in the speech of Agamemnon. The negro dialect of this character is less elaborately developed than is the speech of the other dialect characters, a little negro dialect in Cooper's opinion apparently going a long way to supply all this kind of color that was needed. Cooper speaks of Agamemnon's "Guinea blood," therefore supposedly he was a Guinea negro, though by the first quarter of the nineteenth century the local origins of a particular negro must have been a matter of very uncertain inference. Whatever his origins may have been, Agamemnon does not speak a Virginia negro dialect, but something more like Gullah English, as in the following passage from Chapter XXXII: "O, Masser Richard! Masser Richard! such a ting! such

[1] See also Hutton, *Curiosities of the American Stage*, pp. 95–96, for the negro on the stage, and F. P. Gaines, *The Southern Plantation, A Study in the Development and the Accuracy of a Tradition* (1924), p. 97.

a ting! I nebber tink a could 'appen! nebber tink he die! O, Lor-a-gor! ain't bury—keep 'em till Masser Richard get back—got a grabe dug . . ."

There is an element of unconvincingness in this dialect, but perhaps not more so than in Cooper's other attempts to write dialect, or in fact any forms of his supposedly humorous conversation. Negro dialect characters appear also in Cooper's *Satanstoe* (1845), but the dialect is very thin and badly managed.

It is interesting to note that Irving, in the *Tales of a Traveller*, 1824, did not utilize an obvious opportunity to employ negro dialect. In the *Adventure of the Black Fisherman* the principal character is Black Sam, but he speaks no dialect, only conventional English. If one may hazard a guess to explain this fact, it may be that the only literary negro dialect which Irving had at hand being a very barbarous Gullah dialect, he preferred to avoid dialect altogether to using an English so outlandish.

In *Haverhill*, a novel by James A. Jones, New York, 1831, a negro, supposed to be from the Gold Coast, speaks as follows, Vol. II, p. 190: "Me dig down where dey bury ole massa Billy Brimmer; fine bones braky, braky, get up whole airt [earth] full a bone—tigh-bone, solder-blade, teet, toe-bone; look-a-here, Sang, see wid him own ears." Various other negro dialect passages occur in this story, the latter part of which is laid in the West Indies, but they are all much alike. It was probably through traders and travelers in the West Indies that all these early examples of negro dialect were derived.

In *The Yemassee* (1835), by W. Gilmore Simms, a negro Hector figures largely in the story, the scene of which is laid in South Carolina, near Beaufort. "Da good dog dat," says Hector, Chap. XLI, "dat same Dugdale. But he hab reason—Hector no gib 'em meat for not'ing. Spaniar no l'arn 'em better, and de Lord hab mercy 'pon dem Ingin, eff he once stick he teet in he troat. He better bin in de fire, for he neber leff off, long as he kin kick. Hark—da good dog, dat same Dugdale. Wonder way massa pick up da name for 'em; speck he Spanish—in English, he bin Dogdale." Hector also uses *enty* for *haven't you*, *yerry* for *hear*, and *um* as a generalized pronoun.

Paulding's *Dutchman's Fireside* (1831) contains several negro characters, servants in Hudson river Dutch families, but their dialect, of the older grotesque type, is not highly developed. A few passages of negro speech also appear in *Westward Ho* (1832), but none of any extent. In both of these tales Indian characters appear as well as negro, but the dialect of both is mostly puerile English, with very little red or black color in it.

Even in Longstreet's *Georgia Scenes* (1835), the work of a professed realist, negro dialect is only meagerly represented, the following, p. 48, being typical of the occasional brief passage: "Fedder fly all ober de buckera-man meat, he come bang me fo' true—No massa, I mighty sorry for your wife, but I no cutty chicken open."

A good deal of Gullah negro dialect occurs in Caroline Gilman's *Recollections of a Southern Matron* (1837), a novel descriptive of manners and society in South Carolina. It is interesting to observe that Mrs. Gilman thinks it necessary to apologize "as a matter of taste for the frequent introduction of the negro dialect," but she explains that it "has only been done when essential to the development of individual character."

The action of Poe's *Gold Bug*, published in 1839, takes place at Sullivan's Island, near Charleston, South Carolina. In the story a negro servant, Jupiter, speaks dialect, though the dialect is not very elaborate, consisting mainly in the change of *v* to *b*, of voiceless *th* to *t*, of voiced *th* to *d*, and in the generalized use of certain pronouns. Certain archaisms occur, like *sartain*, *mought*, *ventur*, which possibly may have been derived by Poe from a not very discriminating recollection of New England literary dialect. As is apparent from the following passage, however, Jupiter speaks not a Virginian, but something like a Gullah dialect: "Him rotten, massa, sure nuff . . . but no so berry rotten as mought be. Mought ventur' out leetle way 'pon de limb by myself, dat's true."

In the decade before the Civil War a considerable body of slavery and anti-slavery fiction was published in which negro characters figured more or less, though negro dialect was much less skilfully and generally used in this literature than one might expect. Very often it was intentionally avoided in order not to impair the dignity of an argument. Interest in the negro at this time was not picturesque and realistic but controversial. The most famous negro character in fiction was presented to the public when Mrs. Stowe's *Uncle Tom's Cabin* was published in 1852. There is a certain amount of dialect in this novel, but not in the speech of Uncle Tom. Even in familiar conversation, Uncle Tom expresses himself with very little dialect color, hardly more than enough to enable the reader to place his speech on the low colloquial level. This is one of the various devices employed by Mrs. Stowe to keep Tom in a central and dignified position in her story. Other characters upon whom the weight of doctrine rested more lightly were allowed to speak more dialectally. Thus Uncle Tom's wife, Aunt Chloe, makes use of as complete a negro dialect as Mrs. Stowe had at her command. But the illusion even of Aunt Chloe's speech is very imperfect. It is, in fact, New England literary dialect, slightly adapted to a Southern climate. "Good, plain, common cookin' Jinny 'll do," says Aunt Chloe, Chapter IV "—make a good pone o' bread,—bile her taters *fa'r*,—her corn-cakes isn't extra, not extra now, Jinny's corn-cakes isn't, but then they's fa'r,—but Lor, come to de higher branches, and what can she do? Why, she makes pies,—sartin she does; but what kinder crust? Can she make your real flecky paste, as melts in your mouth, and lies all up like a puff? Now, I went over thar when Miss Mary was gwine to be married, and Jinny, she jest showed me de weddin-pies. Jinny and I is good friends, ye know. I never said nothin'; but go 'long, Mas'r George! Why, I shouldn't sleep a wink for a week, if I had a batch of pies like dem ar. Why, dey warn't no 'count 't all." For verisimilitude this speech would be better adapted, both in language and in content, to the "pie belt" of the North than to the cotton fields of the sunny South. Assisted by a red turban and charcoal it might pass, but as literary workmanship, it is crude.

When by proclamation the negro became a citizen of the United States, it was perhaps a necessary consequence to this great event that he should, at least in literary representations of his speech, utter his thoughts in a language more like that of the body of American citizens than was the Gullah literary dialect. In reality, as the opportunities of conventional education have been opened to him, the negro has acquired conventional English speech with as much facility and as perfectly as any of the numerous races and classes that have entered the American public schools. A negro dialect markedly different from the dialect speech of white people would therefore seem too remote from the real speech of negroes to be useful for literary purposes. For these reasons, probably, when local color became the literary fashion in the decades following the Civil War, the type of negro who figured in the literature of the time was not the sea-islander, speaking an outlandish gibberish, but the plantation darkie, echoing in his own way the courtly address and manner of his white superiors.[1]

Negro dialect characters as they appear in early American plays and novels do not owe anything to imitation of similar characters in British writing. They are apparently the result of direct observation, and for this reason one might expect that West Indian and coast negroes served as models rather than the plantation negroes because the early lines of travel and communication made the West Indian negroes and the coast negroes of South Carolina better known than the negroes of the interior. It was not until the time of the Civil War that the Virginia negro became a familiar folklore figure.

Perhaps the earliest example of negro dialect in English occurs in De Foe, *The Family Instructor*, Vol. II, Part II, Dialogue IV (1715). In this dialogue, a little negro boy, about fourteen years old, is servant to a white boy. The negro boy, named Toby, has been brought from Barbados, and "though born in that island, spoke but imperfect English."

Toby. Me be born at Barbadoes.

Boy. Who lives there, Toby?

Toby. There lives white mans, white womans, negree mans, negree womans, just so as live here.

Boy. What and not know God?

[1] See F. P. Gaines, *The Southern Plantation*, pp. 21 ff., for some further examples of nineteenth-century negro dialect.

Toby. Yes, the white mans say God prayers,—no much know God.

Boy. And what do the black mans do?

Toby. They much work, much work,—no say God prayers, not at all.

Boy. What work do they do, Toby?

Toby. Makee the sugar, makee the ginger,—much great work, weary work, all day, all night.

. . . .

Toby. Yes, yes, teaché me to read; pray teaché me.

In the second part of *Robinson Crusoe*, Defoe has a great deal of the talk of native South American Indians, but it is very little different from his negro English. "But how you makee me know," says one of the Indians, "that God teachee them to write that book." Later Defoe remarks that "it is to be observed that all these natives [of South America], as also those of Africa, when they learn English, always add two *e's* at the end of the words where we use one; and they place the accent upon them, as makée, takée, and the like; nay, I could hardly make Friday leave it off, though at last he did." It would seem from this that Defoe supposed that a tendency to add a final *e* was born in a savage's blood and came out when he tried to speak English. In all probability, however, the savages heard their English masters pronounce the final *e* and merely imitated them. In De Foe's *Life of Colonel Jacque* (1722) a great deal is said about the negroes of Virginia and Maryland; but only a few words of negro dialect are given, *Works*, ed. Maynadier, VI, 210:

"He shook his head, and made signs that he was *muchee sorree*, as he called it. 'And what will you say or do,' said I, 'if I should prevail with the great master to pardon you? I have a mind to go and see if I can beg for you.' He told me he would lie down, let me kill him. 'Me will,' says he, 'run, go, fetch, bring for you as long as me live.'"

Of the same date as these passages from De Foe is another in Cotton Mather's *Angel of Bethesda*, a tract on inoculation for small-pox written about 1721. Mather quotes the words of his negro slave Onesimus, who had been presented to him by his parishioners and who had been inoculated for the smallpox:

"I have since mett with a considerable Number of these Africans, who all agree in One Story; That in their Countrey *grandy-many* dy of the Small-Pox; But now they learn This Way: People take Juice of *Small-Pox;* and *Cutty-skin,* and Putt in a Drop; then by'nd by a little *Sicky, Sicky:* then very few little things like Small-Pox, and no body dy of it; and no body have *Small-Pox* any more."[1]

Mather calls Onesimus "*a Guramantee*-Servant of my own," and elsewhere he remarks that "the more plainly, brokenly, and blunderingly, and like Ideots, they [the negroes] tell their Story, it will be with reasonable Men, but the much more credible." But Mather's negro, his testimony and his speech, were much ridiculed by contemporary critics. It was perhaps the first time the critics had ever seen a record of negro speech, as indeed it is the earliest example in America that this writer has discovered.

Though Uncle Remus and characters like Page's Marse Chan may be said to be classic literary representations of the American negro, expressing himself in his own dialect, no similarly representative Indian character can be placed by the side of these black men. A good Indian, speaking in character, has never been achieved. Ordinarily the Indian in the thrilling fiction in which he frequently appears is presented as speaking very little, his conversation consisting mainly of the exclamation Ugh, Ugh, enriched with some such statement as *Me heap big Indian,* or a request for firewater. In the more dignified style of writing, he speaks entirely out of character. Hiawatha appears only in poetry, and perhaps poetic license justifies the exalted treatment he receives. The same excuse cannot be made for Cooper's Indians. But apparently Cooper made slight effort to provide his Indian characters with an appropriate speech, like his other distinctively American creations. In *The Pioneers*

[1] See Kittredge, *Lost Works of Cotton Mather,* in *Proceedings of the Mass. Hist. Society,* XLV, 431 (1912).

(1823), in the speech of Chingachgook no attempt at dialect is made at all, and in fact the Indian speaks more conventional English than Leatherstocking or Hurry Harry. At one point, Chapter VII, the author says that the "Mohegan now spoke, in tolerable English," but the words that actually appear in the record are the following: "The children of Miquon do not love the sight of blood, and yet the Young Eagle has been struck by the hand that should do no evil." This is the oratorical style of the speech of Logan, and Chingachgook is allowed to speak in no other manner. He is kept dignified by being made unreal.

In some of his other novels Cooper attempted to treat the speech of Indian characters more realistically. In *Satanstoe* (1845), for example, Susquesus speaks as follows:

"Nuttin' see farther than Injin. Red man fly high, too. See from salt lake to sweet water. Know ebbery t'ing in wood. Tell him nuttin' he don't know." "Red man nebber measure land so. He p'int with finger, break bush down, and say, 'There, take from that water to that water.'"

In *Redskins* (1846), a sequel to *Satanstoe*, similar crude Indian dialect is to be found which differs not at all from Cooper's negro dialect. In Chap. VIII, Cooper uses the word *Sago*, and describes it as "that familiar semi-Indian salutation." In a footnote he adds that "the colonists caught a great many words from the Indians," and that "a sort of limited *lingua franca* has grown up in the country that everybody understands." But the only words Cooper mentions, besides *Sago* in the text, are a few in this note, *moccasin*, *squaw*, *pap-poose*, *tomahawk* and *Yankees*. If this *lingua franca* existed, of which Cooper speaks, certainly Cooper made little effort to use it.

The Indian never had a fair chance to be treated in literature as a human being. By the time Indians began to figure in literature, they were idealized out of all recognition. Indian characters appear in a number of early American plays of the period of the Revolution, but in all of them, the Indians speak like Roman senators. The dignity of the Indian seemed in some way to involve the dignity of the new America. Always more or less aloof, in his daily surroundings the Indian rarely lived in intimate relations with white neighbors. He did not become a house or body servant, like the negro, did not adapt himself to the conditions of the white man's life in such a way as to make him an object of personal sympathetic concern to the latter. The relations of the Indian to the white man were moreover seldom relieved by any humorous attachments. In his happier and original state the Indian may have been dignified and impressive, in his degraded condition he was often disgusting, but at no time does he seem to have been amusing. In this respect also he has differed from the negro, who from the beginning has been an unfailing source of entertainment to his white brethren. Nor has the Indian ever taken enthusiastic advantage of such opportunities as he had to learn English. Too proud to make himself ridiculous by inadequate attempts to speak an unknown language, he preferred either to remain silent or to transact necessary negotiations through an interpreter. For these reasons, though the bad Indian might be treated with some degree of unpleasant realism, the good Indian has not figured largely in American literature, except in literature of a poetic or oratorical kind. Thus an accepted and recognized Indian dialect for literary uses has never been developed, because there was no authentic dialect in the practice of Indians in their relations to white men. Indians who learned English learned it so well that comparatively little Indian color was left in their spoken English. Those who did not learn English remained silent in the presence of whites, earning for themselves the frequently applied epithets sullen, morose and impassive, all terms inapplicable to the Indian in his natural surroundings.

A certain degree of antiquarian interest nevertheless attaches to the attempts that have been made from time to time to record the English of Indians. These attempts are not numerous, nor are the records in which they occur extensive. White men frequently studied the speech of the Indians, though not to record the Indian's English but his native tongue. Examples of "Indian talk" are consequently not easy to find, and additions to the citations that follow may be counted as discoveries.

In the *Present State of New England*, by a merchant of Boston, 1675, p. 12, quoted by Kittredge, p. 354, we read that "About the 15th of *August*, Captain *Mosely* with sixty Men, met with a company, judged about three hundred *Indians*, in a plain place where few Trees were, and on both sides preparations were making for a Battle; all being ready on both sides to fight, Captain *Mosely* plucked off his Periwig, and put it into his Breeches, because it should not hinder him in fighting. As soon as the *Indians* saw that, they fell a Howling and Yelling most hideously, and said, "*Umh, umh, me no stawmerre fight Engis mon, Engis mon got two hed, Engis mon got two hed; if me cut off un hed, he got noder, a put on beder as dis.*" Kittredge remarks that "me no *stawmerre fight Engis mon*" is an oracle that defies interpretation. But *stawmerre* is evidently the same word as that which occurs in the passage from Ames's *Almanack*, 1730, quoted below, and it obviously means *understand*. Whether it is merely a corruption of English *understand*, or is a modification of a genuine Indian word, as seems more probable, only one versed in the phonology of American Indian dialects should venture to say.

In the *Present State of New England*, p. 13, occurs also the anecdote of an Indian who drank the blood of his friend who had been executed: "Being asked his reason therefor, his answer was, Umh, umh nu, Me stronger as I was before, me be so strong as me and he too, he be ver strong Man fore he die." Another anecdote by the same writer, p. 14, relates the story of the rescue of an Englishman who had been left for dead; an Indian found him, took him up and said, "Umh, umh poo Ingisman, me save you life, me take yow to Captain Mosee."

Certain passages of Indian dialect in verse occur in Benjamin Thompson's *New England Crisis*, 1676, quoted by Kittredge, p. 357. In this poem King Philip is described with animosity as delivering the following oration:

> "'My friends, our Fathers were not half so wise
> As we our selves, who see with younger eyes;
> They sel our land to english man, who teach
> Our nation all so fast to pray and preach.

Of all our country they enjoy the best,
And quickly they intend to have the rest.
This no wunnegin; so big matchit law,
Which our old fathers fathers never saw,
These english make, and we must keep them too,
Which is too hard for us or them to doe.
We drink, we so big whipt; but english they
Go sneep, no more, or else a little pay.
Me meddle Squaw, me hang'd; our fathers kept
What Squaws they would, whither they wakt or slept.
Now, if you'le fight, Ile get you english coats,
And wine to drink out of their Captains throats.'

"This was assented to, and, for a close
He strokt his smutty beard and curst his foes."

Another passage of six lines of verse in Indian dialect containing genuine Indian words mingled with transformed English words, is contained in Ames's *Almanack*, for March, 1730, see *The Essays, Humor and Poems of Nathaniel Ames*, ed. Sam Briggs, Cleveland (Ohio), 1891, p. 66. It calls for some editing in punctuation and for some ingenuity in interpretation, though there can be little doubt as to its general meaning. The passage, very brief and apparently the only one of its kind in the *Almanack*, is as follows:

"Cunkeechah Netop? what News you speak to me?
Muffy good news; what? you no Stommonee?
By by come Elwipes much as me can wish
Tink nuxt Week den me shan heb it Bish
Where is Tat prace you speak to me? Me ashk it
Me tink some Pokes he cann his Lame Namaskitt."

Under March, 1735, in this *Almanack*, we are informed that "at this time of the year Namasket River is a Market Place." The theme of the verses in the *Almanack* is thus that event so important in the colonial New England settlements, the annual coming of the alewives. In a note to this passage, p. 69, the editor of Ames's *Almanack* gives the following as a free rendering:

"The aborigine having saluted Netop (Englishman) with an inquiry of surprise, continues: What news you speak to me? mighty good news; what? don't you understand me? By and by Alewives (a sort of fish) will come, as much as I could wish. I think next week then I shall have them sure. Where is the place, you ask me? I answer, I think some folks call its name Namasket (river)."

There is room for difference of opinion concerning some parts of this translation, for example, the translation of Bish, line 4, by *sure*. It seems more likely that Bish is merely the Indian pronunciation of *fish*. It will be observed that the labial continuants become stops in this dialect, *v* becoming *p* in *Elwipes*, *b* in *heb*, and *f* becoming *p* in *Pokes*. The *l* in English words appears as *n* in *shan*, l. 4, and *cann* for *call*, l. 6, but as *r* in *prace*, l. 5, and conversely *n* appears as *l* in *Lame*, l. 6. The solution of these puzzles in sound correspondence must be left to the special student of the American Indian languages, but if one may hazard a statement based on the slight evidence afforded by the passages quoted in this chapter, a certain degree of regularity manifested itself in the sound substitutions which the Indians made in their attempts to pronounce English words.

A curious historical interest attaches to a fragment of Indian dialect extracted by Kittredge, p. 333, from the *Farmer's Almanack* for 1797. The statement in the *Almanack* is as follows:

"An Indian who was appointed a Justice of the Peace, issued the following Warrant.—Me High Howder, yu constable, yu deputy, best way yu look um Jeremiah Wicket, strong yu take um, fast yu hold um, quick yu bring um before me. Captain Howder."

By an elaborate collection of evidence, Kittredge shows that this warrant was not a piece of fiction, that it rests on a basis of fact, and that very probably it had persisted in New England tradition from the second half of the seventeenth century.

In Madam Knight's *Journals* (1704–5), pp. 37–38, occurs an anecdote containing both negro and Indian dialect, though the distinguishing marks of neither are numerous. According to the tale, a negro slave in New Haven stole a hogshead from his master and gave or sold it to an Indian. The Indian then sold it, whereupon the theft was discovered and the Indian brought to trial. The judge happened at the time to be in his field gathering his pumpkins, with a brother justice. "Their worships cann't proceed in form without a Bench: whereupon they Order one to be imediately erected, which, for want of fitter materials, they made with pompions—which being finished, down setts their worships, and the malefactor call'd, and by the Senior Justice Interrogated after the following manner. You Indian why did You steal from this man? You sho'dn't do so—it's a Grandy wicked thing to steal. Hol't Hol't, cryes Justice Jun[r], Brother, you speak negro to him. I'le ask him. You sirrah, why did you steal this man's Hoggshead. Hoggshead? (replys the Indian), me no stomany. No? says his Worship; and pulling off his hatt, Patted his own head with his hand, sais Tatapa—You, Tatapa —you; all one this. Hoggshead all one this. Hah! says Netop, now me stomany that. Whereupon the Company fell into a great fitt of Laughter, even to Roreing."

Ponteach (1766) by Robert Rogers, ed. Nevins, p. 181, has several short passages of slightly broken Indian talk—*How much you ask per quart for this strong Rum?*—but for the most part the characters are heroic and speak elegantly.

A few interesting passages occur in *An Account of the Remarkable Occurrences in the Life and Travels of Col. James Smith*, written by himself, Lexington [Kentucky] 1799, reprinted in the Ohio Valley Historical Series, No. 5. Col. Smith was a prisoner among the Indians from 1755 to 1759. During his captivity he kept a journal, from which his book was made. "On my return to camp," he says, p. 20, describing his life as a captive, "I observed a large piece of fat meat: the Delaware Indian that could talk some English, observed me looking earnestly at this meat, and asked me *what meat you think that is?* I said I supposed it was bear meat; he laughed and said, *ho, all one fool you, beal now elly pool*, and pointing to the other side of the camp, he said *look at that skin, you think that beal skin?* I went and lifted the skin, which appeared like an ox hide: he then said, *what skin you think that?* I replied that I thought it was a buffaloe hide; he laughed and said, *you fool again, you know nothing, you think buffaloe that colo?* I acknowledged I did not know much about these things, and told him I never saw a buffaloe, and that I had not heard what color they were. He replied *by and by you shall see gleat many buffaloe;*

He now go to gleat lick. That skin no buffaloe skin, that skin buck-elk skin." The main phonetic characteristic of this dialect is the substitution of *l* for *r*.

Heckewelder, the Pennsylvania missionary to the Indians, gives the following speech of an Indian, Kittredge, p. 362, dating it about 1770. The substance of the speech is the ineffectiveness of the English as contrasted with the Indian manner of choosing wives:

"White man court,—court,—may be one whole year!—may be two year before he marry!—well!—may be then got *very good wife*—but may be *not*!—may be *very* cross! Well now, suppose cross! scold so soon as get awake in the morning! scold all day! scold until sleep!—all one; he must keep *him*! White people have law forbidding throwing away wife, be *he* ever so cross! must keep *him* always! Well! how does Indian do?—Indian when he see industrious Squaw, which he like, he go to *him*, place his two forefingers close aside each other, make two look like one—look Squaw in the face—see *him* smile—which is all one *he* say Yes! so he take *him* home—no danger *he* be cross! no! no! Squaw know too well what Indian do if *he* cross! throw *him* away and take another! Squaw love to eat meat! no husband! no meat! Squaw do everything to please husband! he do the same to please Squaw! live happy!" This speech may be Indian in sentiment, but very little Indian flavor is to be detected in the language of it. Like most later literary visions of Indian talk, it is merely crude and childish English, the English of the half-breed and the hanger-on about missions and white settlements. Not much literary skill is required to write this kind of dialect and very little direct observation of speech. Abundant examples of it will be found in nineteenth century fiction and books of travel, but for genuine echoes of the Indian-speaking voice, we seem to be dependent upon such occasional scraps of dialect as have been preserved in the almanacs and other records of the Colonial period.

Indian characters appear in Charles Brockden Brown's *Edgar Huntly* (1799), but they do not speak in dialog, all the narrative being given in the first person by the narrator.

The following song, by the Indian maiden Chicka, from a musical entertainment, *The Catawba Travelers: or Kiew Neika's Return*, presented at Sadler's Wells in 1797, indicates the existence at least of a type of song similar to the later "coon" song:

"Chicka like Sailor Man,
Tom like'a Chicka too;
He come home, he shakee hand,
And me say how dye do?
Tom no to Ningland go,
Doll nibber come so far—den—
Ickle Chicka happy Squaw,
With a jolly Tar!—

"Tom Shoot a Cockatoo,
Chicka put him in a pot,—
Tom fill a Wamessou,
And pura till he hot;
Him call for Grog, a ho!
Me drinka swipe galore;—hee—ee!
Ickle Chicka happy Squaw,
Wid a jolly Tar.

"But, Doll 'o Wapping is she dead,
Chicka, den a Ningland goes,—
Yellow fedder on a head,
And Silber at ee Nose;
Gold ring on ebery Toe,
Blue Cheek and shinee hair;—Oh la!
Ickle Chicka pretty Squaw,
For a jolly Tar!"[1]

Through the courtesy of Miss Dorothy Dondore.

STYLE

The historian who attempts to discuss any aspect of style finds his first difficulty in the lack of an accepted definition of the subject. Style is a Je ne sais quoi, the man himself, and a thousand other things. But perhaps the real character of style is best revealed in this very multiplicity of definitions. Style is a quality which in the end reduces to individual variation, therefore cannot be summed up in a theoretical generalization. There is in truth a great similarity in the endeavors which have been made to define dialects and the endeavors which have been made to define style. The final analysis in the study of dialects carries one back to the individual as the only reality. General dialects, whether regional or social, are merely abstract summaries of details selected from the habits of speakers who have, among their countless differentiations, certain relatively few habits in common which make these speakers seem homogeneous when attention is directed specially to their similarities. So it is with style, and the various literary styles of a language may be classed merely among its dialect manifestations.

In America, as in any country employing a highly developed idiom, there is and has been an infinity of ways of expression in language. Only here and there can the student observe a more or less generalized tendency in these habits of expression, and these habits, viewed in perspective, may be made the basis for a history of style. Whether stylistic impulses in America have brought something new and altogether unique into existence is obviously a question that permits of no simple and categorical answer. But certainly it is not possible to detach American writing with ease from the whole body of literature written in the English language and to say that by the possession of this and of that precise quality, it has established itself in its specific character. It is a perilous adventure to attempt the description of anything so subtle and diffused as a general manner of expression. If American style has an essential and distinguishing quality, it does not have it as the clear result of conscious choice and intention. It must be something deeply hidden. In a recent stimulating discussion,[1] an endeavor is made to bring to light this hidden quality by contrasting American with British style. The essential quality of British style, as here conceived, is something that may be best described as structural. In British writing the thought and its expression are considered as elaborated together into a compact and mutually dependent unity which gives to this writing a kind of organic architectural character. And this standard and method of literary expression, it is assumed, come to the Englishman from his respectful study not only of the classics of Greek and Latin, but also of the classics of his own literature. American style, on the contrary, rests not upon a basis of structural organization, but is more a matter of points, of successive brilliant moments, of verbal ingenuities and surprises. It is a restless, rapid, animated style, a sparkling if not a profound style. In short, American style, in this study, is taken to be a style of wit, whereas British style is a style of thought and constructive understanding.

That this characterization of American style applies not inaptly to many American writers is beyond question. That it distinguishes recent American writers markedly from recent British writers is not so certain. For the purpose of comparison, manifestly it would be meaningless to compare Burke or Macaulay with American writers of the present day. Like must be compared with like. The tendency of all English writing, within the past two or three generations, has been to move away from the formal structure of the older classics towards a simpler, more rapid and flexible stylistic method. This applies to British as well as to American writers. Formal structure in all modern English writing tends to be replaced by other more lightly moving qualities, and so far as the comparison between British and American writing is concerned, perhaps it may be said that the latter has only traveled a little faster than the former. Certainly when one looks back a generation or two in America, one finds few

[1] *American Style*, by Stuart Sherman, in *Points of View* (1924), pp. 153–170.

striking marks of difference between writing in England and writing in America. A perspective even of a short duration levels many distinctions.

If a new soul and a new style were born in America, one finds it difficult to settle upon a fixed date for this important event. It remains a matter of debate who is rightly to be called the first American man of letters. Early colonial writers like Captain John Smith and the Puritan recorders and historians were neither Americans nor men of letters in any just sense of these terms. Not until one approaches the Revolution in the third quarter of the eighteenth century can one reasonably speak of writers in America as being American. Of these first American writers, the chief historical place is unquestionably occupied by Benjamin Franklin. Franklin was much more than a man of letters, and indeed has come to be regarded in the latter light not because he made a direct bid for literary fame but, like Bacon, whom he in several respects resembled, because his larger activities could not be carried on without the assistance of a literary method and technic. After many generations of Americans have lived, Franklin's own personal life also seems in many respects prophetic of what a definitely typical literary American was to be. In rough outline the story of the poor printer's boy who emerges by rigorous self-discipline and native wit into the bright light of public success might serve for numerous American authors.

American in spirit and in choice of theme Franklin may have been, but when one examines the details of his literary method, one finds no peculiar Americanism in style. It could not have been otherwise with the spiritual background which Franklin has described near the beginning of his *Autobiography*. "From a child," he says, "I was fond of reading, and all the little money that came into my hands was ever laid out in books. Pleased with Pilgrim's Progress, my first collection was of John Bunyan's works in separate little volumes. I afterwards sold them to enable me to buy R. Burton's Historical Collections. . . . My father's library consisted chiefly of books in polemic divinity, most of which I read . . . Plutarch's Lives there was in which I read abundantly and I still think that time spent to great advantage. There was also a book of De Foe's, called an Essay on Projects, and another of Dr. Mather's, called Essays to do Good, which perhaps gave me a form of thinking that had an influence on some of the principal future events of my life." After some excursions into the field of poetry, from which he was rescued by the ridicule of his father, Franklin devoted himself to prose writing. He describes a bad habit of disputatiousness which he had fallen into, caught by reading his father's religious books, and how he was brought to the realization of a more urbane manner of writing. "About this time, I met with an odd volume of the Spectator. It was the third. I had never before seen any of them. I bought it, read it over and over, and was much delighted with it. I thought the writing excellent, and wished, if possible, to imitate it. With this view I took some of the papers, and, making short hints of the sentiment in each sentence, laid them by a few days, and then, without looking at the book, try'd to complete the papers again, by expressing each hinted sentiment at length, and as fully as it had been expressed before, in any suitable words that should come to hand. Then I compared my Spectator with the original, discovered some of my faults, and corrected them. But I found I wanted a stock of words, or a readiness in recollecting and using them, which I thought I should have acquired before that time if I had gone on making verses; since the continual occasion for words of the same import, but of different length, to suit the measure, or of different sound for the rhyme, would have laid me under a constant necessity of searching for variety, and also have tended to fix that variety in my mind, and make me master of it. Therefore I took some of the tales and turned them into verse; and, after a time, when I had pretty well forgotten the prose, turned them back again. I also sometimes jumbled my collections of hints into confusion, and after some weeks endeavored to reduce them into the best order, before I began to form the full sentences and compleat the paper. This was to teach me method in the arrangement of thoughts. By comparing my work afterwards with the original, I discovered many faults and amended them; but I sometimes had the pleasure of fancying that, in certain particulars of small import, I had been lucky enough to improve the method or the language, and this encouraged me to think I might possibly in time come to be a tolerable English writer, of which I was extreamly ambitious."

It has seemed worth while calling attention again to these well-known passages in Franklin's *Autobiography* because in kind they might stand for the normal experience of almost any American man of letters from the time they were written to the present day. What Franklin aspired to become was "a tolerable English writer," and he conceived that the best method of attaining this end was to discipline himself in the best literary traditions of the English language. The thought probably never occurred to Franklin that to be a true American writer he must renounce the whole or any part of British cultural tradition. Franklin's concern in writing was primarily with content, and so it is with every serious writer. Language is merely the mechanical means to convey the content effectively. If therefore one had at hand an adequate mechanical means, as any writer of English was convinced he had in Franklin's day in the language of Shakspere and Milton and Addison, only a pedant or theorist would have refused to use this means. "Nicenesse in wordes," says the Preface to the King James translation of the Bible, "was alwayes counted the next step to trifling." So the first writers of English in America thought when it came to the practical question of using or refusing the heritage of literary expression common to all whose native speech is English. Their purpose was not to escape the literary traditions of the past, but to utilize and to surpass them. The spirit of their endeavor was ambitiously expressed in the following lines from one of Samuel Low's *Poems* (1800), p. 135:

> "The time will come, soon may that time arrive,
> When Roman greatness shall in us revive;
> When Homer's genius here sublime shall soar,
> And a new Virgil grace this western shore."

Homer and Virgil in these lines merely express figuratively respect for the accredited achievements of the past in English literature.

Acceptance of the traditions of good literature by American writers after the Revolution did not carry with it, however, a confessed and absolute submission to older models. On the contrary, critical opinion at least favored a healthy expansion in the use of the English language in America. In this respect as in many others Noah Webster was one of the leaders of opinion. It should be remembered, however, that what Webster advocated was not the construction of a new language in America, but the use of English as it already existed on American soil for all purposes, colloquial or literary. In other words, Webster thought that the "Federal English" which he advocated could find for its basis a better foundation in the English actually spoken and current among the "yeomanry" of New England than in the English of England, or even in the books written in the traditional language of England. But this was a theoretical rather than a practical notion on the part of Webster. It had some following, however, and apparently was one of the tenets of the Philological Society, which flourished but briefly during the year 1788. Among the more important members of this society were Josiah Ogden Hoffman, William Dunlap, the dramatist, and Noah Webster, all persons of distinction. Others, however, as Jeremy Belknap, see Ford, *Notes,* I, 185, treated the Society with scorn. It formed a part of the procession in New York to celebrate the adoption of the Constitution by ten states, see Webster's Diary, July 23, 1788. The procession was "very brilliant but fatiguing," says Webster, adding, "I formed a part of the Philological Society, whose flag and uniform black dress made a very respectable figure." It is difficult now to call to life again the enthusiasm for a new Federal English which gave to these patriotic representatives of it a kind of symbolical place in a great state procession. It was, however, an enthusiasm of sentiment, not of reason. Even Webster, who was the most devoted supporter of the cause, put very little of his theory into practice when it came actually to writing. In his dictionaries he inserted a few New England local words, but his own writings are as Addisonian as those of Franklin. Webster wrote well, but he did so not because of, but in spite of, his theories. The judgment of Jefferson, *Writings*, ed. Ford, VIII, 80, expressed in 1801, that Webster was "a mere pedagogue, of very limited understanding," was severe and unsympathetic, but it is not difficult to see how a man of broad common sense like Jefferson might be annoyed at some of Webster's preachments. American provincialism of thought in the eighteenth century shows more in just such strivings after an unworthy independence than in a frank acceptance of the past achievements of English civilization.

The views which Jefferson held with respect to language, especially with respect to the use of neologisms, have been discussed in the chapter on vocabulary. They were, as one would expect from the man, sensible and liberal views. Jefferson had no notion of discarding in America the good which England had to offer. What he desired to secure in the matter of language was coöperation between England and America. For the good of the English language in England as well as for the good of the English language in America, he counseled an open-mindedness towards innovation such as would permit new adaptations to new circumstances and would permit growth where growth was necessary. Only as a final evil did he permit his mind to dwell on the possibility that the English language of England might become stationary, in which case he adds, *Writings*, ed. Washington, VI, 184, "we shall probably enlarge our employment of it, until its new character may separate it in name as well as in power, from the mother-tongue."

No traces of the beginning of this separation can be found in Jefferson's own writings. He is credited with having coined the verb *belittle*, but this is a stray and doubtful example. Neither in vocabulary nor in syntax does his writing betray any peculiar Americanism. Such local flavor as it has comes from content, not form, and any Englishman of equal good sense and knowledge would have written as he wrote. Jefferson was greatly interested in French thought and French style, as were many other Americans in his day. It is doubtful if any other American has been quite as much at home in France as was Franklin, and it was a common charge against Jefferson by his enemies that he was too much under the influence of French philosophy. This interest also tended to preserve American English from provincial extravagance, encouraging at the same time simplicity and lightness rather than pomposity of style.

In their critical opinions as in their writings, Americans of the first years of the Republic accepted and approved the simple and natural standards of style which entered English literature in the first decade of the eighteenth century. In the meantime Dr. Johnson had appeared and had done his best to free the language of "colloquial barbarisms, licentious idioms and irregular combinations," to reduce it in short to a pompous and formal regularity. In America, however, little respect was shown for the Johnsonian style, and though the reaction against Johnson became marked also in England at the end of the eighteenth century, opinion in America seems to have been independent of opinion in England. In a revolutionary society supposedly based upon simple common rights one ought not indeed to find the artificial and narrowly literary style of Johnson regarded sympathetically. The temptation to do so lay in the fact that it provided an easy method and technic for acquiring literary distinction. To write in the Johnsonian style was much easier than to write in a simpler style. One must record it to the credit of American writers that in this difficult period of their literary development they did not lose sight of the essential element in their new freedom.

Dislike of Dr. Johnson went deeper than it would have done if it had been occasioned merely by his political opinions. It is not to be expected that Americans would think kindly of the author of *Taxation No Tyranny* and of many a jibe by the way at America as the home of uncivilized barbarians, a region interesting only for its "natural curiosities." "A nation scattered in the boundless regions of America," wrote Johnson in his *Journey to the Western Islands*, "resembles rays diverging from a focus. All the rays remain but the heat is gone." When Johnson wrote thus he could not have been thinking of American opinions of his style, for there was heat enough in them. Webster was untiring in his hostility to Johnson. He declared, *Dissertations*, p. xi, that Johnson's pedantry had "corrupted the purity of the English language," and again, p. 32, that "the benefits derived from his morality and his erudition will hardly counterbalance the mischief done by his manner of writing." Webster was of the opinion, p. 30, that it would have been fortunate for the English language if the style of writing had been fixed as it stood in the reign of Queen Anne and her successor, that "few improvements have been made since that time, but innumerable corruptions in pronunciation have been introduced by Garrick, and in stile, by Johnson, Gibbon and their imitators." One may doubt the influence of Garrick in pronunciation, but there can be no question that the learned and artificial style acquired great respect through the example set by Dr. Johnson and his followers at the very time when the first Americans were choosing the style in which they would write.

The views of Hugh Henry Brackenridge on Johnson and on style in general are worth more than a moment's notice. Brackenridge began the publication of his *Modern Chivalry* in 1792, a book which from the point of view of literary virtuosity, had no equal in American literature until the appearance of Irving's *Knickerbocker's History*. *Modern Chivalry* is a medley of satirical, humorous and other sketches on distinctly American subjects, but largely inspired by the reading of Cervantes, Le Sage and Swift. In the Author's Address to the Reader, Brackenridge raises the question of the best means of doing something towards establishing the literary character of the English language, and concludes that "if some work were undertaken with a view to stile, regarding thought as of secondary importance, it might do more to effect so desirable an end, than can be accomplished by all the dictionaries and institutes that were ever made." He therefore undertook this book, "in which stile, language and forms of expression are more regarded than matter." With this program, the author permitted himself the greatest liberty of excursion, both in narrative and in casual comment. He frequently took the reader with him to his literary workshop, discussing purposes and methods of writing with the learning and earnestness of the true artist. "The English language," he declared, Vol. I, Chapter XX, "has not been so well written in England since the time of that literary dunce,

Samuel Johnson, who was totally destitute of taste for the *vrai naturelle,* or simplicity of nature." "Language being the vestment of thought," he says elsewhere in this same chapter, "it comes within the rules of other dress; so that, as slovenliness, on the one hand, or foppery on the other, is to be avoided in our attire, so also in our speech and writing. Simplicity in the one and the other, is the greatest beauty." In another passage, Vol. IV, Chapter II, which must be quoted, he acknowledges his chief admirations among English writers. He repeats the statement that in the writing of his book, style was his primary object, adding, "I will acknowledge at the same time, *entre nous,* that stile is what I never could exactly hit, to my own satisfaction. And in the English language, that of Hume, Swift, and Fielding, is the only stile that I have coveted to possess. For I take it they are precisely the same, according to the subjects of their writing. But the easy, the natural, and the graceful, is of all stiles, whether of manners or of speaking, the most difficult to attain."

Thus early in the annals of American writing, Brackenridge had comprehended the peculiarly American problem of combining informality and art. His own performances were frankly experimental, and in one respect at least his judgment was faulty. He was mistaken in thinking that by style alone he could effectively establish a literary use of the English language. A permanently interesting content is necessary to keep a work alive, and if Brackenridge had devoted as much attention to content as he did to style, his book would not now be known only to the literary or linguistic historian. The book was popular in its own day, but it is more significant as showing the drift of literary thought in Brackenridge's time than for any direct influence which it has exerted upon other writers.

One further early criticism of Johnson may be noted from the pen of Joseph Brown Ladd, a poet of some merit who was born at Newport in 1764 and was killed in a duel at Charleston, South Carolina, in 1786. In his *Literary Remains,* pp. 181–194, appears an essay which must have been first printed very soon after Johnson's death. "Of all modern perversions of taste," he remarks, "the works of

Johnson have done the greatest mischief." The *Rambler* is said to be written "in a swelled, pompous, bombastical language, an affected structure, and verbosity of style." "The swelled, bombastic style succeeds with the lower class of readers, who are by far the most numerous. Hence, every writer, who is deficient in that genius, will affect pomposity and magnificence of language." "At present," concludes the essay, "this alarming revolution of our taste seems to be making hasty strides in common life. There are few readers who think a writer tolerable that is not magnificent. Overseers write florid letters to their employers; and men in business publish sublime advertisements."

The first region of America in which a genuine community interest and effort in literature developed was in Connecticut. In the last quarter of the eighteenth century that group of writers known as the Hartford Wits made what they thought was a new literary discovery of America, not to be sure the discovery of a literary continent already in existence, but of an utterly virgin empire of literary themes waiting to crown them and America with glory.

There was good reason why Connecticut should be the home of the muses in the latter eighteenth century. By that time the State was completely settled and homogeneously civilized. The population had come in from two directions. From the older colony in Massachusetts, pioneer adventurers had entered the valley of the Connecticut within the seventeenth century. Other settlements were made along the Sound, and the two waves of population spreading south and north soon mingled and extinguished the frontier, so far as Connecticut was concerned. The Connecticut Yankee prospered and was happy. He did not grow rich, for his land did not flow with milk and honey. It was a stony and hilly land in the main, cut into numerous north and south ridges with narrow valleys between them and rivers that leaped south into the Sound. But the rivers were full of waterfalls which supplied power for countless small factories, for hoe shops and hat shops, for ax factories, for clock factories, for the making of an infinite variety of Yankee notions.

The valleys were fertile and the hills too brought forth abundantly when strenuous labor had obtained for the seed a lodging place among the rocks. Travelers and contemporary recorders unite in presenting an idyllic picture of busy and humble contentment in the Connecticut of the closing decades of the eighteenth century. Steam and electricity had not yet revealed their possibilities. The organization of business and manufacturing was still on a small scale and humanly comprehensible. The glamour of western riches and adventure had not yet made the farmer and mechanic weary of his simple and hard-working lot. All the boundless energy which later was to play a chief part in subduing the wilderness of central New York, of the Western Reserve in Ohio, of southern Michigan, Wisconsin and northern Indiana and Illinois, all this was still active in the many pleasant villages that nestled in the valleys or perched upon the hill-tops throughout the length and breadth of Connecticut.

In those days Connecticut was not only a happy land, but the people who dwelt in it knew that it was. They were proud of their State, proud of their skill, proud of their learning, proud of their democracy, proud of their country of which they considered themselves to be no inconsiderable part. Noah Webster was only one of many who had visions of this people asserting itself, building upon its own fully developed and harmonious culture a new civilization which should be distinctive for America as British culture was distinctive for England. Certainly such a people could not remain satisfied without some literary achievement to maintain proper balance with the other elements of its greatness. To achieve was the prime necessity in Connecticut, and the Hartford Wits were not sluggish in realizing this new opportunity at their doors, and this pious obligation which rested upon them.

Life at this time and in this place was by no means given over to material things. Every village had its respected representatives of learning and piety. Jonathan Edwards was born in a Connecticut village and educated at Yale. Intellectual interests indeed had advanced so far by the last quarter of the century, that not a little of the rationalist and sceptical color of French philosophy was tolerated even in the opinions of highly respected persons. Plain living and high thinking were the order of the day and the soil was well prepared for the flowering of a literary culture.

The most distinguished members of this Connecticut republic of letters were Timothy Dwight, one of Yale's memorable presidents, Joel Barlow, John Trumbull, and David Humphreys. All these writers were mainly poets. Dwight published his *Conquest of Canaan* in 1785, though it was written eleven years before. It is a long epic poem based on Scriptural sources, but the transition from Canaan to Connecticut was easy for Dwight, and the poem was not lacking in local American allusion and color. Its chief literary models were Pope's *Homer* and Milton's *Paradise Lost*. Dwight's *Greenfield Hill* was published in 1794. It was written in several rhythms, heroic couplets, Spenserian stanzas, blank verse, and octosyllabics, each suggested by the characteristic metrical form of a standard British poet. From the brow of Greenfield Hill where now he would look down upon smoky Bridgeport, the poet looked out upon the world. His feet and his heart were firmly fixed in America, but his vision was not merely of things parochial. When Dwight wrote about Connecticut, he did so with the full realization that he was, as it were, putting Connecticut on the literary map. He was doing for Greenfield Hill what Goldsmith, Thomson, Denham, Milton, Pope and Beattie had done for various regions in England, and in fact he often did this in almost exactly the same words.

The grandiose conception of Columbus seeing in vision the future of the continent he had discovered provided Joel Barlow with the theme for his *Visions of Columbus*, published in 1787. This was later doubled in size and published as an epic poem, *The Columbiad*, in 1807. As an epic worthy of America, *The Columbiad* was designed to out-Homer Homer. Not only was its subject greater, but its style was more refined and its moral purpose was loftier than anything Homer dreamed of. In other words, Barlow did not attempt to create a new style for his American epic but merely to do better what Pope and Milton and Virgil and Homer had done before him. In the *Conquest of Canaan* and *The Columbiad* America was now provided by these industrious sons of Connecticut with two great epic poems.

The first part of Trumbull's *McFingal* appeared in 1775, and the first complete edition in 1782. It is a satirical poem, animated and amusing, but as closely imitative of Butler's *Hudibras* as an independent work well could be. It is abundantly patriotic in spirit and upon this doubtless depended its great contemporary popularity. In the various poems of Humphreys, gathered together as *Miscellaneous Works* in 1790, there is voiced the same high confidence in the future glory of America. As for style, a remark which Humphreys makes in the preface to his writings is conclusive. "Every poet," he declares, "who aspires to celebrity strives to approach the perfection of Pope and the sweetness of his versification."

One turns from the contemplation of the works of these Hartford Wits with a mingled feeling of relief and melancholy. The poems they wrote are so good that one wonders why they are not really good. They exhibit tremendous energy, their themes are promising, they glow with love of man and nature and country, their technic is adequate, and yet scarcely a line from them is now remembered. One cannot lay this failure to the models followed, for they were of the best. Nor would it be just to ask that these poets should have foregone all literary models, should have built upon a new American foundation an entirely new American style. Such an effort would have been exactly opposite to their intention. What they strove to accomplish was the acclimatization in America of an admired, and rightly admired, culture of the old world. The claims of Americanization were best satisfied, in their minds, when American themes were clothed in the best style which the traditions of English literature afforded. Their reasoning, it must be acknowledged, was sound. For its growth and development, literature must have literary sustenance. The cause of their failure is not to be found in technic, but in the spirit in which they went to work at their self-imposed task. A poet must imitate, but must beware of being too imitative. For he must transmute as well as imitate. Intelligence, ingenuity and energy are not a complete equipment for the poet, not at least for the kind of poet who was putting new life into English poetry at the turn of the century. Had this first flowering of American letters in Connecticut occurred a generation earlier, the fame of the poets of this period might have borne some relation to that of Dryden and Pope. If it had come a generation later, a different imaginative spirit would have animated it and have made it perhaps significant and alive even for the present day.

From Connecticut the center of literary effort passed to New York in the first decades of the nineteenth century. In 1807 Irving and Paulding satirized the follies of the city in *Salmagundi*, a series of essays frankly Addisonian. The title *Salmagundi* is not Indian, as it sounds, and there is no taint of the wigwam about the performance. In 1809, Irving published his satirical and humorous *History of New York*. Sir Walter Scott read this book with pleasure and meant to pay it a compliment when he commented on its similarity to Swift. The gentle Irving and the saturnine Swift do not seem much alike temperamentally, but certainly it is true that Irving studied Swift's ironic method before he wrote his *Knickerbocker History*.

Ten years after the publication of the *Knickerbocker History*, the essays of the *Sketch Book* began to appear. By this time Irving's literary art had been completely formed. He wrote nothing better than the *Sketch Book* and nothing markedly different. No elaborate analysis is necessary to show the dependence of the *Sketch Book* upon Addison and Goldsmith. Irving himself would have been the last to deny this dependence. He wrote a life of Goldsmith which shows how harmoniously attuned were the souls of these two kindly essayists. Shortly after the appearance of the *Sketch Book*, the British critic Hazlitt wrote, *Spirit of the Age*, p. 405, that Irving's writings were "very good copies of our British essayists and novelists, which may be very well on the other side of the water, or as proof of the capabilities of the national genius, but might be dispensed with here, where we have to boast of the originals." This criticism was both ill-natured and stupid. Irving's essays were not copies of Addison's or Goldsmith's. They were in the same literary tradition, a tradition which they made more illustrious, but on the ground that one can get along with "the originals," one would have to reject Goldsmith and Steele as well as Irving, for Addison set the fashion for British as well as American essayists. In reality English readers have never done so, but have taken Irving as one of their own, as Americans have taken Addison and Goldsmith. The *Sketch Book* was first published in England, and has there remained popular.

Cooper's first novel, *Precaution,* was published in 1820, one year after the first part of the *Sketch Book* had appeared. "Reading some cheap British novel," says Brander Matthews, *American Literature,* p. 60, "he was seized with the idea that he could do as well himself; and the result was his first book, 'Precaution,' published late in 1820. 'Precaution' was an imitation of the average British novel of the time; it had merit equal to that of most of its models; it was a tale of life in England, and there was nothing to show that its author was not an Englishman. Indeed when the book was republished in London, it was reviewed with no suspicion of its American authorship." But Cooper was not proud of *Precaution* after it was done, and in 1821 he published *The Spy,* the first of his long list of genuinely American novels.

It is customary to speak with condescension of Cooper's style, as of that of Scott, his predecessor and master. But if Cooper was careless, it was not because he was indifferent. Unquestionably Cooper was deeply interested in the whole matter of the technic of expression. The *Pioneers,* published in 1823, might almost be described as an experiment in varying styles of expression. Some half dozen different dialect types are elaborately studied and illustrated in dialog, but in the end all these dialect speeches, even the native American speech of Natty, are put on the more or less humorous, popular level, while high above them shines the elegant and formal style of the polished gentleman as represented by Marmaduke Temple. This formal style is merely the standard or conventional literary language, as Cooper conceived it and as it was applied by him often with a stiffness and severity which belonged to the precise methods of the old school. Cooper was aware of and valued the rich stores of popular idiom in America. From the point of view of dignified literature, however, there was something else which he valued more highly. This was the ancient and pure style of the great masters of English literature, not in their lightest and most playful moments, but when they spoke seriously and with circumspection. It was from the elevation of this style that Cooper viewed the scene and the characters of American life. Genuine Americanism in his conception was a varied thing, and careful cultivation of refined literary tradition no less genuine than the speech of backwoodsmen.

It would be tedious and unnecessary to continue through the whole catalog of classic American authors with the purpose of showing that their artistic allegiance has been overwhelmingly given to the central tradition of classical English literature. Merely raising the question indicates the obvious answer. One cannot always find immediate models for writers as skilful and independent as were Longfellow, Emerson, Hawthorne, Thoreau, Lowell and the other New England masters of the early flowering period of American literature, any more than one can find immediate models for Macaulay or Thackeray or any of the greater names in British literature. Individual variation made these several writers different from each other, but the differences of all, whether British or American, were made on the basis of a common literary aspiration and a common inherited literary tradition. No American writer wanders further from this central tradition than Carlyle, and certainly a conception of English literature broad enough to include Carlyle and Lamb, Browning and Tennyson, would be broad enough to accommodate any American writer. Individual variation has always been characteristic of English literature, sometimes within very wide limits. What holds all these varying units together into something single and homogeneous is a desire and a loyalty not easily definable except in terms of the traditional literary idiom of the English language. Carlyle and Emerson, Lamb and Lowell all felt themselves to be parts of English literature because they all wrote the same language, not identically the same language, but the same language in spirit and feeling. The area of variation between an American writer and his fellow writers,

American or British, has never been permitted to become so great as not to be negligible to any one whose native speech is English and who approaches the writer with the sympathetic intention of getting his message. The Americanism of American literature has always been an Americanism of thought, of scene and of action, not an Americanism of style which would have made this American content intelligible only to those who were prepared to approach it on a limited American plane. All this may seem so obvious as not to call for statement. Its very obviousness, however, seems often to cause it to be overlooked. The feeling for the whole historical tradition of the English language is so immanent in the literary use of the English language in America that one may be as unconscious of its presence as one is of breathing in the living body. It has been indeed the very breath of life to American literature. Localism and nationalism have been, one may say, merely casual symptoms which from time to time enable one to perceive more fully and consciously the main stream of life with which they are contrasted. To call this American attitude towards English style provincial would be to miss the character of it. A writer might be described as provincial if he deliberately set to work to copy the manner and themes of a respected master, as many an American poet, and British poet as well, copied Pope in the eighteenth century. The representative writers of American literature have not done this. They have united themselves to the central tradition of the language as naturally as Carlyle the Scotchman did, or Kipling the East Indian, or as any Canadian, Australian, or South African would who felt impelled to write English. The bond which unites them all is the feeling for the common literary idiom. To prefer this common idiom to some local literary dialect is not provincialism but common sense. The use of the common idiom has not been and cannot be conferred as a privilege granted by favor. The feeling of American writers has always been that a common possession like literary English style calls for no special permissions, the only necessary key of admission being an understanding of what this style is and a willingness to undergo the discipline by which alone one can become a master of the art of English writing.

If one can conceive of American writers as intentionally departing from the central feeling for the English literary idiom, it would obviously be in vocabulary and grammar that the easiest roads to eccentricity would be opened. No tests of rhythm or cadence have as yet been elaborated in general consciousness definite enough to serve as distinctions between different types of expression, whether spoken or written, cultivated or uncultivated. The literary artist unquestionably uses cadences which do not occur in the speech of matter-of-fact persons, when they are discussing matter-of-fact affairs. But only in the rarest instances can one disentangle a cadence of speech and say that it carries with it an accompaniment of precise connotation in the experience of language which enables one to place the user of it in a fixed position relative to all other users of the language. It is quite otherwise, however, with respect to words and grammar. The limits of possible variation in what one calls cultivated language are vast, but they are also very definitely fixed. They are wide enough to include writers as different as Carlyle and Pater, but not wide enough to betray even the most extravagant author into using *done* or *seen* as a past tense, into doing any of the things peculiar to uncultivated use. All this is merely equivalent to saying that literary style rests in the main upon those limited uses of the language which constitute the accepted standards of cultivated speech. And just as American colloquial speech, in its standard use, has constantly endeavored to establish a form of cultivated speech distinctive for those who take an artist's concern in speech, so also in its literary use, American writing when tested by the forms of popular vocabulary and grammar is seen to be something with aspirations and sanctions of its own.

In the preceding paragraphs an attempt has been made to describe the impulse which in general has governed Americans in the practical exercise of the technic of writing. They have not striven to be exclusively American, but above all to be English. They have allied themselves to the central tradition of English literature, and if they have committed sins against this central idiom, it has been by inadvertence, not by intention. To explain just how the feeling for this central idiom has been established would call for a special study of each individual author, but always an important element in the explanation would be the reading and loyal study of the past masters of English literature. Rebellion against this tradition has never gone far, has never been an intentional rebellion, not even in Walt Whitman's most striking and radical departures. In the fifties, Whitman put together a number of observations on English which he published in 1855 as *An American Primer*. In this essay, readers familiar with Whitman's verse will find the same keen and exultant joy in the richness of words as in his poetry. Though words were to Whitman not positive and original things themselves, they were the most direct way of knowledge to a troubled and tumbling wealth of things that pressed upon his consciousness. "In America" says Whitman, "an immense number of new words are needed," and a long catalog follows of the kinds of these needs. "Words are wanted to supply the copious trains of facts, and flanges of facts, feelings, arguments and adjectival facts, growing out of all new knowledge," *American Primer*, p. 9. "The occasions of the English speech in America," he says elsewhere, p. 2, "are immense, profound—stretch over ten thousand vast cities, over millions of miles of meadows, farms, mountains, men, through thousands of years . . . Geography, shipping, steam, the mint, the electric telegraph, railroads, and so forth, have many strong and beautiful words. Mines—iron works—the sugar plantations of Louisiana—the cotton crop and the rice crop—Illinois wheat—Ohio corn and pork—Maine lumber—all these sprout in hundreds and hundreds of words, all tangible and clean-lived, all having texture and beauty." But what these words themselves are Whitman does not pause to say, not even to illustrate. His interest in them was not philological, not even literary, but rather in the sense of life which by their mere existence they gave him. Even in his verse he used very few words which were not ordinarily current in the language. A few novelties like *camerado, imperturbe* loom large because they are so infrequent, and they are Whitmanisms, not Americanisms. In short Whitman was entranced with the vision of a multitudinous life for literary purposes, but well realized that literary purposes could be made effective only when style and language were kept within literary bounds. These bounds he sometimes passed, but some errors he was sure to make in his exuberant desire to test the limits of possible experiment. His eccentricities of style summed up are no greater, however, than those of Browning. He was ejaculatory and apocalyptic, dithyrambic and chaotic, but in detail he respected normal literary experience more than Browning. Browning often shocked his readers into attention by formal and mechanical eccentricity; Whitman does this by a pose of the spirit. Not only what he did, but also the things he avoided doing are significant for Whitman's style. With his theories he might well have attempted to exalt the ungrammatical speech of illiterates for literary purposes. He might have regarded this as the real literary America. He might have used the common, vulgar words of low life, "the slang words among fighting men, gamblers, thieves, prostitutes. . . . These words ought to be collected—the bad words as well as the good. —Many of these bad words are fine." But collecting them and admiring them as fine from the safe distance of the cultivated speech are different matters from using them as expressive of the inmost heart of one's being. Whitman did not use them. He had no desire to degrade the great literary tradition of the English language, to bring it down to an unlettered popular level. The English language in America, he declares, p. 7, is "the body of the whole of the past. We are to justify our inheritance—we are to pass it on to those who are to come after us, a thousand years hence, as we have grown out of the English of a thousand years ago: American geography,—the plenteousness and variety of the great nations of the Union—the thousands of settlements—the seacoast—the Canadian north—the Mexican south—California and Oregon—the inland seas—the mountains—Arizona—the prairies—the immense rivers"—all these have a duty to perform to the English language of the past, an addition to make to the English language of the future. "Never will I allude to the English language or tongue without exultation. This is the tongue that spurns laws, as the greatest tongue must. It is the most capacious vital tongue of all—full of ease, definiteness and power—full of sustenance.—An enormous treasure house, or range of treasure houses, arsenals, granary, chock full with so many contributions from the north and from the south, from Scandinavia, from Greece and Rome,—from Spaniards, Italians and the French,—that its own sturdy home-dated Angles-bred words have long been outnumbered by the foreigners whom they lead—which is all good enough, and indeed must be.—America owes immeasurable respect and love to the past, and to many ancestries, for many inheritances—but of all that America has received from the past, from the mothers and fathers of laws, arts, letters, etc., by far the greatest inheritance is the English language—so long in growing—so fitted," *American Primer*, p. 30. When the radical speaks thus, the conservative may keep silence.

It is plain, however, that the whole story of American style has not been told when one has taken account of the classics of American literature. There is more to be said than that. If serious American literature is to be swallowed up in general English literature, as it seems to have been, one must seek elsewhere for something distinctive and peculiar in the American manner of expression. That this something exists, no one can doubt. There is an Americanism of expression strongly colored and highly flavored, racy of the soil and the people. It has manifested itself, however, on levels different from those on which Emerson and Longfellow and all the other traditionally great writers of America have moved, different from those upon which the serious literary artists in America today are moving. In the attempt to determine these levels, the parallelism between style and dialect will again be useful. In speech one takes account, first of all, of a generalized standard English speech, which is approximately the same among all cultivated persons, whether they are residents of London or Chicago or Melbourne or Vancouver. Individual variations will appear even in the standard speech of the persons from these various places, but not ordinarily by intention or preference. When one speaks the standard English speech one endeavors to speak a language which will make one seem at home wherever native English is spoken. Corresponding to this general standard for the spoken language, English literature has its own standard literary style.

But every speaker, even the most cosmopolitan and completely "standardized" is not only a citizen of the general English world, he is also a native of some local community. If he is a cultivated person, he may speak the standard language when he wishes. But he will not probably always wish to do so. There are times when he will prefer to speak with some more intimate and local flavor. Even if his informal speech is merely the English of colloquial discourse, it will differ in many respects from the more formal, or standard, use of the language. The informal or local speech will often seem more penetrating, more genuine than the standard speech. It will carry with it the direct and close associations of everyday life, and will have the warmth of immediate experience. One can call it better than the standard speech, however, only by assuming that all life should be conducted on the informal and intimate basis, and one could call it worse only by assuming that formal speech is the only justifiable norm and guide to proper expression. The truth is that one is not to be measured by the other. They are two different things, each proper in its own place and when it performs its appropriate tasks. So in style, by the side of the formal literary style there flourishes a more or less popular and informal style. The latter is not a cultivated style, that is, not formed by the studious examination of approved literary models. It arises more directly from experience, is likely to manifest itself in ephemeral writings, which seem exceptionally expressive and vigorous for the short time that they last. Whether or not this kind of writing should be called literature is a matter of definition. Obviously no sharp dividing line can be drawn between familiar literary composition and formal literary composition. The former may pass into the latter by imperceptible degrees, and the relative placing of any individual literary manifestation will depend very much upon the "purity" and severity of one's literary standards. Thus one finds the greatest difference of opinion on the question just how *Tom Sawyer* is to be ranked as a literary monument, whether low, as a popular, bad-boy book, or high among the immortal classics of American literature. But though one may not always know how to rate popular literary compositions, the quality of them is clearly recognizable. Here again the task of the historian is easier than that of the critic. As one looks back over the annals of American literature, one perceives that generations of readers on the whole have made the division clear between popular and classic endeavor in literature. The critic may rebel against these decisions, but for the historian they are the facts given. It is the purpose of the remainder of this chapter to discover the quality of these manifestations of the popular or informal style in American literature.

The region in which a folk tradition of style first developed in America may roughly be given as Kentucky, or in general the new Southwest. The time was the end of the eighteenth century and the early years of the nineteenth century, especially in the period of exalted feeling before and after the war of 1812. The Revolution was over but not forgotten. Towards the end of the eighteenth century the restless Western movement began, opening up possibilities of a new world full of hope, adventure and romance. A generation of men was still living who had become accustomed to a life of hardy endeavor, who by personal effort had justified their right to independence and who were determined to follow the free promptings of their natures, wherever they might lead them. "The Kentucky spirit," says Shaler, *Kentucky*, p. 21, "was the offspring of the Revolution. The combative spirit left by the Revolutionary war was elsewhere overwhelmed by the tide of commercial life; here it lived on, fed by the tradition and by a nearly continuous combat down to the time of the Rebellion." Adventuring into Kentucky had indeed begun before the Revolution. Daniel Boone came to Kentucky from North Carolina in 1769. Others also came in the third quarter of the century, but "the singular feature about all these early wanderings in Kentucky is," to quote Shaler again, p. 65, "that although they had been going on for thirty years or more, many of the explorers returning two or three times to the ground, they were moved more by the spirit of adventure than by any distinct love of gain or idea of permanent settlement. To make a perilous journey into the dark and bloody battle-ground of the Indians, and then to return with many stories of hair-breadth escapes and a scalp or two, seems to have been the motive and end of these numerous expeditions." In the last quarter of the eighteenth century, however, pioneer conditions in Kentucky began to be modified somewhat and a kind of community character to develop. But the circumstances in which the members of the community had grown up, had brought into being, says Shaler, p. 111, "a peculiar sort of man,—a kind that was never known before or since in such numbers in any one country. . . . They had a very peculiar quality of mind. Its most characteristic feature was a certain dauntlessness, a habit of asserting the independence of all control except that of the written law. Their speech was rude and often exaggerated. As a class, they were much like the men of to-day [1885] in the Rocky Mountains, except that they had not the eager desire for gain that takes away from the charm of that people. This advantage made the frontiersman of Kentucky a much more agreeable fellow than his money-seeking kinsman of the far West. He was more sympathetic, more externalized, than the miner of Colorado to-day."

This exuberant Kentucky or Southwestern spirit did not escape the notice of early travelers in America and critics of American life. Timothy Flint, in his *Recollections*, p. 61, describes Kentucky in 1815 as follows:

"As soon as you depart from the Ohio [into Kentucky], and find yourself in the region of hills and springs, you will nowhere see fairer and fresher complexions, or fuller and finer forms, than you see in the young men and women, who are generally exempted from the necessity of labour. . . . The circumstances under which they are born tend to give them the most perfect development of person and form. It struck me, that the young native Kentuckians were, in general, the largest race that I had seen." And he adds later, p. 71, that "There is a distinct and striking moral physiognomy to this people;

an enthusiasm, a vivacity, and ardour of character, courage, frankness, generosity, that have been developed with the peculiar circumstances under which they have been placed." Kentucky sets the tone for all Western and Southwestern life, says Flint, and to be a Kentuckian is a sure way to success in elections for political office all through the West.

Mellish, *Travels*, II, 94, gives an account of the warmth of character of the Kentuckians, the result of observations made in the first decade of the nineteenth century. Fearon visited America and Kentucky in 1817, and he remarks, *Sketches*, p. 234, "I had received an impression that the genuine Kentuckian had many excellent traits of character." He then supports Mellish to the effect that the Kentuckians "resemble the Irish; are frank, affable, polite, and hospitable in a high degree; they are quick in their temper, sudden in their resentment, and warm in all their affections." With his customary caution, Fearon says he does not feel competent to confirm or deny the general claim of the Kentuckians to generosity and warmth of character, but "that they drink a great deal, and gamble a great deal, will be apparent to a very brief resident." An unknown American observer from Virginia gave a highly complimentary picture of the Kentuckians in 1825, in *Letters on the Condition of Kentucky*, ed. Swem, p. 50. "The Kentuckians are in general," he declared, "bold and enterprising; confiding in their friendships; acute and judicious in their traffic, ardent and aspiring in their feelings, energetic in their measures, and intelligent, manly and independent in their manners; the gentlemen are courteous, well-informed and cordially hospitable." In 1828 when Cooper published his *Notions* he remarked, I, 224, that so far as the eye could judge, "men of great stature and strength are about as common in America as elsewhere, while small men are more rare," but he added in a footnote that he had found "what he is almost tempted to call a race of big men in the southwestern states." He noted also a new set of social manners in this region, *Notions*, I, 102, remarking that a New Englander always addresses one as *friend* or *squire*, but that "in the new States to the Southwest" *stranger* is used. The expansiveness of the Kentuckian was not always agreeable to travelers. Beltrami, *Pilgrimage in Europe and America*, 1828, Vol. II, p. 57, speaks of the Kentuckians "whom it is really impossible to endure. It is a pity a people so brave, industrious and active should be so coarse and insolent; one can and must esteem them, but it is a difficult matter to like them." Kentucky, he declares, p. 92, is "the Eden of the United States," the people are "industrious, enterprising and brave," but "insupportable from their insolence and coarseness. They are sometimes amusing, but always exceed all bounds of decent manners." Beltrami's code being that of the courts of Europe, one might imagine that a Salt river roarer would by this standard offend against propriety.

As early as the first decade of the nineteenth century the Kentuckian had taken his place in American folklore. He was a new type of creature, with a shaggy style all his own, superabounding in energy. In the *Knickerbocker History*, Book VI, Chap. III, Irving says that "the backwoodmen of Kentucky are styled half man, half horse and half alligator, by the settlers on the Mississippi, and held accordingly in great respect and abhorrence." The same description of the Kentuckians appears in Paulding's *The Bucktails*, written about 1812, and Thornton, I, 410 ff., gives a number of other citations. In the Salem Gazette for June 12, 1812, a communication from New Orleans says that "half horse half alligator has hitherto been the boast of our up-country boatmen, when quarreling. The present season however has made a complete change. A few days ago two of them quarreled in a boat at Natchez, when one of them jumping ashore declared with a horrid oath that he was a *steamboat*. His opponent immediately followed him, swearing he was an *earthquake* and would shake him to pieces." Another Mississippi navigator, *Analectic Magazine*, IV, 63, 1814, "affirmed himself to be *all alligator* but his head, which was of *aqua-fortis*." In Flint's *Recollections*, p. 78, 1826, we are told that when the warmth of whiskey in a Kentuckian's stomach is added to his natural energy, "he becomes in succession, *horse, alligator* and *steamboat*"; and p. 98, there are others who "claim to be the genuine and original breed, compounded of the *horse, alligator and snapping turtle*." In the

Richmond Whig for Dec. 9, 1828, occurred a description of a "Salt river roarer," sometimes called a ring-tailed roarer, "one of those two-fisted backwoodsmen, *half horse, half alligator* and a little touched with the snapping turtle." He went to see a caravan of wild beasts, and after giving them a careful examination, he offered to bet the owner that "he could whip his lion in an open ring; and he might throw in all his monkeys, and let the zebra kick him occasionally during the fight."

The half horse, half alligator character, the full grown snapping turtle, the yaller flower of the desert, was by this time well launched upon his literary career. Confiding travelers began to note that they met him in the flesh less generally in their travels than they had expected to do. Paul Hover in Cooper's *Prairie* (1827) is one of these tall sons of Kentucky, a daredevil, amiable adventurer, brave but reckless, a bee-hunter by occupation, a lover and a poet, with "a careless, off-hand, heedless manner." He has the gift of eloquence like the rest of his kind. "I deny myself nothing," he declares, Chap. III. "If a bear crosses my path he is soon a mere ghost of Bruin. The deer begin to nose me, and as for the buffalo, I have killed more beef, old stranger, than the largest butcher in all Kentuck."

"You can shoot then," demanded the trapper, with a glow of latent fire glimmering about his eyes; "is your hand true and your look quick?"

"The first is like a steel trap," answered Paul, "and the last nimbler than buckshot. I wish it was hot noon now, grand'ther; and that there was an acre or two of your white swans or of black feathered ducks going south, over our heads; you or Ellen here might set your heart on the finest in the flock, and my character against a horn of powder, that the bird would be hanging head downwards in five minutes and that too with a single ball." This is Kentucky eloquence enfeebled in Cooper's somewhat inadequate literary imitation. It was more torrential when it stood nearer to its immediate popular sources. The romantic and grandiloquent Paul is interestingly contrasted, however, with another southwestern group in the

Prairie, with the family of Ishmael Bush, who is heavy and inarticulate, typical of the low-down, sullen, lazy, shiftless, semi-outlaws of the border.

In J. K. Paulding's *Westward Ho!*, published in 1832, are to be found full length portraits of the free, daring and eloquent sons of Kentucky. The *Life of David Crockett*, supposed to have been written by himself, was ended, incomplete, in 1836, in which year Crockett was killed in a battle against the Mexicans on the Alamo in Texas. Crockett confessed to a certain amount of editorial assistance in the preparation of the manuscript of his *Life*, especially in grammar and spelling. How far this editorial assistance went it is impossible to say, impossible therefore to say who is responsible for the genuinely literary and imaginative quality that has made the autobiography a permanently interesting American book.[1] In it one finds the expansive sentiment, the grandiloquence, the touches of emotional poetry, the wild adventure, the uncouth humor that later was to take completer and more successful literary form in the writings of Mark Twain, Bret Harte and other Pike county celebrities. "Vice does not appear so shocking," says Crockett, p. 344, "when we are familiar with the perpetrator of it." This is a sentiment which could not come out of New England. It underlies the broad charity which made the outcasts of Poker Flat heroically human, which later in the stories of O. Henry, a disciple of Mark Twain and Bret Harte, in many a tale of the lonesome camp and the city slum was to show how the cool and well-regulated virtues of respectable persons may be made to seem contemptible when brought into contrast with the generous hearts and errors of desperadoes and derelicts. The unrepenting but potentially large-minded and warm-hearted sinner was necessary in the melodramatic morality appropriate to the grandiloquent style.

The various notes of the exuberant style are but tentatively sounded, not sustained, in Crockett's *Life*. The transitions are quick and the contrasts violent. At one moment the author is politician and statesman, at the next he is killing bears for his winter's supply

[1] See Tandy, Chapter IV, for a discussion of this question of authorship.

of food. The picturesqueness and artistic possibilities of these contrasts did not escape him, and it would not be safe to take the *Life* as a veracious record of the facts of the times. In the character of the bee-hunter, Edward, one can see obvious traces of the influence of Paul Hover in Cooper's *Prairie*, which had appeared in 1827. Both are graceful, imaginative and poetic Southwest characters. The following picture of the dithyrambic backwoods orator also had its literary predecessors. "I jocosely asked the ragged hunter, who was a smart, active young fellow, of the steamboat and alligator breed," writes Crockett, p. 381, "whether he was a rhinoceros or a hyena, as he was so eager for a fight with the invaders. 'Neither the one nor the t'other, Colonel,' says he, 'but a whole menagerie in myself. I'm shaggy as a bear, wolfish about the head, active as a cougar, and can grin like a hyena, until the bark will curl off a gum log. There's a sprinking of all sorts in me, from the lion down to the skunk; and before the war is over, you'll pronounce me an entire zoological institute, or I miss a figure in my calculation. I promise to swallow Santa Anna without gagging, if you will only skewer back his ears, and grease his head a little.'"

Another sample of this exaggerated and picturesque backwoods eloquence is found in one of the characters of Bird's *Nick of the Woods* (1837). This is a tale of frontier Kentucky life, supposedly in 1782, of a strong romantic flavor. The most interesting character study in the book is that of Ralph Stackpole, Roaring Ralph, a fire-eater and fighter, a horse-thief and a loud-mouthed braggart, a noisy, amusing, helpful, troublesome child of the frontier. He performs amazing physical contortions, jumps into the air, cracks his heels together, and sends forth a stream of prodigious eloquence. He speaks the true Southwest dialect, with an abundance of great words, like *squabblification; aungelliferous madam; splendiferous; you exflunctified, perditioned rascal*, etc. In his later years, Chapter XXXVI, Ralph gave up horse-stealing, "launched his broad-horn on the narrow bosom of the Salt, and was soon afterwards transformed into a Mississippi alligator; in which amphibious condition, we presume he roared on till the day of his death."

Several plays, popularly successful, were built around the character of the Kentucky hero. The earliest of these was J. K. Paulding's *Lion of the West* (1831). The Lion was Nimrod Wildfire, a "humorous, unpolished, generous" son of Old Kentuck who was always "primed for anything, from a possum-hunt to a nigger funeral," *New York Mirror*, Vol IX, p. 102 (1831). He must have a fight every ten days, or he feels "mighty wolfy about the head and shoulders." His sweetheart has "no back-out in her breed, for she can lick her weight in wild-cats, and she shot a bear at nine years old."

The name and the hero of this play were suggested to Paulding by the comedian James H. Hackett, who had offered a prize of three hundred dollars for "an original comedy whereof an American should be the leading character." The judges, Bryant, Halleck and P. M. Wetmore, gave Paulding's *Lion of the West* first place. The original play apparently was never published, but it was acted often and served as the basis for several adaptations, see W. I. Paulding's *Literary Life of James K. Paulding*, p. 219. One of the earliest of these revisions is reviewed in the *New York Mirror*, Vol. IX, p. 102 (1831), and an outline of the plot is given. This review seems to be now the fullest extant source of information concerning the play. At the time of appearance of the play, Paulding found it necessary to write to David Crockett to say that the play had not been written as a take-off of the Representative from Tennessee. Crockett replied unorthographically but with dignity. The character of Nimrod Wildfire was one of Hackett's most successful parts. "I have repeatedly acted the character in that drama," he said, "in every principal city of the United States with applause, and in every theatrical engagement I made for twenty years following." Similar characters appeared in *Tecumseh* (1836) by R. Emmons. Three expert riflemen, Ralph, Arthur, and Franklin, figure in this play, see Reed, *Realistic Characters*, p. 103. Like all Kentuckians, they drink much whiskey, but become intoxicated only on patriotic occasions, such as the Fourth of July and Washington's Birthday. Ralph declares that he is "part horse, part alligator, a touch of the steamboat, and a sprinkling of an earthquake," and he never does anything by halves but always "goes the whole hog."

A volume could be filled with examples of this expansive eloquence taken from the more or less popular literature of newspapers and magazines of the mid-decades of the nineteenth century. Old Dan Tucker, who combed his hair with a wagon wheel, is of this heroic origin. Drake's poem to the American Flag, which first appeared in the *Croaker Papers* in 1819, begins with this bit of cosmic imagery:

"When Freedom from her mountain height
Unfurled her standard to the air,
She tore the azure robes of night
And set the stars of glory there!"

Still more magnificent in his self-glorification was one described in a parody in the *Knickerbocker Magazine*, Vol. 51, p. 215 (1858), supposed to combine "the sublime and mystic":

"Ye cannot count me as I run,
I play with stars at pitch and toss;
I am the uncle of the sun,
Half alligator and half hoss."

From this imaginative flight to Emerson's "Hitch your wagon to a star" the distance is not great. Both passages are in the spirit of the popular American imagination of the years preceding the Civil War. A robustious eloquence, a torrential flow of words, grand in sentiment, striking in figure, not without humorous coloring, this was the note to catch the popular ear of the time. The style took its origin in a genuinely native and independent desire for self-expression. Perhaps grandiloquence is not ordinarily characteristic of the popular mind. On the contrary, a certain decent modesty is commonly demanded by the people one of another. One must restrain oneself, not get "too gay" or "too fresh." Extremes of manner are not encouraged, are condemned except in the favored few. The person, however, who is favored with the gift permits himself and is permitted any extravagance. He has the poet's licence to be a harebrained scamp, to be a wag, a cut-up, a spouting fountain of fiery eloquence. When the creative fancy breaks loose in the popular orator, it sets no limits to its eruptions.

In American society, especially between the War of 1812 and the Civil War, an exceptionally favorable occasion was offered for this kind of popular self-expression. It was a period of active and rapidly changing experience. The world was full of great opportunities. One man was as good as another and need not stop to say to himself, when he felt the stirrings of the god within, that this sort of thing was meant for his betters, not for him. Nothing was too good for an American citizen, no attitude too magnanimous, no charity too broad, no comedy too fantastic, no poetry too fine, no thought too profound. This impulse toward the bold and the magnificent in self-expression has been characterized as the Kentucky spirit. It was more than that, it was a national spirit. It showed itself most strikingly along the path of adventure, down the Ohio and up the Missouri and across the Rockies to the gold fields of California, but it is implicit in various forms of American expression, some of which must be further noticed. Nor did these developments in popular eloquence take place without direction and approval. Timothy Flint wrote an essay on the style and eloquence of the pulpit, the bar and the press, "in the Three Great Divisions of the United States," *Western Monthly Review*, III, 639–647 (1830),[1] in which he characterized the New England style as restrained and critical, the Southern style as self-confident and expansive, and the Western style as mixed, a compound of New England restraint and Western exuberance. But the restraint is very little evident in what Flint calls the Western style. "The eloquence of the East," he says, "is sober, passionless, condensed, metaphysical; that of the West is free, lofty, agitating, grand, impassioned . . . the West defies and transcends criticism." "What orator," asked a bold Kentuckian, "can deign to restrain his imagination within a vulgar and sterile state of facts?"[2]

Another defense and analysis of Western eloquence is contained in the following passage:

[1] See Rush, *Literature of the Middle Western Frontier*, p. 205. [2] Rush, p. 206.

"The literature of a young and free people will, of course, be declamatory, and such, so far as it is yet developed, is the character of our own. Deeper learning will, no doubt, abate its verbosity and intumescence; but our natural scenery, and our liberal political and social institution, must long continue to maintain its character of floridness. And what is there in this that should excite regret in ourselves, or raise derision in others? Ought not the literature of a free people to be declamatory? . . . Whenever the literature of a new country loses its metaphorical and declamatory character, the institutions which depend on public sentiment will languish and decline. . . . For a long time the oration, in various forms, will constitute a large portion of our literature. A people who have fresh and lively feelings will always relish oratory." [1]

The feat of making the eagle scream and of twisting the lion's tail at Fourth of July and other patriotic celebrations was one of the accomplishments of the old-fashioned orator. The following toast was given at Waterville, Maine, on July 4, 1815: "The Eagle of the United States—may she extend her wings from the Atlantic to the Pacific; and fixing her talons on the Isthmus of Darien, stretch with her beak to the Northern Pole," *Proceedings of the American Antiquarian Society*, New Series, 19, 31. Patriotic toasts of this kind were a regular feature in the Fourth of July celebrations of the early nineteenth century, first thirteen toasts, one for each of the original colonies, then an indefinite number of voluntary toasts. It is not easy to determine just how large an element of humor entered into these displays of flamboyant eloquence. They were not downright parodies, nor on the other hand is it conceivable that they were composed or heard in deadly earnest. Perhaps they can be best characterized as part of the noisy sport of the old-fashioned Fourth of July. The occasion was one of jubilant freedom, not to say license, in eating and above all in drinking, but in explosive oratory as well. Charles Sprague, in An Oration Delivered on Monday, Fourth of July, 1825,

[1] Daniel Drake, *Discourse on the History, Character, and Prospects of the West* (1834), pp. 32–33, 45.

before the officials and citizens of Boston, began with this trumpet blast:

"Why, on *this day*, lingers along these sacred walls, the spirit-kindling anthem? Why, on *this day*, waits the herald of God at the altar, to utter forth his holy prayer? Why, on *this day*, congregate here the wise, and the good, and the beautiful of the land?—Fathers! Friends! it is the Sabbath Day of Freedom! The race of the ransomed, with grateful hearts and exulting voices, have again come up. in the sunlight of peace, to the Jubilee of their Independence!"

The pastor of the First Universalist Church in New York, Abner Kneeland, touched a still higher note in the opening paragraph of his Oration, July 4, 1826, before the societies of New York assembled to celebrate the day:

"Freemen! Friends! and Fellow-citizens!

One hundred times has the sun crossed the equator, and the earth has made fifty complete revolutions in its orbit, since the Genius of Liberty, beholding with indignation the cruel arm of the oppressor, and hearing with sympathy the cries of the oppressed, arose in the majesty of her strength and, waving her broad pinions from Maine to Georgia, she took the trump of fame, and with a blast that thrilled like electricity through every American heart, pronounced these memorable words—'Sons and Daughters of Columbia, scorn to be slaves!'"

Infinite variations in the major key were played upon these patriotic themes. Mr. Cathcart of Indiana, remarked in the House of Representatives, Feb. 6, 1846, that "those convenient sources of poetic fancy, the American eagle and the British lion, have been so often drawn upon, that the roar of the one and the scream of the other now fall powerless," and then proceeds with a spreadeagle flight of his own: "From the apex of the Alleghany to the summit of Mount Hood, the bird of America has so often been made to take flight, that his shadow may be said to have worn a trail across the basin of the Mississippi; and the poor lord of the beasts has become so familiar with the point of a hickory pole and of an ash splinter, that he has slunk away to his lair, and there let him lie for the balance of my allotted hour," Thornton, II, 985. Another example of this patriotic bombast may be cited from the speech of Samuel C. Pomeroy of Kansas, in the Senate, May 5, 1862:

"The proudest bird upon the mountain is upon the American ensign, and not one feather shall fall from her plumage here. She is American in design, and an emblem of wildness and freedom. I say again, she has not perched herself upon American standards to die here. Our great Western valleys were never scooped out for her burial place. Nor were the everlasting untrodden mountains piled for her monument. Niagara shall not pour her endless waters for her requiem; nor shall our ten thousand rivers weep to the ocean in eternal tears. No, sir, no. Unnumbered voices shall come up from river, plain and mountain, echoing the songs of our triumphant deliverance, wild lights from a thousand hilltops will betoken the rising of the sun of freedom," Thornton, II, 987.

The date of the following, quoted in that rich mine of illustrations of American life, the *Knickerbocker Magazine*, 46, 212 (1855) is a few years earlier:

"Sir, we want elbow-room!—the continent, the whole continent, and nothing but the continent! And we will have it! Then shall Uncle Sam, placing his hat upon the Canadas, rest his right arm on the Oregon and California coast, his left on the eastern seaboard, and whittle away the British power, while reposing his leg, like a freeman, upon Cape Horn! Sir, the day *will*—the day *must* come!"

Another sample from the *Knickerbocker Magazine*, 51, 209 (1858), was taken from the Jackson, Tennessee, "Madisonian." The concluding sentence will suffice:

"The wild and mysterious hyperbolical phantasm of enthusiasts would create a furor and stampede, run riot over the safeguard of American liberty—the constitution—stab to the very vitals the great incentives which clustered around the spot that gave birth to the mighty instrument, mock their primitive fathers and mothers, sing the requiem to the death knell of Liberty, and gormandize over the destruction of the confederacy."

This grandiloquent style colored most of the serious political oratory of the ante-bellum generation. That it has completely died out of American oratory, one would fain believe, but must be content with knowing that tall talk has become much less common and less extravagant than it was formerly.[1] The artificial character of American oratory has frequently been noted. Brackenridge, in *Modern Chivalry*, Vol. IV, Chapter IX (1815), declared that the bar was the only real school of eloquence in America because the lawyer was always confronted with the concrete problem of winning his cases in order to make a living. On the other hand, the public speaker in an American deliberative assembly must always strive to please a many-headed and incomprehensible multitude at home. He cannot speak only to the point of a subject under discussion, but in order to avoid possible offense, must speak in general terms in which glittering ornament is substituted for solid content. A somewhat similar comment was later made by Charles Francis Adams

[1] But occasional examples are still met with, as in the following prayer, reported as having been delivered at the inauguration of the governor of Arizona in the *New York Times*, January 30, 1923:

"O, Thou Eternal Jehovah, on this inaugural day, as this grand old Roman assumes the gubernatorial responsibilities of this great Commonwealth, we stand as hopeful, happy expectants of better days for Arizona. We pray that he may have wisdom to steer the ship of State over the breakers of extravagance and the deep seas of indebtedness which now confront him.

"During his tenure of office spare him the unjust, unreasonable criticism of disgruntled mugwump Democrats, shrewd and designing Republican politicians and sensational headlines of newspapers. Grant that he may have the support and co-operation of all sections, from every hilltop high and valley low, from desert waste and city full, from these rich and fertile valleys where the lowing herds come winding o'er the lea and the plowman homeward plods his weary way, from the golden West, where the sun gilds the Western hills and the beautiful Colorado winds its way like a silver thread on its way to the ocean; from the north, where the snow-capped mountains and waving pines kiss the skies and aurora borealis shines at midnight like the noonday sun; from the East, where the quivering, glimmering rays of the coming sun prophesy the approach of the coming day and the stars pour their lustre on the mountain slopes; from the sunny South, where the notes of the nightingale are more melodious than the lays and lutes of Olympus and the song of the mocking bird sweeter than the sound of the dulcimer that is heard in the shadow of death.

"Grant, O Lord, that the banner of peace and prosperity may wave over Arizona until every State in the Union shall point with pride to this, the youngest, fairest daughter and brightest star that shines in the galaxy of States and that Arizona may be regarded as the playground of the angels."

in 1861, *A Cycle of Adams Letters*, ed. Ford, I, 8. The characteristic of the English House of Commons, he remarked, is that "it is in essence a real deliberative body, whilst our House has ceased to be one. We speak to the people and not to the audience. Hence we make orations and not speeches. I know not how this can be remedied in America. Some members of Parliament tell me that it is perceptibly growing even here. So it must be, in proportion to the control which the people exercise over their representatives."

Whatever the amount of truth in this criticism of democratic oratory, it evidently fits better the conditions of political life in the old days of Andrew Jackson, of Tippecanoe and Tyler too, than it does political life to-day. A great change has come over the spirit of public discussion in America and much of the older grandiloquence and rustic picturesqueness has passed away. The flourishing period of American oratory was that which produced the three who by the test of popular fame are counted the greatest American orators. These were Daniel Webster, who died in 1852, John C. Calhoun, who died in 1850, and Henry Clay, who died in the same year as Webster. These three were orators in the old-fashioned grand style. In their public utterances they addressed no mere human beings, but made their appeals directly to the throne of truth and the bar of justice. The senatorial dignity which they assumed was partly necessitated by the more formal code of conduct of the older generation, but still more was it cultivated as a refuge in which public speakers of pretensions to good taste, still remaining grand, could escape the crude bombast of the still more popular style of oratory. Perhaps they did not altogether escape the latter evil. Even the best of the orations of the old school were turgid, too much given to rhetorical attitudinizing, too ostentatious and mechanical in feeling. Webster was a man of massive personality, of great political wisdom, endowed by nature with a powerful mind which rigorous discipline enabled him to use effectively. For a long generation he produced upon his contemporaries the impression of greatness. In him seemed to be figured the grand outline of the future political life of the country, just beginning to take shape. His name has thus been intimately bound with the best American patriotic tradition, and one hesitates even to seem to lay irreverent hands on the expression of his genius. But Webster did not differ from other great men in being the child of his own generation. It is true that oratory from its very nature demands a magniloquent manner of expression, less pleasing than formerly, now that oratory itself is less whole-heartedly practised than once it was. One may indeed read the orations of Webster with regret that his ample flights are no longer possible, but it is true that what once was eloquent now seems overblown. Thus the famous Liberty and Union oration leads to this climax:

"When my eyes shall be turned to behold, for the last time, the sun in heaven, may I not see him shining on the broken and dishonored fragments of a once glorious union—on States dissevered, discordant, belligerent—on a land rent with civil feuds, or drenched it may be, in fraternal blood! Let their last feeble and lingering glance rather behold the gorgeous ensign of the republic, now known and honored throughout the earth, still full high advanced; its arms and trophies streaming in their original luster, not a stripe erased or polluted, nor a single star obscured,—bearing for its motto no such miserable interrogatory, as, 'What is all this worth?' Nor those other words of delusion and folly, 'Liberty first, and Union afterward'; but everywhere, spread all over in characters of living light, blazing on all its ample folds, as they float over the sea and over the land, and in every wind under the whole heavens, that other sentiment, dear to every true American heart—Liberty and Union, now and forever, one and inseparable!" This is perhaps magnificent, but no longer possible to the enfeebled children of a later generation. But Webster's theatrical skill was nowhere more effectively displayed than in the supposed speech of John Adams, introduced into a Discourse on Adams and Jefferson, August 2, 1826. The scene was deliberately arranged. Hancock is supposed to be presiding over the solemn sitting. A person not yet ready to pronounce for absolute independence is on the floor, with moderate eloquence urging reasons for delay. This speaker having finished, Adams "would commence with his accustomed directness and earnestness"—"Sink or swim, live or die, survive or perish"—and so through the rest of the words which the powerful elocution of Webster must have made intensely moving. But the echoes of Webster's voice have faded, his pose seems now lifeless and exaggerated. As in uproarious comedy, the contagion of the moment was necessary to make this oratory effective.

Even genuine feeling had to struggle hard to find a way through such an encumbering eloquence. "I migrated to the State of Kentucky," said Henry Clay, in his last speech in the Senate, in March, 1842, Benton, *Thirty Years' View*, II, 401, "nearly forty-five years ago. I went there as an orphan, who had not yet attained his majority—who had never recognized a father's smile—with an imperfect and inadequate education, limited to the means applicable to such a boy;—but scarcely had I set foot upon that generous soil, before I was caressed with parental fondness—patronized with bounteous munificence—and I may add to this, that her choicest honors, often unsolicited, have been freely showered upon me; and when I stood, as it were, in the darkest moments of human existence—abandoned by the world, calumniated by a large portion of my own countrymen, she threw around me her impenetrable shield, and bore me aloft, and repelled the attacks of malignity and calumny, by which I was assailed. Sir, it is to me an unspeakable pleasure that I am shortly to return to her friendly limits; and that I shall finally deposit (and it will not be long before that day arrives) my last remains under her generous soil, with the remains of her gallant and patriotic sons who have preceded me." Thus spake Zarathustra, but never any ordinary mortal.

Another of these demi-gods is portrayed at length in Baldwin's *Flush Times in Mississippi*, pp. 197 ff. He was the Mississippi statesman, Sargent Smith Prentiss, "in the flower of his forensic fame" in 1837. He had, says Baldwin, "the talent of an Italian improvisatore, and could speak the thoughts of poetry with the inspiration of oratory, and in the tones of music. The fluency of his speech was unbroken—no syllable unpronounced—not a ripple in the smooth and brilliant tide. Probably he never hesitated for a word in his life. His diction adapted itself, without effort, to the thought; now easy and familiar, now stately and dignified, now beautiful and various as the hues of the rainbow, again compact, even rugged in sinewy strength, or lofty and grand in eloquent declamation." When he spoke in public, "ladies surrounded the rostrum with their carriages." He reminded his Southern friends of Byron. He was the idol of Mississippi. On his first appearance in the House, he delivered a speech, "which if his fame rested upon it alone, for its manliness of tone, exquisite satire, gorgeous imagery, and argumentative power, would have rendered his name imperishable." Faded now are these imperishable glories, all melted away like the snows of other years.

How large a place the fame of the orator occupied among the aspirations of American youth in the second quarter of the nineteenth century can be readily seen by examining the many readers, speakers, and books of selections of the time. In McGuffey's *Rhetorical Guide or Fifth Reader* (1844), intended for the highest classes, in the part devoted to prose, orations occur much more frequently than any other kind of composition, the nearest rivals being essays of the school of Addison and Irving. Among the orations are found examples from British as well as American orators. Webster is represented by five orations, including the Supposed Speech of John Adams, which has probably been recited by a larger number of American boys than any other monument of English literature. In Sanders's *School Reader*, Fifth Book, 1848, orations are still more numerous, among the orators represented being Edward Everett, Fisher Ames, Edmund Randolph, Webster, Calhoun, Henry Clay, Madison, Jackson, besides Black Hawk, Black Thunder, and other Indian orators not specified by name. After illustrative citations from Indian orations, the prophecy is made, p. 216, that they "will be as enduring as the swan-like music of Attic and Roman eloquence, which was the funeral song of the liberties of those republics."

In all these schoolbook collections a great many of the orations are placed in the mouths of Indians. The patriotic orations all turn on the greatness and future glory of America. In them there was obviously no place for the pathetic and elegiac strain, and this lack the melancholy fate of the Indians in America abundantly supplied. The Indian became in time a stock figure for elegiac treatment. Freneau's *Indian Burying Ground* and *The Dying Indian* are early examples, Percival's *Grave of the Indian Chief* is romantically melancholy, and tombs of Indians and Indian epitaphs were zealously described by the American antiquaries of the first half of the last century. As to Indian oratory, beginning with the earliest accounts, travelers and students of Indian customs have much to say about it. Undoubtedly the business of the tribe was often conducted by a method of public discussion. The eloquence of this oratory, however, seems to have impressed observers little before eloquence became an American obsession. To discover the actual stylistic quality of Indian oratory, as it was delivered, in the early colonial and national periods is not easy. None of it could be known except as it was interpreted, and the interpretation usually passed through several mediums, first that of the oral interpreter and then that of the literary transcriber. That the Indian vocabulary was concrete and metaphorical is certain, this being the general character of all slightly developed languages. But the idea of winter when translated into the phrase, "the time of frozen waters," or of summer as "the season of standing corn" may well seem more dignified and poetic in the translated phrases than they were intended to be in their originals. For the Indians, only those qualities of style were present in their speech which they felt to be there. The sentimental adapter of Indian speech, however, was hampered by no philological or ethnological scruples. His aim was to make Indian speech interesting to white people, not to reproduce it accurately, and as the Indian style of oratory readily lent itself to grandiloquent expansion, the path of the literary interpreter was clearly indicated. The first specimen of alleged Indian eloquence to become widely known was the supposed speech of Logan, which Jefferson printed in his *Notes on Virginia*, written in 1781 and 1782, and where he challenges "the whole orations of Demosthenes and Cicero, and of any more eminent orator, if Europe has furnished more eminent, to produce a single passage, superior to the speech of Logan." It is not impossible, however, that Demosthenes and Cicero had something to do with the composition of the speech of Logan. The glorification of Indian oratory became more and more general after the publication of this speech, and it reached its height in the third and fourth decades of the nineteenth century. In Knapp's *Lectures on American Literature* (1829), the first history of American literature, the chapter on American oratory begins with a glowing account of the eloquence of the Indians. Cooper's *Last of the Mohicans*, in which the exalted figure of Tamenund moves, had appeared in 1826. Thatcher's *Indian Biography* appeared in two volumes in 1832, and Stone's *Life of Red Jacket* appeared in its first edition in 1840. Both of these books make a great deal of the Indian as orator. Ethnologists of more recent date, though they take account of the Indian custom of speechifying, have not so much to say about Indian eloquence. The Indian as Ciceronian orator, as in some other respects, seems to have been more the victim than the cause of American tradition.

The general conditions which permitted the display oratory of the days of Webster and Calhoun have changed, in all probability never to return. In the first half of the nineteenth century, politics in America fought its combats within a definitely limited arena. The population of the country was then not great, it was still relatively homogeneous, and it was in the main settled along the Atlantic seaboard and in the neighboring row of states inland. It was possible for political affairs in such a society to be conducted with a good deal of personal and familiar feeling. One could appeal to the people because a single language, a single set of emotions and associations, was intelligible to the people. With the growth of the country to the West and Southwest, however, with the coming of vast armies of immigrants from lands in which English speech and traditions were unknown, with the rise of the great self-centered cities of the East and West, North and South, it has become increasingly difficult to find a form of expression in public speaking which shall be both intimate and comprehensive. The most recent developments in internationalism at the expense of nationalism, if they go far enough, may also affect the practice of oratory. Will they provide a new grand idea for a new and exalted oratory? In the many speeches and messages of President Wilson the notion of world politics certainly inspired more eloquence than the notion of American politics. The idea has imaginative appeal. Whether or not it has solidity, only time or the touchstone of a new Lincoln can tell. If it has solidity, however, one may safely prophesy that the expression of it will take a form derived not from American popular style but from the standard literary style.

The great event which pricked the bubble of American grandiloquent oratory was the Civil War. Confronted with the dreadful seriousness of that experience, the theatrical forensics of the second quarter of the century were seen to be inadequate for a genuinely great occasion. The final blow was given to the old-fashioned oratory when Lincoln, himself a student of the older oratory, in a five-minute speech of intense sincerity and incredible simplicity, on the field of Gettysburg set a new mark for all later generations of public speakers in America.

Another manifestation in America of the exuberant popular style appears in that kind of expression called slang, a thing of many aspects, readily recognized in experience though not always clearly definable. Slang does not flourish under all conditions. It requires an appropriate atmosphere for its successful growth. In general it is found in the speech of persons whose social relations are extensive, varied and animated. It is the product of the city rather than the country, of sophisticated rather than naïve society. Historically it does not appear extensively in American records before the middle decades of the nineteenth century, and then it was an accompaniment of the free and easy life which was developing in the picturesque politics of the time and in the new settlements of the West and Southwest. On June 26, 1812, a few days after the declaration of war with England, Governor Caleb Strong of Massachusetts, spoke of England as "the bulwark of the religion we profess," *Proceedings of the*

American Antiquarian Society, New Series, XIX, 24. The phrase *bulwark of our religion* as applied to England struck the heated fancy of the time as exquisitely grotesque and humorous. It spread like measles, for a decade bulwark and England were synonymous terms, and a new slang word had come into existence. Like most slang, however, it also soon passed out of existence. Society in America, however, had developed conditions in which slang could flourish and from this time the student of American slang finds himself plentifully provided with material. A new spirit of the times had come into being.

The ephemeral campaign and political literature of the third and fourth decades of the last century was particularly rich in this expressive popular lingo. Its variations are illustrated by Kendall (Timothy Tickle) in his *Doleful Tragedy of the Raising of John Burnham,* or *The Cat Let Out of the Bag* (1832). This play has as its theme the trickeries and betrayals of trust of a group of politicians organized ostensibly to oppose the Masonic order but really to secure office for themselves. The play gives an interesting picture of "canting slang and rotten-cored profession," the inner meaning of both now calling for not a little antiquarian annotation. Some of the phrases apparently at the time rich in connotation are *equal rights; light; the old Handmaid; giant claims; loaves and fishes*, or more briefly, *loaves*, meaning the spoils of office; *outrage; the depravity of human nature; raise the wind*, meaning to secure money for publicity purposes; *the blessed spirit; to go the whole, to go the whole hog; a rush, a rush light*, from the name of a politician named Rush; *the star gazer; divan*, a secret political organization; *a rouser*, a mildly sensational lie, preparatory to a *thumper; come back or edge; Jacks and cable tows.* These and many other words and phrases like these in the play well illustrate how the highly colored vocabulary of one day becomes feeble and even meaningless as soon as the exciting causes of the moment have passed away.

Politics being in the first half of the nineteenth century the most exciting of American pastimes, it was natural that slang should take its rise in political journalism and debate. But other groups of persons whose associations were intimate and animated have also developed extensive slang vocabularies. This has been especially true of sports, or activities with sporting associations, such as card playing, horse racing, prize fighting, baseball, golf, dog raising, college life, in fact any situation in which personal contacts were close and exhilarating. Slang has flourished also in certain not too stable regions of the American business world, especially in that generically known as Wall Street. The language of these various activities, of the stock market, of the gambling table or racing field, readily becomes merely professional and technical. Words in business may originate strikingly and picturesquely, with the full flavor of slang, but by constant use as the definite names of definite things they lose their picturesque flavor and become merely literal names of things or ideas. If the social situation remains as it was, however, that is, exciting and intimate, new slang terms will be constantly invented to give expression to experiences as they are freshly realized. By the time a professional slang word or phrase is put on record, however, it will probably already have passed into the class of literal English, or by discontinuance, have passed altogether out of use. The technical slang of sports, trades and occupations consequently has little significance for the student of the idioms of general English speech. Occasionally words pass from professional slang into general use, but in the main the slang of a profession is like the rest of its technical vocabulary, limited to the relatively small group in which it circulates.

But political and professional activities have not been the only ones to produce slang in America. In ordinary social intercourse, in the relations of the man in the street to his neighboring man in the street, slang has flourished and continues to flourish. This slang of social conversation belongs naturally to the language of familiar and colloquial experience. All American conversation is not colored by slang, and the greater the degree of formality and conventionality, the less favorable are the conditions for slang. The peculiar province of slang lies on the lower popular level, and on that level it has been elaborately developed. Certain writers like George Ade and

Wallace Irwin have even utilized this slang for literary purposes, have written in what practically amounts to a slang dialect. The thought clothed in this form has been simple and humorous, but the combination of a familiar content and an amusing form has been irresistible to the American public. Successful slang writers have built up not inconsiderable literary reputations and very considerable fortunes. British literature has nothing parallel to this slang literature of America. Whatever the relative proportions of slang in British and in American speech may be, certainly slang has not been printed as much in England as in America. Here it is a recognized form of public entertainment. In a popular magazine like the *Saturday Evening Post*, for example, one can count on a certain proportion of slang in any issue, both the specialized slang of baseball and other professions and the general slang of social relationships. These slang words and phrases may be colored with the peculiar quality of slang merely from their grotesque sound associations or they may be striking and picturesque metaphors. Slang words of the former type are such words as *oodles*, "abundance," *flabbergasted*, *spondulics*, *mollycoddle*, *biff*, *blooey* (an automobile is *blooey* when it fails to run just right), *dinky*, *dotty*, *scrumptious*, *skeezicks*, *snoop*, *foozle*, *frazzle*, *woozy*, *blurb*, *mugwump*. Word perversions of this type are well illustrated in many of the creations of Lewis Carroll's humorous poems. Thus *burble* seems to have been suggested by *gurgle* and *bubble*, *tulgy* by *bulge*, *frabjious* by *joyous*, *beamish* by the alliteration with boy and by *gleam* and *beam*, *vorpal* by *vortical*, a vorpal blade being a whirling blade, *slithy* by *lithe* and *slimy*.

These words depend for their effect upon a violent contrast between the sound of a conventionally expected word and of the word actually heard. They cannot be reduced to definite pictures and may be described as humorous word echoes. They are much more characteristic of British than of American slang, the violent contrasts of concrete images found in the latter being generally offensive to British taste, except as exotics. The commonly occurring slang words in British use are words like *bally*, *bash*, *bloke*, *lugs*, *swank*, *tizzy*, a sixpence, or feeble metaphors like *beastly, blooming, priceless.* Another kind of British slang is that which rests upon abbreviation of frequently occurring conventional phrases, such as *snatch a hasty*, that is, a hasty lunch or tea, *wait a sec, ever so*, ever so much obliged, *future*, for future wife, *digs*, for diggings, *Aussie* for Australian, *brolly* for umbrella, etc. This kind of slang is of course not unknown in American use, but the genuine expert in American slang would probably regard it as weak and effeminate, entirely too obvious and infantile in method to be deserving of his notice.

Examples of striking picturesque metaphor in American slang are legion. It is in this direction that the artist in slang exerts himself. No metaphor is too remote for him, no allusion too subtle. Novelty is the very breath of life to the artist in slang. This quest for freshness naturally causes the slang of the moment to become archaic with the passing of the moment. Illustrations must almost necessarily belong to the history of slang, but antiquated examples are just as useful for illustrating the psychological processes as the last word. Thus *warm* or *hot society*, meaning gay society, is vigorously self-explanatory; *bunch*, a number of persons or a number of anything not usually tied in bunches suggests its metaphorical origin. A *lemon* can be an unpleasant person, experience, remark, anything not sweet or agreeable. A hat may be a *scream* by the same process as that which the poet employs when a smile becomes a summer's day. Or a hat becomes a *lid.* One can *freeze on to* a thing when one holds it fast, as water freezes to cold metal. The science of bacteriology has brought certain new ideas within the limits of popular apprehension, especially the notion of germs. The germ, however, becomes a *bug*, and so a person with a particular fad or notion is said to have that *bug*, or to be *bug house* in a certain direction. Some slang has local associations, like *tenderfoot, cinch, corral*, and an infinite number of words from the West. Sometimes slang is complicated in its suggestiveness, like *cackleberry*, meaning *egg*. This word might be reduced to a mathematical formula as follows:

$$\frac{\text{cackle}}{\text{huckle}} + \frac{\text{berry}}{\text{egg}} = \frac{\text{egg}}{\text{cackleberry}}$$

The metaphor sometimes depends on a phrase, as in *nobody home*, meaning you do not get me, you have not caught on, you are off the trolley, etc., or *Good night* as a general expression of finality. Or it may be a generalization derived from an individual or personal quality, as in *Jonah*, meaning anything or any person that brings bad luck, or the reverse *mascot*, something which brings good luck, usually a living animal, from La Mascotte, the luck-bringing heroine of a French comic opera popular in America in the last quarter of the nineteenth century.

To exhaust all the psychological types and sub-types of American slang would be a tedious and unprofitable undertaking. The same general qualities would be found in all of them, a keen sense of immediacy, of intimate social understanding, of soul-satisfying completeness, of violent and comic incongruity. With all its vivid differentiation, the psychology of slang is relatively simple. Its quality always depends primarily on contrast heightened to the point of the grotesque. To this is commonly added an abnormally active sense of community life of the social group in which the slang circulates. A common understanding is supposed, not the common understanding of ordinary experience, but something special, like the feeling for the "gang" or the "set" or the "swim."

The picturesque metaphor of slang as it has been used in popular American expression has certain manifest virtues, but also obvious limitations. It is usually concrete, direct and vigorous, but it makes the mistake of saying everything and leaving nothing to the imagination. It is too adequate, too pat. A hat is a lid by a very appropriate metaphor. A hat fits a head as a lid fits a pot—nothing could be more apt or more final. But when one gets the point, there is nothing more to get. The metaphor leaves nothing unrealized, nothing to be imagined. It is like a remorselessly precise epithet, so completely satisfactory that it removes the situation from further human interest. The literary value of such a style is obviously low. One can admire or smile at the ingenuity employed in securing so striking a metaphor or epithet, but the mechanical perfection of the complete adaptation of the image to its purpose can have only a momentary and mechanical interest. This character of finality is found not infrequently in popular speech. Persons of limited but absolutely certain experience sometimes express themselves with a picturesque precision and conclusiveness of effect which seems as unsought and unescapable as a happening in the world of nature. Their figures are on the same level imaginatively as the platitude in the intellectual world. The striking metaphors of slang are imaginative platitudes, fatal to genuine poetry. As slang always arises in concrete and familiar situations, in it a highly effective machinery of expression is applied to a relatively low order of thought.

As it has occurred in American popular style, slang cannot therefore be taken as evidence of an unusual elevation in the imaginative activity of the American mind. Slang is not the seed and promise of greater things to come, but a trivial by-product of things already existing. Lowell's confident expectation, expressed in the introduction to the Second Series of the Biglow Papers two generations and more ago, has not been realized. He regarded American extravagance of expression as "more fitly to be called intensity and picturesqueness, symptoms of the imaginative faculty in full health and strength, though producing, as yet, only the raw and formless material in which poetry is to work. By and by, perhaps, the world will see it fashioned into poem and picture, and Europe, which will be hard pushed for originality erelong, may have to thank us for a new sensation." And he adds later, that "it may well be that the life, invention, and vigor shown by our popular speech, and the freedom with which it is shaped to the instant want of those who use it, are the best omen for our having a swan at last." But the omen of popular speech did not really point in the direction of poetic swans. Slang uses have been abundant and striking in American speech because among the people American social contacts have been varied and rapid, because American popular life during the past three or four generations has been forced in a genial atmosphere of prosperity, of good nature, of pleasant adventure. This liking for a cataclysmic figurative expression in America has sometimes been accounted for as a survival of the Elizabethan spirit. It was not that, for it does not vigorously manifest itself until the beginning of the nineteenth century. One may say, however, that the social conditions which explain the verbal ingenuities of the Elizabethan writers were in some respects similar to those which have favored the development of a violent metaphorical style in popular American speech. The verbal eccentricities of the Elizabethans, however, are not the measure of their greatness. From the literary point of view, they are merely defects negligible in the light of more admirable imaginative achievements. So also American slang is merely the iridescent froth blown from the surface of the deep but troubled ocean of American imaginative experience. Whether or not these profounder imaginative experiences have been otherwise and more adequately recorded in literature is another question, but certainly it is true that they have not been recorded in slang literature, nor is it true that American slang is an index of the existence of them.

Besides the hyperbolical style of oratory and of picturesque exaggeration, American popular expression has employed only one other manner, one which in many respects seems the exact opposite to the exuberant style. This second manner may be described as the reluctant or rustic philosophic style. In this style, under cover of an apparent handicap, for example, that of unconventional, even ungrammatical and illiterate language, the philosopher nevertheless succeeds in uttering sagacious or penetrating or poetic criticisms of life and of men. On the spoken side the method is well described in Mark Twain's "How to Tell a Story." The main requirement, according to Mark Twain, in successful story telling before an audience is a drawl and an appearance of utter guilelessness and simplicity. This is of course a dramatic device, useful for grotesque contrast. The story teller's seeming obtuseness causes the hearer to realize the more keenly the sagacity or comedy of the story. The pose was one peculiarly adapted to American taste and convictions. If all men are created free and equal, if one man is as good as another, and maybe a little better, obviously there is no reason why the wisdom and eloquence of the homespun philosopher may not be as excellent as that of the polished man of letters. If this conviction is seasoned with a dash of scepticism, with some sense of an amusing contrast, the pose is no less interesting. The rustic philosopher, it may be assumed, is only the victim of circumstances. If essentials are the only things that count, his crudities are then merely the accidents which set off more clearly by contrast his native virtues.[1]

The first successful exponent of reluctant rustic wit appeared in the character of Major Jack Downing in the letters contributed to newspapers by Seba Smith. These letters began to appear in the *Daily Courier* of Portland, Maine, in 1830, and immediately gained wide popularity. They were later collected and published as a volume, *My Thirty Years Out of the Senate*, by Major Jack Downing (1859). Before 1830 the upland Yankee, uncouth in body and speech, but wise and masterful beneath his unpromising exterior, had already figured in comedies and plays, where indeed he had become something of a comic stock figure. In Major Downing, however, the character was first amplified sufficiently to make it self-supporting. This rustic philosopher and his numerous imitations was as distinctly a product of New England as the half-horse half-alligator orator was of the Southwest. Jack Downing was a simple-minded villager from Downingville, situated "jest about in the middle of Down East." Here Jack grew up in the great traditions of the Revolutionary War, passed on to him by his grandfather. His mother declared he was "the smartest baby that she ever see," and before he was a week old, he showed that he was "real grit, and could kick and scream two hours upon the stretch, and not seem to be the least bit tired that ever was." When he was six years old he went sliding on the ice, barefoot, because he had no shoes. "I carried a great pine chip in my hand," he explains, p. 26, "and when my feet got so cold I couldn't stand it no longer, I'd put the chip down and stand on that a little while and warm 'em, and then at it to sliding again." From this it will be seen that Jack's pedigree is not altogether unmixed with a strain of the horse and alligator

[1] For an historical account of some of these early American humorists, see Tandy, *The Cracker-box Philosophers in American Humor and Satire*, New York, 1925.

breed. When Jack had grown up to be right smart of a boy, he set out to make his way in the world. "So I tackled up the old horse," he says, p. 33, "and packed in a load of ax-handles and a few notions, and mother fried me some doughnuts and put 'em into a box along with some cheese and sassages, and ropped me up another shirt," and off he drove for Portland. He had not been in Portland long before he happened to "blunder into the Legislater" and thus the setting for his activities is made complete. He writes back letters to the folks at Downingville, commenting in the tone of doughnuts and sausages on the men and policies of the Jacksonian era.

Though Jack Downing has long since been forgotten by all except the literary historian, the literary device which his letters illustrate still has a familiar ring. Major Downing was the immediate spiritual ancestor of Hosea Biglow and a host of other minor rustic critics of life and manners. As the abundance of these characters shows, the American sense of propriety was not shocked by this seemingly irreverent way of treating serious things. Since the momentous affairs of life were not supposedly in the hands only of an accredited higher class, decorum could not be violated by treating them in a lowly way. There seemed indeed a special piquancy in emphasizing the lowliness of the treatment. The most simple-minded could scarcely be as simple as Josh Billings or Petroleum V. Nasby or Artemus Ward were made to seem. The style lent itself to extravagance, but inevitably the extravagance of the method employed caused the span of life of these various characters to be very brief. Illiterate spelling and bad grammar cannot in themselves be made permanently interesting devices, though the pose of simplicity, sufficiently varied, has never failed of its effect. Senator Sorghum and Farmer Corntossel still find a place for their wise and humorous sayings in the lower right-hand corner of the newspaper page, and new disguises for the old trick are continually being devised. The native illiterate has also provided the model for the foreign dialect philosopher, as in the musings of Peter Finley Dunne's Mr. Dooley, and in the wise and childlike sayings of Wallace Irwin's Japanese schoolboy writing about things American to his friends in Japan.

The popularity of this device seems now, however, to be on the wane. Rusticity and illiteracy are not now as amusing as they were a few generations ago in America. In a day when it was some distinction to be able to spell, when a Congressman like Davy Crockett must acknowledge humbly that he could not spell and punctuate, great possibilities of comic contrast lay in the pose of illiteracy. But society has now become more uniform. The illiterate person to-day is likely not to seem amusing, but merely stupid or unfortunate.

To the question whether these two popular literary styles, the exaggerated hyperbolical style and the reluctant simple style, also exaggerated in its different way, are the beginnings of what may develop in America into a new and genuinely individual literary style, the answer must be in the negative. For one thing, the popular styles have already had the chance to realize themselves in works of lasting literary significance and have failed to do so. For over a hundred years, that is throughout the whole of the productive period of American literature, these styles have been in existence, but in them no single work has been written which Americans cherish as expressing their national literary aspirations. The life of writings of this kind has always been short, though it may have been hilarious while it lasted. But writings in exaggerated popular styles must necessarily be parasitic in their nature. An extremely violent style or an extremely simple style can only be extreme when contrasted with a normal and moderate central style. The extreme style can be endured only for a moment as a grotesque parody of the sane and normal literary experience to which one must always return as providing the test of values by which the worth of all eccentricities is measured. Like its past, therefore, the future of American literary style will doubtless be determined by respect for moderation, for tradition, for good workmanship, for a more dependable perfection in the difficult art of writing than can come from demonic seizures or from the rude simplicity that often accompanies vivid personal contacts.

AMERICAN SPELLING

Though seemingly a mechanical matter of intrinsically little importance, from the time of the early grammarians to the present day of simplified spelling boards and societies, English spelling has claimed a large share of attention in all critical discussions of the language. And though American customs in spelling have never differed widely from British, such differences as have existed have nevertheless been treated as though they were matters of some moment, as though the Americans had really done something startling to spelling. What they might have done is, of course, quite a different affair from what they have done. English spelling at any time within the last three hundred years has offered great opportunities for the exercise of ingenious reform, and consequently as great opportunities for restraint in the exercise of reform. On the whole, Americans, like the British, have been conservative in their treatment of spelling, and the notion that American spelling is radical and revolutionary seems indeed to be mainly a survival from eighteenth and early nineteenth century political feeling.

At first thought it would appear that spelling, being merely the symbolic representation of speech by means of visible signs, should be very directly under the control of the practical intelligence. And in fact, to a large extent it is so. Nothing is easier than the pastime of devising schemes of spelling which, by all tests of common sense, are better in many respects than the spellings which happen to be in current use. The difficulty lies not in the invention of reasonable reforms, but in securing their general acceptance. The spelling of the English language became fixed in approximately its present form during the sixteenth and seventeenth centuries. The sounds of the language have changed in many respects since the close of the Middle English period, but the changes in spelling have not kept pace with the changes in pronunciation. Supported by the authority of the schools, and of the dictionaries when they came to be made, literary tradition has fixed the conventional English spelling in an almost impregnable position. A few changes in detail have made their way, but of the many proposals for a thoroughgoing reform of English spelling that have been urged from time to time during the past three centuries, none has ever acquired much more than a theoretical significance, even in America.

So long as the American colonies remained appendages to the mother country, little special attention seems to have been paid in them to the matter of spelling. It was doubtless generally assumed that spelling was a blessing, of more or less qualified character, to be received without question, as other gifts were received from across the water. With the establishment of the colonies in an independent position, however, a new attitude was taken with respect to the English language as it was then spoken and written. To the American reformers and revolutionists of the end of the eighteenth century, the time seemed unusually propitious for the advent of a reign of reason. In spelling, it was obvious then, as now, that the most logical and rational method of reform was one which called for a reconstruction of the alphabet and such invention of new characters as would make possible the representation of the sounds of the language with precision and regularity. As early as 1768 Benjamin Franklin had elaborated *A Scheme for a New Alphabet and Reformed Mode of Spelling,*[1] which contained only six new symbols, but which utilized the traditional symbols in a new and independent manner. Except for two passages of verse, each of six lines, which he transcribed into his phonetic alphabet as illustrations of its workings, and a letter in phonetic script, addressed to an English correspondent who thought there would be "many inconveniences, as well as difficulties," that would attend the bringing of the new letters and orthography into common use, Franklin seems not to have done anything with his alphabet. Of the difficulties which stood in the way of securing a general acceptance of a new alphabet, Franklin was fully aware, but

[1] *Works*, ed. Bigelow, IV, 198–209.

he declared that "whatever the difficulties and inconveniences now are, they will be more easily surmounted now, than hereafter; and some time or other it must be done." [1]

Several other early proposals for a reformed system of spelling in America may be noted. William Thornton, in *Cadmus*, 1793, proposed a full scheme of reform, and he exhorts the citizens of America, having now "corrected the dangerous doctrines of European powers," to correct also the language in which the life of the New World is to be expressed. "The American Language will thus be as distinct," declares Thornton, "as the government, free from all the follies of unphilosophical fashion, and resting upon truth as its only regulator. I perceive no difficulties: if you find any, I trust they are not without remedy." James Ewing's *Columbian Alphabet*, "being an attempt to new model the English alphabet," which appeared at Trenton, in 1798, and William Pelham's *System of Notation*, Boston, 1808, a very elaborate attempt to record the language phonetically, are entitled to mention at least as among the curiosities of orthographical literature.[2]

A few years after its first publication, when Noah Webster

[1] *Works*, ed. Bigelow, IV, p. 208. From the letter in phonetic script mentioned above.

[2] As evidence of the early and continued interest in orthographic reform, some further titles may be appended: *Monalpha*, by Amasa D. Sproat, Chillicothe, Ohio, 1807, an 8-page folder outlining a kind of visible speech alphabet; *Sketch of a plan and method of Education* [with a new alphabet], by Joseph Neef, Philadelphia, 1808; *Elements of Orthography, or an attempt to form a complete system of letters* . . . The first proposition of this idea was published in the *Columbian Magazine*, of July, 1791. Since which time the subject has laid dormant. By J. G. Chambers, Zanesville, Ohio, 1812; *Orthography Corrected*, by Thomas Embree, Philadelphia, 1813; *Philosophy of the Human Voice*, James Rush, Philadelphia, 1827; *An Essay on Learning to Read and Write the English Language*, by W. R. Weeks [Proceedings American Lyceum, Sept., 1832], New York, 1832; *Key to the new system of Orthography*, by Abner Kneeland, Boston, 1832; *Something New*, comprising a new and perfect alphabet containing 40 distinct characters, by M. H. Barton, Boston, 1833; *A New System of Orthography*, by N. Nash, Philadelphia, 1836; *Pantography*, by B. J. Antrim, Philadelphia, 1843; *New Project for Reforming the English Alphabet* . . . by Ezekiel Rich . . . praying the assistance of Congress . . . Feb. 19, 1844. Read and laid upon the table. [28th Congress. 1st Session. H. R. Doc. No. 126]; *Thoughts on a Reform of the English Alphabet and Orthography*, New York, 1846; *Orthography become Phonography*. A homographic introduction to the English language, by J. P. Hart, New Haven, Ct., 1847; *Analytic Orthography*, by S. S. Haldeman, Philadelphia, 1860. Later treatises are legion.

entered upon his campaign for nationalizing the English language in America, for creating a Federal English, he took up with enthusiasm Franklin's project for a phonetic alphabet. Franklin's interest in the matter had not died out, and he eagerly welcomed the arrival of this new disciple. In 1786 Webster drew up "a plan for the purpose of reducing the orthography of the language to perfect regularity, with as few new characters and alterations of the old ones as possible," which he submitted by letter to Franklin, Ford, *Notes on the Life of Noah Webster*, II, 455. In reply, Franklin gave the proposal his general approval, and declared that the reformation was "not only necessary but practicable." Webster did not shut his eyes to the fact that various attempts to promulgate a phonetic alphabet in England had "proved fruitless," but he added, "I conceive they failed through some defect in the plans proposed, or for reasons that do not exist in this country." In America, "the minds of the people are in a ferment, and consequently disposed to receive improvements," so much so, in Webster's opinion, that he is led to hope that "most of the Americans may be detached from an implicit adherence to the language and manners of the British nation," *Notes*, II, 456. While lecturing in New York in 1786, Webster wrote to a correspondent, *Notes* I, 114, that "the Chairman of Congress, many other members, and about one hundred of the first ladies and gentlemen in the city are my hearers and the number is increasing. They fall in with my plan, and there is no longer a doubt that I shall be able to effect a uniformity of language and education throughout this continent." If this statement now seems absurd, it does so not as an ideal but in the expectation Webster expressed of the early realization of the ideal.

In furtherance of his plan, Webster suggested to Franklin that he secure the approval of Washington, who had expressed, he says, "the warmest wishes for the success of my undertaking to refine the language," and who would, he thinks, "undoubtedly commence its advocate" if he were made acquainted with the new phonetic alphabet. Thus gently Franklin is shown how he could make himself useful. With the support of "a few distinguished characters" who might give such weight to the undertaking as to crush the opposition of "the enemies of our independence," Webster recommended to Franklin that the alphabet be then presented to Congress for action by that body. What Webster apparently had in mind was the creation of a fiat language, and the hope he seems to have cherished for the success of such an undertaking is characteristic of the pathetic faith of men in the early days of the American republic in the power of government to cure all the evils of life by edict and decree. To Webster's program of action, Franklin gave only a qualified assent. He asked for further discussion, and remarked that he had "formerly consider'd this matter pretty fully, and contriv'd some of the means of carrying it into Execution, so as gradually to render the Reformation general," *Notes*, II, 457.

One is not surprised to find that the proposed reformation became general neither suddenly nor gradually. In itself the project was not novel, and it has seemed worth while dwelling on it for a moment only because its failure shows how little effect theoretical reforms of language had upon men's minds, even in the days when their minds were most open to innovation and reform. With all its respect for Franklin's wisdom and good sense, the American public was not ready to follow him into schemes of reform which called for a complete reconstruction of so complicated a set of social habits as were involved in spelling. Nor was Franklin himself enough of a zealot to follow up his suggestions in solitary enthusiasm. The discipleship of Webster seemed promising at the start, but Webster was above all a practical, not a theoretical reformer. Even while he was toying with the idea of a phonetic alphabet, he was engaged in preparing and advertising to the public his elementary books of instruction for which no sale could have been expected, had they made use of an invented phonetic alphabet. He yielded to practical necessity, for if Dr. Franklin did not succeed with his project, how could any one else, he asks some years later, hope for success. "The attempts are vain." [1] In his *American Spelling Book*, Webster made no attempt at all to indicate pronunciations by means of reformed spell-

[1] *Brief View*, p. 6. See also *American Dictionary* (1828), Introduction (unpaged).

ings. He divided the words into syllables, and this he thought was the easiest, and therefore the best way of indicating the true pronunciation. As a further aid, he sometimes placed numerals over the vowels which referred to the several qualities which the same symbol might have. Still later he expressed himself as convinced that the only practicable way to indicate English pronunciation was by the use of diacritics and special markings, his point of departure being the sounds of the alphabet as they are indicated in the names of the letters.

In a note to the Preface of the dictionary of 1806, p. vi, Webster remarked, somewhat disingenuously, that "in the year 1776, Dr. Franklin proposed to me to prosecute his scheme of a Reformed Alphabet, and offered me his types for the purpose. I declined accepting his offer, on a full conviction of the utter impracticability, as well as inutility of the scheme. The orthography of our language might be rendered sufficiently regular, without a single new character, by means of a few trifling alterations of the present characters, and retrenching a few superfluous letters, the most of which are corruptions of the original words." These views remained unchanged in the *American Dictionary* of 1828, where Webster repeated in the Introduction that "the mode of ascertaining the proper pronunciation of words by marks, points and trifling alterations of the present characters, seemed to be the only one which can be reduced to practice." This was the characteristic contribution of the Webster dictionaries to the popular understanding of phonetics in America and remains to-day the chief obstacle in the way of securing a treatment of the subject in elementary books which is based on scientific principles.

One other compromise experiment by Webster may be noted, not because of its greater success, but because its wider circulation in one of Webster's books brought it to the attention of a larger circle of observers. In his *Collection of Essays and Fugitive Writings*, published in 1790, Webster attempted a reform of English spelling without using any new symbols, his innovations being the omission of silent letters and the application of analogy to groups of spellings for the purpose of getting rid of anomalies. Thus for *ch* = *k* (karacter), *s* = *z* (reezon), *o* = *u* (abuv), *ea* = *ee* (reeder), etc., Webster printed only the latter symbol—or at least theoretically printed only the latter symbol, for his actual practice was very inconsistent. The liberty he here took with English spelling "waz taken," he says, "by the writers [why not riters?] before the age of Queen Elizabeth, and to this we are indebted for the preference of modern spelling over that of Gower and Chaucer," *Essays*, p. xi. The man who admits "that the change of *housbonde, mynde, ygone, moneth,* into *husband, mind, gone, month,* iz an improovement, must acknowledge also the riting of *helth, breth, rong* [wrong], *tung, munth,* to be an improovement. There iz no alternativ." "Every possible reezon," he continues, "that could ever be offered for altering the spelling of wurds, stil exists in full force; and if a gradual reform should not be made in our language, it wil proov that we are less under the influence of reezon than our ancestors." But alas for the influence of reason! The spelling of the *Essays* was greeted with scorn and ridicule. Even Webster's friends would not follow him. Jeremy Belknap was very severe in "reprobating" the innovations of Webster, "critick and coxcomb general of the United States," Ford, *Notes*, I, 297. In acknowledging the receipt of a copy of the *Essays*, Ezra Stiles, president of Yale, expressed the opinion that Webster had "put in the pruning Knife too freely for general Acceptance," *Notes*, I, 288. Others refused to read even those writings of Webster which were not written in the offensive spelling. Not being of the stern stuff of which great reformers are made, Webster soon yielded even this modified scheme of spelling reform. It is amusing to find him employing occasional reformed spellings in his diary about the year 1790, but the fever soon passed and in later entries the cherished principle of analogy was almost forgotten. Webster was too shrewd a Yankee not to see that the advocacy of what seemed to his contemporaries to be extreme reforms, even though they were essentially reasonable, might cause him to be regarded as visionary and doctrinaire, a kind of reputation that would have been fatal to his influence and to the reputation of his elementary educational books. His desire "to correct popular errors" and his patriotism were beyond question both sincere, but these ideals were combined in his character with a very keen business sense and an ear for popular approval which sometimes served to check the purer impulses. It was made very evident to him that though America in 1790 was patriotic, her patriotism was not of a kind to lead her to reject altogether the bonds of association which held her to the literature of the English race. Spelling then as now was not merely a rational, but also an emotional matter, and the emotions which centered about it were not political, but civilizational and traditional in the widest sense. In determining the forms which American spelling was to take, Webster undoubtedly exerted some influence, but this influence operated through his spelling books and dictionaries, not through the radical proposals of the phonetic alphabet or the modified, but still radical experiments of the *Essays*. The main result of these radical proposals has been to leave a vague traditional feeling on the part of some Englishmen that American spelling is extreme and grotesque.

Webster's spelling books preceded his dictionaries. His first dictionary appeared in 1806, but his first speller was Part I of *A Grammatical Institute of the English Language, Comprising An easy, concise, and systematic Method of Education, Designed for the Use of English Schools in America. In Three Parts.* Part I, containing a "new and accurate standard of pronunciation" was published at Hartford, in 1783. The book which was most commonly used in American schools for elementary instruction in English before Webster's Grammatical Institute appeared was Thomas Dilworth's *Guide to the English Tongue,* the work of an English schoolmaster which was often reprinted in America. This book of Dilworth's was devised as "a speedy way of teaching Children to read," and it contained tables of words for spelling, a grammar, short passages for reading, "adorned with proper sculptures" [i.e., engravings], and it concluded with a set of prayers for children, very much after the fashion of the older primers in use in church schools. A glance at Dilworth shows that if this was the book generally employed for elementary instruction in English, there was every reason, besides the patriotic one of teaching American children from American books, for the composition of a book to take its place. And yet Webster's speller in its earliest edition, not only in construction and outward appearance, but also in method, closely resembled Dilworth. Though he thought that "for America in her infancy to adopt the present maxims of the old world would be to stamp the wrinkle of decrepit age upon the bloom of youth," these sentiments did not prevent him from recording such orthodox spellings as *honour*, *favour*, and even expressly commending them, see the *Grammatical Institute*, p. 11. But these spellings soon disappeared in the succeeding editions of the book, which gradually came to be modified also in content. Beginning with the edition of 1789, the First Part of the *Grammatical Institute* was called the *American Spelling Book*, a title which was long retained.

In the edition of 1798, described on the title page as the seventeenth, 124 of the 156 pages of the book are taken up with the elements of pronunciation, spelling, and reading. Then follows a short introduction to grammar, pp. 125–137, a few further passages for reading, and in an appendix, "A Moral Catechism or Lessons for Saturday," and a brief "Federal Catechism," containing a short explanation of the Constitution of the United States and the principles of government. In later editions the grammatical section was omitted, Webster having treated this subject more fully in the second part of his *Grammatical Institute*, but the moral parts he seems to have regarded as important and in some editions he amplified them. They contain precepts of a general kind, both of spiritual and worldly application, but much less exclusively pious and religious than in older books like Dilworth's. This change is one of the many results of the secularization of education in New England, but is indicative also of Webster's own rationalist opinions at this period of his life. The hold of these sentiments on popular interest may be seen from Samuel Woodworth's *Deed of Gift*, a comic opera, published in 1822. In this play, Mrs. Barton, a village bluestocking in Massachusetts, continually quotes wise sayings from Webster, and also continually uses big words out of their proper senses. Though not himself held up to ridicule, Webster shares to some extent in the absurdity of Mrs. Barton.

Webster's procedure in the American Spelling Book was on the whole very conservative. Acknowledging that the orthography of the language was not yet settled with precision, he did not attempt a complete reform, but established his spelling on the authority of the "most approved authors of the last and present century." While granting that the spelling of such words as *publick, favour, neighbour, head, prove, phlegm, his, give, debt, rough, well* has the "plea of antiquity in its favour," he records his conviction that "common sense and convenience will sooner or later get the better of the present absurd practice," and will bring about the "more rational and easy" spellings *public, favor, nabor, hed, proov, flem, hiz, giv, det, ruf, wel.* Nevertheless he had not the courage of this conviction, and in the body of the book he retained in general the more conservative spellings. In the spelling of names of places peculiar to America, he allowed himself more liberty. In these he thought "the orthography should coincide with the true pronunciation." "To retain old difficulties may be absurd," he continues, "but to create them, without the least occasion, is folly in the extreme." In the revised edition of the *American Spelling Book* he returned to this point and discussed it more in detail. "The orthography of Indian names," he remarks, "has not, in every instance, been well adjusted by American authors. Many of these names still retain the French orthography, found in the writings of the first discoverers or early travelers, but the practice of writing such words in the French manner ought to be discountenanced. How does an unlettered American know the pronunciation of the names Ouisconsin or Ouabasche, in this French dress? Would he suspect the pronunciation to be Wisconsin and Waubash? Our citizens ought not to be thus perplexed with an orthography to which they are strangers. Nor ought the harsh guttural sounds of the natives to be retained in such words as Shawangunk,[1] and many others. Where popular practice has

[1] Webster records the word as pronounced Shongum, and gives this as a variant spelling in his lists (see edition of 1831, pp. 135, 140). Only the spelling Shawangunk has persisted and this spelling has determined the pronunciation of the word.

softened and abridged words of this kind, the change has been made in conformity to the genius of our language, which is accommodated to a civilized people, and the orthography ought to be conformed to the practice of speaking. The true pronunciation of the name of a place is that which prevails in and near the place."[1]

The spellings of the *American Spelling Book* which call for comment are not numerous. Following his guiding principle of economy, Webster consistently omitted the final *k* in words like *magic, tragic, havoc*, etc., including *hassoc*, in which word the conventional spelling has restored the final *k*. He omitted the *u* in *favor, flavor, honor, savior*, etc., but gives *behaviour*,[2] perhaps an oversight, since the form *behavior* is the only one recorded in his dictionary, both in the edition of 1806 and 1807. Other rationalized spellings are *chesnut tree*, p. 111, *turky*, p. 23, *enrol*, p. 24, *hoop*, to cry out, p. 39, *sley*, p. 40, *meter, miter, niter*, etc., p. 46, *opake*, p. 52, *rallery*, p. 66, *musketoe*, p. 63, *whurr*, p. 102. In the spelling *pannel, empannel*, pp. 22, 28, the double consonant is retained to indicate the shortness of the accented vowel. But one is surprised to find *waggoner*, p. 27, and *waggon* persists even in the dictionary of 1807, though it is changed to *wagon* in the *American Dictionary* of 1828. One notes also *phrenzy*, p. 47, *buccanier, cannonier*, p. 97, though these last spellings are analogically justified by being grouped with *brigadier, cavalier, financier*, and others in which the French orthography has persisted. A spelling *teint*, p. 36, pronounced *tint*, seems not to be intended for the common word, meaning "shade of color," since it is recorded as a special form in the dictionary of 1807, where it is defined as "a touch of a pencil." On the whole one must admire the restraint which Webster exercised in making up his lists. He followed simplifying tendencies wherever he found sufficient authority for doing so, but indulged in few experimental innovations of his own.

The popularity of the book was doubtless due in large measure to the fact that it presented an orderly, and as far as convention at all permitted, an economical and systematic guide to English spell-

[1] From the preface of the revision made in 1803.
[2] Revision of 1803, edition of 1831, p. 91.

ing. It is historically significant therefore, not as a radical book, but because it became so widely used. In fact the *American Spelling Book* became so generally accepted as a standard that it made any thoroughgoing reform of spelling more than ever impossible. In a note to the Preface of the 1803 revision, dated March, 1818, Webster says that "the sales of the American Spelling Book, since its first publication, amount to more than five millions of copies, and they are annually increasing." A few years later, the publishers stated that one million copies were sold annually. If we remember that in 1820 the state of Illinois numbered less than 100,000 inhabitants, that the whole population of the state of New York was less than one-third of that of the present city of New York, that the whole of Massachusetts contained fewer inhabitants than Boston now does, we begin to realize the enormous consumption of these spelling books. Writing in 1837 and in answer to a letter of inquiry, Webster gave the number of copies sold to date as "at least fifteen millions." By 1865 the total circulation had been about 42,000,000 copies. From 1876 to 1890, during which time the book was under the control of D. Appleton and Company, the sales were "about eleven and one-half million copies," Ford, *Notes*, II, 448–449. "The present generation of living men and women," says a writer in the year 1865, quoted in Ford, *Notes* II, 448, "when they go back in memory to their early school days find their thoughts resting upon this, as their only and all-important text-book." The spelling match became indeed a great social and national pastime, rivaling in interest the singing school and horse racing in pioneer and village life. It is not too much to say that for the average American citizen, especially in the North and West, throughout at least three generations, Webster's spelling book was almost the solitary means of approach to the elements of literary culture. Other spelling books appeared, some rivals, some imitations, but none ever approached the *American Spelling Book* in popularity. The term American in the title may have had something to do with this, but the Americanism of the author, as has been pointed out, affected his spelling very little. It appeared mainly in the introduction of some statistical and encyclopedic matter, and in the lists of names of towns, rivers, and mountains in America. In these latter Webster's genius for spelling shows at its best. If one compares Webster's simple and reasonable spellings with the cumbersome and multifarious proper names which give early books of American travel and description so odd an appearance to modern eyes, one realizes the extent of his achievement in normalizing and simplifying the orthography of American place names. In almost all instances his spellings are those which have become familiar in present use. Where they differ it is usually in the names of places which at the beginning of the nineteenth century were but little more than names, for example, *Illenois*, *Missorie*, *Chickaugo*, *Chatanuga*.

Webster began his career as a maker of dictionaries with the publication of *A Compendious Dictionary of the English Language*, published at New Haven, in 1806. This work, he declares, in words that have become familiar in the business of making dictionaries, contains five thousand words not "found in the Best English Compends." It also contains certain encyclopedic matter, such as tables of money, weights and measures, measurements of time, a list of the post-offices in the United States, statistics of population, and chronological tables. The dictionary proper gives the spelling, pronunciation and definition of the words, but not their etymologies. This dictionary was intended to contain "a complete vocabulary of English words now in use, . . . for the daily use of adults." In the year following, Webster published a briefer form of it, *A Dictionary of the English Language compiled for the use of common schools in the United States*, New Haven, 1807. This abridgment was designed to contain "all the words which common people have occasion to use," and being cheap, Webster hopes it will be well received "by the great body of farmers and mechanics in the United States," Preface, p. iv. In the preface to this dictionary, Webster repudiates the authority of Johnson as a guide in spelling, as he had often done before, and in fact repudiates all literary authority, since "authorities equally respectable for different modes of spelling may be cited without end, leaving the inquirer unsatisfied, and the real truth undiscovered." "I have adopted," he continues, "a different mode of deciding doubtful questions of this sort, and by tracing out the radical words and primitive spelling, have endeavored to ascertain the real orthography. By pursuing this principle, we arrive at a point which cannot be disputed, thus gradually settling controversies and purifying our language from many corruptions introduced by ignorance or negligence, during the confusion of languages under the first Norman prince. Without recurring to the originals, in the manner here stated, it is impossible, I apprehend, to adjust the orthography of many words in the language, or to purify it from numerous barbarisms," p. v. It was a large and bold undertaking which Webster announces in these words, and we turn to the dictionary itself with some curiosity to see how much of the "real truth" thus defined Webster thought it proper to reveal to the common people, farmers and mechanics.

The most significant of Webster's spellings in this dictionary of 1807 are simplifications arising either from the omission of silent letters or the application of the principle of analogy. The final syllable of words like *honor, favor, savior, behavior* is consistently spelled without *u*. In final syllables *k* is also omitted in *arrac, music, physic, burdoc, cassoc, hassoc, hommoc* (*hummock*), *logic*, and so generally. But in this, as in many of his principles, Webster was not altogether consistent, for he spells *almanack, traffick, trafficker*. In monosyllabic words the combination *ck* is regularly retained, as in *dock, sick, thick*, etc., though he permits a choice between *zinc* and *zink, talc* and *talck*. Final double consonants are simplified, as in *bur*, and in the final element of compounds and polysyllables, as in *cat-cal, epaulet, etiquet, farewel, fore-tel, gavot, palet* (for palette), *skilful, wind-fal, wool-fel*, but often they are not, and besides these spellings one finds *charr* (the fish, but *char*, verb), *tarif* or *tariff*, and with considerable regularity double consonants in final stressed syllables, as in *brunett, gazell* (but *gazette*), *giraff*, and others. Webster also strove to omit final silent *e* when not needed to indicate the length of a preceding vowel, as in *ax, carmin, definit, disciplin, doctrin, examin, famin, granit, imagin, libertin, nightmar, opposit*, etc., though for some of these words he also records a form with *e*, and for some words which would seem to belong in this class, *e.g.*, *missile*, *missive*, *motive*, he records only the forms with *e*. In *maiz* the *final e* is omitted on the assumption that the spelling *ai* indicates a long vowel. Silent consonants are omitted in some words, either without remark or with express approval as useful reforms, e.g., *altho* (also *tho*), *benum*, *chesnut*, *crum*, *diaphram*, *dipthong* (*diphthong* is not recorded), *ile* (for *aisle*), *ieland* (for *island*), *istmus* (beside *isthmus*), *num* (for *numb*), *sodder* (for *solder*), *thum* (for *thumb*). Among the analogical simplifications are (1) a generalization of the use of *k* for that sound, as in *ake*, *aker* (or *acre*), *checker* (for *chequer*), *grotesk*, *kalender*, *kaw* (for *caw*), *mosk* (for *mosque*), *musketoe*, *oblike*, *oker*, *opake*, *picturesk*, *skirrous*, *skreen* (but inconsistently *scate* beside *skate*); (2) *cion* for *scion*, according to the rule that *c* is a continuant before *e* and *i;* (3) *oo* for long *u*, as in *accooter*, *behoove* (beside *behove*), *choose* (beside *chuse*), *croop*, *groop*, *lagoon* (or *lagune*), *loom* (or *loam*), *oosel* (or *ousel*), *ragoo* (for *ragout*), *soop* (but also recorded under *soup*), *surtoot* (or *surtout*), *toor* (or *tour*), *troop;* (4) *e* for the short vowel in words written *ea*, *eo*, as in *bed-sted*, *bredth*, *fether*, *lether*, *lepard*, *sted*, *stelth*, *thred*, *trechorous*, *tred*, *welth*, *wether*, *yest* (for *yeast*); (5) *o* for the long value of that vowel, as in *cloke*, *coke* (beside *coak*), *jole* (beside *jowl*), *mold* (for *mould*), *molt*, *soe* (for *sew* and *sow*), *wo* (or *woe*); (6) *u* for *o* when the latter was historically an orthographic substitution for the former, as in *spunge*, *tun*, *tung* (for *tongue*), *tunnage*; (7) *o* for *io* in *fashon*, *parishoner*, *u* for *ui* in *juce*, *nusance*, *e* for *ei* in *plebean*, *i* for *ui* in *guillotin*; (8) derivatives formed on simple words without alteration, as in *bell-foundery* from *founder*, *cloisteral* from *cloister*, *deanry* from *dean;* (9) single letters for digraphs, as in *asafetida*, *diarrhea*, *economy*, *ecumenical*, *fetus*, *maneuver*, *pean*, *phenix*. Besides these there are some miscellaneous simplifications, as *battoe* for *bateau*, *batteau*, *chapt* for *chapped*, *controller* for *comptroller*, *cookt* for *cooked*, *demain* for *demesne*, *epitomy* for *epitome*, *glast* for *glassed*, *hainous* for *heinous*, *leggin* for *legging*, *lettice* for *lettuce*, *liver* for the French coin, *melasses* for *molasses*, *pleet* for *plait*, *prairy*, *raindeer* (*reindeer* rejected as "false spelling," but *rane* also recorded), *segar*, *silvan, sirup, skilful, sley* (for *sleigh*), *stiptic, strait* (for *straight*), *substract* (for *subtract*, on the ground that *substract* is etymologically more correct), *taffety* (beside *taffeta*), *tailor* (but *taylor* also recorded), *ticken* (for *ticking*), *turky, vittle, vultur, wimmen* (defended as the correct etymological spelling of *women*, from the Old English form *wif-mon*).

On the whole, Webster's improved spellings in the dictionary of 1807 were unreasonable neither in number nor character, though many of them were records of Webster's personal opinions rather than statements of established conventions. One may question the advisability of making an elementary dictionary, or in fact a dictionary of any kind, the exponent of theories of reform in spelling, but if this is done, the reforms ought to be carried through systematically and formally, not merely suggested here and there as preferences of the compilers. In this book Webster wrought mainly as an educator, not as an unbiassed recorder of words, and he seems to have introduced his reforms more or less casually with the intent of showing what he thought American spelling ought to be, not what it was.

Twenty years later, Webster was ready to proceed with the publication of his most important work, *An American Dictionary of the English Language*, published at New York in 1828, in two large quarto volumes. The book shows a considerable modification of Webster's earlier views. He is still convinced that it is "not only important, but in a degree necessary, that the people of this country should have an American Dictionary of the English language," but he no longer desires to emphasize the differences between American and British English. He now finds that the body of the language is the same in America as in England, and that it is "desirable to perpetuate that sameness." National pride and patriotism are no longer made the justification for his interest in American speech, but the simple necessity that "a number of words in our language require to be defined in a phraseology accommodated to the condition and institutions of the people in these states, and the people of England must look to an American Dictionary for a correct understanding of such terms," *American Dictionary* (1828), Preface. Other considerations "of a public nature, which serve to justify the attempt to furnish an American Work which shall be a guide to the youth of the United States," Webster passes over with the discreet remark that they "are too obvious to require mention." One point, however, he dwells upon, and that is the innovation he has started in citing Franklin, Washington, Adams, Jay and other American writers as authorities on the same page as Boyle, Hooker, Milton, Dryden and other British men of letters. Franklin and Washington, Webster thinks, "present as pure models of genuine English as Addison or Swift," and he mentions various others whose style is "equaled only by that of the best British authors, and surpassed by that of no English compositions of similar kind." But the Americanism reflected in the sentiment thus expressed is quite a different matter from the narrow patriotic zeal which was rampant in the years immediately following the Revolution.

A similar modification of his earlier theories of reform is to be noted in the body of Webster's *American Dictionary*. Many of the simplifications recorded in the earlier dictionaries and spelling books are not found at all in the quarto of 1828, or if mentioned, are given second place. Thus the quarto has only *accouter*, *soup*, etc., though occasional reforms are retained, as in the second spelling *groop* for *group* and *croop* for *croup*. Some other of the reformed spellings like *lether*, *fether*, etc., are retained as second choices, but the conventional spellings *leather*, *feather*, *bedstead*, *meadow*, *spread*, *stealth*, etc., are either the only ones recorded or are given first place. The double consonant of simple words is generally restored in compounds like *bellwether*, *catcall*, instead of earlier *belwether*, *catcal*. The final consonant of the first element of *chestnuttree* is restored, and final *e* in words like *definite*, *doctrine*, *examine*, *famine*, is generally recorded, though here, as frequently, Webster is far from being consistent. Other returns to conventional spelling are *basin* (not *bason*), *boil* (a tumor, in the dictionary of 1806 given as *bile*), *dandruff*, *cutlas* (not *cutlash*), *lettuce* (instead of *lettice*), *parishioner* (instead of *parishoner*), *pomace* (instead of *pumice*), *taffeta* (rejecting *taffety*), *women* (rejecting *wimmen*), and many others. Curiously enough the spelling *wagon* appears first in the dictionary of 1828, being spelled *waggon* in all Webster's earlier books. Words of foreign origin are less drastically anglicized than they had been in the earlier dictionaries, for example in *bateau, chamois* (for which three spellings are given), *guillotin, livre,* and others. Conventional spellings like *ache, acre, aisle* are given the head positions, though frequently the reformed spellings, such as *ake, aker, aile, ile,* are given under separate heading with expression of opinion in their favor. In general the three points of orthography on which Webster seems to have placed most stress were the omission of *k* in many words like *music, public,* etc., which were spelled *ck* in Johnson's dictionary; of *u* in end-syllables of words like *error, honor, superior,* etc.; and the writing of *center, meter, scepter, sepulcher,* etc., instead of *centre, metre, sceptre, sepulchre,* etc. With respect to the words of the second group, his procedure was regular, but in the first and third groups he permitted himself all sorts of inconsistencies, many of them inexcusable in a lexicographer who had set himself the task of reducing the spelling of the language to uniformity. An elaborate collection of instances of irregularity was made by Cobb, *A Critical Review of the Orthography of Dr. Webster's Series of Books for Systematick Instruction in the English Language,* New York, 1831.

On the other hand, Webster introduced some new reforms into the *American Dictionary,* though the principle upon which the reforms were based was generally etymology, not analogy or economy. It is difficult to clear Webster of the charge of pedantry in his treatment of etymological spellings. He spells *bridegoom* for *bridegroom,* on the basis of the Anglo-Saxon original of the word and in defiance of centuries of good usage, because he thinks that "such a gross corruption or blunder ought not to remain a reproach to philology." For similar reasons he changes *build* to *bild, furlough* to *furlow, island* to *ieland* (recorded also in the earlier dictionaries), *nightmare* to *nightmar, parsnip, turnip,* to *parsnep, turnep* (because of Anglo-Saxon *næpe*), *ribbon, riband* to *ribin* (on the ground that the word has no etymological connection with *band*), *selvage* to *selvedge.* Apparently none of Webster's etymological reforms has passed into general use.

The *American Dictionary* was not received with universal approval. Many persons resented Webster's tinkering the language, especially in the matter of spellings. He also introduced an element of confusion in estimating the value of his work by reason of the extraordinary inconsistency of the spellings he employed. He often failed to follow even his own simplest rules, not only in one publication as compared with another, but even in the head-forms and definitions of the authoritative dictionary of 1828. For the apostle of regularity to violate regularity was a sin scarcely to be forgiven. Webster held on to some of his reformed spellings to the end, but the sequence of his publications shows a gradually diminishing endeavor to present a comprehensively American, as distinguished from British system of spelling. Even his three cardinal reforms, as illustrated in *music, honor* and *center*, did not pass unquestioned, and his severer critics, as for example, Lyman Cobb, advocated a return to the Johnsonian spellings *musick, honour* and *centre*. Spelling books of the Johnsonian tradition, however, enjoyed only a moderate popularity. In the main the spellings advocated by Webster were followed by all other makers of spelling books in America, whose number, after the first quarter of the nineteenth century, was legion. But they differed from each other, so far as they did differ, not in exploitation of new spellings, but of new theories and methods of teaching the accepted spelling. Webster indeed complained more than once that the multiplying of authorities, that is, of text-books, was bringing confusion into American education. Doubtless it would have been pleasing to him if he could have maintained a monopoly in this profitable commodity of spelling books. But trade rivalries soon became very keen, and the resultant confusion was more a confusion of the market place than in spelling itself.

It is scarcely necessary to follow Webster's spelling book and his dictionary through their later and numerous modifications and revisions, after they passed from his personal control, but it may be pointed out that in general the changes were in the direction of gradually getting rid of Webster's peculiarities of orthography, and of bringing American and British spelling into closer accord. In this the publishers were unquestionably responding to a popular demand, and Webster's project of a distinctive American spelling for the American people was doomed to failure because the people did not want such a spelling. It was one of Webster's merits, however, that both by his publications and by ceaseless lecturing, advertising and sometimes wire-pulling, he succeeded in arousing a great popular interest in spelling and in the language in America, an interest so great that dictionary making became a profitable publishers' undertaking. The battle of the dictionaries which followed the publication of Webster's quarto of 1828 reflects therefore not only popular interest, but also to a very considerable extent the commercial rivalries of opposing publishing houses.

Of the later endeavors to reform English spelling in America, the most important has been that of the Simplified Spelling Board. This Board was organized January 12, 1906, and as it enjoyed the financial support of Andrew Carnegie, it was able to conduct a vigorous campaign of publication. Its first publication was a list of common words now spelled in two or more ways, issued March 21, 1906. Numerous other bulletins and documents were later sent forth, the aim of the Board not being to establish a thoroughgoing reform at once, but by a campaign of publicity to lead the public to accept reforms gradually. After a life of two decades, it cannot be said that the movement has brought success within sight. The program of education still continues with diminished ardor, and the public, as ever, remains reluctant. In its many publications, however, the Board has collected a very considerable body of information and sensible suggestion on the whole matter of spelling reform which in time may bear fruit. Corresponding to the American Simplified Spelling Board is the British Simplified Spelling Society, organized later than the Board and much more radical in the reforms which it has recommended and which it has exemplified in its publications. The most important of the publications of the Simplified Spelling Board is the Handbook of Simplified Spelling, issued in 1920.

The question of the present differences between standard British and standard American spelling is of so little linguistic importance that it scarcely calls for discussion. It is true that some Englishmen still seem to think that American spelling is grotesquely different from British spelling, though persons who cherish this opinion are likely also to think of Chicago as a suburb of Philadelphia, or of American Indians as still walking the streets of Kansas City. The notion is probably a survival from early nineteenth-century controversies in America over spelling, at which time some justification for it was given by Webster's proposed new spellings. But these new spellings were theoretical reforms advocated by Webster, and the only ones which were general in actual practice in America, like the spellings *music, center* and *honor,* were such as found abundant authority in British usage and might have been general there as readily as they have become general in America. There are various reasons to account for the almost complete harmony between British and American spelling. In the first place, English spelling was pretty well fixed by the year 1600, and consequently the spelling which all emigrants to America brought with them was the one which custom had established in most instances for English spelling everywhere. Then again Americans have always read British books with little or no sense that these books might be regarded as belonging to a speech different from their own. The forms of English spelling have been uninterruptedly familiar—and very rarely hateful—to Americans, so much so that nowadays American publishers, with the publisher's keen professional sense of what offends, often choose to offend the least easily offended by employing in books meant to circulate in England as well as America the three or four spellings which are sacred in British use. To the American these spellings are in the main matters of indifference, and during the food conservation efforts of the Great War, almost every American household displayed a placard stating that "in honour bound" the members of the household would do all they could to save food. Among other examples of British spelling cited by Professor Brander Matthews, "As to American Spelling," in *Parts of Speech*, p. 298, where some of the emotional aspects of the attitude of the British towards their spelling are entertainingly set forth, are *almanack* with a *k*, *waggon* with two *g*'s, *traveller* with two *l*'s, *defence* for *defense*, and so with some similar words, and *theatre*, *centre*, etc., for *theater*, *center*, etc. The British objection to American spelling, as thus summarized, Professor Matthews declares to have been fully and fairly stated as it was deduced "from a painful perusal of many columns of exacerbated British writing." By search one might perhaps add some further words to this list, for example, *tyre* for *tire*, *storey*, *storeys*, of a house, *shew* for *show*, *kerb* for *curb*. Yet the most exhaustive search and the inclusion of words which might occur even only rarely in British spelling, as *chymist* for *chemist*, *chace* for *chase*, *cyder* for *cider*, could not bring together more than a trifling number of words as compared with the whole body of spellings common to British and American English. In the main the so-called British spellings are survivals from older spellings which have been leveled out in American spelling, either through analogy or in the quest for economy and simplicity of spelling. Yet it would be a mistake to suppose that all Englishmen thought as one about their archaic spellings. The style book of the Oxford University Press, known as *Authors' and Printers' Dictionary*, originally compiled by F. Howard Collins and revised by Horace Hart, prefers *story* to *storey*, and declares that though *tyre* is usual, *tire* is correct. It spells *almanac* without *k*, except in a few archaic and traditional titles. It does, however, insist on *centre*, *theatre*, etc., on *defence*, *offence*, etc., on *honour*, though it says nothing about *errour*, *favour*, and *candour*, and many similar words, which apparently may be spelled *error*, *favor*, *candor*, and it specifically rejects *tenour* for *tenor;* it definitely retains *colour* as a military term and in *coloured*, *colourist*, but nothing is said about the noun, which apparently may be spelled *colour* or *color*, as it is given in the *New English Dictionary*. The spelling *show* is prescribed for most uses, but *shew* is to be used in Scotch law and in citations from the Bible and the Prayer Book. When one begins to examine the details of British spelling in this way it soon becomes apparent that it is a wise and rare Britisher who knows what British spelling is. One needs at hand a printed style book to enable one always to make sure that one is following the orthodox faith. In the style book of the Oxford Press mentioned above, in the first few pages under the letter *a*, we learn that *advertise* and *affranchise* must be spelled with *s*, not *z*, but *anglicize*, *appetize* and many others, must be spelled with *z*, while *apprise*, "to inform," must have *s*, and *apprize*, "to value," must have *z*. Only one whose business it is to remember technical details would think of burdening his mind with minutiæ of this sort, and certainly when the Britisher's heart glows with pride and patriotism as he rises to the defense, or defence, of the beloved institution of British spelling, it cannot be with such matters that his mind is filled. It is filled merely with those half dozen words like *honour*, *centre*, *defence*, *waggon*, *traveller*, which indeed serve sufficiently as rocks upon which to found his faith. To attack this faith would perhaps be both inexpedient and futile. Since spelling is merely a conventional system of symbolic representation of speech, it would seem that the wisest thing to do would be to permit in spelling as wide a choice as civilized persons usually permit in other conventions. If not maintained by extraneous enthusiasm and prejudices, the less worthy conventions will the more readily pass away, leaving behind no occasion for difference either of opinion or of practice.

AMERICAN DICTIONARIES

No account of the English language in America would be complete without some notice of the American dictionary. Unlike the sewing-machine, the dictionary was not an American invention. But if America cannot claim the dictionary by the right of discovery, she may be said to have made at least the popular English dictionary peculiarly her own by right of use and occupation. Since the day of Dr. Johnson there has been no lack of English dictionaries, either in England or America, but in America the special conditions of an unlettered immigrant population and the elaborate development of general elementary education, both offering opportunities for the exercise of commercial pushfulness, have given to the annals of popular dictionary making peculiar animation and variety. It is in the tradition of American life that a household cannot be regarded as adequately equipped for the business of the day without a Webster's Unabridged. The American child passed by natural progression from the spelling book to the dictionary, but the dictionary one never outgrew. As the newer dictionaries have become more elaborate than their predecessors, and as all of them took on more and more the character of cyclopedias of information, they have acquired reverence as indispensable sources of information concerning all those things about which the average citizen feels that he should know.

But if Noah Webster did not invent the dictionary, neither did Dr. Johnson. Johnson's dictionary appeared in 1755, in two large folio volumes. Various partial and specialized dictionaries had appeared earlier, though none that approached Johnson's monumental work in size and in scholarship. Obviously, however, the original edition of Johnson's dictionary, both because of its cost and its unwieldiness, was not a book for popular circulation. It soon passed into modified and abbreviated editions, and these were the forms of it most commonly known. The first complete American edition of Johnson, from the eleventh London edition, was published in two volumes at Philadelphia in 1818. To this was added Walker's *Principles of English Pronunciation,* as was commonly done in American editions of Johnson after Walker's dictionary had appeared. Johnson's *Dictionary of the English Language,* in miniature, 3d American edition, Boston, 1810, is typical of abbreviated forms of Johnson. It contained 276 pages, about six inches tall. Other hands, more or less pious, were laid upon Johnson's work from time to time, and later editions frequently announced themselves as Johnson's *English Dictionary,* as improved by Todd and abridged by Chalmers, with Walker's pronouncing dictionary combined. Todd's edition of Johnson appeared in 1818, but even after the publication of Webster's *American Dictionary* in 1828, the combination of Johnson, Todd, Chalmers and Walker was held in respect and esteemed invincible.

A smaller dictionary extensively used in America in the eighteenth century was Entick's *Spelling Dictionary,* first published at London in 1764. This was revised in 1787 by William Crakelt, who added a "catalogue of words of similar Sounds, but of different Spelling and Significations," and lists of this kind are commonly found in later popular dictionaries. The dictionary itself gives the accents of words but does not indicate the quality of the sounds. Dr. Johnson had done no more than this, and the chief advance in the making of dictionaries in the second half of the eighteenth century by Perry, Sheridan, Walker and others, lay in the direction of orthoepy. Entick's dictionary was partly cyclopedical, containing besides a grammatical introduction, a list of proper names of men and women, "a List of all the Cities, Boroughs, Market-Towns, and Remarkable Villages in England and Wales," and a "Succinct account of the Heathen Gods and Goddesses, Heroes and Heroines, etc., deduced from the best authorities." Comparison of some of Webster's early publications with Entick shows that he learned a good deal, especially in method and arrangement, from Entick's dictionary.

In the last three decades of the eighteenth century, the English dictionary gained new life and interest through the attempt to record the living and audible forms of the English language more exactly than was possible in the conventional historical spelling. Hitherto dictionaries had not attempted to do more than indicate the accents of words and their division into syllables. The list of pronouncing dictionaries of the English language begins with Kenrick's *New Dictionary*, 1773, which was not unknown in America, but not nearly so generally used as several others. More popular was William Perry's *Royal Standard English Dictionary*, first published at London, in 1775. This had been preceded by Perry's *Only Sure Guide to the English Tongue*, which, in spite of its expansive title, is only a simple pronouncing spelling book. The *Only Sure Guide* was republished in America by Isaiah Thomas, at Worcester, Massachusetts, who comments with pride, in the advertisement to his fourth edition, on the fact that he "was the first person who ventured to print this work in America." This fourth edition had been revised by comparison with Perry's *Royal Standard English Dictionary*, which in the meantime Thomas, noticing its scarcity in America, had also published. This first American Worcester edition of Perry appeared January 1, 1788, "Being the First Work of the kind printed in America." The vaunt was justifiable, for no dictionary had been printed before in America. It was dedicated to the American Academy of Arts and Sciences by the publisher. Besides the traditional material of dictionaries, it contained a system of pronunciation, "intelligible to the weakest capacity," a grammar of English, Scripture proper names in the Old and New Testament with their pronunciations, names of the principal cities, rivers, mountains, etc., in the known world, also the names of "the ancient and modern poets, philosophers and statesmen," with their pronunciations. Yet withal the book is not very large, containing 596 pages of thirty-eight lines to the page, the words being arranged in double columns. The number of words defined and pronounced is something over thirty thousand.

After Perry's *Royal Standard English Dictionary* the next important dictionary was Sheridan's *General Dictionary of the English*

Language, published in two volumes in 1780. Sheridan's dictionary was the first pronouncing dictionary to acquire what, for lack of a better term, may be described as social distinction. None of the pronouncing dictionaries of the eighteenth century approached the subject of pronunciation in the spirit merely of the impartial scientific observer and recorder. They were all the exponents of systems of pronunciation. One formed one's pronunciation on Sheridan or Walker or Perry, or whatever sure guide one felt inclined to follow. But neither among professional writers on the subject nor among the conscientious lay speakers of the language was there any inclination merely to follow nature. This attitude of mind persisted late, as is shown in the controversies which arose in America over the relative merits of Webster and Worcester, nor has it altogether died out to-day. Many persons still think that pronunciation is a kind of fine art, like playing the piano, which one acquires at its best only by following an authorized disciplinary method, by acquiring a system. Persons who would scorn to regulate their other social acts by the prescriptions of books of conduct, will yet regulate the social activity of speech by the rules of the dictionary. Unwilling to make decisions for themselves and perhaps perplexed by the very great variety in practice which they observe in actual speech, they simplify the situation by accepting as final the statements of some dictionary maker who has confidence enough to set himself up as an authority. Such an authority was Sheridan, although his rule was by no means undisputed. Webster was particularly violent and insistent in his denunciation of Sheridan, who had brought into his authoritative description of the English language, Webster thought, many of the corruptions of the stage and court as these corruptions flourished in Great Britain. As a matter of fact it was no part of Sheridan's intention to present an extreme form of the English language, whether the speech of a small and fashionable class of courtiers or the public and professional speech of actors. Sheridan doubtless thought he was describing the English language as it had become established in certain forms of general social custom of which he approved, and no doubt in the main he did so. It has always been the fashion with critics of speech to reject that of which they do not approve or with which they are unfamiliar as the speech of corrupt society, either at its highest or its lowest level. In Sheridan three pronunciations especially were made the objects of criticism. One was the treatment of the ending *-ciation* as a dissyllable instead of a trisyllable, *enunciation* being pronounced *enunshashun;* the second was the treatment of *tu* in stressed syllables in the same way as in unstressed syllables, *tutor* being pronounced with [tʃ] as in *nature;* the third was the failure to recognize any sound like "the Italian *a*" in English. Sheridan thus acquired the reputation of not being altogether a safe authority in pronunciation, and as safety in so delicate a matter as the guidance of speech is a first requisite, he failed to gain a wide or lasting popularity. In America Sheridan was little used, and in England also he was soon replaced by Walker, his immediate and more popular successor. Timothy Dwight reflected the common opinion of the eighteenth century that dictionaries made usage, and also the very general distrust of Sheridan, when he declared, *Travels*, I, 468, that the pronunciation of *tu* as [tʃ] was "foisted upon the language by Sheridan."

A version of Sheridan somewhat widely used was that by Stephen Jones, *A General Pronouncing and Explanatory Dictionary of the English Language for the use of Schools, Foreigners learning English, etc. In which it has been attempted to improve on the plan of Mr. Sheridan.* The edition from which this title was taken is the First Philadelphia Edition, Philadelphia, 1806. This was a reprint of the fifth British edition, the first having appeared in 1798. The improvement attempted in this dictionary consists mainly in replacing certain pronunciations of Sheridan's by those of Walker, though "the Italian *a*," perhaps through the influence of Perry, is more extensively employed by Jones than by Walker. So far as the Philadelphia edition is concerned, there is nothing whatever American about the book, except perhaps the easy manner in which an American publisher appropriated the property of a British author.

Walker's *Critical Pronouncing Dictionary and Expositor of the English Language* appeared in a single volume in 1791. It contained prefixed an essay on the Principles of English Pronunciation, by far the most elaborate and discriminating discussion of pronunciation that had so far appeared in an English dictionary. The success of Walker's book was immediate and wide and lasting. For two generations it was the leading authority on pronunciation and it was edited and published in countless forms and adaptations. Older dictionaries incorporated as much of Walker as they could, and Johnson for spelling and Walker for pronunciation was a combination frequently made. The first American edition of Walker appeared in 1803, and there were numerous later editions, abridgments and partial appropriations. It became a common article of trade. "Novels and useful histories," remarked a competent observer in the *Gentleman's Magazine*, XLVI, 914, November, 1796, "are the best articles to be considered here [in the South in America] after Dictionaries." The popular success of Walker probably stimulated the production of American dictionaries when they began to appear at the beginning of the new century. Pickering, *A Vocabulary* (1816), p. 42, notes with satisfaction that "there is a general and increasing disposition to regulate our pronunciation by that of Walker." The earliest American dictionaries, however, were small books, published to sell for a low price and to be used in schools. The beginnings of American lexicography are therefore rather humble, reflecting the needs and conditions of popular education, not the high life of Sheridan and Walker.

The first English dictionary made and published in America was the work of Samuel Johnson, Jr., son of Samuel Johnson, first president of King's College, the present Columbia University. Johnson was a native of Guilford, Connecticut, where he was born on March 10, 1757, and where he died August 20, 1836. His dictionary was a very modest affair of 198 pages, containing in all something less than five thousand words. The title page is without date, but 1798 was doubtless the year of publication. Of this book only two copies are known to be in existence, one in the Yale University Library, imperfect, and one in the British Museum, and doubtless the original edition, which was not followed by a second, was small. The book was intended to be used as a schoolbook, and its title reads: "A School Dictionary, being a compendium of the latest and most improved dictionaries, and comprising an easy and concise method of teaching children the true meaning and pronunciation of the most useful words in the English language, and in which the parts of speech are distinguished and explained and a special rule is given for spelling derivatives and compound words. By Samuel Johnson, Jun'r. Published according to Act of Congress, New Haven. Printed and sold by Edward O'Brien, who holds the copyright for the States of Connecticut and New York." The author was a schoolmaster and says in his Preface that he undertook to prepare his dictionary because he had often felt the want of a "sizeable School dictionary." He does not pretend that there is anything original in his work but characterizes it as a "collection from previous authors of established reputation." Who these authors were Johnson does not say, but one may surmise that they were mainly Dr. Johnson and Perry. As the dictionary was intended to supplement the common school books, that is the spellers, it omitted many familiar words, and thus took on somewhat the character of a dictionary of hard words. Pronunciations are indicated very crudely by diacritical marks, and the author confesses that "the differences of the sounds of the vowels are not so accurately pointed out in the following work as they are in the Grammatical Institute by the ingenious Webster." As the supply of marks ran out in the printing of the book at *enhance*, the author explains at this point that "the want of a supply of accented types obliges the printer to omit the accents in such words as are easily pronounced by the division only."

Two years after the publication of this first dictionary appeared *A Selected pronouncing and accented Dictionary*, Suffield [Conn.], 1800, by John Elliott and Samuel Johnson, Jr. Elliott was pastor of the church in East Guilford. Two editions of this work, with slight variations, appeared in 1800, see Steger, p. 23. In the Preface, the authors object to the extant dictionaries, both because of their size and cost, and also "from their want of delicacy and chastity of language. Many words, there found, are highly offensive to the modest ear, and cannot be read without a blush, and delicacy is one of the principal objects of early instruction: and this object is totally defeated by the indiscriminate use of vulgar and indecent words." In the division of syllables and pronunciation of words, the standard avowed by the authors was "the practice of men of letters, and Gentlemen of the first abilities, and experience, in school education in modern times." As in Johnson's first dictionary, pronunciations are indicated by diacritical marks, but occasionally a word is spelled in brackets as it should be pronounced, as *sugar* [*shugar*], *chamois* [*shammy*]. The authors give a list of words spelled differently but pronounced alike, and also a list of vulgar errors, p. 30–31, in pronunciation.

In the same year appeared Caleb Alexander's *Columbian Dictionary of the English Language*, Boston, 1800. This was the first dictionary to boast of its Americanism. On the title page, Alexander declares that his book contains "many new words of general use, not found in any other English dictionary." Detailed examination of the book, which is only a small volume of about five hundred and fifty pages, does not bear out this statement. Practically all the words are in Perry and Walker, even picturesque words like *widow-hunter*, one who hunts up widows with jointures, *sneak-up*, one who creeps up, etc. But *telegraph* is in Alexander, though not in Perry or Walker, and *ducape*, a kind of silk, is in Perry and Alexander, but not in Walker. On the whole, Alexander seems to stand somewhat closer to Perry than to Walker. Only a very few distinctively American words are given, e.g., *dime*, ten cents; *dollar*, one hundred cents; *Yanky*, a New Englander. Alexander gives *freshet* in the American sense of a sudden rise of water due to rainfall, and also a fresh-water pool, as Perry and Walker do. But it is difficult to see the grounds of criticism in the *Portfolio*, I, 247, 325 (1801), on Alexander's "wigwam words," for there are none such in the dictionary, not even the word *wigwam*. Most is made over the word *coquette*, with the second syllable pronounced [-kwɛt]. It was enough, however, to arouse violent opposition at this time if one merely announced one's intention of making a dictionary specially for America and for Americans, for the animosities which center about innovations in language are likely to be stronger than the facts themselves warrant.

In the matter of pronunciation, also, Alexander announced himself as bringing a special message to Americans. "Could any means be used, or any plan devised, to alter and unite Americans," so he writes in his Advertisement, "in giving similar sounds to all the vowels and consonants, and their various combinations, the event would be happy." But Alexander, reflecting on the differences in opinion between Sheridan and Walker, was not very hopeful of attaining this desired end. "In spite of the most learned dissertations, and the best rules, some would pronounce *tūne,* others *tshône,* some *tuesday,* others *tshôsday;* some *vôl'-um,* others *vôl'-yum;* some *pĭc'-ture,* others *pĭc'-tshur;* some *vĕn'-due,* and others *wĕn'due;* and each would have his admirers and followers. . . . Not despairing, however, of doing a *little* to fix a *uniform* and *permanent* standard of pronunciation, no pains have been spared in dividing and accenting the words according to the practice of the most *approved* and *polite* speakers." This was no more than any other dictionary maker would have attempted to do. Alexander seems to have felt some feeble desire to record speech as he heard it. He was a patriotic son of New England, satisfied with his native land, but his dictionary was too traditional and imitative to acquire significance as an historically important document.

Webster began his career as a dictionary maker with the publication of his *Compendious Dictionary of the English Language,* Hartford and New Haven, 1806. The book has a long descriptive title which sounds several familiar notes. Five thousand words are said to be added "to the best English compends," the orthography is, "in some instances," corrected, the pronunciation marked by an accent or other suitable direction, and the definitions of many words amended and improved. In actual fact the book is a rather slight work of about four hundred pages, with few departures from earlier works of similar character. In the preface, however, Webster presented several ideas which were more fully realized in his later dictionaries. He advocated a greater attention to the history of the language as providing safer authorities than modern writers, a method of deciding questions of present use by the appeal to historical use which might be carried very far. He also advocated reforms in spelling, and asserted with respect to pronunciation, p. xi, "that a living language admits of no fixed state, nor of any certain standard of pronunciation by which even the learned in general will consent to be governed." He thinks that from the nature of the human mind, pronunciation is mutable, and he shows how different authorities speak differently on the same point. He also defends the importance of etymology in dictionary making, and has a good deal to say about new words. "Some words are either new in the United States," he observes, p. xxii, "or what is more usual, English words have received a new sense. Words of these kinds, when in general use in a state or number of states, or sanctioned by public authority in laws and judicial proceedings, are admitted into this work. When the use is local, that circumstance is noted [but the number of words thus marked local is very small]. Thus the system of taxation in Connecticut has converted *fourfold* into a verb, as have the laws of New York and Pennsylvania, the word *docket*, and the practice of courts in many states, the word *default*. The system of ecclesiastical polity in some states, has given a new meaning to *association* and *consociation*—the course of commercial transactions and the system of finance have originated new terms, as *dutiable*, *customable*, *irredeemable*. The farmer *girdles* his trees, the planter *gins* his cotton, or stocks up the *rattoons* of his sugar cane; although the language of England furnishes him with no words with meanings suited to his ideas. The merchant imports *romals*, *humhums*, *baftas*, and *gurrahs;* new species of cloths in this country; some perhaps destined to be of durable use, with their foreign names; others, with their names, to slide into disuse and oblivion. *Lots* and *locations* of lands, with *located* and *unlocated rights*, form, in this country, a new language, to which the British people are strangers." Webster then speaks of inventions and new discoveries, and adds that "in each of the countries peopled by Englishmen, a distinct dialect of the language will gradually be formed; the principal of which will be that of the United States." In fifty years from this time, the American branch of English "will be spoken by more people than all the other dialects of the language, and in one hundred and thirty years, by more people than any other language on the globe, not excepting the Chinese." He thinks the various dialects of English will remain mutually intelligible because of printing, but that the differentiation will be great.

On the whole, this first dictionary of Webster's is interesting more as showing the directions to which his mind was turning than as realizing in the treatment of detail any new ideas. In the year following, Webster published a condensation of his *Compendious Dictionary*, entitled *Dictionary for Schools*, New Haven, 1807. The dictionary of 1806 he declares to be too expensive for common schools, and he believes that "an abridgment of that work, containing all the words which common people have occasion to use, and sold at a less price, will be received by the great body of farmers and mechanics in the United States." The *Dictionary for Schools* contains 306 pages, and the *Compendious Dictionary* slightly over 400 pages, and the page of the *Compendious Dictionary* is also five lines longer than that of the *Dictionary for Schools*. At the conclusion of the *Dictionary for Schools*, Webster gives a three-page chronological Table of Remarkable Events, and this is the only encyclopedic matter included in the book. In the *Compendious Dictionary* he had given, "for the benefit of the Merchant, the Student and Traveller," tables of moneys, weights and measures, the divisions of time among the Jews, Greeks and Romans, an official list of the post-offices of the United States, the number of the inhabitants in the United States, and finally, "New and interesting Chronological Tables." In the preface to his *Dictionary for Schools*, Webster notes, p. iii, improvement in education in the United States, "particularly in common schools, in which are taught the branches of learning necessary for the yeomanry of the country." The British pocket dictionaries being all imperfect, Webster felt impelled to supply his countrymen with a proper book. "Some of them [the British dictionaries] contain obscene and vulgar terms, improper to be repeated before children; others abound with obsolete words, or terms of art, which are of no use to common people; some of them are extremely faulty in the manner of marking the accent, making no distinction whatever between the long and short vowels; all of them contain some words not used in this country, or not in the same sense as in Great Britain; and what is very important, all of them are deficient in a multitude of words which are sanctioned by the best usage." He repeats here also the opinion previously expressed in his Dissertations, "that two nations, proceeding from the same ancestors, but established in distant countries, cannot long preserve a perfect sameness of language." He grants that the language of the United States is English, but already feels strongly the need of a dictionary of the American language.

Webster's interest in the making of dictionaries grew as he acquired greater leisure for carrying on such pursuits. He began, as has just been pointed out, with the compilation of cheap elementary dictionaries, and with the income derived from the sale of these, but more especially from the sale of his American Spelling Book, he felt himself to be set free to proceed to more ambitious undertakings. The chief labor of his life, *An American Dictionary of the English Language*, in two quarto volumes, was published at New York, in 1828. Three years intervened between the time of completion of the copy of the book and the date of publication. "When I finished my copy," so Webster wrote in words that recall the earlier words of Gibbon, "I was sitting at my table in Cambridge, England, January, 1825. When I arrived at the last word I was seized with a tremor that made it difficult to proceed. I, however, summoned up strength to finish the work, and then, walking about the room, I soon recovered."[1]

Despite its historical importance as the most significant contribution to the growth of English lexicography between Dr. Johnson and the appearance of the first volume of the *New English Dictionary*, Webster's *American Dictionary* can be said to have been only

[1] Steger, p. 39.

partially successful. The book was broadly conceived, but in parts executed with an inadequate scholarship and with a stubbornness of personal conviction that seriously impaired the noble design. In the form which Webster gave it, it has not become an American classic, and if it were not for elaborate publishers' revisions of Webster's work, revisions with which he had nothing to do but which nevertheless did retain what was genuinely good in the dictionary of 1828, Webster's name would probably now be unknown in the land.

Webster considered that in the composition of his dictionary he was making contributions of importance to English lexicography especially in etymology, orthography, pronunciation, definition of words, and what for lack of a better name may be called Americanization. Each of these aspects of his book calls for a word of comment. In etymology Webster was least successful and most ambitious. He rightly analyzed the situation as he observed it in his day and found that all preceding dictionaries were altogether inadequate on the side of etymology. This inadequacy he attempted to supply, and as a preliminary, he developed a complete explanation of the origin and relationships of languages. He spent ten years in the comparison of "radical words" and in forming "a synopsis of the principal words in twenty languages, arranged in classes, under their primary elements or letters." From these studies Webster thought that he had derived the "genuine principles" on which languages are constructed. The value of these principles may be inferred when one observes that on Scriptural evidence Webster accepts the notion of a single, unified language as the primitive language of mankind, the notion that "before the dispersion, the whole earth was of one language and of one or the same speech." This primitive language he takes to have been Chaldee, and much of his etymologizing consists in showing the supposed relations which exist between later languages and original parent Chaldee. Sir James Murray, *Evolution of English Lexicography*, p. 43, is therefore unjust to Webster when he says that Webster "had the notion that derivations can be elaborated from one's own consciousness." Webster did not derive his etymologies from his inner consciousness, but from Chaldee.

Nor did he make these derivations without employing a certain amount of scholarly machinery and critical method. But his critical method was crude and unsound. His endeavor was to discover what he considered to be "radical words," the primitive units from which all languages were derived. To do this he made lists of words in various languages which had somewhat similar meanings and which looked alike in their consonant framework. Thus the name of "the *Russ* or Russians is clearly recognized in the *Roxolani* of Pliny and Ptolemy"; that the Teutonic races formerly dwelt in the East is proved by an assumption of identity in English *crag* and the proper name *Cragus* in Pliny, of *Perga* in Pamphylia and Teutonic *burg* or *bergen;* in Thymbreck, the name of a small stream near the site of Troy, "we recognize the English *brook*." In establishing these identities Webster paid little attention to vowels, the changes in vowels being so common and so meaningless that "little or no regard is to be had to them, in ascertaining the origin and affinity of languages." With unfortunate complacency, Webster criticizes adversely the opinions of Sir William Jones on this point, remarking that "it is obvious that Sir William Jones had given very little attention to the subject." Even in his treatment of consonants, however, Webster had worked out no systematic principles of identities and correspondences. He does recognize that certain consonants have undergone changes which may be reduced to regular or general statement, for example, the vocalization of an earlier *g* in English *bow*, *buy*, *lay*, *say*, *fair*, *flail*, etc. But ordinarily Webster is content to assume a radical identity between two words if they exhibit only a moderate degree of similarity in their consonantal structure. Thus "the Saxon *carc*, 'care,' *cærcian*, 'to care,' 'to cark,' is connected in origin with the Latin *carcer*, 'a prison,' both from the sense of *straining*, whence holding or restraint." Disregarding the very dubious Anglo-Saxon scholarship here exhibited, and recalling the relation of *cark* as an etymological doublet of *charge*, of which Webster knew nothing, one notes that Webster had no clear notion of the relation between *cark* and *carcer* beyond that suggested by the fact that the two words sounded alike and could be made to mean something alike. "No part of my researches," says Webster, "has given me more trouble or solicitude than that of arriving at the precise radical significance of moral ideas; such, for example, as hope, love, favor, faith." In short it was really spiritual, not phonological truth in which Webster was primarily interested, and he seems to have thought, as Plato makes Socrates think in the *Cratylus* that the truth of a word, that is the primitive and original radical value of the word, was equivalent to the truth of the idea. This is, to be sure, the literal and original meaning of the word etymology, but not at all the sense which attaches to that word in the science of linguistics. Writing, or at least publishing, in the second quarter of the nineteenth century, Webster can scarcely be excused for not knowing that Grimm's *Deutsche Grammatik* was in existence, that the comparative relations of words in languages of the same group are to be determined by the tests of regular phonetic rules or laws, not by casual external similarities or by subtle spiritual interpretations. Webster's work in etymology illustrates the extreme isolation and provincialism of American scholarship in the early years of the nineteenth century. This condition, however, was soon to change, and before the close of the second quarter of the century, pilgrims to Germany had brought to America a realization of a new content and method in scholarship which at once made Webster's efforts seem futile and antiquated. But Webster was not one of these pilgrims. He apparently never realized that his dictionary was not altogether adequate. It was unfortunate for Webster's fame that his book had scarcely appeared before it was necessary to disburden it of its errors in order that its better parts could be properly utilized. These etymological crudities were retained in all editions of Webster until the edition of 1864, the first to be designated as Unabridged. In this edition the department of etymology was put under the direction of C. A. F. Mahn, a German scholar of ability, and the edition is frequently referred to as the Webster-Mahn.

In orthography Webster regarded himself as not merely a recorder but also as a reformer. His fundamental ideas were the same as those which had previously appeared in his spelling books and earlier dictionaries. They were based upon notions of economy, of the value of regularity to be secured by following analogy, and in some instances, of faithfulness to earlier obscured forms of words. The omission of *u* in *honor*, *neighbor*, etc., and of final *k* in *music*, *public*, etc., are examples of spellings favored for reasons of economy. The preference of *meter*, *specter*, etc., to *metre*, *spectre*, etc., of *mold*, *molt* to *mould*, *moult*, *thred* to *thread*, of *lether* to *leather*, was defended by Webster on the ground that the preferred spellings followed the more common, therefore the more natural analogy. Webster did not often modify spellings to bring words into harmony with their etymological originals, but some of his most impracticable spellings are of this kind. Thus *bridegroom* he would spell *bridegoom*, because the second element of the word is derived from Old English *guma*. The singular *woman* Webster took to be derived from *womb* and *man*, therefore with some propriety spelled *woman*. But the plural as written looks as though it were *womb* and *men*. The true source of the plural Webster takes to be Old English *wifmen*, and this plural he would write as pronounced, *wimen*. It should be remarked, however, that Webster advocates the spelling *wimen* only as the counsel of perfection, and that he records *women* as the conventional form. Disregarding these comparatively few fantastic etymological spellings, one finds that Webster's spellings on the whole were sensible and reasonable. Many of them have passed into unquestioned American use, and many others have failed to do so not from any theoretical defect in the spellings, but because language is only in part under the control of judgment and reason.

The treatment of pronunciation in the *American Dictionary* shows no advance over Webster's treatment of this subject in his earlier dictionaries and in his spelling books. Many distinctive and some provincial New England pronunciations are retained, as [ɑː] in *ask*, *past*, *dance*, etc., [uː] in *tube*, *duke*, etc., *deaf* with the vowel of *leaf;* words with *au* as in *saunter*, *taunt*, etc., are given with [ɑː]; but *sauce*, contrary to Webster's earlier opinion, has [ɔː]. In some instances, Webster recognized popular pronunciations, as when he gave *shamois*, *shammy*, *chamois*, with no indication of preference for one of these as compared with the others. The indication of pronunciation is not more precise than in the spelling book, though the method employed is somewhat different. Instead of figures placed above the vowels to indicate their quality, diacritical marks alone are used. Occasionally words are spelled out to indicate their pronunciation, as *spens* for *spence,* but this principle is not frequently or consistently used. It is unfortunate that Webster did not provide a more adequate system for recording sounds, for undoubtedly Webster's spelling books and dictionaries have added greatly to the difficulty in securing the popular acceptance of any later more precise and economical methods of indicating pronunciation.

It is a commonly accepted view that Webster's chief contribution in his *American Dictionary* lay in the definition of words, not merely new American words, but in general the vocabulary of the language. Sir James Murray, *Evolution of English Lexicography,* p. 43, says that "Webster was a great man, a born definer of words." In this respect lexicography in the nineteenth century has made some of its greatest advances, and Webster's definitions have been vastly improved upon, at least, for comprehensiveness, by those of the *New English Dictionary.* Modern dictionaries are not the work of one man but are coöperative efforts in which the detailed knowledge of specialists in various subjects is incorporated. Moreover the modern library has on its shelves a much richer collection of works of reference than that which was available to the scholar of Webster's day. Webster prided himself specially on his definitions of scientific terms, but obviously his definitions of terms, for example of electricity, steel, etc., could not go beyond the state of knowledge of his day. One must admire nevertheless both the courage and the skill of Webster in his definitions. He was not afraid to attack any term nor did he often fail to give a definition which was clear, and true at least to the elements of the subject defined. In this part of his work especially Webster's Yankee ingenuity stood him in good stead. He was a good definer of words because he wanted to know about all things, not merely about them in general, but with the detailed knowledge which comes from taking ideas apart and putting them together again. In this connection it is in point to recall the variety of Webster's intellectual interests, that he was active as grammarian, lexicographer, essayist, newspaper editor, educator, lawyer, politician, farmer, and always as scientific observer. His published writings covered a wide range of subjects, including not only educational and literary works but more technical treatises, such as the elaborate *History of Pestilential Diseases*, published in two volumes in 1799, the important *Rights of Neutrals*, published in 1802, and in the same year a discussion of *Banking Institutions and Insurance Offices*. He was a not infrequent contributor to the learned journals of his day and he was actively interested in various learned societies. The parallel between Webster and Franklin is in a number of respects close, and in the definitions of his dictionary Webster reveals a clearness of mind, soundness of judgment and catholicity of interest that puts him intellectually in the same class with Franklin.

Webster's definitions, however, are also illustrative of one of the constant limitations of the man. He was so possessed with the notion of the importance of New England that he often fell into a garrulous provincialism not pardonable in one who set out to write an American, not merely a New England dictionary. Much of this comment is now historically interesting or amusing, but Webster's American contemporaries often found it annoying, even New Englanders, if they were highly cultivated and cosmopolitan, doubtless being willing to forget that there was such a thing as American provincialism. Thus there is a flavor of rusticity in the comment added at the end of the definition of *sauce*, that "sauce consisting of stewed apples is a great article in some parts of New England; but cranberries make the most delicious sauce." Under *spell* we learn that the word means in New England, "a short time, a little time," a use said to be not elegant. It also meant in New England "a turn of gratuitous labor, sometimes accompanied with presents. People give their neighbors a spell." This apparently Webster considered to be not inelegant. As a verb one of the meanings of *spell* is given as "to take another's place or turn temporarily in any labor or service," and this is said to be a "popular use of the word in New England."

It may have been so, but were the popular and inelegant uses of New England any more important in a supposedly national American dictionary than the popular and inelegant uses of any other parts of the country? Webster, in short, did not sufficiently discriminate between two of his interests. He was interested mainly in the preparation of a general standard American dictionary, but also in the study of New England provincialisms, and this latter interest sometimes crept in where it did not belong.

Webster's patriotism may likewise be said to have had some flavor of provincialism. Words current in American use should undoubtedly find a place in any dictionary of the English language, whether that dictionary is published in America or England. If the English dictionaries before Webster's were defective in this respect, the defect arose from ignorance, not conscious neglect. Peculiar American words or uses, however, constitute only a small part of any dictionary which is at all satisfactory as a dictionary of the English language, and Webster's dictionary is significant because of its general value as an English dictionary. Webster's insistence on the Americanism of his dictionary betrays a local self-consciousness which the situation did not warrant. It did not in fact carry him very far. Aside from the definition of a certain number of words peculiar to America or common to England and America, but with uses peculiar to the latter, the Americanism of the *American Dictionary* consists merely in the use of illustrative quotations of the meanings of words taken from American writings. With pride and satisfaction Webster places Franklin, Washington, Adams, Jay, Marshall, Irving, and other Americans as authorities on the same page as Boyle, Hooker, Milton, Dryden, and other names great in English literature. The satisfaction seems somewhat irrelevant and puerile. In a dictionary it is of no great importance whether quotations illustrating the meaning of a word are taken from one reputable author or another. The important thing is merely that they shall illustrate the word defined. No one would question that Washington or Franklin used many words, the common words of the language, as clearly and exactly as any other writer of English used these words. It seems therefore rather an empty distinction to quote Washington, Franklin and other Americans merely for the sake of putting their names on the same page as the names of Boyle, Hooker, Milton, and Dryden when almost any writer of English would have served equally well.

Before the appearance of Webster's dictionary of 1828 only two other lexicographical adventures in America call for notice. For the most part, after the appearance of Walker's dictionary, American publishers were content to reprint Walker, either in full or abridged, and either as an independent authority or buttressed with the august name of Dr. Johnson. The *New Critical Pronouncing Dictionary of the English Language*, by An American Gentleman, published at Burlington, New Jersey, 1813, was the work of Richard S. Coxe, a native of New Jersey and a graduate of Princeton, concerning whom little further is known. His dictionary was acknowledgedly based on Johnson and Walker, and on the whole it offers much less of interest than one might expect from its title. The same must be said of *The American Standard of Orthography and Pronunciation and Improved Dictionary of the English Language*, by Burgiss Allison, also published at Burlington, New Jersey, in 1815. This book also followed Walker, and its Americanism did not extend much beyond the title page. Both Coxe's and Allison's dictionaries are considerably larger than the earlier school dictionaries, from which one may infer that the making of dictionaries in America was growing in dignity at least as a commercial undertaking.

After Webster the most distinguished name in the annals of American dictionary making is that of Joseph Emerson Worcester. In 1830, two years after the publication of Webster's *American Dictionary*, Worcester published his *Comprehensive Pronouncing and Explanatory Dictionary of the English Language.* This is an octavo book of four hundred pages, and it was intended not merely for rustics and laborers but for the use of cultivated speakers and writers. Worcester had previously edited "Johnson's Dictionary, as improved by Todd and abridged by Chalmers, with Walker's Pronouncing Dictionary combined," and while engaged in this task, he formed the plan for his own dictionary. Another labor which Worcester also performed before publishing his dictionary of 1830, was an abridgement of Webster's *American Dictionary*, which he characterized, in the Preface to his own dictionary, p. vii, as "a work of vast learning and research, containing the most complete vocabulary of the language that has yet appeared, and comprising numerous and great improvements upon all works of the kind which preceded it, with respect to the etymology and definition of words." Worcester thus in a way grew up in the shadow of Webster, a relationship which led later to many bitter charges and counter-charges when rivalry interrupted the friendly relations between the two.

Worcester's claims to distinction in his dictionary of 1830 are not numerous, but are well founded. He makes the usual boast of having added many new words to his dictionary. In spelling he followed a middle course between Webster and the British dictionaries. His definitions are very brief, but well phrased. He avoided Webster's many errors in etymologizing by not giving any etymologies, and in general he showed greater common sense and better judgment than Webster. The most distinctive part of the book lies in the treatment of pronunciation, which was made "a leading object, and has received particular attention." The pronunciations are carefully indicated, and for words differently pronounced by different authorities, a list of variorum pronunciations, selected from twenty-six different earlier dictionaries and treatises on pronunciation, is given. On the whole the book impresses one as being a discriminating and scholarly piece of work.

Worcester's dictionary grew in size in later editions. The edition of 1846 was entitled *A Universal and Critical Dictionary of the English Language*, and this larger form then frequently appeared later in an abbreviated form, the date of copyright of this abridgment being 1850. The next important edition of Worcester's dictionary was the quarto edition of 1860, which in essentials established the final form of Worcester. Webster's dictionary had been published in the preceding year in an elaborate Pictorial Edition, and it was at this time and later that "the battle of the dictionaries" was at its height.

Partisanships in the choice of dictionaries were aroused partly by the fact that there really was a choice between the two main claimants, Worcester standing on the whole closer to British use and Webster, in some respects, standing for a local and somewhat provincial American use. But unquestionably feeling was also aroused by the methods employed in the advertising and selling of the two books. This latter subject is a chapter in the history of American business methods which must be left to the student of morals. As the last edition of Worcester appeared in 1886, and as the book is now practically no longer in use, the interest of the subject is now exclusively historical and ethical. It is now impossible to revive any of the violent hostilities and preferences of the mid-decades of the nineteenth century. In the *Poet at the Breakfast Table* (1872), Chapter I, Holmes remarks that a certain word is "considered vulgar by the nobility and gentry of the Mother Country, and it is not to be found in Mr. Worcester's Dictionary, on which, as is well known, the literary men of this metropolis are by special statute allowed to be sworn in place of the Bible. I know one, certainly, who never takes his oath on any other dictionary, any advertising fiction to the contrary, notwithstanding." Worcester may have been the Bible of Bostonians two or three generations ago, but it does not seem that the British characteristics of Worcester were pronounced enough to account for the failure of so good a book to continue in general use. A little editing might easily have removed the objectionable features. If one balances the faults of the Webster of 1828 against the faults of the Worcester of 1830, the totals are greatly in favor of Worcester. One must conclude that the success of Webster has been due largely to judicious editing, manufacturing and selling.

The special student of phonetics may be interested in two books of the middle of the nineteenth century which are best classed as among the curiosities of dictionary making. The first of these is *An Explanatory and Phonographic Pronouncing Dictionary of the English Language*, edited by William Bolles, 1847, a book of 944 folio pages. The book does not use a phonetic type, but indicates pronunciations by superior figures. It differs from earlier dictionaries in that it attempts to give the pronunciation of all words, not merely those which are supposedly difficult or concerning which there is a difference of opinion. It is not a book of much originality or fineness of observation but it is interesting as an endeavor to give a complete phonetic record of the language. Strangely enough it nowhere mentions Webster or Worcester. A good deal is said about Walker and Sheridan, and though the book boasts of additions to Walker's number of words, so far as ideas concerning pronunciation are concerned, it is dependent mainly on Sheridan.

The other book is the *American Phonetic Dictionary of the English Language, Adapted to the Present State of Literature and Science; with pronouncing vocabularies of Classical, Scriptural and Geographical Names*, Designed by Nathaniel Storrs, compiled by Dan S. Smalley, with a general introduction by A. J. Ellis, Cincinnati, 1855. "In presenting to the world its first Phonetic Dictionary," says the Preface, "the compiler feels confident that the simple but appropriate dress with which he has clothed the spoken language cannot fail to commend itself to the favourable consideration of every friend of human progress." The book is intended "to represent, by means of a phonetic alphabet, that pronunciation of the English language which is supported by the greatest number of competent authorities" and to define the meanings of words as they are used by standard writers. Words are arranged in alphabetical order and are then phonetically transcribed, the definitions also being in phonetic type. The phonetic alphabet is a good one, and it was devised by Benn Pitman, Elias Longley, and A. J. Ellis and others. The book was published by the aid of a bequest left for this pupose by Nathaniel Storrs, a Boston school principal. It was published in Cincinnati because the Longleys were established there as phonetic publishers, especially of Pitman shorthand books. The phonetic alphabet used in the dictionary differs but slightly from the one devised by Isaac Pitman, but the changes, such as they were, are the only features of the book that can be called American. It is not a record of American speech, but merely a phonetic record of a generalized kind of English speech, published in America. It has now little present interest, neither has it been historically significant. To invent and illustrate a phonetic alphabet may be an interesting undertaking, but to carry the use of a phonetic alphabet through a whole dictionary, as the compiler of the *American Phonetic Dictionary* has done, has the ironic result of proving just the opposite of what the compiler intended. It proves that even a phonetic alphabet does not hold the mirror up to nature, but that after all it is only an approximate, therefore conventional, representation of real speech, like the traditional alphabet.

Of later American dictionaries it is not necessary to speak in detail. *The Century Dictionary* first appeared in six volumes in 1889–1891, and it remains the most elaborate American attempt in the field of lexicography. In 1894 *The Century Cyclopedia of Names* was added, and in 1897, *The Century Atlas of the World.* In 1911 the book was published in a revised edition of twelve volumes, ten being devoted to the dictionary and the eleventh and twelfth to the *Cyclopedia* and *Atlas*. Obviously a dictionary in twelve volumes is not a popular handbook, and as a scholarly dictionary, the *Century* unavoidably must be compared with the *New English Dictionary.* If one may qualify in matters of scholarship, one may say that the *Century* is a convenient and practical scholarly dictionary and the *New English Dictionary* is a thorough and scientific scholarly dictionary. In plan the two differ in that the *New English Dictionary* pays much more attention to the historical aspects of the English language, its most important contributions being the citations of passages illustrating the uses of English words from Middle English to modern times.

In conjunction with the *Century Dictionary* must be named the *Standard Dictionary*, first published in two volumes, Volume I in 1893, Volume II in 1894. In subsequent editions this book has undergone changes in content and size, but none so extensive as to alter its original character. Like the *Century* it may be described as holding a middle course between a learned and a popular dictionary. It is not merely a practical desk book, and on the other hand, it cannot be said to exhaust the supplies of present scholarly information.

Both the *Century* and the *Standard* have numerous practical and ingenious features which enhance their value as useful books. Together with the *New International*, the latest revision of the old Webster, they are the three most commonly used dictionaries in America. These three dictionaries illustrate the disappearance of the individual in the making of modern dictionaries, and the emergence of what may be called the syndicate or composite dictionary. The older dictionaries depended for their value upon a name, the name of Johnson, or Sheridan, or Walker, or Webster, or Worcester. The modern dictionary is a large and costly publication, the work of numerous scholars, specialists and compilers whose names are altogether unknown to the persons who use the dictionaries. In other words, the dictionary has been slowly moving away from the conception of the dictionary as some person's description of a "system" of the English language, from the statement of what an "authority" thinks the language ought to be, to an attempt to record the language as it has existed and as it exists in all its complexities and infinite variations of practice. The complete realization of this latter ideal is impossible, whether for an individual or for a syndicate, but it is obviously in this direction that the chief advances in American lexicography are still to be made.

The dictionary of "Americanisms" is a special kind of dictionary which has flourished with vigor in America. The Americanisms contained in these dictionaries were gathered not for the purpose of contrast with "Briticisms," but with the central body of English usage which supposedly was established most soundly and rightfully in the speech of England. The use of the term Americanism goes back to the eighteenth century, but the idea of a corresponding type of expression, to be designated Briticisms, was apparently so recent that a word was not needed for it until much later. The earliest citation in the *New English Dictionary* is for 1883, but Tucker, *American English*, p. 42, "though he will not assert positively that he invented this now well accepted word," believes nevertheless that his use of it in a paper read before the Albany Institute, June 16, 1882, is the first on record. But Americanisms almost necessarily imply Briticisms. So also do Scotticisms, and a diligent reading of the eighteenth-century discussions of language would very probably reveal some stray instances of the use of the word Briticisms. The first dictionary of Americanisms was Pickering's *Vocabulary or Collection of Words and Phrases which have been supposed to be peculiar to the United States*, published in 1816, the materials having been collected some ten or more years earlier, during the author's residence in England. Pickering's *Vocabulary* called forth a *Letter*, by Noah Webster, 1817, in which Webster rose with patriotic indignation to the defense of American English. Bartlett's *Dictionary of Americanisms, a Glossary of Words and Phrases usually regarded as peculiar to the United States*, may be described as the classic example among books of this kind. It was first published in 1848, towards the close of the picturesque half century of American life. It appeared with enlargements in later editions, a second in 1859, a third in 1860, and a last edition in 1877. After Bartlett must be mentioned the slighter work of Elwyn, *Glossary of Supposed Americanisms*, published in 1859. Farmer's *Americanisms, Old and New*, 1889, was the work of an Englishman, who expanded his subject by including "numerous Anecdotal, Historical, Explanatory and Folk-Lore Notes." A more specialized glossary was Norton's *Political Americanisms*, 1890. Another book in the older fashion is Clapin's *New Dictionary of Americanisms*, 1902. The main defect of all these books is their lack of critical and scientific method. Their subject was not clearly defined, their collections being consequently heterogeneous, nor were the examples of supposed Americanisms which they contained systematically verified for time and place of occurrence in a way to enable the reader to determine the degree of their authenticity. These defects of method were corrected in Thornton's *American Glossary*, which appeared in two volumes in 1912. Though Thornton's *American Glossary* is by no means final so far as inclusiveness is concerned, as indeed it makes no pretense to be, it does supply a sound method by which later students of the subject must profit.

Several works not actually in dictionary form may be mentioned here because they discuss mainly vocabulary and because their indexes provide useful lists of words. The first of these is De Vere's *Americanisms*, published in 1872. Mencken's *American Language* has much more to say about vocabulary than any other subject and is well indexed. Tucker's *American English*, 1921, separates the collections of the older books into two groups of false and genuine Americanisms. Less extensive though no less interesting as human documents than the books that have been mentioned are Lowell's prefaces to the first and second series of the *Biglow Papers*, 1848 and 1864, and *Americanisms and Briticisms*, by Brander Matthews, published in 1892. As the controversial and personal interests in the study of Americanisms seem now to be receding, perhaps the coming generation may see further advances in the scientific study of the subject. Above all richer collections of words are needed, with illustrative passages showing their use in context. The study of Americanisms will thus serve its most useful purpose in making definite and detailed our knowledge of the past of American life, preparatory to the compilation of a genuine dictionary of Americanisms.

Blue